The Russian Orthodox Community in Hong Kong

The Russian Orthodox Community in Hong Kong

Religion, Ethnicity, and Intercultural Relations

Loretta E. Kim and Chengyi Zhou

LEXINGTON BOOKS
Lanham • Boulder • New York • London

Published by Lexington Books
An imprint of The Rowman & Littlefield Publishing Group, Inc.
4501 Forbes Boulevard, Suite 200, Lanham, Maryland 20706
www.rowman.com

86-90 Paul Street, London EC2A 4NE

Copyright © 2021 by The Rowman & Littlefield Publishing Group, Inc.

All rights reserved. No part of this book may be reproduced in any form or by any electronic or mechanical means, including information storage and retrieval systems, without written permission from the publisher, except by a reviewer who may quote passages in a review.

British Library Cataloguing in Publication Information Available

Library of Congress Cataloging-in-Publication Data

Names: Kim, Loretta E., 1978- author. | Zhou, Chengyi, author.
Title: The Russian Orthodox community in Hong Kong : religion, ethnicity, and intercultural relations / Loretta E. Kim and Chengyi Zhou.
Description: Lanham : Lexington Books, [2021] | Includes bibliographical references and index. | Summary: "Russian Orthodox Christianity is the cornerstone of a diverse cultural community in modern Hong Kong. This book explores the contributions that this group has made to the social landscape of Hong Kong from the British colonial period to the current era of integration into China"— Provided by publisher.
Identifiers: LCCN 2021025701 (print) | LCCN 2021025702 (ebook) | ISBN 9781793616739 (cloth) | ISBN 9781793616746 (ebook)
Subjects: LCSH: Russians—China—Hong Kong—History. | Orthodox Eastern Church—China—Hong Kong—History. | Minorities—China—Hong Kong—History. | Orthodox Parish of Apostles Saints Peter and Paul (Hong Kong, China) | China—Church history. | China—Relations—Russia. | Russia—Relations—China.
Classification: LCC DS796.H79 R875 2021 (print) | LCC DS796.H79 (ebook) | DDC 281.9/4705125—dc23
LC record available at https://lccn.loc.gov/2021025701
LC ebook record available at https://lccn.loc.gov/2021025702

Contents

List of Figures and Table	vii
Acknowledgments	ix
Conventions and Abbreviations	xi
Note to Readers	xiii
Map	xv
Introduction	xvii
1 Sino-Russian Relations, Christianity in Greater China, and Religious and Ethnic Minorities in Hong Kong	1
2 Foundation and Revival	27
3 The Russian Language Center	55
4 The China Orthodox Press	79
5 The OPASPP as a Hong Kong Community	123
Epilogue	163
Glossary: General Terms, Places, Institutions, and Texts	173
Bibliography	217
Index	257
About the Authors	269

List of Figures and Table

FIGURES

Figure A.1	Key Russian Orthodox Church Sites and Areas of Community Activity in Hong Kong	xv
Figure 2.1	Iconostasis of the Church in Kowloon Tong	34
Figure 2.2	Iconostasis of the Church in Sheung Wan	46
Figure 3.1	Poster for the Russian Language Center	59
Figure 4.1	Comparison of the Format of the 2006 and 2007 Liturgical Calendars	91
Figure 4.2	Format of the 2015 Simplified Chinese Calendar	93
Figure 4.3	Format of the *Eight Church Modes* Book	94
Figure 4.4	Format of the *Divine Liturgy of Saint John Chrysostom* Service Book	95
Figure 4.5	Format of the Prayer Book	96
Figure 4.6	Format of the *300th Anniversary of the Russian Ecclesiastical Mission* Service Book	98
Figure 5.1	Logo of the Orthodox Parish of Saint Apostles Peter and Paul	124
Figure 5.2	Russian Bazaar Doll Cut-Out Board	148
Figure 5.3	Display of Dolls at the Russian Bazaar	149

TABLE

Table 4.1	Number of Publications in Traditional Chinese and Simplified Chinese Scripts, 1998 and 2005–2016	84

Acknowledgments

We would like to thank the following institutions and individuals for their support and substantial contributions to this research:

- The Orthodox Parish of Apostles Saints Peter and Paul, particularly the Very Reverend Dionisy Pozdnyaev and Mrs. Kira Pozdnyaeva, Father Anatoly Kung (Kung Cheung Ming), Father Anton Serafimovich, Mr. Roman Kremnev, and Mrs. Svetlana Kremneva
- Father Dmitry Lepeshev
- Staff of the Russian Learning Center, especially Mrs. Irina Ustuygova, Ms. Tatiana Pugacheva, Mrs. Anastasia Kraeva
- Dr. Alexander Dmitrenko
- All the persons interviewed, both identified by their true names and by pseudonyms
- Professor Cindy Chu for the inspiration and encouragement to study the importance of the Russian Orthodox Church in China
- Professor Nadieszda Kizenko for sharing her valuable expertise throughout the research, writing, and editing process
- Hong Kong Institute for the Humanities and Social Sciences, University of Hong Kong for providing research funding through the Sin Wai-Kin Junior Fellowship. Special thanks are due to Institute Director Professor Angela Ki-Che Leung, Ms. Joan Cheng, and Ms. Louise Mak
- The Institutional Review Board of the University of Hong Kong for assessing and granting permission to conduct interviews, with particular thanks to Professor John Bacon-Shone, chairman of the Human Research Ethics Committee
- School of Modern Languages and Cultures, University of Hong Kong, particularly Ms. Zena Cheung, Ms. Shirley Chan, and Ms. Lucilla Cheng

- Dr. Song Gang of the School of Chinese, and Professor John Carroll and Dr. Oscar Sanchez-Sibony of the Department of History, University of Hong Kong
- Dr. Alvin Wong of the Department of Comparative Literature, Dr. Vivien Wei of the School of Chinese, and Ms. Georgina Challen, Faculty of Arts, University of Hong Kong
- Dr. Nikolai Mukhin for his expert editing and concordance of Cyrillic and Chinese terms
- All our editors, especially Mr. Eric Kuntzman, Ms. Alexandra Rallo, Ms. Kasey Beduhn, and Ms. Mikayla Mislak, for their guidance and support throughout the research, writing, and production process
- All our formal and informal reviewers who provided essential critiques to improve our work
- Mrs. Jay Ann Ogena and Mrs. Evelyn Ramiro for making Loretta Kim's work–life balance possible
- Family members of the authors, including Madam Zheng Qiping and Mr. Zhou Yonghai, Mr. Yu Yiqi and Yu Yau Shing, Mr. Zhang Dapeng and Madam Gu Shengmei, Mr. Yeungki Kim, Dr. Lawrence Zhang, Dr. Eugenia Kim, and Oliana, Cato, and Minerva Zhang

Conventions and Abbreviations

TRANSLITERATION

The following languages are Romanized according to these systems.

- Chinese: Hanyu Pinyin
- Church Slavonic: ALA-LC (Library of Congress) Romanization with Diacritics
- Japanese: Revised Hepburn
- Korean: Revised Romanization
- Russian: ALA-LC (Library of Congress) Romanization without Diacritics

NAMES

East Asian names are cited in "surname + given name" order.

Russian names are given in "given name+(patronymic)+surname" format. The patronymic, as implied by the parentheses, will only be included for most now-deceased persons, and for some living persons, based on whether they prefer it mentioned.

Orthodox clergy will be introduced by their full religious names. For second and subsequent citations, archpriests and priests will be referred to by title and surname, and clerics ranking bishop and above will be referred to by title and religious name.

ABBREVIATIONS

Most of the following abbreviations have been created to represent organizations concisely for second and subsequent citations. If an organization has an official abbreviation, it is employed instead of one that the authors have designated for it.

- BRI: Belt and Road Initiative
- CEFR: Common European Framework of Reference for Languages
- CCP: Chinese Communist Party
- COP: China Orthodox Press
- CUHK: Chinese University of Hong Kong
- DECR: Department of External Church Relations
- DPRK: Democratic People's Republic of Korea
- HKBU: Hong Kong Baptist University
- HKC: Hong Kong-born Chinese
- HKCC: Hong Kong Christian Council
- HKSAR: Hong Kong Special Administrative Region
- HKU: University of Hong Kong
- HSBC: Hongkong Shanghai Banking Corporation
- MAPRYAL: Mezhdunarodnaia assotsiatsiia prepodavatelei russkogo iazyka i literatury [International Association of Teachers of Russian Language and Literature]
- OCA: Orthodox Church of America
- OCSLE: Orthodox Cathedral of Saint Luke the Evangelist
- OFASC: Orthodox Fellowship of All Saints of China
- OPASPP: Orthodox Parish of Saint Apostles Peter and Paul
- OMHKSEA: Orthodox Metropolitanate of Hong Kong and South East Asia
- PRO: [Hong Kong] Public Records Office
- PRC: People's Republic of China
- RCA: Russian Culture Association
- RLC: Russian Language Center
- ROC: Russian Orthodox Church
- ROCOR: Russian Orthodox Church Outside of Russia
- ROK: Republic of Korea
- SAR: special administrative region
- TORFL: Test of Russian as a Foreign Language
- USSR: Soviet Union (Union of Soviet Socialist Republics)

Note to Readers

Since the Orthodox Parish of Saint Apostles Peter and Paul and the Russian Language Center have placed many of the images related to their communities online and update these repositories continuously, readers are welcome to consult these websites:

- "Orthodox Church in Hong Kong," https://orthodoxy.hk (this website may be viewed in English, Russian, Simplified Chinese, and Traditional Chinese)
- "Orthodoxy in China," http://www.orthodox.cn (Chinese) http://www.orthodox.cn/index_en.html (English)
- "Russian Language Center," http://rlc.edu.hk

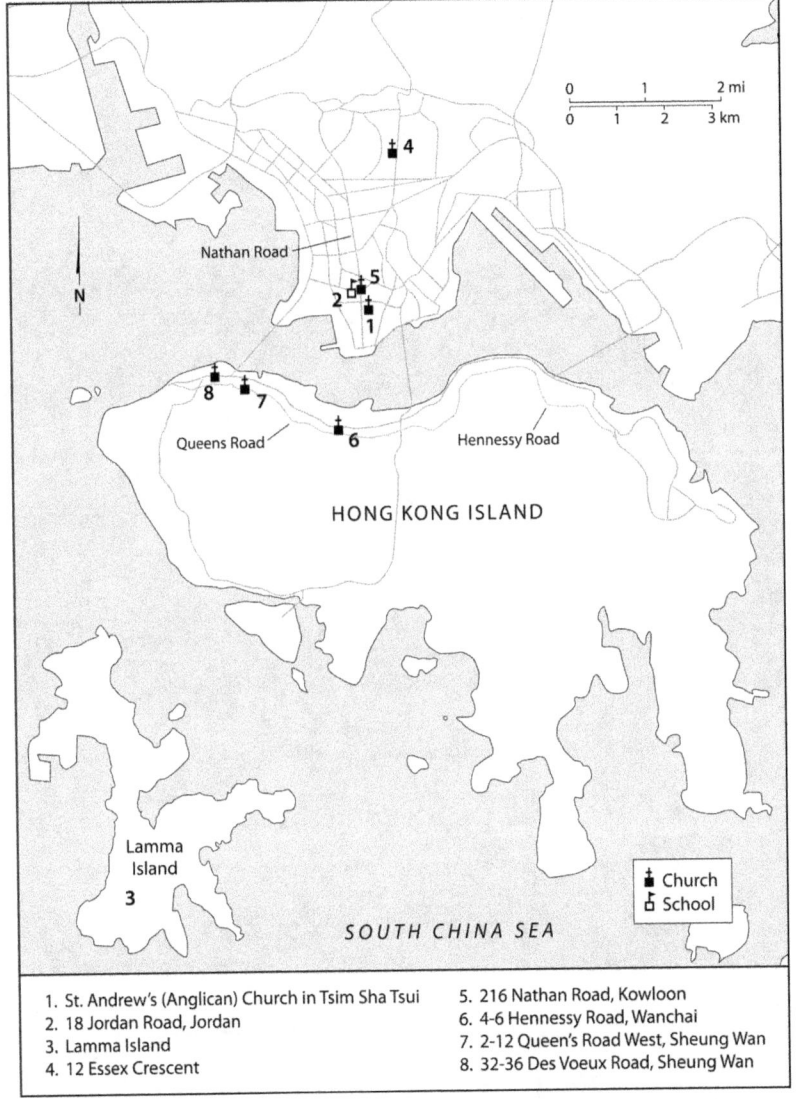

Figure A.1 Key Russian Orthodox Church Sites and Areas of Community Activity in Hong Kong.
Source: Map by Bill Nelson.

Introduction

The Orthodox Parish of Apostles Saints Peter and Paul (OPASPP) organizes an event that takes place in the Hong Kong Cemetery annually.[1] Professional historian Kira Pozdnyaeva, who is also the wife of the OPASPP's chief pastor, archpriest Father Dionisy Pozdnyaev, leads the tour of graves of Russian persons who lived and died in Hong Kong. This tour teaches participants about a facet of Hong Kong's regional history and specifically about the presence of a population that most current Hong Kong residents do not know about. This tour is important because it not only revives the memories of Hong Kong that are not commonly remembered, but also because it draws attention to the region's polyethnic, multinational society of the past that is comparable but also dissimilar to Hong Kong today. Furthermore, the cemetery tour reminds participants that Hong Kong has been a society of religious and cultural diversity since the early twentieth century.

In this book, we examine the development of the Russian Orthodox community. which has existed in Hong Kong since the early twentieth century. The congregations preceding the OPASPP were based in Kowloon, the subregion directly north of Hong Kong Island, from the 1930s through the 1970s. Now the members of the OPASPP meet for worship and fellowship in a commercial building in Sheung Wan, a district in northern Hong Kong Island near the Victoria Harbor and famous for shops selling dried seafood products and ingredients for Chinese herbal medicine. Housed in a suite of rooms that includes a sanctuary, offices, and the Russian Language Center (RLC) on one floor of the building since July 2016, the OPASPP represents the Moscow Patriarchate, the head administrative unit of the Russian Orthodox Church (ROC).[2]

Although the ROC is the largest of the autocephalous Orthodox Churches in the world, with more than 90 million members as of 2020, it has not attracted substantial numbers of believers in East Asia, including Hong Kong.[3] Moreover, Orthodox Christianity is relatively less significant in Hong Kong, as determined by the number of adherents and other indicators of influence like the presence of church-affiliated institutions like schools and hospitals, than Roman Catholicism and mainline denominations of Protestant Christianity. Russian Orthodox and Greek Orthodox believers altogether make up the smallest subgroup of Christians in Hong Kong.

However, instead of concluding that the Russian Orthodox community constitutes a negligible subpopulation in Hong Kong society and therefore does not merit much attention, we take the opposite view and instead of evaluating conventional metrics such as the number of members, adopt the approach of assessing its impact by focusing on its presence and continual growth even as a minority group. Our work of contemporary history concentrates on how the OPASPP has developed since its founding in the first decade of the twenty-first century. As seen throughout the book, religious practice and sociocultural life have been equally important for the formation and sustenance of a community whose members are brought together by a diverse range of motivations. Spirituality matters to many of these individuals, but others belong because they value Russian language and culture.[4] In this regard, we define "community" for this case-study broadly to include people who are parishioners of the OPASPP, regular participants in activities and events organized by the OPASPP and the RLC, and audiences for the publications produced by the China Orthodox Press (COP). The RLC and COP, as affiliate institutions of the OPASPP, are key components of this community because they introduce Orthodox Christianity without imposing the requirement of belief on their target audiences. Furthermore, they facilitate the OPASPP's role as not only a religious institution but also as a source of information about Russian society and culture in Hong Kong. We also demonstrate that the current Russian Orthodox community in Hong Kong is significant for the ROC's mission in the People's Republic of China (PRC) because it is not subject to direct governance and regulation by the PRC government. The parish clergy and laypersons have therefore been able to transmit knowledge about Orthodox Christianity that is not politically censored before dissemination to believers in mainland China, Taiwan, and other Sinophone communities by producing the content in Hong Kong. The relative freedom of expression is a critical asset in sustaining relations between China and Russia that has been maintained, with intermittent interruptions, since the seventeenth century.

With a dual emphasis on the Russian Orthodox community's position in and beyond Hong Kong, this book makes three interrelated contributions to our understanding of religion, ethnicity, and culture in modern China. The first major point of our research is that Orthodox Christianity has enduring influence as a conduit of Sino-Russian relations. Spreading the faith is the principal objective of Orthodox missions, but the influence of promoting contact between Russian and Chinese cultural groups has been arguably greater. The OPASPP is one of several Russian Orthodox parishes in the PRC so it is not alone in transmitting knowledge about Russian spirituality, history, and culture. However, because it is not subject to laws applicable in mainland China circumscribing the functions of religious leaders and performance of religious practice, the OPASPP can take a proportionately larger role in facilitating intercultural relations. The second is that inculturation can generate social institutions that are neither predominantly for Chinese nor primarily for foreigners. The OPASPP, like parishes in other non-Orthodox-dominant societies, has adapted its practices to align with norms based in non-Christian cultures. It has initiated more ethnic Chinese believers into the congregation through conversion and produced Chinese-language publications about Orthodox theology and traditions. At the same time, the OPASPP has been an "ethnic church" for expatriate Russians and other Slavic believers living in Hong Kong. It is therefore distinctive in Hong Kong because for most Christian denominations in this region, inculturation has been exemplified and most studied in churches serving and led by native (ethnic Chinese) people. The third and final argument of this study is that there are many communities in Hong Kong which are "double minorities." Dominant perceptions of Hong Kong as a "British colonial society" or a "Chinese society" in political, social, and cultural terms have marginalized many groups and individuals in both the annals of history and in daily life. The Russian Orthodox community, as seen in chapter 2, originally consisted of mostly heritage believers, those who were born into Orthodox Christian families and raised in the faith, from the Russian Empire/Soviet Union (USSR). With the sweeping political changes affecting Hong Kong and mainland China, much of this community dissipated through out-migration to other countries from the 1950s to 1970s. It was revived by a parish that serves as a spiritual and cultural home for heritage believers and that introduces Russian language and culture as well as the Orthodox faith to converts. This change is like what has been experienced by many Orthodox populations around the world. Since outside of Russia and Eastern Europe, Orthodox Christians are minorities within the Christian populations of their home countries, being a religious minority group in Hong Kong is not the main defining feature of the Russian Orthodox community.[5] Being a group that is associated primarily with people who are ethnic minorities and foreigners by nationality does pose significant challenges to how this community has developed its identity as being both genuinely local and a microcosm of sociocultural interaction between Hong Kong as a part of China and Orthodox communities in other areas of the world.

AREAS OF SIGNIFICANCE

All three main ideas of this book connect to three areas of significance, which will be discussed further in chapter 1: Sino-Russian relations, Christianity in Greater China, and religious and ethnic diversity in Hong Kong. Orthodox communities, including but not limited to ROCs, are active not only in the PRC, of which Hong Kong is a special administrative region (SAR), but also the Republic of China (Taiwan). In the PRC mainland (the country excluding Hong Kong and Macau, also a SAR), the Chinese Communist Party (CCP)-led state exerts full control over religious practice and expressions of religious faith. Only registered believers are permitted to worship in Christian churches. This regulation implicitly discourages and obstructs the conversion of people to Christianity, which is still considered as a foreign religion and therefore a potential source of cultural values that are contrary or harmful to Chinese social norms. Legal restrictions constrain the amount and forms of influence that the Moscow Patriarchate and other foreign religious authorities such as the Roman Catholic Vatican can exercise over church administration, training of clergy, and religious education. As of 2020, Russian Orthodox congregations are permitted to worship legally in the dioceses of Beijing, Harbin, and Shanghai, and in churches in Hebei, Hubei, Jiangsu, Jiangxi, Liaoning, Shandong, Zhejiang provinces, and the Xinjiang Uyghur Autonomous Region and the Inner Mongolia Autonomous Region.

In Taiwan, which remains a contested political territory between the PRC and the Republic of China, there are no legal or political restrictions on the freedom of religion within the general bounds of civil law. The recorded history of the Orthodox community in Taiwan began in 1771 when two Russians, one being the son of a priest, introduced precepts of the faith to the people they met after they came to the island of Taiwan by boat. They left Taiwan to continue their seafaring journey. The next encounter was in 1895 with the presence of Japanese Orthodox believers, including three professional missionaries. In 1901, Father Semyon (n.d.) founded the first church in Taiwan known as the Taipei Orthodox Church. This church was an initiative of the Russian Orthodox mission in Japan and overseen by the mission leader Nicholas of Japan (Ivan Dmitrievich Kasatkin, 1836–1912). The Japanese colonial government in Taiwan (1895–1945) granted official recognition to the church in 1917. Worship and other church activities were disrupted during World War II (1939–1945). In 1957, a new church was established in Taipei, but the community gradually lost its religious and social coherence, with gatherings mostly held in homes. A revival began in the late 1990s with the contributions of non-Taiwanese and Taiwanese believers. Father Pozdnyaev and another Russian representative discovered that some Russians were worshipping together in 1999. Father Pozdnyaev then began to visit Taiwan about once every two years to hold services. In the 2000s and to the present, the Russian Orthodox community has regained legal status as a religious organization and in 2012, the Parish of Christ the Savior in Taipei was reactivated under the leadership of a Canadian priest.[6] In 2016, the Taiwan Orthodox Church, as a constituent of the Moscow Patriarchate, attained its status as a legal corporate body.[7]

Hong Kong occupies a middle ground between the PRC mainland and Taiwan in terms of religious policy and religious organization. Although political administration in Hong Kong is based on an independent judiciary system, and other features of governance that distinguish the region from other areas of the PRC, the national (central) government exercises considerable and constant influence over how laws are interpreted and what political actions are permitted or banned in Hong Kong. However, as in Taiwan, religion itself is not considered as politically or socially problematic. Hong Kong residents may hold religious beliefs of their own choice and conduct religious practices according to those principles if they otherwise act legally. This state of freedom differs from how religions of foreign origin like Christianity must be altered to promote "Chinese values" in mainland China which means that the publicly expressed ideas and activities of those religious groups must adhere to the political guidelines of religious belief and practice, as determined by the CCP. Christian churches exist in two forms: "patriotic" (officially sanctioned) and "underground." Patriotic churches are expected to adjust their views and to tailor their actions to avoid any overt conflict or criticism of Communist political values. Underground churches attempt to avoid political censorship and surveillance of their operations, but these organizations and their members risk being accused of crimes and being deprived of their resources.

There is no theoretical difference between the PRC mainland and Hong Kong because the CCP and PRC central government officially permit religious pluralism. However, the underlying expectation behind tolerance of religion in mainland China is that foreign religions will not only be "politically correct" but also to "become Chinese." Changing religions to conform to the preferences of a Chinese nation–state and society is exemplified in a placard introducing objects of Chinese Christianity in the Minzu University of China museum. Part of the English translation provided on the placard with the Chinese text describes Christianity as follows:

> Christianity, when it is adopted among the Han, Yi, Buyi, Korean, Lisu, Nu, Tujia, Zhuang often takes on a distinctly Chinese form, and is significantly changed by China's traditional religious pluralism. Furthermore, many of the Chinese understandings of Christian concepts are markedly different from the traditional European ideas, creating various forms [*sic*] Christianity that are distinctly and unmistakably Chinese.[8]

Embedded in this description of Chinese Christianity are the implications that Christianity itself is of limited value to Chinese people and that the exclusivity of belief in Christianity as a monotheistic religion has been tempered by China's historical and ever-present proclivity for pluralistic faith. In other words, these interpretations of Christianity's scope and practice are that most Chinese (members of the Han ethnic majority) are not attracted to Christianity. Listing several ethnic minorities such as the Yi and Zhuang as the principal groups of adherents is a deliberate means to marginalize the religion. Emphasizing the "markedly different" concepts of Christianity serve to neutralize the religion as a force of social and cultural change. At most, Christianity, by this description, advances the ambiguous corpus of "Chinese morals" irrespective of the religion's genesis outside of China. State control over Christian churches is therefore designed to discourage expressions of religious faith and minimize the possibility that religious organizations will develop social and political influence that will threaten the PRC's legitimacy as a secular atheist state.

Despite the different political and legal environments in which they exist, Christian churches in both mainland China and Hong Kong function as local institutions while also belonging to an international faith community. Legal ROCs in mainland China observe the regulations that constrain any religious belief or practice which would be regarded as politically sensitive so that they can serve congregants who are subject to PRC laws. However, although they are only open to registered believers or with special permission to nonbelievers, these churches do provide information about their activities to audiences outside of their congregations and maintain relations with one another as well as with parishes in Hong Kong and outside of the PRC. Likewise, although it does not have any political or legal obligation to do so, the OPASPP incorporates features into worship that are relevant to its location into a Chinese-majority society such as using Chinese language for singing and reciting and performing rituals with Chinese elements such as chalice and cloths for Holy Communion with Chinese character designs and kolivo for the Saturday of the Souls, or Memorial Saturdays taking place before the first Sunday of Great Lent, made with sweet rice instead of boiled wheat or barley as it would be served in most Orthodox churches.[9] The OPASPP also extends its reach beyond its congregation by welcoming members of Hong Kong's general public and foreign visitors for tours, lectures, and other events held in the church.

The similarity of purpose driving religious institutions and life in both Hong Kong and mainland China is also related to the cultural diversity that has been significant to these places. The dominant understanding of diversity in modern China has been related to ethnicity because of the Ethnic Identification Project conducted in the PRC mainland from the 1950s onward that divided China's population into 1 ethnic majority group and 55 ethnic minority groups, but preceding the modern notion of ethnicity, language, religion, and material culture been variables of diversity and identity throughout China's history.[10]

Hong Kong, due to its exceptional political status from 1841 to 1997 as a British colony, a territory under Japanese occupation during World War II from 1941 to 1945, and as a SAR after 1997, has often been treated separately from mainland China in academic and popular conversations about China's diversity. "China Studies" and "Hong Kong Studies" have evolved as two distinct intellectual fields because of the political divergence, but also because of the presumption that their societies have been shaped by disparate factors, with the urban–rural divide and political elite and masses being prominent for mainland China and race and profound economic inequality stratifying Hong Kong. Religion remains one area in which there is little direct comparison of how diversity manifests in China. A major underlying reason for the emphasis on contrasting what diversity means in Hong Kong as compared to the mainland is the legacy of Hong Kong as a cultural and economic entrepôt from 1841 to 1997 under British colonial rule. Although Christians are minority groups in both contemporary Hong Kong and the PRC mainland, about 12 percent of Hong Kong's population as calculated from church membership records and about 3 percent of the mainland population,[11] many residents of Hong Kong are also affected by Christianity even if they are not affiliated with churches as actual or prospective members. Parents of all religious backgrounds, including atheists, regard Christian primary and secondary schools, the overwhelming majority founded before 1997, as respected providers of education. The Hong Kong Baptist University (HKBU), founded in 1956 as the Hong Kong Baptist College, became a public tertiary institution in 1983 but retains its original mission of education based on Christian precepts.[12] Most private hospitals in Hong Kong were established as medical outlets of Christian missions.[13] The lack of overt restrictions on practicing Christianity is furthermore evident in how the government permits Christian groups to hold large-scale events such as conferences that attract local and foreign participants.

The example of Christianity's influence on daily life supports the view that diversity in Hong Kong is expressed through the coexistence of various ideas, institutions, and types of people. Hong Kong maintains a reputation as an international metropolis, due in large part to successful branding by the regional government, as "Asia's World City," where people can take advantage of full access to the Internet, relatively easy formation of new companies, and the convenient connections by air and sea to mainland China, Southeast Asia, and Northeast Asia.[14] Although about 90 percent of the current population identifies as ethnic Chinese, Hong Kong's businesses and the general public take pride in the city's historical reputation as an ethnically heterogeneous society where "East Meets West" and which has combined the strengths of Chinese culture with values regarding education, health, and civic life adopted from Great Britain, Western Europe, North America, and Australia.[15]

Such impressions of Hong Kong, as espoused by the region's residents and by foreign observers, largely promote a superficial rather than substantial interpretation of social diversity. In the simplest terms, pre-1997 Hong Kong society was diverse because several ethno-national groups pursued common economic interests under colonial rule by a distinctly foreign power. Since 1997, Hong Kong is an official territory of the PRC with some privileges that will distinguish it from mainland Chinese cities until 2047. If this special status remains in effect, its significant but diminishing importance as a financial center should accommodate the presence of transient expatriates and service providers such as foreign domestic helpers from Southeast Asia who diversify the population. However, as Hong Kong has gone through these major changes in political and economic status, how and why Hong Kong is a diverse society has become contentious as the meaning of being a "Hong Kong person" or colloquially, "Hong Konger" has also been variously defined according to different criteria such as place of birth, ethnicity, duration of residence, and personal attachment.[16] These criteria are also considered in combination, such as some people believing that only people who are born in Hong Kong and who are ethnic Chinese can be authentic Hong Kongers whereas other people think that anyone who has lived in Hong Kong for seven years, the minimum length of time for a person not born in Hong Kong to be eligible for permanent residency and who self-identifies as a Hong Konger is legitimately entitled to claim that identity.[17]

Many of these debates, whether carried out in public political forums or privately among friends, reflect the reality that people who are not ethnic Chinese, whether by self-identification or as commonly recognized by others, have ambiguous positions in Hong Kong's past and present. The concept of "ethnic minority" in Hong Kong often refers to non-Chinese groups, such as Indians and Pakistanis, many who have lived in Hong Kong for several generations but who are socially marginalized because they hold low socioeconomic status. Several charitable organizations and civic rights groups strive to assist these "ethnic minorities."[18] "Foreigners," people who are considered non-native by any criteria, whether birth or duration of residence, are generally subcategorized by place of origin, profession, and wealth. The term "expatriate" generally applies to people from the United States, Europe, British Commonwealth countries, and East Asia who reside in Hong Kong for definitively limited periods of time and who hold relatively high socioeconomic status. Another subcategory of "foreigner" encompasses people who perform low-wage jobs, especially work that has little or no social prestige, and who are treated as permanent outsiders to Hong Kong society, irrespective of how long they live in the city.

In addition to Orthodox Christianity being overlooked in common perceptions of religious life in Hong Kong because of its "double minority" status, the Russian Orthodox community has also been an underexplored subject of intellectual and popular understanding because Russians and people from other Slavic countries have not been included or confined to stereotypes in conceptions of Hong Kong as a polyethnic, multicultural society. Many people in Hong Kong, whether of Chinese or ethnic background, consider Russian/Slavic people as "exotic" based on fascination with essentialized differences between Chinese and Russians, which has been perpetuated by political and economic rivalry between the Soviet Union/post-1991 Russia and the PRC. Others usually think of Russians as being sojourners in Hong Kong's past. Vestiges of Russian businesses established in the 1920s and 1930s belong to sentimental nostalgia. Russian/Slavic people who are living in Hong Kong today are either invisible in the general social class of "expatriates," often because they are mistaken as being Western European or North American or are considered as foreigners who are temporarily present in Hong Kong for tourism or business.[19]

Our study of the Russian Orthodox community points out that Russians and other Slavic persons who believe in Orthodox Christianity do not constitute exclusive subpopulations that are defined and isolated by nationality, religion, or culture. In other words, Russian/Slavic persons in present-day Hong Kong should be viewed as residents of the region, rather than just as a group of foreigners. Just as the Russian/Slavic populations in Shanghai during the early and mid-twentieth century built up commercial enterprises that enriched the city, Russian/Slavic people in Hong Kong have benefited the region's economy and society through their work and cultural activities.[20] The personal relationships that Russian/Slavic persons in Hong Kong form with residents of other ethnic and national backgrounds, such as through school attendance and membership in clubs and other types of social organizations, also contribute to the social diversity of the region, similarly to how Shanghai was a cosmopolitan metropolis before 1949 and how it is today.

Extending beyond the OPASPP's relevance to the religious and social life of Hong Kong, we consider this book as a case study of how a ROC mission is currently operating in East Asia. Based in Hong Kong, the OPASPP is a unique node in not only the exchange of cultural ideas and practices between Russia and China, but concomitantly within the Orthodox Christian community in East Asia. OPASPP clergy have more freedom than PRC mainland clergy to travel outside of China. They can visit churches and participate in events that occur in neighboring areas of East Asia, Russia, and other parts of the world. Father Anatoly Kung (Kung Cheung Ming), who is one of the very few ethnic Chinese priests in the ROC and one of the officiants at the OPASPP, was educated in Russia and spent extensive periods there during his previous career in business. He is familiar with Russian culture through his proficiency in Russian language and lived experiences in Russian society. Father Kung also maintains an international network of fellow clerics and lay believers, which is possible because his writings about religious life and translations of Orthodox liturgical texts are accessible to a worldwide audience. The COP, which is the main subject of chapter 4, produces publications in Russian, English, Simplified Chinese, and Traditional Chinese, including works by Father Pozdnyaev and by Father Kung.

In addition to textual publications, interpretation of Orthodox Christian thought and practice, are also transmitted between Hong Kong and fellow Orthodox institutions in other countries through interactions between layman believers. Many ethnic Chinese converts to Russian Orthodox Christianity first developed interest in the faith when they visited Orthodox churches in Russia or read Russian literature, which will be seen in case studies presented in chapter 5. Similarly, while formal relations between Orthodox parishes in East Asia are mutually respectful but limited in practice, individual OPASPP members do visit churches when they are traveling in other countries. They also learn about variations in customs, such as holiday traditions, specific to ethnic and national groups through digital media and indirect contact with fellow believers via email, messaging, and other forms of communication.

The OPASPP also contend with some challenges that are unique to its status being within the PRC but not in the mainland. Since Hong Kong is the only place in the PRC without any restrictions on missionary work, the OPASPP has the ability to spread information about the faith and attract converts but must do so with highly limited material and human resources.

Another challenge is how to balance inculturation of religious practice with preservation of Russian customs and values. The OPASPP is responsible for promulgating not only Orthodox Christianity but also Russian culture which is easier done in some areas of the world, especially where there are demographically stable populations of Russian expatriates and persons of Russian heritage. In contrast, in Hong Kong, the segment of the Russian expatriate population with Orthodox backgrounds is highly divided between practicing and nonpracticing believers. This group is also not socially cohesive. Many Russians in Hong Kong prefer to socialize with non-Russian friends and colleagues. Therefore, the OPASPP serves as a spiritual center for only some of the city's Russian/Slavic persons, and has difficulty incorporating and retaining parishioners who are not Russian/Slavic or who are not related to Russian/Slavic persons by marriage. The OPASPP embraces the challenges of serving heritage believers, or "cradle Orthodox Christians," and also "seeker converts" (individuals converting on their own) and "intermarriage converts" (individuals converting through affiliation and marriage with Orthodox partners) and has adapted in many ways to be a religious and social home for its parishioners and people who want to learn more about the theological and cultural characteristics of Russian Orthodox Christianity but approach the parish without the explicit intent of conversion.

Since the political and social conditions in neighboring countries of East Asia differ greatly from those in Hong Kong and mainland China, this book does not presume to draw in-depth comparisons or to suggest that what occurs in Hong Kong is necessarily relevant or transferable to other East Asian Orthodox communities. However, the imperative of political and cultural adaptation is one that all these groups have faced throughout the history of Orthodox Christianity's presence in their societies. At present, Orthodox Christianity is also practiced in neighboring countries of East Asia, the Democratic People's Republic of North Korea (DPRK, North Korea), South Korea, and Japan.[21] The government of North Korea, like the PRC center, exerts direct control over all aspects of church operations. Kim Il-sung (1912–1994) permitted some religious institutions to operate after the country was founded as a Communist state in 1948. Kim Jong-il (1941–2011), Kim Il-sung's son and successor as head of the DPRK government, authorized the opening of the ROC of the Life-Giving Trinity in Pyongyang in 2006.[22] The church is formally a parish under the Moscow Patriarchate, but the DPRK government provides financial support for the church's expenses, including clergy salaries and operational costs, and determines who can join the clergy by choosing the students who will be permitted to attend Russian seminaries and be ordained.

In Japan and the Republic of Korea (ROK, South Korea), Orthodox churches enjoy the rights accorded to other civic bodies including freedom of expression about political and social issues. Clergy can enact mandates from Church central authorities with little or no government interference. Believers do not fear religious persecution and can practice their faith openly. Russian Orthodox and Greek Orthodox missionaries introduced Orthodox Christianity to Japan in the nineteenth century.[23] From that period to the present, the Orthodox community in Japan, which has continually been a significant minority in both the total population and within the Christian subpopulation, developed indigenized practices and customs, such as services conducted fully in Japanese and churches staffed primarily by Japanese clergy.[24] The ROC has been more important and influential than the Greek Orthodox Church. The Japanese Orthodox Church has been recognized as an autonomous church (Church of Japan) by the Moscow Patriarchate since 1970.[25] It consists of the Tokyo Archdiocese, Eastern Japan Diocese, and Western Japan Diocese, and administers the Tokyo Orthodox Seminary.[26]

Sharing a similar history with Japan of both Russian Orthodox and Greek Orthodox missions introducing the faith in the late nineteenth century, but with a much smaller population of believers, the Korean Orthodox Church, or Metropolis of Korea, which is under the Ecumenical Patriarchate of Constantinople, is now the predominant Orthodox body in South Korea.[27] There are also parishes formerly under the Holy Synod of the ROC and now belonging to the Patriarchal Exarchate in Southeast Asia. Also, as in Japan, Orthodox believers constitute a minority within the total Christian population in South Korea. Among the 30 percent of South Korea's total population (51.3 million as of 2019) who claim to be members of Christian denominations, only an estimated 4,000 people are Orthodox Christians.[28]

Studies of Orthodox Christianity in Japan and Korea have largely developed separately from the body of scholarship about the religion and the communities formed around it in China. This book alone cannot bridge that gap. However evidence from Hong Kong is intended to facilitate future comparisons among these states and societies that do share philosophical values, such as the traditions of Confucian and Buddhist thought, and have engaged with Russia as a regional neighbor, both in adversarial and cooperative terms.[29] Inspiring more cross-cultural or macro-studies of Russian Orthodox communities in East Asia will also link these groups and their interpretations of faith and culture to those farther afield in the Orthodox world. In particular, the adaptation of Russian Orthodox Christianity in North America is fertile ground for understanding both facets of the OPASPP's mission as a spiritual center for heritage believers and for converts. Studies on a very local scale, like David B. Cole's thesis on the establishment of the Church in the state of Oregon, are similar in scope and the emphasis on how the preservation of Russian/Slavic culture was a key impetus for the community to develop.[30] The subfield of Russian Orthodox inculturation in Alaska also holds potential for comparison. The evolution of Orthodox Christianity that intersects with Alaskan Native worldviews and how Orthodox culture indigenized together with spiritual beliefs during the twentieth century bear similarities to how Orthodox beliefs and cultural practices are translated linguistically and conceptually for Chinese/Sinophone people in Hong Kong.[31]

METHODS AND SOURCES

This book builds upon the foundation of research about the ROC in China by representatives of the OPASPP and scholars specializing in Russian Orthodoxy as a topic of theology, philosophy, history, and sociology. The OPASPP clergy and church office have produced an abundant literature about the previous Orthodox communities and the history of the currently active parish, as seen in chapter 4.³² In this book, we do not intend to duplicate these narratives or supplant them with entirely contrasting perceptions of the same events and general development of the church. Details from these insider interpretations are important to our analysis and we respect the values and interests reflected in them. The "added value" of our research for the existing body of knowledge about the ROC in Hong Kong, is that we examine the parish and its religious activities as part of a community that has spiritual and secular functions and in the broader context of Hong Kong's social development during the late twentieth century to the present. Since new evidence for this analysis is generated perpetually and through social media and other sources, we acknowledge that our study is grounded in a historical perspective as we reflect mainly on how Russian Orthodox community has developed in the past twenty years.

Even though the OPASPP is a central subject, this book was not formulated as a study of church history or missiology. As social historians of China, we started with the motivation to understand how Russian Orthodox Christianity shapes facets of life in Hong Kong. Just as Christopher Munn introduces Carl T. Smith's path-breaking work on Chinese Christians in Hong Kong as "primarily of social and cultural history, not of religious or church history," we expect that our findings about the Russian Orthodox community will be most relevant and meaningful to readers who share our interest in China Studies.³³ Also like Smith's work, and described by Munn as a strength rather than a weakness, our book takes the approach of providing details which help readers form multiple types of understandings about the topic rather than a "single narrative sweep" that may be expected from historical research about a single city or a relatively small segment of a society.³⁴ While not written with the disciplinary standards of missiology and church history in mind, we expect that our case study will shed light on how the Hong Kong mission is both unique and representative of broader developments in twenty-first century missions.³⁵ Our book also contributes a piece of what constitutes "Church history" for the ROC, which Eugene I. Lyutko has regarded as particularly complicated due to the intertwining of theological and political concerns throughout its history.³⁶

The bulk of evidence analyzed in our research are primary source materials generated by the OPASPP, RLC, and COP. These three institutions have generously permitted us to access their publications, which range from books and articles to flyers and postcards. They also produce significant amounts of digitally born media that are generally available for public viewing. The changes in how information is created and disseminated by these three pillars of the Russian Orthodox community could be the subject of another book because they have been so dynamic. Therefore most of the citations in chapters 2 through 5 are representative rather than exhaustive.

To reflect the ongoing changes in Hong Kong's ROC as a living institution and social community, we conducted interviews for this study primarily in 2017, with some conducted in 2018 and 2019 to follow up and update some content. While every effort was made to encourage interviewees contributing data included in chapters 3 to 6 to identify themselves either by their actual names or by pseudonyms, some persons asked that their experiences be disassociated from them as individuals and instead used to substantiate a general phenomenon. The authors followed standard, approved research protocol to conduct such interviews but have decided to respect such wishes for further anonymization. Interested readers may contact Loretta Kim, the corresponding co-author, for further details about the interview-derived content of this book.

CHAPTER OUTLINE

The first two chapters situate our topic and arguments in the context of relevant concepts and the development of the Russian Orthodox community from the 1930s to the present. In chapter 1, we discuss the three areas of significance for our case study: (1) Sino-Russian relations, (2) Christianity in Greater China, and (3) religious and ethnic minorities in Hong Kong. We will pinpoint specific foci in each area and explain how our study is related to them. Chapter 2 will then give an overview of the community's evolution from its inception as marked by major milestones. This section of the book is not an uncritical "potted history," because much of the content is not well-known outside of the community but is presented in relation to the well-established framework of Hong Kong's political history based on the chronological change from British colonization to mainlandization, the current phase of developing Hong Kong into a standard Chinese society. We begin this chapter with the significance of the Russian Orthodox mission taking root in Hong Kong during the 1920s and 1930s. In the 1940s, the Hong Kong parish became active as a period of involuntary dormancy due to the Japanese occupation during World War II. From the 1950s to 1970, large-scale out-migration by Russian/Slavic residents of Hong Kong affected the composition and resources of the community. Starting in the late 1990s, Father Pozdnyaev re-established the mission and has led the rejuvenation of parish and the wider community life since then.

Chapters 3, 4, and 5 each examine one institution of the community and an area of significance. The RLC and Sino-Russian relations is the subject of chapter 3 because it is an important channel of transmitting information about Russian culture to non-Russian persons in Hong Kong. Since the RLC is a legal corporate entity distinct from the OPASPP and is the most publicly visible component of the community, it fosters wide participation in Russian-language classes and activities. This chapter discusses how the RLC plays an important role in educating and promoting awareness of Russian culture and now it provides services for both Orthodox believers, such as Russian-language instruction for discounted or no charge for church members, as well as for Hong Kong residents who do not know the school is associated with a church. Chapter 4 focuses on the COP and the community's transmission of knowledge about Orthodox Christianity to Chinese-literate audiences. The first section introduces how Hong Kong has been an important marketplace of ideas because publication and trade have been relatively unrestricted for most of its colonial and post-1997 history. The OPASPP and COP have made use of these conditions to generate Chinese-language content about Orthodoxy, including histories of Orthodox Christianity, the ROC, and the ROC in China, texts for liturgical practice, translations of theological classics, and tools for understanding Orthodox Christian culture and life. This chapter demonstrates how Hong Kong functions as a vital source of information for Christians throughout Greater China. Chapter 5 discusses how the OPASPP is a center for people seeking spiritual enrichment and information about Russian society and culture, and its significance as a case study for understanding the experiences of people who belong to religious and ethnic minority groups in Hong Kong. This chapter addresses the relative invisibility of Russians and other Slavic persons in Hong Kong and how the OPASPP plays an important role in performing outreach about both religious and secular facets of historical and contemporary Russian life. As Michael Khordarkovsky concluded from evidence about conversions of non-Christians within the Russian empire from the eighteenth and nineteenth centuries that "Religious conversion was also a process of exchange, as a Russian Orthodox sense of identity was itself further crystallized in the encounter with non-Christians."[37] In this vein, the OPASPP functions as a meaningful site, through the physical space of the church and parish facilities, and as a source of spiritual and cultural guidance, by its clergy, for a variety of Hong Kong residents including those seeking "tradition" as a key element of religious practice whether as heritage believers or converts, a "home away from home" from Russian/Slavic societies, and those who value the Russian cultural elements that are embedded in the OPASPP's religious services and social activities. This chapter furthermore demonstrates that a group that may be considered as a minority because of religion and ethnicity is nevertheless important in maintaining social and cultural diversity both within an urban area like Hong Kong and to connect this region to other parts of the world.

NOTES

1. This event often takes place during the annual Russian Culture Week, co-sponsored by the OPASPP and the OPASPP-affiliated Russian Language Center, as well as other community organizations in Hong Kong. More discussion of Russian Culture Week will be included in chapters 3 and 5.

2. According to the Constitution of the Russian Orthodox Church, the supreme bodies of church authority and governance are the Local Council comprised of both clergy and lay members, the Council of Bishops that convenes once every two years and the Holy Synod with a membership of 14 bishops headed by the Patriarch. These bodies have legislative, executive, and judicial powers in their own competence. The Local Council of the Russian Orthodox Church has the highest power of ROC and makes all the important decisions of the ROC as its legal organ such as the election of the patriarch. The Council of Bishops and the Holy Synod oversee a Supreme Church Council and General Church Court. The ROC headquarters, presently at the Danilov Monastery in Moscow, oversees all the subunits, including deaneries, monasteries, convents, and religious educational institutions.

Eparchies, exarchates, and metropolitan districts are the major subunits of the Church. A bishop governs each eparchy (diocese) or exarchate. A metropolitan (bishop) or archbishop oversees large eparchies and self-governing branches of the ROC such as the Church of Japan and the Russian Orthodox Church Outside of Russia (ROCOR), now based in the United States. Each bishop oversees an eparchial assembly that meets once a year, an eparchial council that meets once every six months, and an eparchial court. The bishop also supervises vicar bishops who administer vicarates, and the deaneries. Each deanery consists of several parishes. A parish archpriest or priest heads each parish, and presides over a parish assembly, parish council, and a parish audit committee.

About the historical background of ROCOR and its relations with other Orthodox bodies, see Katja Richters, *The Post-Soviet Russian Orthodox Church: Politics, Culture and Greater Russia* (London: Routledge, 2012), and Ciprian Burlacioiu, "Russian Orthodox Diaspora as a Global Religion after 1918," *Studies in World Christianity* 24, no. 1 (April 2018): 4–24. ROCOR has maintained a website in Russian and English but it is currently defunct. For a layperson introduction on the Internet, see *Orthodox Wiki*, "Russian Orthodox Church Outside Russia," accessed August 27, 2017, https://orthodoxwiki.org/Russian_Orthodox_Church_Outside_Russia.

3. For a simple explanation about the organization of Eastern Orthodox Churches and their jurisdictions, see World Council of Churches, "Orthodox churches (Eastern)," accessed February 18, 2021, https://www.oikoumene.org/church-families/orthodox-churches-eastern.

4. Russian culture, like other cultures, is not static or bound in immutable traditions. We will use the term flexibly, respecting various definitions and interpretations, such as presented in the now classic work by James H. Billington, *The Icon and the Axe: An Interpretive History of Russian Culture* (New York: Vintage Books, 1970), and for examples of more recent scholarship, Nicholas Rzhevsky, ed.

The Cambridge Companion to Modern Russian Culture (Cambridge: Cambridge University Press, 2012). Regarding "Russian Orthodox tradition," as an aspect of Russian culture, see Vera Shevzov, "The Russian Tradition," in *The Orthodox Christian World*, ed. Augustine Casiday (London: Routledge, 2012), 15–40. This volume includes chapters about Orthodoxy in North America and Australia but not about East Asia.

5. The term "Russia" will refer to both the historical Soviet Union and the current Russian Federation, when referring in general to the place of origin for persons who claim Russian, or formerly Soviet, nationality because they were born or otherwise enjoy the right of citizenship in the Soviet Union/Russian Federation. "Soviet Union" and "Russian Federation" will be used to refer to those specific states or time periods.

6. The Orthodox Metropolitanate of Hong Kong and South East Asia (OMHKSEA), representing the Ecumenical Patriarchate of Constantinople, established the Holy Trinity Parish of Taipei in 2004.

7. The current church maintains a website in Russian, see Pravoslavnaia Tserkov' v Taivane (Ofitsial'nyi sait patriarshego podvor'ia russkoi pravoslavnoi tserkvi-Khram vozdvizheniia kresta gospodnia) [Orthodox Church in Taiwan, official site of the Patriarchal Metochion of the Russian Orthodox Church-Temple of the Exaltation of the Holy Cross], accessed March 14, 2017, https://orthodox-church.com.tw, and in Chinese, see Taiwan Jidu Zhengjiaohui [Orthodox Church in Taiwan (Moscow Patriarchate)], accessed March 14, 2017, http://orthodoxchurch.tw/%E5%8F%B0%E7%81%A3%E6%AD%A3%E6%95%99%E6%9C%83. About the Parish of Christ the Savior, see Christ the Savior Church, Catholic Archdiocese of Taipei, accessed February 18, 2021, https://taipei.catholic.org.tw/taipei/eng/deanery/2/.

8. Minzu University of China Museum, "Jidujiao [Christianity]," permanent exhibit.

9. Kolivo, also known as koliva, is a special food that is usually arranged on a tray with a cross to honor the deceased. See Mary Paloumpis Hallick, *Treasured Traditions and Customs of the Orthodox Church* (Edina, MN: Light and Life Publishing, 2001), 57.

10. About the Ethnic Identification Project and Chinese conceptions of ethnicity, see Thomas S. Mullaney, *Coming to Terms with the Nation: Ethnic Classification in Modern China* (Berkeley: University of California Press, 2011). For a comprehensive examination of personal and communal identity, see Ge Zhaoguang and Michael Hill, *What Is China?: Territory, Ethnicity, Culture, and History* (Cambridge, MA: Belknap Press of Harvard University Press, 2018) or the original Chinese publication, Ge Zhaoguang, *He wei Zhongguo?: Jiangyu, minzu, wenhua yu lishi* [What Is China?: Territory, Ethnicity, Culture, and History] (Hong Kong: Oxford University Press, 2014).

11. Statistics for religious affiliation in the annually published *Hong Kong Yearbook* vary, but Christians are consistently identified as less than 20 percent of the total population. About the number of Christians in mainland China, see *The Economist*, "Protestant Christianity is booming in China: President Xi does not approve," Daily chart, September 15, 2020, accessed February 18, 2021, https://ww

w.economist.com/graphic-detail/2020/09/15/protestant-christianity-is-booming-in-china.

12. Regarding the university's Christian mission, see the university's website, "Hong Kong Baptist University Vision and Mission," accessed April 10, 2019, https://www.hkbu.edu.hk/eng/about/mission.jsp.

13. Christian hospitals include St. Teresa's Hospital in Kowloon and the Hong Kong Adventist Hospital with campuses in Hong Kong Island and Tsuen Wan, New Territories.

14. See Brand Hong Kong, "Brand Hong Kong," accessed December 21, 2018, www.brandhk.gov.hk/en/index.html.

15. The Hong Kong government provides open access to demographical statistics. The latest data shows that 6.8 million out of 7.2 million people were identified as ethnic Chinese in 2016. For the most recent figures, which are updated periodically, see the Hong Kong [Special Administrative Region] Government Census and Statistics Department, "Demographic Characteristics," accessed July 19, 2018, https://www.censtatd.gov.hk/hkstat/sub/gender/demographic/index.jsp. Statistics in this category consider both gender and other traits such as ethnicity.

16. See Loretta E. Kim, "From Residency to Citizenship: Chinese Nationalism and Changing Criteria for Political and Legal Interpretations of Hong Kong Identity in the Post-1997 Era," in *Reimagining Nation and Nationalism in Multicultural East Asia*, eds. Sungmoon Kim and Hsin-Wen Lee (London and New York: Routledge, 2018), 123–40.

17. The seven-year rule does not apply to some groups like foreign domestic workers who are ineligible for permanent residency even if they remain in Hong Kong for decades.

18. Among these groups, Hong Kong Unison is a prominent organization that specifically advocates for the rights and socioeconomic advancement of ethnic minorities in Hong Kong. See "Hong Kong Unison," accessed November 20, 2018, http://www.unison.org.hk.

19. The modifier "Russian/Slavic" is intended to be inclusive of Russians who are Slavic, Russians who are non-Slavic, and Slavic persons who are not Russian.

20. Russian commercial activities in Shanghai during the first half of the twentieth century encompassed many areas including several light industries, trade, and services ranging from food production and sales to insurance. See Wang Zhicheng, *Jindai Shanghai Eguo qiaomin shenghuo* [The life of Russian émigrés in modern Shanghai] (Shanghai: Shanghai cishu chubanshe, 2008), 524–67.

21. For a comprehensive history of Orthodox Christianity in East Asia, see Kevin Baker, *A History of the Orthodox Church in China, Korea and Japan* (Lewiston, NY: Edwin Mellen, 2006).

22. Since information about North Korea is highly restricted, most sources about this church are highly general and not suitable for academic analysis. See, for example, Embassy of Russia (Russian Federation) to the DPRK, "Orthodox Church of the Live-Giving (sic.) Trinity in Pyongyang," accessed June 16, 2018, http://www.rusembdprk.ru/en/russia-and-dprk/orthodox-church-in-pyongyang, and Spiegel Online, "North Korea Builds an Orthodox Church," accessed June 20, 2018, https://www

.spiegel.de/international/kim-jong-il-and-religion-north-korea-builds-an-orthodox-church-a-431310.html.

23. About the Greek Orthodox missions in Japan, see Otis Cary, *Roman Catholic and Greek Orthodox Missions*, vol.1 of *A History of Christianity in Japan* (Rutland, VT and Tokyo, Japan: Charles. Tuttle Company, 1976).

24. The Orthodox population in Japan ranges from 10,000 to 20,000 believers, based on different sources. Father Timothy Ware estimated that there were 25,000 believers as of 2015. See Timothy Ware, *The Orthodox Church: An Introduction to Eastern Christianity*, 3rd ed. (London: Penguin Books, 2015), 183. This broad estimate confirms that this group is a minority in a country of 126.9 million people (as of 2019). See the "Japan" entry in United Nations Population Fund, "World Population Dashboard," accessed June 16, 2019, https://www.unfpa.org/data/world-population-dashboard.

25. For the Church's website, see Orthodox Church of Japan, "The Orthodox Church of Japan," accessed June 19, 2018, http://www.orthodoxjapan.jp (in Japanese).

26. For descriptions of the dioceses and individual churches, see Michael Van Remortel and Peter Chang, eds. *St. Nikolai Kasatkin and the Orthodox Mission in Japan: A Collection of Writings by an International Group of Scholars about St. Nikolai, his Disciples and the Mission* (Point Reyes Station, CA: Divine Ascent Press, Monastery of St. John of Shanghai and San Francisco, 2003), particularly Eleonora Sablina, "Pathways of a Pilgrim from Russia," 37–80.

27. Russian Orthodox clergy founded a Korean Church in 1898, which was maintained until the 1950s when it almost died out but was then revived by Archimandrite Sotirios (Trambas) who served as Bishop until 2008. See Ware, *Orthodox Church*, 183. The COP has published a bilingual publication about the concise history of Orthodoxy in Korea from 1900 to the present. The cover of this book includes the title in three languages: Russian on top, Korean *hangeul* in the middle, and Chinese characters on the bottom. The Russian text of the book is on the verso of each page, and the corresponding Korean text is on the recto. See Choi Jiyoon (Pilateus), *Kratkii Ocherk Istorii Koreiskoi Pravoslavnoi Tserkvi / Hanguk jeonggyohoe yaksa / Hanguo Zhengjiaohui lüeshi* [A short history of Orthodox Christianity in Korea] (Hong Kong: China Orthodox Press, 2015).

28. For the current population of South Korea, see the "Korea, Republic of" entry in United Nations Population Fund, "World Population Dashboard," accessed June 16, 2019, https://www.unfpa.org/data/world-population-dashboard.

29. Recent works about social and cultural relations include Olga V. Solovieva and Sho Konishi, eds., *Japan's Russia: Challenging the East-West Paradigm* (Amherst, NY: Cambria Press, 2021), and Alyssa M. Park, *Sovereignty Experiments: Korean Migrants and the Building of Borders in Northeast Asia, 1860–1945*, Studies of the Weatherhead East Asian Institute, Columbia University (Ithaca, NY: Cornell University Press, 2019).

30. David B. Cole, "Russian Oregon: A History of the Russian Orthodox Church and Settlement in Oregon, 1882–1976" (master's thesis, Portland State University, 1976), page number, PDXScholar (Paper 2334).

31. About Orthodox missions in Alaska, see Michael Oleksa, *Orthodox Alaska: A Theology of Mission* (Crestwood, NY: St. Vladimir's Seminary Press, 1992), and

Sergei Kan, *Memory Eternal: Tlingit Culture and Russian Orthodox Christianity Through Two Centuries* (Seattle: University of Washington Press, 1999).

32. For example, "Kitaiskaia Avtonomnaia Pravoslavnaia Tserkov'" [Chinese Autonomous Orthodox Church], accessed March 21, 2017, http://www.orthodox.cn/localchurch/pozdnyaev/5_ru.htm (this website is also available in English).

33. Carl T. Smith, *Chinese Christians: Elites, Middlemen, and the Church in Hong Kong* (Oxford: Oxford University Press, 1985; repr., Hong Kong: Hong Kong University Press, 2005), xi.

34. Smith, *Chinese Christians*, xiv.

35. About the development and definition of missiology as an academic field, see Paul Kollman, "At the Origins of Mission and Missiology: A Study in the Dynamics of Religious Language," *Journal of the American Academy of Religion* 79, no. 2 (June 2011): 425–58.

36. Eugene I. Lyutko, "Church History and the Predicament of the Orthodox Hierarchy in the Russian Empire of the Early 1800s," *Slověne* 6, no. 2 (2017): 385–99.

37. Michael Khodarkovsky, "The Conversion of Non-Christians in Early Modern Russia," in *Of Religion and Empire: Missions, Conversion, and Tolerance in Tsarist Russia*, eds. Robert P. Geraci and Michael Khodarkovsky (Ithaca, NY: Cornell University Press, 2001), 116–17.

Chapter 1

Sino-Russian Relations, Christianity in Greater China, and Religious and Ethnic Minorities in Hong Kong

This chapter places our study of the Russian Orthodox community in Hong Kong, as consisting of the Orthodox Parish of Apostles Saints Peter and Paul (OPASPP), the Russian Language Center (RLC), and the China Orthodox Press (COP), in the context of salient understandings and ongoing developments in the three areas of significance stated in the book's Introduction. For readers who are familiar with one or more of these fields, this chapter serves to elucidate which aspects that we consider as most relevant to our inquiry. Readers who are new to these topics will find that our descriptions are given to be representative but not exhaustive explanations that will orient and provide adequate background for the following three chapters.

Each area comprises a section of this chapter. The first section is about the elements of Sino-Russian relations that have been prominent in primarily English-language scholarship. Our study contributes to the growing awareness about how cooperative contact has been an integral element of relations between China and Russia, which research on trade, intermarriage, and acculturation of Russians as ethnic minority people in China have shown.[1] We also relate our work to the cumulative perceptions of the ROC as an institution of Russian diplomacy to China and the exchange of knowledge and cultural practices between Chinese and Russian states and societies. The second section is about how this book addresses the need for more understanding of Orthodox Christianity in China. Since other religions and denominations of Christianity have received more scholarly attention, many questions about how Orthodox Christianity, including but not limited to the ROC, has developed as a non-native religion in Greater China remain to be answered. Our link between this area and the COP highlights the fact that the Russian Orthodox community in Hong Kong has been a critical hub of creating and disseminating information about faith and culture. The COP's work also exemplifies that although Hong Kong is a city of 7.5 million people on the geographic periphery of China, it is still important because it remains a place where ideas about religion and society in modern China are developed. The third area, about how this study is about religious and ethnic minorities in Hong Kong, is the topic of the final section. Research on religion in Hong Kong has revealed the diversity of faiths in the region, from Daoism and Buddhism, which are considered native, and Islam, Hinduism, and Judaism, which are deemed foreign in origin but have been the spiritual cores of communities that are important to Hong Kong's past and present. Within scholarship on Hong Kong Christianity, the overwhelming focus on Anglican (Episcopalian), Roman Catholic, and Protestant churches has created an opportunity to see another dimension of the faith which we have taken in this book as one step of building up a more comprehensive field of study.

SINO-RUSSIAN RELATIONS

Contact between China and Russia is a well-established area of research. Countless studies analyzing state-to-state, group-to-group, and individual-to-individual interactions abound in English, Chinese, and Russian languages, and the disciplines represented in this body of scholarship include most of the social sciences and much of the humanities. Therefore, this section will focus on two major aspects that are derived from what can be broadly observed but are also subject to reconsideration as more publications are produced and new themes emerge.

The first of these aspects is that "conventional understandings" of Orthodox Christianity as a part of Sino-Russian relations have been limited by temporal and geographic scope, focusing on pre-1949 evidence from major cities like Beijing and the Sino-Russian borderland which adjoins Siberia and Manchuria/Manchukuo (Northeast China).[2] Only in a few works about Orthodox Christianity in Southern China has Hong Kong been mentioned as a place with an Orthodox presence.[3] One notable example is the citation by Oxford-educated Serge Nikolaevich Bolshakoff (1901–1990), listing Hong Kong as well as the Philippines, Indonesia, and Indochina as places still under ROCOR jurisdiction in the 1950s. This citation appears in a section of Bolshakoff's article describing Russian Orthodox missionary activity in Manchuria and Xinjiang (Turkestan), two regions for which he gives proportionately more details, contributing to the bias toward northern China.[4]

The second aspect is that many studies have concentrated on Orthodox Christianity as a tool of political relations and treated it as a marginal or tangential element of social and cultural relations between Chinese and Russians. More scholarship in the past twenty years has demonstrated that

Orthodox Christianity should be evaluated not just as a religion but also as a means of communicating values and customs since the seventeenth century. This book contributes to this evolving approach which treats the ROC and its adherents in a more comprehensive context that includes but also distinguishes the impact of Orthodox institutions, communities, and individuals in China.[5]

The ROC is prominent in many narratives of Sino-Russian relations that begin in the seventeenth century. A very concise summation of their common premise is that the Russian tsardom-then-empire expanded its administrative control and economic extraction of material resources in North Asia, while the Qing empire (1644–1911) intended to keep foreigners out of its domain except for sanctioned visits and economic activities in frontier zones.[6] After these states reached a truce about the boundary that would demarcate their territories and settled other terms of engagement with the 1689 Treaty of Nerchinsk such as about the daily administrative operations of monitoring people, goods, and animals moving from one side to another of the border, the ROC gained a formal foothold in China through the missions, about 18 to 20 by different counts, that were sent to serve as representatives of the Church and to transmit information about China back to the Russian government. In doing so, the ROC played a similar role that it did as the spiritual and cultural arm of the Russian enterprise of territorial expansion in Central Asia and Siberia.

Studies about the missions and the institution of the Russian Ecclesiastical Mission from 1715 to 1956, have revealed that they had many purposes and generated a variety of conclusions about their significance.[7] These missions, by any quantitative or qualitative analysis of their activities, were not successful in achieving the primary objective of mass conversion of Chinese to Orthodox Christianity even though they maintained a stable presence in China until the late nineteenth century.[8] Confined in Beijing with little opportunity to leave their home base, the earliest missionaries tried to spread their faith to some members of the imperial elite and the small population of people, known as the Albazinians, who were supposed to be Orthodox Christians because of their forefathers had been Russian subjects.[9] Also affecting the mission operations were that the Orthodox clerics served tours of duty typically lasting a decade or shorter, and returned to Russia after completing them rather than coming to China intending to stay for as long as possible like their Roman Catholic counterparts.

The Russian Ecclesiastical Mission, which Gregory Afinogenov has described as "an institution so dysfunctional that it eventually came to stand for the failures of Russia's China policy," also achieved mixed results in training Russian students to learn Manchu and Chinese languages.[10] According to Afinogenov, among the factors hampering the educational objectives of the institution was that the presence of two groups under separate administration. The missionaries, led by an archimandrite, represented the Holy Synod and the Russian students were accountable to the College of Foreign Affairs, meant that teachers and their pupils did not necessarily share common goals and sources of motivation.

Aside from studies that focus on the missions, the role of Orthodox Christianity has been a relatively minor topic in general studies of Sino-Russian relations which have been largely analyzed on a state-to-state level and concentrated on diplomacy, trade, and other forms of control and competition over material and human resources from the sixteenth through nineteenth centuries.[11] Although the North Hostel, also known as the Russian Hostel, which was the residence and working headquarters of the missions, was the unofficial consulate of the Russian empire, it does not feature much in discussions about how Sino-Russian political and economic relations developed.[12] However, the importance of the missions and of Orthodox Christianity more broadly has come to light as perceptions of contact between China and Russia as being more than a "clash of civilizations," with conflict and inherent differences at the fore, have given way to more holistic appraisals of what such interactions exemplify about modes of interstate relations and conceptions of foreign cultures and societies.[13]

Orthodox Christianity is embedded in what may be considered the crucial first stage of Sino-Russian relations during the imperial age in several ways. The timing of the "official" beginning of Sino-Russian relations remains ambiguous, but in scholarly consensus, generally falls sometime in the sixteenth or seventeenth centuries, depending on what types of interactions are regarded as constituting substantial contact. However, Kevin Baker points out that Orthodox Christians were present in China starting in the thirteenth century, a claim which shifts the timeline profoundly.[14] Kenneth Scott Latourette dates first contact between Russians and Beijing in his comprehensive history of Christian missions in China to the "late sixteenth century" but emphasizes that the Russians were "not officially received."[15] He makes a more overt observation about the impact of political factors on the Russian Orthodox mission in China with his explanation that the mission that started in 1914 was forced to end in 1926 because of the Russian Revolution (1917–1923).[16]

Less examined has been the impact of Orthodox Christianity on indigenous inhabitants of regions that became China's borderlands during the Qing. The lack of attention to this topic can be attributed to the comparative scarcity of sources about these borderland populations' social and cultural lives, and the difficulty of constructing complete narratives from such limited evidence. However justified, the paucity of such research skews the metrics of measuring the missions' influence only by what they could but failed to achieve in their immediate field of activity, which was restricted by the imperial government. The passing references to Orthodox Christians south of the border also differentiate what research on missions in Central Asia and Siberia has discovered about the discrepancy between the theoretical transformation of heart and mind that colonized populations would undergo after converting to Orthodox Christianity and becoming proper imperial subjects and the realities of Orthodox Christian faith and culture being interpreted and adapted by those groups in ways that defied the expectations that they would become more loyal to the tsar and more "Russian" in thought and demeanor.[17] More often implied than explicitly affirmed in related studies of Sino-Russian borderlands is that neither the Chinese state nor social communities accommodate the "Siberian model of expansion," in which the religion took root in conquered areas because settlements needed churches which needed priests who could enforce religious and cultural codes.[18] Although conversion to Orthodox Christianity was supposed to be perceived a privilege, from the perspective of the putative converts, because they would no longer have to pay tribute to the Russian tsar in the form of material resources, many indigenous populations in Central Asia and Siberia resisted conversion or engaged in practices of Orthodox Christianity concomitantly with their native faiths.[19] James Forsyth describes some Mansis and Khantys pretending to be Christian by wearing and "acting Russian" during the eighteenth and nineteenth centuries to avoid being punished by Russian colonial authorities but having only nominal knowledge of Christianity as one of many such cases.[20] Since the Sino-Russian border remained porous despite legal modification through successive treaties and the presence of physical barriers and routine patrols conducted to prevent illegal crossings, some natives of northernmost areas of the Qing realm also learned about Orthodox Christianity, including those who pursued conversion for a combination of political and social capital like the Daur leader Gantimur who became an Orthodox Christian, a Russian prince, and the progenitor of the Gantimurov family.[21] With more investigations about other cases of people from the Qing side of the shared borderland encountering Orthodox Christianity, interesting comparisons with studies about Central Asia and Siberia may be possible.

However, a common conception that differentiates China from other targets of Russian influence through Orthodox Christianity, and which would explain why research on the sixteenth to eighteenth centuries remains narrow in scope is that "systematic work" by Russian Orthodox missions did not begin until the nineteenth century and gained momentum into the early twentieth century.[22] Although this turning point does not coincide with a substantial expansion in the number of Chinese believers much less clergy, the missions changed their orientation and engaged in contact with not only non-elite Chinese but also with Russians in the nineteenth and early twentieth centuries to increase the efficacy of evangelization.

This mission by Archimandrite Innocent (Ivan Apollonovich Figurovskii) from 1896 to 1931 was more effective at reaching a broader base of potential converts by spreading knowledge through youth education and publication, performing social work, and establishing a library and a press.[23] Archimandrite Innocent was personally instrumental in altering the form and function of the mission by preaching in railway cars in Manchuria and using the cars as makeshift schools.[24] He also oversaw a broader agenda of providing charity for indigent Albazinians, who were recipients of support from the missions since the seventeenth century, and other groups while performing religious services in Chinese and earning income from businesses to fund the charitable activities.[25]

The reach of Orthodox Christianity also spread literally during this time with the establishment of churches and schools in various parts of China. This is evident in the description of the 1909 mission published by the Christian Literature Society for China and the China Continuation Committee as consisting of 1 bishop, 2 archimandrites, 10 priests (of whom 3 were Chinese), 6 deacons (including 2 Chinese), 3 psalm readers, 10 monks, 7 nuns,[26] and of the 1914 mission including 32 mission centers in Zhili, Hubei, Hunan, Jiangsu, Mongolia, 500 students in Orthodox schools, and 5,035 baptized Chinese.[27] The Church of the Holy Iveron Icon (St. Ibervel Church) of Harbin built in 1908 was one of these new churches which also served as a tribute to Russian victims of the Russo-Japanese War (1904–1905).[28] The "religious manifest destiny" to spread Orthodox Christianity as the dominant if not sole form of Christianity in China remained important to the ROC missions, even if it could not be realized beyond the enclaves of Beijing and in Northeast China where most of the churches and clergy were present.[29] What the missions did manage to achieve with their work in these locations was to acquire knowledge for detailed studies of China. Transfer of knowledge about China occurred regularly with the change of mission personnel but by the nineteenth century, Russian Sinology yielded comprehensive knowledge of Chinese language as exemplified by the publication of *Museum Sinicum* by Theophilus Siegfried Bayer (1689–1749) in 1730.[30] *Museum Sinicum* was not only the first Latin–Chinese lexicon published but was the first European study of Chinese language. Sinologists who were Russian or non-Russian but sponsored by the Russian imperial state also studied Chinese philosophy, history, and literature.[31] However, the ostensible gains of this era were tempered by setbacks caused by political forces and other factors. James J. Stamoolis claims that the Russian Orthodox mission suffered greater proportional losses during the Boxer Rebellion than Catholic and Protestant missions, attesting to the breadth of the Orthodox institution.[32] The number of Chinese joining the faith dwindled to less than 100 persons per baptismal cycle by the second half of the nineteenth century,[33] but attrition of both newly and previously baptized Chinese leaving the faith appeared severe in Archimandrite Innocent's calculation that there were less than 200 Orthodox, including Albazinians, by 1856.[34] Despite such setbacks, the resilience of the missions was not inconsequential. In 1902, the ROC attained two milestones positively affecting its financial condition and administrative authority. The incumbent mission obtained double the amount of funds it had received previously. Archimandrite Innocent was promoted from archimandrite to Bishop of Pereslavl and assumed greater responsibilities for Mongolia and Tibet as well as China proper.[35]

The importance of the nineteenth century and early twentieth century missions in our understanding of Sino-Russian relations is not exclusively in the details or the impression that the ROC reached the apex of its presence in China, even if any substantive increase in its influence as a religious institution is debatable, but in contrast to what may be considered as the series of crises that Russian Orthodox missions faced from the 1910s to the 1950s. This narrative of successive struggles fits into the parallel frameworks of political revolution in both China and Russia, the tenuous modes of military and political cooperation between the governments in power in this period, and ultimately the "Sino-Soviet splits" that happened not only between the USSR and the PRC but also with the Nationalist government under Chiang Kai-shek's rule as Chiang turned away from Russian advisors and toward German ones.[36] Perhaps mirroring the gradual political dissolution of the Qing state, the ROC in China became more regionally oriented in 1946 with the establishment of the East Asian Exarchate in Harbin. Three quasi-independent ROCOR bodies subsequently formed the Exarchate in Harbin led by Metropolitan Nestor (1884/1885–1962), the Ecclesiastical Mission in Beijing headed by Archbishop Viktor (Svyatin) (1893–1966), and the diocese in Shanghai led by Bishop John (Maximovitch) (1896–1966).[37]

Although Russian Orthodox missions continued officially until after the PRC was founded in 1949, the ROC adapted to the PRC's official constraints on organized religion with mixed results. Feodor Du Runchen (1886–1965) was ordained as the first ethnic Chinese bishop in 1950. First known as Bishop Simeon of Tianjin, he later served as Bishop of Shanghai.[38] Four years later, in 1956, the Moscow Patriarchate Holy Synod closed down the Russian Ecclesiastical Mission and left all churches in China under the authority of the East Asian Exarchate.[39] This discontinuation of official missions in the 1950s was the first step in the process of disassociating Orthodox Christianity in China from Russian leaders and institutions. In 1957, the Moscow Patriarchate granted full autonomy to the Chinese Autonomous Orthodox Church. Vasily Yao (Yao Fu'an, 1888–1962) in Moscow to be the Bishop of Beijing.[40] Bishop Vasily failed to establish himself as an efficient leader to oversee measures to reorganize church governance and rebuild congregations. Concomitant with the disintegration of official relations between the USSR and the PRC during the late 1950s and the Great Proletariat Cultural Revolution (1966–1976), the ROC diminished in capacity. In 1964, the PRC government closed the Church of the Dormition in Beijing.[41] The following year, Bishop Simeon died, and the PRC authorities closed down the Cathedral of the Icon of the Mother of God "Surety of Sinners" in Shanghai.[42] The last Russian cleric, archpriest Viktor Chernykh (1887–1967) from Harbin left the PRC to return to Moscow in 1966.[43] With economic liberalization in the 1980s, circumstances changed. The Protection (Pokrov) of the Theotokos Church of Harbin reopened on October 14, 1984 to conduct divine services.[44] The Chinese priest Father Grigorij Zhu Shipu (1924–2000) resumed his ecclesiastical duties in 1986. Gradual but measured allowances for religious practices have fostered the revival of Russian Orthodox Christianity in China, which will be discussed further in chapter 2.

These events and their consequences have mainly been studied separately from how Chinese and Russians interacted more generally in the twentieth century, whether in regions of "China proper" and "Russia proper" and the borderlands, and how Orthodox Christianity affected the development of Chinese regional cultures.[45] Our study of the Russian Orthodox community in Hong Kong engages with precedent scholarship that has focused upon and enriched our understanding of ways in which Chinese–Russian interaction has been cooperative or mutually beneficial, rather than competitive or antagonistic as studies of diplomatic and military relations tend to stress, and how social and cultural synergy has been possible between two groups that are often seen as rivals or adversaries in the international political arena or as being incompatible civilizations. Also related to the third area of significance, about religious and ethnic minorities in Hong Kong, is the subject of how a Russian ethnic group evolved in mainland China. Orthodox Christianity is discussed in scholarship about the "Russian ethnic minority" (*Eluosi zu*) but as an inherent cultural trait rather than more explicitly as part of their historical development as a social subgroup in Chinese society.[46]

CHRISTIANITY IN CHINA

Orthodox Christianity has also been overlooked in many general and comparative studies of Christianity in China. Omission may be considered inadvertent, as most scholarly attention has concentrated on the Roman Catholic and Protestant Churches, but the absence of such information from crucial texts of the field suggests to the reader that Orthodox Christianity has not mattered at all.[47] Two reasons may explain the relative lack of analysis about Orthodox communities in China. The first is that the association with Orthodox

Christianity with foreigners, both those literally outside of China and people considered as temporary residents of China, has not inspired studies of how it has social and cultural impact on the Chinese places where its institutions have existed and still exist. The second is that Orthodox Christianity may be politically sensitive because of its connection to contentious relations between China and Russia as introduced in the previous section. Orthodox Christian clergy in contemporary China are not "agents of empire" like Archpriest Ioann Vostorgov (1867–1918) who intended to preserve the Russian imperial order by bringing the inhabitants of Siberia under the ROC's control and was an active participant in developing strategies to proselytize in China and Japan.[48] However, the ongoing emphasis on atheism as the core of PRC social values affects how communities of faith are perceived and may be examined within the proper political parameters.

As of now, Hong Kong remains exceptional because foreign religious practices were not explicitly forbidden or severely regulated from the start of British colonial administration to the present. However, akin to Orthodox communities being concentrated in Northeast China, Northwest China, and Inner Mongolia, as well as ethnic Russians and other Slavic heritage believers in mainland China, Orthodox Christianity has been a marginal part of Hong Kong's social and cultural landscape, significantly overshadowed by Chinese religions like Daoism and Buddhism, and Catholic and Protestant churches.

We do not suggest that Orthodox Christianity, and the ROC in particular, has been insufficiently studied in absolute terms. Many overview histories have been published in Chinese and Russian.[49] Chinese-language translations of Orthodox theology and writings of Orthodox religious leaders are published and marketed as works of philosophy. This genre will be discussed more in chapter 4. There are also "grassroot histories" about Orthodox Christians in China such as a self-published account of the Du family documenting their history based on their ancestor Du Bining but also about their heritage as Albazinians and the cultural practices of Orthodox families developed over 300 years.[50] Descriptions of Orthodox Christianity in research on the Russian ethnic minority vary from a few nominal details to analysis of how the faith has shaped their social and cultural identities.[51] In-depth studies of Orthodox Christianity's impact on regional culture are limited, but two representative works by Tang Ge and Zheng Yongwang, incidentally published in the same year, have proven that certain elements of life in Northeast China originated in Orthodox Christian communities.[52]

Our book is one drop in the proverbial bucket, but we aim to show that the ROC is important to incorporate more comprehensively into the understanding of Christianity in China because religious communities have enhanced cultural diversity and stimulated constructive contact between people who may otherwise belong to different social groups through the channel of faith.

Setting aside the question of whether missionary work has been effective in China, a question which is often answered with ambiguous metrics, it is clear that Orthodox missionaries were interested in the intersection of faith and culture.[53] The propensity of China's governments to be wary of foreign religions makes the subject of cultural clash as a major consequence of religious proselytization.[54] However, just as current developments in work on Christianity in China that have revealed important findings about how time, region, gender affect the spread and acceptance, we view the ROC as a significant actor in how a "foreign religion" has adapted to social and cultural conditions in China.[55]

Two factors must be considered in integrating the ROC more meaningfully into the general field. First, political control over Christianity plays a great part in how and why the ROC may still not be well-integrated into the general history of Chinese Christianity, despite its presence since the seventeenth century through the missions. Orthodox Christianity in the PRC mainland fits Sabrina P. Ramet's "simple co-optive nationalist" framework for Church–State relations in the Orthodox world in which the Church hierarchy is co-opted and follows the regime's nationalist line.[56] Working with and against this limitation, there are many directions to be pursued in order to understand how the ROC has responded to policies about religious belief and practice. A second factor is the orientation of the field to think about inculturation, or nativization, of Christianity in terms that have been primarily based on Roman Catholic and Protestant cases.[57] Inculturation of Christianity in China has concentrated on the training of Chinese clergy and translations of the Bible and other texts into Chinese languages.[58] Analysis of inculturation has also been evolving to demonstrate that Christian missionaries were genuinely interested in understanding "native" belief systems and that inculturation affects how the practice of religions by people who are perceived as "not quite (ethnic) Chinese" such as Muslims in Northwest China have tried to maintain their faith and distinct ethnic identities while being members of a Chinese society.[59]

Although Hong Kong has been very different from the PRC mainland in many ways since the late nineteenth century, we believe that the OPASPP's history in Hong Kong also illustrates how the ROC has adapted and developed within a Chinese-majority society and polity, albeit with exceptional legal protection that allows religious groups to maintain their own leadership and to operate with little direct interference from government authorities. The presence of a Russian Orthodox community in Hong Kong from the early twentieth century onward gives evidence for examining how Orthodox Christianity has adapted to local social and cultural norms that speaks to two important questions. The first question is how do "Chinese" or "Asian" elements fit into the practices of Russian Orthodox Christianity in Hong Kong?

The terms Chinese and Asian in this question are deliberately in quotation marks as fluid concepts that are subject to individual as well as collective interpretation. The second and related question is how has the ROC in Hong Kong adapted to serve a polyethnic congregation? The ROC throughout East Asia has demonstrated respect for the communities in which the faith is practiced, such as reflected in how liturgical vestments are designed to incorporate symbols that are meaningful to Japanese or Chinese culture rather than originally to Russian culture.[60] This book shows that by adopting and adapting these elements, the OPASPP intends to a diverse group of believers.

Moreover, this book contributes to the expansion of what may be conceptualized as "Sinicization" of foreign religions and in doing so, also blurs the boundaries between "expatriate churches" and "native ethno-religious communities" in China, both the mainland and in Hong Kong. Sinicization has been interpreted differently from inculturation/nativization as being more overtly connected to how Chinese governments have attempted to make foreign cultures more politically acceptable such as the CCP's drive to exert ideological and administrative control over the practice of religions like Christianity and Islam.[61] Although the imperative of remaining legally and politically sanctioned is essential to the existence of any community, Sinicization is important when considering that religious groups strive for stability and growth based on holding a favorable position in the "spiritual marketplace," a term developed by Amy Slagle, or religious marketplace, as described by Philip Hammond.[62] Although the OPASPP has a relatively small share of the Hong Kong "marketplace," it is the spiritual home and social center for Russian Orthodox Christians in Hong Kong. The OPASPP is also an important part of the Russian Orthodox network in China's Guangdong province, directly north of Hong Kong. In Guangdong, there are Orthodox communities at the Icon of the Mother of God "Joy of All Who Sorrow" Church in Guangzhou and the St. Sergius of Radonezh Parish in Shenzhen.[63] Clergy and parishioners of the OPASPP furthermore belong to the broader Eastern Orthodox Christian community in East Asia. The OPASPP is one of two Eastern Orthodox Christian parishes in Hong Kong. The other congregation meets at the Saint Luke Orthodox Cathedral in Central, the district to the east of Sheung Wan.[64] The cathedral is the regional seat of the Orthodox Metropolitanate of Hong Kong and South East Asia (OMHKSEA). The Hong Kong Legislative Council recognized OMHKSEA as a legal corporate body with an ordinance approved in January 1997.[65] In line with the official terminology of this legislation, this church will be subsequently referred to as Orthodox Cathedral of Saint Luke the Evangelist (OCSLE) to differentiate it from the OPASPP.

The OPASPP may be commonly regarded as one of Hong Kong's "expatriate churches" because a significant number of its members are not Chinese by ethnicity and/or nationality, but we show in chapters 3 through 5, that inculturation both links this group to the past of the ROC in China and also differentiates it from other Orthodox Christian communities. One of many ways in which we see continuity as a method of the OPASPP's mission is that through their work of translating texts and writing about Orthodox culture and social values, Father Pozdynaev and Father Kung are transmitting knowledge between Russophone, Sinophone, and Anglophone audiences like Father Iakinf (Nikita Yakovlevich Bichurin, 1777–1853) did as head of the ninth ROC mission to the Qing empire by relaying information about China through writing to the Russian empire.[66] At the same time, the OPASPP has developed its own practices that are unlike other Orthodox parishes in other parts of the world such as about how new believers are integrated into the community. Some of the terminology about subcategories within the community is relevant, like Amy Slagle's differentiation of "Cradle Orthodox Christian," "seeker convert," and "intermarriage convert" within her study of congregations in Pennsylvania and Mississippi.[67] OPASPP parishioners may be similarly classified according to these terms. However, the reasons and ways in which converts join the community are specific to Hong Kong and a Chinese cultural context. Likewise, the incorporation of local languages into liturgical practices and the training of indigenous clergy and lay staff is culturally specific, so any commonalities that can be identified between the OPASPP and parishes in the PRC mainland as well as other parts of the world, are not conclusive indicators that there are international or intercultural consistency among missions. Nevertheless, it is meaningful to see how the Russian Orthodox community has developed in Hong Kong as it has been going through the major transition from colonial governance to the framework of autonomy within a state since 1997, which influences how all religious bodies, including the ROC, operate in the region.

RELIGIOUS AND ETHNIC MINORITIES IN HONG KONG

Conditions in Hong Kong have changed profoundly in the past five years, but our book is predicated on the as-yet operative features of law and administration of religion that differentiate the region from the PRC mainland. According to the framework that applies to governance until 2047, when the "fifty years of no change" period ends, the Hong Kong SAR (HKSAR) government upholds the freedom of spiritual belief and practice of religion among the rights granted to residents. In a publication available online in English and Chinese, the two official languages of the region, the HKSAR government publicizes the presence of several faith communities in the region: Buddhism, Daoism, Sikhism, Hinduism, Judaism, Islam, and Christianity. The paragraph on Christianity in this official fact sheet cites the diversity within the Christian population with various denominations represented. Absent in this description is Eastern Orthodox Christianity.[68] The Basic Law of the Hong Kong Special Administrative Region of the People's Republic of China (Basic Law), which informs the establishment of specific policies and is considered as a "regional constitution" (subordinate to the PRC constitution), includes an article ensuring the rights of religious organizations to hold property, operate institutions to provide social services like schools and hospitals, and perhaps most crucially, "to maintain and develop their relations with religious organizations and believers elsewhere."[69]

In contrast, the main purpose of the PRC's government organs administering religion has been to ensure that religious institutions do not promulgate beliefs that contradict socialist ideology and that they remain ultimately accountable to government authorities, to whom they must be more loyal than to the leaders of their faiths, or must solely be loyal to, for religions of foreign origin.[70] A representative example of the latter is the Roman Catholic Church. Chinese "patriotic" Catholics must not declare allegiance to the Vatican. For Orthodox Christians, the major restrictions on the practice of religion are that people under the age of eighteen cannot pursue religious education and conversion, and that only foreigners and registered believers may congregate at churches. Originally created in 1951 as the Religious Affairs Bureau, the State Administration for Religious Affairs (SARA) was a functioning department under the State Council until 2018. SARA was closely connected with the United Front Work Department of the Communist Party of China and charged with overseeing the operations of China's five officially sanctioned religious organizations: (1) Buddhist Association of China, (2) Chinese Taoist Association, (3) Islamic Association of China, (4) Three-Self Patriotic Movement (Protestant), 5) Chinese Patriotic Catholic Association. SARA was dissolved in 2018, placing all religious affairs directly under the United Front Work Department in the National Religious Affairs Administration unit.[71]

Church–state relations in Hong Kong are also affected by how religious organizations have been critical social actors that express views on political matters as related to the populations that they serve. The end of colonial governance and start of mainlandization before and after 1997 has raised new questions about their roles and responsibilities and the disagreements that occur about the political and social rights about segments of the population that have been economically marginalized and rely on church-based welfare.[72] The British colonial government did not have a specific unit to administer religious affairs, and did not interfere with the social services provided by the Anglican (Episcopalian) and Roman Catholic Churches and the

Hong Kong Christian Council after formal understandings were established in the 1980s.[73]

Although not mentioned in the HKSAR government fact sheet about the presence of multiple religions, the two Orthodox parishes in present-day Hong Kong are thriving religious communities. Both churches are located on Hong Kong Island which is the commercial and political center of the region. The OPASPP is also one of the few Russian Orthodox parishes in the Greater PRC (mainland, Macau, and Hong Kong) area that have full-time clergy and active congregations. ROC churches in Beijing, Shanghai, and Tianjin have relatively continuous histories in the twentieth century, with intermittent periods of inactivity due to government restrictions. Churches that have undergone significant revival in the past twenty years include the St. Innocent of Irkutsk Church in Ergune (E'erguna), Inner Mongolia which was rebuilt in 1999 and consecrated in 2009. Father Pavel Sun Ming has been the pastor of this church since 2018, and Father Alexander Yu Shi succeeded Father Zhu Shipu in 2016 as pastor of the Protection (Pokrov) of the Theotokos Church in Harbin. Other churches, such as St. Nicholas Church in Urumqi and the St. Nicholas Church in Ili, hold services but the appointments of clergy and other details about their operations remain unclear due to general government restrictions on the Xinjiang region where both churches are located.

However, despite these strengths, the OPASPP and the Russian Orthodox community more broadly occupy a unique position different than the Roman Catholic and Protestant churches, or organizations of "native religions" like Buddhism and Daoism or "foreign religions" like Islam and Judaism.[74] Religious organizations that operate schools and hospitals, and churches with mainly ethnic Chinese congregations have greater visibility in Hong Kong because their social impact is measurably greater by the number of people involved and the breadth of influence they have in the daily lives of residents.[75] In chapters 3 through 5, we focus on how the Russian Orthodox community has been making social contributions to Hong Kong and China that are similar but more importantly different from other faith-based groups. Teaching Russian language and culture, publishing about theology and philosophy, and introducing facets of Russian society are all important ways in which this community is more than just a religious group.

This book also addresses the division between "visible ethnic minorities" or those distinguishable by physical features from the Chinese majority and "invisible ethnic minorities" such as Japanese and Korean residents, as well as people from mainland China who are able to assimilate into mainstream society if they learn the Cantonese language which is the predominant Chinese language used in Hong Kong and adopt material customs and values that would make them not overly distinguishable from "Hong Kong Chinese" (HKC), a flexible concept generally describing Chinese of Guangdong ancestry who are born and educated in Hong Kong.⁷⁶ This division is persistent in studies of Hong Kong and of general perceptions regarding the post-1997 social hierarchy which is highly disadvantageous for particular ethnic minorities who are South Asian.⁷⁷ Although Russians and other Slavic groups, as visible ethnic minorities with relatively neutral status, are not usually targets of social discrimination, adjustments to life in Hong Kong and the need for an environment in which they feel comfortable and accepted matters to members of the Russian Orthodox community of these backgrounds. Chinese converts to Orthodox Christianity face other challenges as they pursue journeys of faith that differentiate them from their family members and friends and make them minority members of a society in which they are otherwise part of a majority.

In the next chapter, we discuss how the areas of Sino-Russian relations, Christianity in China, and religious and ethnic minorities in Hong Kong intersect in the formation of the Russian Orthodox community from the 1930s until 2018 within the context of Hong Kong and the ROC in social and political transition.

NOTES

1. Among these areas, the subjects of trade and intermarriage has particularly been evolving and shedding light on how Russian and Chinese people form social networks. See, for example, Rachel Yuexin Lin, "The Opportunity of a Thousand Years: Chinese Merchant Organizations in the Russian Civil War," *Kritika* 19, no. 4 (2018): 745–68, and Chen Yuping, "Zhong E hunyin jiating guanxi luetan" [Brief discussion on Chinese–Russian marriage and family relationship], *Chizi*, no. 7 (2015): 48.

2. This bias seems to be related to the presence of ethnic Russians, including expatriate and native-born people, in these places. For example, see Serge Bolshakoff, *The Foreign Missions of the Russian Orthodox Church* (London: Society for Promoting Christian Knowledge; New York: The Macmillan Co., 1943), 62–69, and Yue Feng, *Dongzhengjiao shi* [History of Eastern Orthodox Christianity], 2nd ed. (Beijing: Zhongguo shehui kexue chubanshe, 2005), 315–23. More discussion of ethnic Russians will follow in this chapter.

3. Works in Russian language about Hong Kong in general are also highly limited. One such work is P.M. Ivanov, *Gonkong: Istoriia i sovremennost'* [Hong Kong: history and modernity] (Moscow: Nauka Glavnaia redaktsiia vostochnoi literatury, 1990).

4. Sergei Bolshakoff, "Les Missions étrangères dans l'Eglise orthodox russe," (Foreign missions of the Russian Orthodox Church), *Irénikon* 28 (1955): 172.

5. We stress that Russian Orthodox communities are subgroups of a faith that have very different social and spiritual characteristics. For the emphasis on heterogeneity rather than homogeneity in the organization and identities of Orthodox Christians, see Paul W. Werth, "Orthodoxy as Ascription (and Beyond): Religious

Identity on the Edges of the Orthodox Community, 1740–1917," in *Orthodox Russia: Belief and Practice under the Tsars*, Valerie A. Kivelson and Robert H. Greene (University Park, PA: Pennsylvania University Press, 2003), 239–51.

6. The Tsardom of Russia, founded in 1547, became an empire in 1721 during the reign of Peter the Great (r. 1682–1725). Among many of the works that set the basic paradigms for Sino-Russian relations, see Alexandre Ular, *Un Empire Russo-Chinois* [A Russian-Chinese empire] (Paris: Félix Juven, 1902).

7. Representative works include Eric Widmer, *The Russian Ecclesiastical Mission in Peking during the Eighteenth Century* (Cambridge, MA: East Asian Research Center, Harvard University Press, 1976), Sergei Leonidovich Tikhvinskii [S. L. Tikhvinskii] et al., eds., *Istoriia Rossiiskoi Dukhovnoi missii v Kitae: Sbornik statei* [History of the Russian Ecclesiastical Mission in China: collected articles], Predisl. S. L. Tikhvinskogo [With a preface by S. L. Tikhvinskogo] (Moscow: Izd-vo Sviato-Vladimirskogo bratstva, 1997). For an older, classic overview, see Nikolai, *Pravoslavnaia missiia v Kitae za 200 let ee sushchestvovaniia: istoriia Pekinskoi Dukhovnoi missii v pervyi i vtoroi periody ee deiatel'nosti* [Two hundred years of the Russian Orthodox Mission in China: the history of the Beijing Ecclesiastical Mission in the first and second periods of its activities] (Kazan: Tipografiia Imperatorskogo universiteta [Kazan: Imperial University Printing House], 1887), and the Chinese translation often cited in Chinese-language works on Russian Orthodox Christianity, Nigula Aduolaciji, *Dongzheng jiao zai Hua liang bai nian shi* [200 years of history of the Orthodox Church in China], trans. Yan Guodong and Xiao Yuqiu (Guangzhou: Guangdong renmin chubanshe, 2007). More recent works include Xiao Yuqiu, *Eguo chuanjiao tuan yu Qingdai Zhong E wenhua jiaoliu* [The Russian Orthodox Mission in Beijing and Sino-Russian cultural exchange in the Qing dynasty] (Tianjin: Tianjin renmin chubanshe, 2009), Zhang Xuefeng, *Qingchao qianqi Eguo zhu Hua zongjiao chuandaotuan yanjiu* (Research on Russian religious missions in China during the Early Qing) (Xinbei: Hua Mulan wenhua chubanshe, 2012), and Ouyang Zhesheng, "Eguo Dongzhengjiao chuanjiao tuan zai jing huodong shu ping (1716–1859)" [Review of the Russian Orthodox mission in Beijing (1716–1859)], *Anhui shixue*, no. 1 (2016): 124–33.

8. See *Handbook of Christianity in China, Volume One: 635–1800*, ed. Nicolas Standaert (Leiden and Boston: Brill, 2000), 367–74, including a bibliography of significant works regarding the imperially sponsored missions.

9. The term "Albazinian" (also known as Albazins) broadly refers to Cossack soldiers who occupied the fort of Albazin, originally a Daur walled city called Yaksa and the descendants of those soldiers. The Qing government housed the Russian Orthodox missionaries in the Russian Hostel (Eluosi guan). See Cai Hongsheng, *Eluosi guan jishi* [Accounts of the Russian Hostel] (Guangzhou: Guangdong renmin chubanshe, 1994).

10. For his general explanation about why the Russian Ecclesiastical Mission did not function properly, see Gregory Afinogenov, *Spies and Scholars: Chinese Secrets and Imperial Russia's Quest for World Power* (Cambridge, MA: The Belknap Press of Harvard University Press, 2020), 71–75.

11. See John F. Baddeley, *Russia, Mongolia, China, being some record of the relations between them from the beginning of the XVIIth century to the death of the Tsar*

Alexei Mikhailovich, A.D. 1602–1676, rendered mainly in the form of narratives dictated or written by the envoys sent by the Russian tsars, or their voevodas in Siberia to the Kalmuk and Mongol khans & princes; and to the emperors of China; with introductions, historical and geographical, also a series of maps, showing the progress of geographical knowledge in regard to Northern Asia during the XVIth, XVIIth, & early XVIIIth centuries, the texts mainly taken more especially from manuscripts in the Moscow Foreign Office Archives (London: Macmillan, 1919); Joseph Sebes, S. J., *The Jesuits and the Sino-Russian Treaty of Nerchinsk (1689): The Diary of Thomas Pereira, S. J* (Rome: Institutum Historicum S. I., 1961); Vincent Chen, *Sino-Russian Relations in the Seventeenth Century* (The Hague: Martinus Nijhoff, 1966); N. F. Demidova and V. S. Miasnikov, eds., *Russko-kitaiskie otnosheniia v XVII veke: Materialy i dokumenty, 1608–1691* [Russo-Chinese relations in the seventeenth century: Materials and Documents, 1608–1691], 2 vols, (Moscow: Nauka, 1969); Robert H. G. Lee, *The Manchurian Frontier in Ch'ing History* (Cambridge, MA: Harvard University Press, 1970); Mark Mancall, *Russia and China: Their Diplomatic Relations to 1728* (Cambridge, MA: Harvard University Press, 1971); Liu Minsheng, Meng Xuanzhang, and Bu Ping, eds., *Shiqi shiji Sha-E qinlüe Heilongjiang liuyu shi ziliao* [Historical materials on the invasion of the Heilongjiang river basin by Russian Tsarist forces during the seventeenth century] (Harbin: Heilongjiang jiaoyu chubanshe, 1992); S. C. M. Paine, *Imperial Rivals: China, Russia, and Their Disputed Frontier, 1858–1924* (Armonk, NY: M. E. Sharpe, 1996).

12. For the general history of the North Hostel, see Boris Pavlovich Voinarskii, *Bei-guan': Rossiiskaia dukhovnaia missiia v Kitae* [Bei-guan: The Russian Ecclesiastical Mission in China] (Tianjin: Ideal Press, 1939) and Meng Ssu-ming (Meng Siming), "The E-luo-ssu kuan (Russian Hostel) in Peking," *Harvard Journal of Asiatic Studies* 23 (1960–1961): 19–46.

13. About Samuel P. Huntington's framework of the "clash of civilizations," see *The Clash of Civilizations and the Remaking of World Order* (New York: Simon & Schuster, 1996). For the broader significance of Sino-Russian relations, see Alexei D. Voskressenski, *Russia and China: A Theory of Inter-State Relations* (London: Routledge, 2002) and Susanna Soojung Lim, "From Albazin to Nagasaki: Russia's First Contacts with China and Japan, 1685–1813," in *China and Japan in the Russian Imagination, 1685–1922: To the Ends of the Orient* (London: Routledge, 2013), 31–55.

14. See Baker, *History of the Orthodox Church in China*, particularly chapter 4 entitled "The First Orthodox Christians in China 1242 to 1689."

15. See Latourette, *History of Christian Missions in China* (London: Society for Promoting Christian Knowledge, 1929), 199.

16. Latourette, *History of Christian Missions*, 741–42.

17. For a concise and cogent summary about three predominant themes in case-specific and comparative studies of the history of Orthodox Christianity in Central Asia and Siberia during and following the Russian imperial age, namely the ROC as a channel of political administration for the Tsarist Empire, Orthodoxy as a dimension of cultural practice and social geography in areas targeted for the spread of the faith, and the impact of religion on the formation and promulgation of social categories

in the Russian imperial domain, see Niccolò Pianciola, "Orthodoxy in the Kazakh Territories (1850–1943)," in *Kazakhstan: Religions and Society in the History of Central Eurasia*, trans. Susan Finnel, eds. Gian Luca Bonora, Niccolò Pianciola, and Paolo Sartori (Turin, London, Venice, and New York: Umberto Allemandi, 2010), 237–54.

18. For this model of expansion, see James Forsyth, *A History of the Peoples of Siberia: Russia's North Asian Colony, 1581–1990* (Cambridge: Cambridge University Press, 1992), 42. This model is also illustrated in the primary source documents in Basil Dmytryshyn, E. A. P. Crownhart-Vaughan, and Thomas Vaughan, eds. and trans., *Russia's Conquest of Siberia, 1558–1700: A Documentary Record* (Portland: Oregon Historical Society Press, 1990).

19. See I. S. Gurvich, *Narody Dal'nego Vostoka SSSR v XVII–XX vv. Istoriko-etnograficheskie ocherki* [The peoples of the Soviet Far East from the seventeenth to the twentieth century: Historical and ethnographic essays] (Moscow: Nauka, 1985) and Khodarkovsky, "The Conversion of Non-Christians," 115–43.

20. *History of the Peoples of Siberia*, 155.

21. About Gantimur's decision to migrate from Manchuria to Siberia and pledge loyalty to the Tsar in 1653 and the dispute it caused between the Qing and Russian governments, see Loretta E. Kim, *Ethnic Chrysalis: China's Orochen People and the Legacy of Qing Borderland Administration* (Cambridge, MA: Harvard University Asia Center, 2019), 76–78.

22. Ware, *The Orthodox Church*, 183. About the ROC missions in the nineteenth century, also see Latourette, *History of Christian Missions*, 486–88. Latourette believes that 1901 to 1914 was a key period of growth for ROC missions in China. See *History of Christian Missions*, 566.

23. See V. G. Datsyshen, *Mitropolit Pekinskii Innokentii* (Figurovskii) [Metropolitan Innocent (Figurovsky)] (Gonkong: Bratstvo Sviatykh Apostolov Petra i Pavla [Hong Kong: Brotherhood of SS Peter & Paul], 2011).

24. The archimandrite's use of train cars for spreading the faith can be juxtaposed with the speculation that Russian immigrants involved in the building and operation of the Chinese Eastern Railway during the late nineteenth and early twentieth centuries influenced the popular (non-mission-based) spread of Orthodox Christianity in Manchuria/Northeast China. Song Yanchen, ed., *Zhongguo diyu wenhua tonglan – Heilongjiang juan* [Overview of Chinese regional cultures – Heilongjiang volume] (Beijing: Zhonghua shuju, 2014), 250.

25. A report about the mission in 1897 describes the archimandrite's work as religious and community leader. See [Archimandrite] Innocent. "The Russian Orthodox Mission in China." *The Chinese Recorder* (American Presbyterian Mission Press) 47, no. 10 (1916): 681.

26. Donald MacGillivray, ed., *The China Mission Year Book: Being "the Christian Movement in China," 1910* (Shanghai: Christian Literature Society for China and the China Continuation Committee, 1910), 425.

27. Donald MacGillivray, ed., *The China Mission Year Book: Being "the Christian Movement in China," 1915* (Shanghai: Christian Literature Society for China and the China Continuation Committee, 1915), 583–84.

28. James Carter, "The Future of Harbin's Past," *Itinerario* 35, no. 3 (December 2011): 77.

29. Regarding case studies that exemplify "manifest destiny" as a framework for justifying Orthodox missions in Eastern Europe and Central Asia, see Paul W. Werth, *At the Margins of Orthodoxy: Mission, Governance, and Confessional Politics in Russia's Volga-Kama Region, 1827–1905* (Ithaca, NY: Cornell University Press, 2002), and Robert P. Geraci, "Going Abroad or Going to Russia?: Orthodox Missionaries in the Kazakh Steppe, 1881–1917," *Of Religion and Empire: Missions, Conversion, and Tolerance in Tsarist Russia*, eds. Robert P. Geraci and Michael Khodarkovsky (Cornell University Press, 2001), 274–310. For an example of the explicit expression of "manifest destiny" in relation to Northeast China, see Wirt Gerrare, *Greater Russia: The Continental Empire of the Old World* (New York and London: Macmillan, 1903), 287–88.

30. Theophilus Siegfried Bayer, *Museum Sinicum: in quo Sinicae linguae et literaturae ratio explicatur*, 2 vols. (Petropoli: Typogr. acad. Imperatoriae, 1730).

31. Orthodox missionaries' intellectual interest in China became more sophisticated even when gradually detached from the original purposes of communicating and persuading Chinese people to accept Orthodox beliefs and practices. Findings in Sinology also contributed to the definition of "Russian" identity. See David Wolff, "Know Thine Enemy, Know Thyself: Russian Orientology in the Borderlands," chapter 5 of *To the Harbin Station: The Liberal Alternative in Russian Manchuria, 1898–1914* (Stanford, CA: Stanford University Press, 1999), 146–167.

32. Stamoolis, *Eastern Orthodox Mission Theology*, 42.

33. Pechatat' Dozvoliaetsia Hachal'nik Missii Episkopi Innokentii [Printing allowed by the Head of Mission Bishop Innocent], *Kratkaia istoriia Russkoi pravoslavnoi missii v Kitae: sostavlennaia po sluchaiu ispolnivshegosia v 1913 godu dvukhsotletnego iubileia ee sushchestvovaniia* [A short history of the Russian Orthodox Mission in China: compiled in 1913 on the occasion of the 200th anniversary of its existence] (Peking: Tipografiia Uspenskago monastyria, 1916), 142.

34. See "The Russian Orthodox Mission in China," 680. For a more optimistic figure that there were 200 believers by 1980, see Samuel Couling, ed., *The Ecnyclopaedia Sinica* (Shanghai: Kelly and Walsh, Limited, 1917).

35. See Alexander Lomanov, "Russian Orthodox Church (Republican China)," in *Handbook of Christianity in China, Volume Two: 1800 to the Present*, ed. R. G. Tiedemann (Leiden and Boston: Brill, 2010), 554–55.

36. About political relations between China and Russia for the twentieth century, see Voskressenski, *Russia and China*, chapters 5 and 6 (124–82), Li Qifang, *Zhong E guanxi shi* [History of Sino-Russian relations] (Taipei: Lian jing chuban shiye gongsi, 2000), and Yang Chuang, *Bai nian Zhong E guanxi* [A century of China and Russia relations] (Beijing: Shijie zhishi chubanshe, 2006), and studies with more specific topics like Bruce A. Elleman, *Diplomacy and Deception: The Secret History of Sino-Soviet Diplomatic Relations, 1917–1927* (Armonk, NY and London: M.E. Sharpe, 1997).

37. Alexander Lomanov, "Chinese Orthodox Church (People's Republic, Hongkong, Macao, Taiwan)," in *Handbook of Christianity in China, Volume Two: 1800 to the Present*, ed. R.G. Tiedemann (Leiden and Boston: Brill, 2010), 826.

38. Ibid., 828.
39. Ibid., 829.
40. Ibid., 830.
41. Ibid., 831.
42. Ibid. The *South China Morning Post* newspaper featured an obituary with a picture about Bishop Simeon's death. Hong Kong Public Records Office, Carl Smith Collection, 168597.
43. Ibid., 832.
44. Ibid.
45. Recent works about subjects that emphasize the social and cultural synergies that form between Chinese and Russian people include the late nineteenth-century to early twentieth-century history of Chinese and Russian communities in the Amur River region in Victor Zatsepine, *Beyond the Amur: Frontier Encounters between China and Russia, 1850–1930* (Vancouver: University of British Columbia Press, 2017). Many studies approach this topic from the presence of Chinese in modern and contemporary Russia, including Felix B. Chang and Sunnie T. Rucker-Chang, eds., *Chinese Migrants in Russia, Central Asia and Eastern Europe*, Routledge Contemporary Russia and Eastern Europe Series 28 (London and New York: Routledge, 2012); and Song Xiaolü, "Zai Eluosi zou gangsi—1994–1999 nian Mosike de Zhongguo shangren" [Walking the wire in Russia—Chinese merchants in Moscow, 1994–1999], *Zhongguo xiangzhen qiye*, no. 3 (2000): 24–33; Olga Alexeeva and Michael Black, "Chinese Migration in the Russian Far East: A Historical and Sociodemographic Analysis," *China Perspectives* 75, no. 3 (2008): 20–32; Yu Tao, *Huashang taojin Mosike: yige qianyi qunti de kuaguo shengcun xingdong* [Chinese businessmen in Moscow: the survival behaviour of a transnational migration group] (Beijing: Social Sciences Academic Press, 2016). Some of these studies connect the past with the present to demonstrate the continuity of China–Russian relations such as Lee Chinyun, "From Kiachta to Vladivostok: Russian Merchants and the Tea Trade," *Region* 3, no. 2 (2014): 195–218 and Vera Skvirskaja, "'Russian Merchant' Legacies in Post-Soviet Trade with China: Moral Economy, Economic Success and Business Innovation in Yiwu," supplement, *History and Anthropology* 29, no. S1 (2018): S48–66.

About Orthodox Christianity as part of the regional cultures of Northwest and Northeast China, see Zheng Yongwang, *Eluosi Dongzhengjiao yu Heilongjiang wenhua: Longjiang dadi shang Eluosi Dongzhengjiao de lishi* [The Russian Orthodox Church and Heilongjiang culture: the historical echo of the Russian Orthodox Church in Heilongjiang] (Harbin: Heilongjiang chubanshe, 2010), especially how Orthodox Christianity was introduced to Heilongjiang from the late nineteenth century to 1949 through a narrative based on personal accounts, 123–480.

46. About the history of Russians in the late imperial–early modern period, see Tatiana A. Pang, "The 'Russian Company' in the Manchu Banner Organization," *Central Asiatic Journal* 43, no. 1 (1999): 132–39, Yang Duojie, "Qingdai Beijing de Eluosi qiren" [Russian bannermen in Qing dynasty Beijing], *Shijie bolan*, no. 22 (2008): 54–59. More references to sources about the contemporary era will be given in the third section of this chapter.

47. See, for example, Daniel H. Bays, *Christianity in China: From the Eighteenth Century to the Present* (Stanford University Press, 1999), which did not mention Orthodox Christianity as even a keyword in the index. In the subsequent revised edition, Russian Orthodox Christianity appears in an appendix. See Daniel H. Bays, *A New History of Christianity in China*, The Global Christianity Series (Chicester: Wiley-Blackwell, 2011), 209–16. Other seminal works that do not discuss Orthodox Christianity or have very brief references to it include Archie R. Crouch et al., eds., *Christianity in China: A Scholars Guide to Resources in the Libraries and Archives of the United States* (Armonk, NY: M.E. Sharpe, 1989); Yao Mingquan and Luo Wei, *Zhongguo Jidujiao jianzhi* [A brief history of Christianity in China] (Beijing: Zongjiao wenhua chubanshe, 2000); Kathleen L. Lodwick, *How Christianity Came to China: A Brief History*, Understanding World Christianity Series (Minneapolis, MN: Fortress Press, 2016); Luo Weihong, *Christianity in China*, trans. Zhu Chengming (Beijing: China Intercontinental Press, 2004); Anthony E. Clark, *China's Christianity: From Missionary to Indigenous Church*, Studies in Christian Mission 50 (Leiden: Brill, 2017); Huang Guangyu, *Jidujiao zhuan xing Zhongguo ji nian: 1807–1949* [Chronicle of Protestant missions' development in China (1807–1949)] (Guilin: Guangxi shifan daxue chubanshe, 2017).

48. See Aileen Friesen, "Building an Orthodox Empire: Archpriest Ioann Vostorgov and Russian Missionary Aspirations in Asia," *Canadian Slavonic Papers* 57 (2015): 56–75. The relationship of Russian states and the ROC has also been subject to various interpretations. For the argument that the Church was not just a branch or a subordinate institution to the Russian imperial state, see G. L. (Gregory L.) Freeze, "Handmaiden of the State? The Church in Imperial Russia Reconsidered," *Journal of Ecclesiastical History* 36, no. 1 (1985): 82–102. In more social than overtly political terms, being an Orthodox Christian was seen as a condition of membership in a Russian nation or "proto-nation" during the imperial period. See Vera Shevzov, "Letting the People into Church: Reflections on Orthodoxy and Community in Late Imperial China," in Valerie A. Kivelson and Robert H. Greene, eds., *Orthodox Russia: Belief and Practice under the Tsars* (University Park, PA: Pennsylvania State University Press, 2003), 59–77.

49. See for example, A.V. Telyuk, ed., *Pravoslavie v Kitae* [Orthodoxy in China] (Blagoveshchensk: Izd-vo OAO Amurskaia iarmarka, 2013) and Yue Feng, *Dongzhengjiao shi*. Other general histories of Orthodox Christianity in Russia will also be introduced in chapter 4.

50. Du Zhongqi, *Du Bining zai Zhongguo: gui si nian Eluosi houyi "zongjiao xungen zhi lü"* [Du Bining in China: "The journey for seeking religious roots" by descendants of Russians in the *Gui si* year (2013)] (n.p.: Self-published, 2014).

51. See *Eluosi zu jianshi* bianxie zu, ed. *Eluosi zu jianshi* [A brief history of the Russian ethnic group] (Ürümqi: Xinjiang renmin chubanshe, 1987); Li Fengbo, "Xinjiang Eluosi zu renkou de shuliang biandong yu fengbu bianqian yanjiu (1949–2000 nian) [Research on the demographic change and distribution of the Russian ethnic group in Xinjiang (1949–2000)], *Xibei renkou*, no. 1 (2006): 60–63; Yu Chunjiang, "Zhongguo Eluosi zu minzu guocheng yanjiu—yi Neimenggu E'erguna shi Shiwei Eluosi minzu xiang wei ge'an yanjiu" [Research on the ethnicization of

China's Russian ethnic group—a case study of the Shiwei Russian Ethnic Minority County of Ergun City in Inner Mongolia] (master's thesis, Zhongyang minzu daxue, 2009); Gao Liqin and Teng Chunhua, "Xinjiang Eluosi zu wenhua bianqian yanjiu" [Research about the cultural development of ethnic Russians in Xinjiang], *Xinjiang daxue xuebao* 38, no. 5 (2010): 73–77; Li Ting, "Xi Xinjiang Eluosi zu de wenhua bianqian" [Analysis of the cultural development ethnic Russians in Xinjiang], *Yuwen xuekan*, no. 13 (2011): 78–80; Wen Guannan and Hu Boya, "Ha'erbin hua e houyi de xianzhuang diaocha" [Investigation on the current situation of the Chinese–Russian descendants in Harbin], *Heilongjiang shen shehui zhuyi xueyuan xuebao*, no. 4 (2011): 45–49; Zhang Xiaobin, *Neimenggu Eluosi zu* [Ethnic Russians in Inner Mongolia] (Hulunbuir: Neimenggu wenhua chubanshe, 2015); Zhu He, "Dui Zhong E hunyin he jiating guanxi de chanshi" [Explanation on Chinese–Russian marriage and family relationship], *Shanxi qingnian*, no. 20 (2017): 202.

52. Tang Ge, *Eluosi wenhua zai Zhongguo: Renlei xue yu lishi xue de yanjiu* [Russian culture in China: anthropological and historical research] (Harbin: Beifang wenyi chubanshe, 2010) and Zheng, *Eluosi Dongzhengjiao yu Heilongjiang wenhua*.

53. Yue Feng, "Dongzhengjiao chuanjiaoshi yu Zhongguo wenhua" [Eastern Orthodox missionaries and Chinese culture], *Shijie zongjiao wenhua*, no. 2 (1995): 37–39.

54. See, for example, Jacques Gernet, *China and the Christian Impact: A Conflict of Cultures* (Cambridge: Cambridge University Press, 1985). Many studies do not focus on conflict such as Wu Zhenchun, *Jidujiao yu Zhongguo wenhua* [Christianity and Chinese culture] (Beijing: Shangwu yinshuguan, 2015) and Lo Lung-Kwong and Tang Xiaofeng, *Jidu zongjiao yu Zhongguo shehui: lishi huisu yu quyu yanjiu* [Christianity and Chinese society: a historical review and regional research] (Beijing: Zongjiao wenhua chubanshe, 2018).

55. Some works that illustrate but cannot, by nature of its breadth, represent the full scope of the field include, for time and region, Alan Richard Sweeten, *Christianity in Rural China: Conflict and Accommodation in Jiangxi Province, 1860–1900* (Ann Arbor: Center for Chinese Studies, University of Michigan, 2001), David E. Mungello, *The Spirit and the Flesh in Shandong, 1650–1785* (Lanham, MD: Rowman & Littlefield, 2001), and Brent Fulton, *China's Urban Christians: A Light That Cannot Be Hidden* (Eugene, OR: Pickwick Publications, 2015); for gender, Pui-lan Kwok, *Chinese Women and Christianity, 1860–1927* (Atlanta: Scholars Press, 1992) and Ji Li, *God's Little Daughters: Catholic Women in Nineteenth-Century Manchuria* (Seattle: University of Washington Press, 2015); for ethnicity and sub-ethnicity, Jessie G. Lutz and Rolland Ray Lutz, *Hakka Chinese Confront Protestant Christianity, 1850–1900: With the Autobiographies of Eight Hakka Christians, and Commentary* (Armonk, NY: M.E. Sharpe, 1998) and Philip L. Wickeri, and Yik-fai Tam, "The Religious Life of Ethnic Minority Communities," in *Chinese Religious Life*, eds. David A. Palmer, Glenn Shive, and Philip L. Wickeri (New York: Oxford University Press, 2011), 50–66.

56. For all four of the frameworks that she has identified, see Sabrina P. Ramet, *Nihil Obstat: Religion, Politics, and Social Change in East-Central Europe and Russia* (Durham, NC: Duke University Press, 1998), 6–19.

57. About inculturation, see Aylward Shorter, *Toward a Theology of Inculturation* (Maryknoll, NY: Orbis Books, 1988) and Peter Schineller, *A Handbook on Inculturation* (New York: Paulist Press, 1990). A study of Orthodoxy's adaptation in Africa that has inspired our work is John N. Njoroge, "Towards an African Orthodoxy: A Call for Inculturation," *Ortodoksia* 56 (2016): 65–85.

58. See, for example, about the transition from missionary-led to native-pastor-led Christianity, Lee Kam Keung, *Jindai Zhongguo mushi qunti de chuxian* [The emergence of the community of pastors in modern China] (Taipei: Wanjuanlou, 2020), and about the translation of not only how to communicate about "God" but the concept of the supreme deity, Timothy Man-kong Wong, "The Rendering of God in Chinese by the Chinese: Chinese Responses to the Term Question in the *Wanguo Gongbao*," in *Mapping Meanings: The Field of New Learning in Late Qing China*, eds. Michael Lackner and Natascha Vittinghoff (Leiden: Brill, 2004), 589–614.

59. About missionaries' knowledge of Chinese religions as part of the inculturation process, see Timothy Man-kong Wong, "Protestant Missionaries' Images of Chinese Buddhism: A Preliminary Study of the Buddhist Writings of Joseph Edkins, Ernest John Eitel, and James Legge," *The HKBU Journal of Historical Studies* 1 (1999): 183–204, Eric Reinders, *Borrowed Gods and Foreign Bodies: Christian Missionaries Imagine Chinese Religion* (Berkeley: University of California Press, 2004). About inculturation of Roman Catholic institutions in Hong Kong, with broader implications for China as a whole, see Chu, Cindy Yik-yi. *The Chinese Sisters of the Precious Blood and the Evolution of the Catholic Church* (London: Palgrave Macmillan, 2016). About Muslims in China, see Jonathan N. Lipman, *Familiar Strangers: A History of Muslims in Northwest China* (Seattle: University of Washington Press, 1998).

60. Yang Jia, "Dongzhengjiao jisi fushi de dongyahua chutan" [A preliminary inquiry into the Asianization of Orthodox liturgical vestments] (conference paper, 2014 PhD Candidates Academic Conference on Social Change and Cultural Adaptation—Religious Study in Asia–Pacific, Peking University, Beijing, October 2014).

61. Benoît Vermander, "Sinicizing Religions, Sinicizing Religious Studies," *Religions* 10, no. 2 (2019): 137, https:/doi.org/10.3390/rel10020137.

62. See Amy Slagle, *The Eastern Church in the Spiritual Marketplace: American Conversions to Orthodox Christianity* (DeKalb, IL: Northern Illinois University Press, 2011), and Philip E. Hammond, *Religion and Personal Autonomy: The Third Disestablishment in America* (Columbia, SC: University of South Carolina Press, 1992).

63. For the Guangzhou church website, see Orthodox Fellowship of All Saints of China (OFASC), "Icon of the Mother of God 'Joy of All Who Sorrow' Church in Guangzhou," *Orthodox Christianity in China*, accessed January 17, 2017, http://www.orthodox.cn/contemporary/guangdong/guangzhou_en.htm. For the Shenzhen church website, see Orthodox Fellowship of All Saints of China (OFASC), "St. Sergius of Radonezh Parish," *Orthodox Christianity in China*, accessed March 31, 2017, http://orthodox.cn/contemporary/guangdong/shenzhen_en.htm.

64. Saint Luke Orthodox Cathedral is registered as the Orthodox Cathedral of Saint Luke the Evangelist, and formerly known as Apostle and Evangelist

Luke Orthodox Cathedral. See Orthodox Church in Hong Kong, Saint Luke Orthodox Cathedral, http://www.omhksea.org/metropolis-of-hong-kong/hong-kong, and http://orthodox.cn/contemporary/omhksea_en.htm, both accessed March 03, 2021.

65. Hong Kong Legislative Council, *The Orthodox Metropolitanate of Hong Kong and South East Asia Ordinance (Cap. 1163), L.N. 562 of 1996*, operated 2 January 1997, accessed November 29, 2019, https://www.elegislation.gov.hk/hk/cap1163.

66. Father Iakinf is often lauded as the founder of Russian Sinology. About him and other missionary Orientalists, see David Schimmelpenninck van der Oye, *Russian Orientalism: Asia in the Russian Mind from Peter the Great to the Emigration* (New Haven, CT: Yale University Press, 2010), chapter 6, "Missionary Orientology," 122–52.

67. Slagle describes the dissimilar motivations and processes of conversion by seeker converts, who are individuals pursuing their interest in the faith, and by intermarriage converts, who join the faith because they want to be partners with Cradle Orthodox Christians and raise children as Orthodox Christians in *The Eastern Church*, chapter 3, "Processes of Catechesis and Socialization for Orthodox Converts," 61–83.

68. GovHK, "Xianggang bianlan—Zongjiao yu fengsu" [Hong Kong: The Facts—Religion and Custom], May 2016, https://www.gov.hk/sc/about/abouthk/factsheets/docs/religion.pdf.

69. Article 141, Chapter VI Education, Science, Culture, Sports, Religion, Labour and Social Services (Basic Law Cap 6 Art 141), https://www.basiclaw.gov.hk/pda/en/basiclawtext/chapter_6.html. See also Article 18 "Freedom of thought, conscience, and religion," https://www.cmab.gov.hk/doc/en/documents/policy_responsibilities/the_rights_of_the_individuals/iccpr3/Article18-e.pdf. Article 32 is also relevant for protecting freedom of conscience. About the expected interpretation of the Basic Law in relation to religion, see Iris Y. L. Tsang, "Zongjiao ziyou yu Jibenfa" [Religious freedom and the Basic Law], in *Xianggang de zongjiao* Hong Kong religions], eds. Hong Kong Catholic Social Communications Office (Hong Kong: Holy Spirit Study Centre and Hong Kong Catholic Social Communications Office, 1988), 118–25.

70. John Powers, *The Buddha Party: How the People's Republic of China Works to Define and Control Tibetan Buddhism* (Oxford: Oxford University Press, 2017), 12–13.

71. About SARA and the National Religious Affairs Administration, see National Religious Affairs Administration, accessed January 15, 2021, http://www.sara.gov.cn/gjzjswjhtml/index.html, The United Front Work Department of CPC Central Committee, accessed January 15, 2021, http://www.zytzb.gov.cn/html/index.html.

For analyses of the transition between SARA and the current mode of administration, see Huang Lanlan and Li Qiao, "China's New Regulation for Religious Groups Emphasizing Party Leadership Could Better Serve Communities: Observers," *Global Times*, January 20, 2020, accessed February 2, 2021, https://www.globaltimes.cn/content/1177478.shtml and Alex Joske, "Reorganizing the United Front Work Department: New Structures for a New Era of Diaspora and Religious Affairs Work," *China Brief* 19, no. 9, *The Jamestown Foundation*. May 9, 2019, accessed January 15,

2021, https://jamestown.org/program/reorganizing-the-united-front-work-department-new-structures-for-a-new-era-of-diaspora-and-religious-affairs-work/.

72. See Chun-wah Kwong, *Hong Kong's Religion in Transition: The Restructuring of Religions During Hong Kong's Incorporation into Mainland China (1983–1998)* (Waco, TX: Tao Foundations, 2000), Beatrice Leung and Shun-hing Chan, *Changing Church and State Relations in Hong Kong, 1950–2000* (Hong Kong: University of Hong Kong Press, 2003) and Ka Shing Ng, "Religion and Social Welfare in Hong Kong: An Overview," *Journal of Graduate Students of Letters* 14 (December 2014): 249–66, http://hdl.handle.net/2115/57709. For historical context about how religious communities exercised political and social influence, see Smith, *Chinese Christians*, and his article, "The Hong Kong Situation as it Influenced the Protestant Church," in *A Carnival of Gods Studies of Religions in Hong Kong*, ed. Chan Shun Hing (Hong Kong: Oxford University Press, 2002), 338–50. About the most recent conflicts between the social justice mission espoused by some church-based organizations and government actions, see Ned Levin, "Hong Kong Democracy Protests Carry a Christian Mission for Some," *The Wall Street Journal*, updated October 3, 2014, accessed October 25, 2016, https://www.wsj.com/articles/hong-kong-democracy-protests-carry-a-christian-mission-for-some-1412255663, and Ng Ka Shing, "Changing Church-state Relations in Colonial and Post-colonial Hong Kong," *Ta bunka syakai kenkyū* [Journal of global humanities and social sciences], no. 4 (March 2018): 251–74, http://hdl.handle.net/10069/38009.

73. See Leung and Chan, *Changing Church and State Relations*, 23–46.

74. About Buddhism in Hong Kong, see Tang Ka-jau, *Ershi shiji Xianggang fojiao zhi fazhan* [Development of Hong Kong Buddhism in the twentieth century] (Hong Kong: Xianggang fojiao yu wenhua lishi xuehui, 2007) and Ankur Barua, and M. A. Basilio, *Buddhism Flourishes in Hong Kong: The History of Buddhism in Hong Kong Dates Back to the Fifth Century A.D* (Saarbrücken: VDM, Verlag Dr. Müller, 2010). About Daoism, see Yau Chi-On, and Ngai Ting Ming, *Daofeng bainian: Xianggang Daojiao yu daoguan* [The Daoist wind in a century: Hong Kong Daoism and Daoist temples] (Xianggang: Peng ying xian guan Daojiao wenhua ziliaoku, Liwen chubanshe, 2002), Zhong Guofa, *Xianggang Daojiao* [Hong Kong Daoism] (Beijing: Zongjiao wenhua chubanshe, 2010), and in a comparative perspective, Kwong Chun-wah, *The Public Role of Religion in Post-colonial Hong Kong: An Historical Overview of Confucianism, Taoism, Buddhism and Christianity*, vol. 53 of *Asian Thought and Culture* (New York: Peter Lang, 2002). About Islam, see Paul O'Connor, *Islam in Hong Kong: Muslims and Everyday Life in China's World City* (Hong Kong: Hong Kong University Press, 2012) and Wai-Yip Ho, *Islam and China's Hong Kong: Ethnic Identity, Muslim Networks, and the New Silk Road* (New York: Routledge, 2013). About Judaism, see Zhou Xun, "Collaborating and Conflicted: Being Jewish in Secular and Multicultural Hong Kong," In *Judaism, Christianity, and Islam: Collaboration and Conflict in the Age of Diaspora*, ed. Sander L. Gilman (Hong Kong: Hong Kong University Press, 2014), 99–114, "'Cosmopolitan from Above': A Jewish Experience in Hong Kong," *European Review of History/Revue Européenne D'histoire* 23, no. 5–6 (2016): 897–911, and Elihai Braun, "Hong Kong Virtual Jewish History Tour," Jewish Virtual Library: A

Project of AICE, accessed March 3, 2021, https://www.jewishvirtuallibrary.org/hong-kong-virtual-jewish-history-tour.

75. About the relationship between religion and social services in Hong Kong and more generally in China, see Chan Shun Hing, "The Development of Christian Social Services in Hong Kong," in *A Carnival of Gods Studies of Religions in Hong Kong*, ed. Chan Shun Hing, 351–68 (Hong Kong: Oxford University Press, 2002), Tong Wai Ki et al., *Li wu ji shi: Xianggang Daojiao cishan shiye zonglan/Reaching out with Benevolence: Overview of Taoist Charitable Work in Hong Kong* (Hong Kong: Xianggang Daojiao lianhehui, 2011), and Li Pingye and Wang Xiaozhao, *Jidu zongjiao zai dangdai Zhongguo de shehui zuoyong ji qi yingxiang* [Social effect and impact of Christian religion in contemporary Chinese society] (Xianggang: Lun jin shenxue chuban youxian gongsi, 2011). The Hong Kong Christian Service is a major religious social welfare organization. See "Hong Kong Christian Service," accessed January 17, 2021, http://www.hkcs.org/about/overview-e.html.

76. About Japanese in Hong Kong, see Sone Akiko, "'Being Japanese' in a Foreign Place: Cultural Identities of Japanese in Hong Kong" (master's thesis, Chinese University of Hong Kong, 2002). About Koreans in Hong Kong, see Higuchi Kenichiro and Kwong Yan Kit, "Honkon zaijū korian no gengo kyōiku to gengo shiyō" [Language education and language use of Koreans living in Hong Kong], *Journal of the School of Culture-Information Studies (Sugiyama Jogakuen University)* 9, no. 2 (September 2009): 71–79. About mainland Chinese immigrants, see Law Kam-yee and Lee Kim-ming, "Citizenship, Economy and Social Exclusion of Mainland Chinese Immigrants in Hong Kong," *Journal of Contemporary Asia* 36, no. 2 (2006): 217–42.

77. About South Asians in Hong Kong, see Caroline Plüss, "Constructing Globalized Ethnicity: Migrants from India in Hong Kong," *International Sociology* 20, no. 2 (2005): 201–24 and John Nguyet Erni, and Lisa Yuk-ming Leung, *Understanding South Asian Minorities in Hong Kong* (Hong Kong: Hong Kong University Press, 2014).

Chapter 2

Foundation and Revival

Nostalgia is a dominant theme in the history of Russians in Hong Kong. The cemetery tour described at the beginning of the Introduction is the first opportunity for many participants to understand the individual and collective experiences of Russian residents of Hong Kong. By the nature of the tour, Russian life is framed in the past tense, as are conceptions of "Old Hong Kong" as a cosmopolitan British colony. Similarly, a document in the Carl Smith Collection of the Hong Kong Public Records Office (PRO) describes an Easter week gathering for the Russian community in Hong Kong "scarcely numbering more than 100" and lacking a place of worship, but "given use of a room in church/hall of St. Andrew's Church, Kowloon" in 1933.[1] This record also notes that the services were held "by a Russian priest from the north." This ostensibly modest citation of the ROC in Hong Kong, by remaining in existence, is a milestone in a historical narrative of the region as a British colony that has always focused on the proliferation of Roman Catholic and Protestant churches.[2]

In this chapter, we examine the Russian Orthodox community, comprised of both people who are Russian and those who are not, in two periods of history. The two periods are based on the existence of an active church, or multiple churches, from the 1930s to the 1970s, and then from the late 1990s to the present. The title of this chapter "Foundation and Revival" refers to both of these periods, which can be considered as two phases in one historical narrative or as the subjects of subjective narratives that are linked by the common cause of Orthodox spiritual life. In either interpretation, both which we explore in this part and the subsequent chapters of the book, the development of the Russian Orthodox community has been influenced by the political environment of Hong Kong, the former by British colonialism and the latter

ORIGINS OF THE RUSSIAN ORTHODOX COMMUNITY IN HONG KONG: THE 1930S TO THE 1970S

Religion is an important and oft-cited topic in histories of colonial Hong Kong.[3] Places of worship were considered landmarks and worthy of citation in travelogues and handbooks for prospective visitors. In Bruce Shepherd's 1893 guide for foreign visitors, he wrote a section describing St. John's Cathedral, two Roman Catholic churches, the Church of the Immaculate Conception and St. Joseph's Church, Union ("Scotch") Church, a church for sailors (St. Peter's Church), and the German Bethesda Chapel.[4] This *Handbook to Hongkong*, and later titled *The Hong Kong Guide*, reflected the active presence of Christians as of 1893, albeit in small numbers, a fact that would change significantly in the twentieth century. William Legge, nephew of the eminent Scottish missionary and Sinologist James Legge, also published a guidebook in 1893 describing the Union Church otherwise known as the Scotch Church, St. John's for Church of England services, Roman Catholic cathedral in Gleanealy Ravine with a spire more like an Islamic minaret. Carl Crow, in his study published originally in 1913 with subsequent editions including the 1921 third edition, describes St. John's Cathedral (the St. John's in Legge's reference), St. Peter's [Church] for sailors, St. Stephen's [Church] for Chinese, and a Jewish synagogue, two mosques, and a Sikh temple, as well as the church-affiliated schools like St. John's College by the Roman Catholic Christian brothers and the Italian Convent for girls' education and orphans.[5]

Implied in these sources and other publications about religion in Hong Kong are that "local society" was in fact bifurcated into the cosmopolitan elite and middle class, dominated by the British population but also with other European groups included, and a middle- and lower- class community of "native" Chinese. Christianity was the religion of heritage for most of the former, and a new foreign faith that influenced the lives of the latter through charitable organizations that provided material and spiritual sustenance. In between the Anglo-European and Chinese subpopulations of Hong Kong were the Eurasians, who straddled the margins of both and also developed a rich culture based on the combination of social and cultural elements from their paternal and maternal origins.[6]

Russians and other Slavic peoples are largely marginalized in these academic and popular memories of Hong Kong during the mid-nineteenth to late twentieth centuries. Unlike contemporaneous accounts of mostly involuntary migration from Russian territories to China and trade that benefited both

Russian and Chinese stakeholders, the faint traces of a Russian presence in Hong Kong are limited to rare references to Russians as refugees passing through Hong Kong ports and as sojourners who established small businesses on Hong Kong Island and then eventually re-migrated to North America, Australia, and even farther to Western Europe.

Although considered insignificant in the general historical narrative of Christianity in China as discussed in chapter 1, the development of a Russian Orthodox community in Hong Kong occurred at a critical moment in Orthodox Christian history, just as the USSR (Soviet Union) government constrained the practice of religion from 1917.[7] The government confiscated church property, imprisoned and executed clergy and lay believers, and undermined the coherence of the Orthodox Church by creating a pro-government, socialist church called the "Renovationist" Church, or Living Church. F[8] The decimation of Orthodox institutions is most evident in the number of operating churches, which Jane Ellis has estimated as decreasing from 80,000 in 1914 to 6,000 in the mid-1980s.[9] The USSR government, which promoted atheism, did not lift restrictions on the ROC's political stances and the general practice of religion until October 1990.

Religious life in mainland China was similarly subject to disruptive political and social pressures. As introduced in the previous chapter, from 1911 to 1949, foreign and civil wars and the whims of regional and local governments affected whether religious organizations could function. After 1949, like the USSR, the PRC government promoted atheism and the dispelling of "superstition." To uphold these principles, the PRC suspended religious activities and eroded communities of faith. Russian Orthodox churches in Beijing, Tianjin, Shanghai, Hankou, and Harbin were affected to different degrees and varying times by specific policies and general movements like the Cultural Revolution (1966–76).[10]

By comparison to the USSR and mainland China, Hong Kong was a liberal and stable religious marketplace. Unlike the Russian imperial government's direct control over the Moscow Patriarchate from 1721 to 1917, Hong Kong's colonial government, representing the British imperial center, generally permitted religious organizations to manage their own affairs and condoned religious practice as an aspect of social and cultural life. Key developments under British rule (1843–1941, 1941–1997) include the establishment of bodies for "indigenous religions" like the Hong Kong Buddhist Association in 1945, the Hong Kong Taoist Association in 1961, and the Confucian Academy in 1930,[11] and the Hong Kong Chinese Churches Union in 1915 and the Hong Kong Christian Council (HKCC) in 1954.[12] The Roman Catholic Church established parishes in Hong Kong in 1841, which is prior to the start of British colonial administration, but it was not until 1946 that Hong Kong became a diocese.[13]

From the 1930s to 1970s, we stress that a key difference from previous missions in China and other areas of Northeast Asia, like Siberia, Korea, and Japan, however, was that the ROC was not trying to replace indigenous religions through active conversion in Hong Kong. A ROC community evolved to serve primarily persons who were joining it already as believers. The clergy did not face problems common in missions like resistance from the leaders of religions supplanted through imposition of the Orthodox faith and the need to monitor and deter converts from passively or overtly continuing to espouse their former beliefs and religious practices, such as with Buriat and Kalmyk lamas in the Lake Baikal and Caspian Sea regions, respectively.[14]

That heritage believers formed almost an exclusive core of the early ROC in Hong Kong reflects a broader view that Russians formed a tight-knit ethnocultural group in China, even if they developed commercial and social relations with Chinese and other peoples during the twentieth century. Antonina Riasanovsky (née Antonina Fedorovna Podgorinova, 1895–1985) fictionalized her multi-phase migration from Siberia to Manchuria where she met and married her husband in Harbin, and onward to the United States, where she settled in Eugene, Oregon.[15] Her novel *The Family*, written under the pseudonym Nina Federova, portrays characters who represent various types of Russian emigrants such as formerly wealthy people with connections to the Russian imperial nobility and young children and adolescents who have lost most of their immediate family members and must rely on the kindness of distant relatives or other Russians they meet in China.

Another glimpse of Russian life in China that demonstrates relative seclusion, whether by choice or circumstance, is vivid in the memoir of Tatiana Erohina (Tatiana Erokhina), now a retired language instructor who settled in the United States during the late 1950s.[16] Erohina describes the hardships that her family encountered in Dairen (Dalian) during the 1930s and 1940s, including the sudden death of her father and the increasing poverty that stalled their migration out of China. Erohina left mainland China in 1954, passing through Shanghai and then through Hong Kong on the way to São Paulo, Brazil. Erohina's memoir is deeply nostalgic and concentrates on the theme of how Russians in economic and political duress nevertheless managed to sustain a strong sense of community, ethnic identity, and traditional customs including use of Russian language. The memoir contains only one chapter about Hong Kong, where Erohina said she did not do or see much because she was an indigent refugee. She does not mention any details about the Russian Orthodox church or Russians affiliated with the church in this chapter.[17]

These memoirs and other records of first-hand experiences suggest a major contrast between the past and present. Many people in Hong Kong today do not know that there are Orthodox churches in Hong Kong. Physically imposing Baptist, Methodist, and Catholic churches occupy prime locations throughout the region. However, to date, the Orthodox churches of the OPASPP and OCSLE are not housed in freestanding, fit-for-purpose buildings and not as visible. Knowledge of the Russian Orthodox community is also uncommon because many of the members joined to become part of a sociocultural group for Slavic people. People without Slavic–Orthodox heritage are certainly welcome to visit the OPASPP and to participate in its worship services and activities. However, both Slavic and Orthodox populations, separately and as they overlap, are not highly visible.

In contrast, in the early twentieth century, Orthodox Christian émigrés from Russia and mainland China formed a discernible and tight-knit community in Hong Kong. The presence of Russians in Hong Kong started with a brief encounter in the mid-nineteenth century. After its defeat in the Crimean War (1853–56), the Russian imperial government viewed Hong Kong as a channel to Southeast Asia. In September, John Bowring (1792–1872), the fourth governor of Hong Kong, accepted 270 prisoners of war from the Russian frigate *Diana* that sunk off the coast of Japan. These prisoners remained in Hong Kong until the British–Russian peace treaty of 1856 was concluded and they were permitted to repatriate. Admiral E.V. Putiatin (1803–1883), who had completed a navigational survey of Japan from 1852 to 1855, then came to establish the first Russian consulate in Hong Kong in 1856 that moved to Johnston House, formerly the residence of two colonial governors and the Hongkong Shanghai Banking Corporation (HSBC) canteen, in 1860. The Russian consulate then moved to Pedder's Hill in 1877 and operated until 1917 when it was closed by the USSR government. The then-Crown Prince Nicholas (later Nicholas II, r. 1894–1917) visited Hong Kong twice in April 1891, holding a formal meeting with incumbent governor William Des Vœux (1834–1909) during the first visit and on the second visit, riding the tram to the Peak and buying antiques on Queen's Road Central. The crown prince's activities in Hong Kong cemented the Russian empire's political presence and relations with the British colony.[18]

Many Russians came to Hong Kong to move away from political instability and persecution during the late 1910s and 1920s when the imperial state became increasingly unstable and lost its authority to the Russian Soviet Federative Socialist Republic. They established their presence in Hong Kong as participants in the local government and economy and as visiting foreigners. In 1909, the Russo-Chinese Bank, known as the Russo-Asiatic Bank from 1910 onward, opened a branch in Hong Kong. In November and December 1912, the Russian pilot Aleksandr Aleksandrovich Kuzminskii (1881–1930) gave paragliding demonstrations to Hong Kong audiences. The community grew from 36 residents in 1921 to 127 residents in 1931.[19] Some Russians worked for the Anti-Piracy Guards force established by the

Hong Kong colonial government in 1914 and made part of the police force in 1930.[20] Many of the original 28 Russian members had substantial experience deterring pirates in Siberia. Russians also established businesses such as the Queen's Café and Cherikoff Bakery.5F[21]

These people and their experiences evoke recollections on the personal and collective scales. In the most recent decade, the history of Russians in Hong Kong has been gaining renewed interest as a topic of local history and culture. Local newspapers and magazines regularly publish numerous articles about Russians in Hong Kong from past eras, often portraying them as a glamorous and tragic diaspora group, forced to set up new lives in a British colony after leaving their homeland and becoming second-class residents as refugees and as non-Western Europeans.[22] Russian contributions to the culture and society of "Old Hong Kong" are crucial elements of preserving a positive image of the British colonial period.

The first ROC mission in Hong Kong was a religious enterprise undertaken and upheld by one clergyman in the midst of Russian migration and settlement in Hong Kong. Dmitry Mikhailovich Uspensky (1886–1970, hereby known as Father Uspensky) began his tenure as head of the Hong Kong parish in 1933. Father Uspensky was a 1907 graduate of the Vladimir School of Theology and was ordained at the Cathedral of the Assumption in his home diocese of Vladimir-Suzdal in January 1914. Father Uspensky visited Hong Kong and reported to Bishop Viktor, head of the Russian Spiritual Mission in Beijing, that there should be a spiritual center for believers in southern China.[23] Bishop Viktor agreed and assigned Father Uspensky to establish a parish in Hong Kong. Father Uspensky negotiated with W.W. Rogers, the incumbent rector of St. Andrew's (Anglican) Church in Tsim Sha Tsui to hold Orthodox Christian services there.[24] Bishop Viktor, by Decree no. 37, which he signed on July 10, 1934, gave official authority to churches in southern China and the Philippines.[25] A principal signatory of the subsequent charter that stated guidelines for the administration of the general community formed by the churches and ratified separately by Bishop Viktor on November 18, 1934, April 22, 1935, and May 1, 1937 as it came into effect for all four of the geographic regions within the jurisdiction, Father Uspensky became the head of the Hong Kong deanery and the Church of Saints Peter and Paul. In 1934, he also became the officiant for the Icon of the Mother of God "Joy of All Who Sorrow" Church in Guangzhou, the Church of the Holy Trinity in Macau, and the Church of the Iberian Icon of the Mother of God in Manila.[26] As pastor of the Hong Kong church, Father Uspensky played an important role in the non-Soviet (White) Russian community in Hong Kong and in the general region of southern China and Southeast Asia.[27]

Throughout the 1930s and into the early 1940s, divine services continued to be celebrated at St. Andrew's Church until a chapel for the ROC community was opened at 8 Middle Road, Tsim Sha Tsui of Kowloon.[28] The church also held services at 18 Jordan Road, Kowloon in 1938 and 1939.[29] Southern Kowloon became a hub of commercial and cultural activity for Russians in Hong Kong. After participating in church services, Russian families could enjoy meals at restaurants serving Russian cuisine and purchase breads to take home. The church itself was the center of social and community activities. An association for women parishioners to arrange decorations for the church formed, as well as the choir that performed during services, a charity, and a foundation for planning the construction of a permanent church building.

Japanese occupation of Hong Kong (1941–1945) stopped the effort to build a new home for the Church of Saints Peter and Paul, even though blueprints were reportedly ready for the church to be built at the 18 Jordan Road location.[30] In 1945, the Church of Saint Peter and Paul moved to 12 Essex Crescent in Kowloon Tong. 12 Essex Crescent was first established as a property through a lease signed on July 1, 1898 as New Kowloon Inland Lot Number 725. The map illustrating the dimensions of the lot that became part of the lease agreement was signed by Harold T. Creasy (1873–1950), Director of Public Works from 1923 to 1932.F[31] The move to the Kowloon Tong property was an important milestone for the community, and one of which there are still extant memories preserved in images like figure 2.1 of the church iconostasis.[32]

However this year was also the start of a period in which significant changes occurred in the jurisdiction and leadership of the Hong Kong community that were in turn related to the general changes in the ROC's general operations in China after World War II.[33] The Russian Ecclesiastical Mission in China (also known as the Beiping/Beijing mission) accepted the authority of the Moscow Patriarchate in 1945, and the Orthodox community in Hong Kong followed, as did the Harbin and Xinjiang eparchies. Many Russian refugees from the north of China, who lived in Hong Kong at that time, disagreed with the decision of the parish, so they did not become members of the parish.[34] Later in 1945 and 1946, many of these refugees left for destinations in North America and Australia. In 1949, the PRC government assumed control over all religious institutions and affairs. Archbishop Viktor remained as head of the Beijing mission until 1956 but could only maintain limited contact with the Moscow Patriarchate. By 1955, the ROC Holy Synod included the Hong Kong deanery of Hong Kong in the Beijing diocese of the East Asian Exarchate. Soon after this administrative change, the Exarchate was abolished at the same time the Russian Ecclesiastical Mission in China was terminated and Archbishop Viktor left China.

Many Russian Orthodox Christians refused to submit to Bishop Simeon of Shanghai or to Bishop Vasily of Beijing in the aftermath of this change. They

Figure 2.1 Iconostasis of the Church in Kowloon Tong.
Source: OPASPP, "History of Parish," https://orthodoxy.hk/parish/history_of_parish. Permission granted by the Saint Apostles Peter and Paul Orthodox Church in Hong Kong.

were against any contact with the Moscow Patriarchate and supported the ROCOR, prompting the question of whether the Church of Saints Peter and Paul should remain as part of the Moscow Patriarchate or change its affiliation to the ROCOR. It was ultimately decided that the church would continue to be a unit of the Moscow Patriarchate.[35] Father Uspensky maintained his congregation, housed at St. Andrew's Church. The ROCOR established a separate church called the Church of the Holy Resurrection, located on the third floor of 216 Nathan Road, Yaumatei. The founding of this church, registered by a French national in Hong Kong as the "Hong Kong Orthodox Association" deepened the rift in China's Orthodox community that started with the ambivalence of believers about the PRC state assuming control over religious affairs.[36]

The endurance of the Russian Orthodox Church through decades of war and financial circumstances which required moving from one physical address to one another and borrowing space from other churches is a phenomenon largely attributable to the two priests who led the congregations during this period. Father Dmitry Uspensky is more well-known of the two. He is generally regarded a prominent historical figure of the Russian community in Hong Kong, and a notable personality in Hong Kong's general history. His memory lives on in photographs, oral histories, and his family members' accounts of his service in Hong Kong. But equally important to sustaining the small community was Father Elias (Ilia) Wen (Wen Zizheng, 1896–2007), one of the few Chinese native clergy in the history of the ROC and when he passed away at the age of 110 years, was the oldest living ROC clergyman.[37]

Father Uspensky was a quintessential career missionary, serving outside of Russia for most of his life. He served in Khabarovsk and other outposts in the Russian Far East before assuming an assignment in Tianjin in 1920. He originally was with the intention of serving in Manchuria (Northeast China), but because Russian migrants headed further away from political turmoil within Russian territory and went toward southern China, he took what amounted to a hardship post in the peripheral region of Guangdong–Hong Kong which as introduced earlier, he identified as an area that needed support for Orthodox Christian believers. As described in an expressly laudatory page on the current OPASPP website, he was an "apostle of China" because he devoted decades of service to believers on Chinese territory and then in, as Hong Kong was considered, a place where pastoral care of fellow Russians in transient and disadvantaged circumstances was more essential than converting native Chinese to Orthodox Christianity.[38]

Each priest contributed to the foundation of a Russian Orthodox community in different and complementary ways. Father Uspensky assumed all the customary duties for the maintenance of his church and served as a spiritual and social leader for his parishioners. He continued church operations under tight financial constraints and by contemporary standards, in understaffed circumstances. His dedication to Hong Kong, as demonstrated by his tenure effectively ending not with retirement but in death, was partially motivated by his opposition to communism.[39] As autochthonous histories of the parish community attest, Father Uspensky was also steadfast in his commitment to helping both Russians who were passing through Hong Kong on their way to more stable countries for permanent immigration, and Russians who considered the British colony to be their long-term home. His leadership benefited both Russians who valued the spiritual dimension of church life and those who were primarily interested in the cultural communion that the church provided. Since the revival of the parish during the last decade, the OPASPP clergy has similarly ministered to congregants who participate in church services and activities to sustain their religious beliefs and to gain social belonging.

Father Wen, a latecomer in comparison to Father Uspensky, was another founding father of the Russian Orthodox community in Hong Kong by setting the precedent of a Chinese clergyman serving as a pastor. A convert to Orthodox Christianity as a young child, Father Wen received formal education at the Russian Orthodox Mission College in Beijing from 1905 to 1916 and then completed further studies at the Russian Theological Seminary, also in

Beijing, from 1916 to 1925. Starting his career at the Bogoyevlensky Church (Church of the Holy Epiphany) in Shanghai, where he was first ordained as a deacon in July 1924 and then as a priest in November 1931, Father Wen continued his ministry in Shanghai at St. Gabriel's Church, taught Chinese language and catechism courses at the church-affiliated school, and became a member of the Shanghai Chinese Orthodox Association in 1935.[40] He served as rector of the Cathedral of the Icon of the Mother of God "Surety of Sinners" in Shanghai until 1949. From February 1949 to October 1957, he served in Hong Kong as pastor of the Church of the Holy Resurrection. After the Church of the Holy Resurrection was closed in 1957, Father Wen spent the rest of his career and affiliation with the ROC until his death at the Holy Virgin "The Joy of All Who Sorrow" Cathedral in San Francisco. Father Wen played a more limited role in the development of Orthodox Christianity in Hong Kong because he was in residence for only eight years. However he proved by his example that a non-ethnic Russian and non-native Russian speaker could master the doctrine, customs, and language of Russian Orthodox Christianity. His proficiency in all aspects of spiritual leadership meant that he was effectively indistinguishable from a priest born and trained in Russia. He was also a role model for prospective ethnic Chinese converts.

Although both priests served Hong Kong parishioners in the same capacity, their relationship was one of simultaneous existence rather than active cooperation. When Archbishop (formerly bishop) John of Shanghai, as head of the (Russian) Orthodox Church in China, visited Hong Kong in July 1949, he only conducted services at the Church of the Holy Resurrection on July 17 and 18 with Father Wen. When he was the guest of honor at a tea held at Tkachenko Restaurant on 3 Hankow Road in Tsim Sha Tsui, the guest list included Father Wen, the restaurant owner A.P. Tkachenko, and other Russian and Chinese local notables but not Father Uspensky.[41] The exclusion of Father Uspensky can be explained as a matter of factional politics. Archbishop John was visiting Hong Kong en route to the United States with his superior, Metropolitan Anastasius of the ROCOR. Father Uspensky would not be expected to participate in a ROCOR-sponsored event, and most likely would not have accepted an invitation to do so.

The ostensible absence of personal memories or documentation about conflicts between Father Uspensky and Father Wen suggest that they maintained very separate lives as pastors. Father Wen's tenure in Hong Kong was itself a point of contention for Father Uspensky's parishioners because he was transferred out of mainland China due to political circumstances rather than because of his own intention to serve in the British colony and because he was affiliated with the ROCOR, which was a branch of the church that was defying the Moscow Patriarchate as the true sole authority. Also, unlike Father Uspensky, who remained in Hong Kong for several decades, Father

Wen served a short tour of duty before moving on to his next post in the United States which became the place of his long-term spiritual and pastoral calling until his death

The coexistence of two Russian Orthodox congregations ultimately weakened or at minimum, deterred from the development of a stable community with the financial and human resources to continue religious and social activities after the mass departure of ethnic Russians from Hong Kong in the 1950s onward. Father Uspensky maintained his spiritual and political loyalty to the Moscow Patriarchate at the expense of relations with many Russians who opposed the Soviet regime. Father Wen did not express an explicit political orientation, but he filled the niche as pastor to believers who wanted to continue their religious practice as Russians living outside of Russia who did not support the incumbent Soviet government. His own identity as a Chinese person did not seem to pose any disadvantage in leading his congregation. Members of his church regarded him as a respected spiritual leader who placed their interests and needs in the center of religious life. However, after Father Wen left Hong Kong, the Church of the Holy Resurrection closed too.

General waves of out-migration from Hong Kong continued to affect the Church of Saints Peter and Paul in the 1960s. The land at 12 Essex Crescent changed hands, with property rights transferred to Chan Bing Yim from Lai Wai Suen.96F[42] By 1968, the church was on the verge of being closed because the congregation was very small. Weakened by advanced age and ill health, Father Uspensky was no longer able to celebrate the divine services, but he was still asked to act as confessor and spiritual guide because church members did not want a new pastor to be appointed.[43] In November 1968, Bishop Juvenaly (Poyarkov) of Zaraisk (Moscow Patriarchate) visited Hong Kong on his way to Tokyo. During this visit, he awarded Father Uspensky with a pectoral cross. On November 28, 1968, Bishop Juvenaly celebrated the Divine Liturgy at the Saints Peter and Paul Church. This event was the first episcopal service in Hong Kong since 1945, when Bishop John of Shanghai had been the celebrant.

The parish community faced major obstacles with the passing of Father Uspensky on January 17, 1970. His Holiness Patriarch Alexy I (1877–1970), Metropolitan Nikodim (1929–1978), and Metropolitan (formerly Bishop) Juvenaly sent telegrams of condolence to the parishioners in Hong Kong. Bishop Germogen (Orekhov) (1858–1918), who was based in Podolsk, and Archpriest Arkady Tyshchuk (1931–2012), stationed in Tokyo, officiated at Father Uspensky's memorial service. Father Uspensky was buried at the Hong Kong Colonial Cemetery in Happy Valley near his wife and older daughter.[44] The parish council decided to close the church in June 1970 due to both the lack of a new pastor to replace Father Uspensky and the difficulties of maintaining the church with insufficient funds. Twenty-four members out of 36 present (with 12 abstentions) voted against asking the Moscow Patriarchate for financial help. After its official closure in September that year, the congregation sent the church utensils to the Parish of the Holy Trinity in Melbourne, Australia. In the late 1970s, the Hong Kong colonial government decided to destroy part of the Colonial Cemetery to construct new roads there. Father Uspensky's second daughter, Adelaide Dmitryevna Fogt, asked Governor Murray MacLehose (1917–2000, in office 1971–1982) to permit her to transfer the remains of her father to another place. The colonial administration transferred them, along with the remains of his relatives, closer to an old chapel located at the Colonial Cemetery that was not affected by construction. Memorial services in commemoration of Father Uspensky have been conducted at the gravesite until the present day.

RUSSIANS AND ORTHODOX CHRISTIANITY IN HONG KONG FROM THE 1930S TO 1970S

Starting the mission in Kowloon rather than on Hong Kong Island was of symbolic as well as material importance. Kowloon was a territory that separated "Hong Kong proper" from the New Territories, which consisted largely of *de facto* autonomous villages, and was part of an extended buffer between the colony of Hong Kong and China. The mission could not afford to rent or purchase real estate on Hong Kong Island where most non-Chinese residents were clustered. Instead, Father Uspensky and his parishioners worshipped in Kowloon, which was still a physically distant place, accessible then only by ferry and not by car or public transportation as it is today, from Hong Kong Island.

The establishment of the ROC in Hong Kong as a marginal member of the region's Christian community also fits into the greater narrative of Russians in China during the mid-twentieth century. Whether in mainland Chinese cities like Harbin and Shanghai, where they could form substantial subpopulations among other foreigners, or in Hong Kong, where they stood out as a distinct minority within a racial minority as well as being minorities by national origin, the history of Russians during this period can be seen in two intertwined veins. The first perspective is that despite the hardships of war and migrant life, Russians were able to survive successfully and eventually return to their homeland or move away from China, which functioned as a way station, to North America, Australia, or Western Europe. The second focal theme is that Russians were subject to extreme discrimination and other adverse conditions that made them perpetual outsiders in both Chinese society and China's foreigner society.

Both types of narratives inform conventional understandings why the Russian Orthodox mission in Hong Kong was suspended after Father Wen's transfer to the United States and Father Uspensky's death. Hierarchization of foreigners in China was a practice that both foreigners and Chinese espoused and reinforced. As Robert Bickers has argued, Russians in China from the late 1910s suffered two disadvantages.[45] White Russians, as opponents of the Communist Revolution and the losers of the civil war, lacked political status and support from what would be their home government, and by extension, their host government in China. As refugees remaining in China because they lacked credentials to leave, their immobility was a political and social handicap. Most Russians also came to China without adequate resources to be financially independent. British and other Europeans viewed the professions that Russians could adopt easily while living in China as undesirable and disgraceful. Russians who worked as police, petty traders, and prostitutes were confined to the margins of colonial society. Social relations between Russians and other Europeans were subject to strictures, such as general apprehension about British men marrying Russian women.F[46]

In the Carl Smith Collection cited at the beginning of this chapter, documents about the Russian community in Hong Kong illustrate the life of Russians in Hong Kong in ways that suggest that they had meaningful social connections with people of other ethnic and national backgrounds. The stereotype that Russians were ostracized is especially not evident in marriage and death records. Elizabeth A. Touching married Michael A. Koodiaroff in a ceremony at Union Church on May 22, 1933. Touching was given away by a Mr. J. Watson, who is not identified specifically as a relative or friend. Her bridal attendant was an unmarried woman (titled Miss) D. Goroskenko and the groom's best man was D. A. Kaluzhny.119F[47] Documents commemorating deaths include 1937 obituary for a "leading member of (sic) Russian Orthodox community" named Anastasia Goldin, whose husband Constantine Golden (Goldin) managed the Majestic Theater and the May 29, 1951 obituary for Niculau Theodor Turin who died at age 50, six years after he moved from Guangzhou (Canton) to Hong Kong.120F[48] The memorial service, which was described as an "Orthodox funeral" in the record, of Mr. Turin, who had been an employee of the Dairy Farm Ice and Cold Store company at his death, was officiated by Reverend Father Iles. He is identified as Russian and the funeral was held at St. John's Cathedral, so it is possible that "Father Iles" was a reference to Elias (Ilya) Wen. Other references to deaths recorded in the collection are May 16, 1951 memorial service of Tatiana Ivanovra Belanovsky, the spouse of N.A. Belanovsky and "Russian housewife," held at the Colonial Cemetery, and the October 23, 1965 requiem mass held for V. V. Vaganoff officiated by Father Uspensky and attended by Mr. and Mrs. Gavidoff, and Mr. and Mrs. Birinkoff.121F[49] The death of Father Uspensky in 1970 is also recorded in the Hong Kong public records, with details such as that he was mourned by his daughter Adelaide Fogt and his grandchildren, and that a requiem mass was held on January 25, 1970 at the Russian Orthodox Church at 12 Essex Crescent. 122F[50] One document refers to Father Uspensky as the vicar of the Russian Orthodox Church and that he was buried in the Colonial Cemetery.123F[51]

Similarly, although Russians were regarded as a European population that was different and thus unequal to the British, accounts of their experiences suggest that discrimination did not deter some from achieving a satisfactory standard of living. Nona Pio-Ulski Langley has discussed her parents' experience as Russians migrating through China and arriving in Hong Kong after the Japanese occupation of Shanghai in 1937.[52] Langley's father, George Pio-Ulski, worked as a hotel orchestra musician and later gained employment with Hongkong Tramways. His wife, Lila Nozadze, was born as a refugee child on her mother's journey to Vladivostok to reunite with her father. The Pio-Ulski family lived in a comfortable house in the Morrison Hill neighborhood on Hong Kong Island and were active members of the Russian Orthodox community. Their happiness, Langley recalls, came at the cost of the family speaking in Russian only at home and changing their surname to Parks. Langley remained in Hong Kong until 1974 and gave up her job at the HSBC to join her family as immigrants to Perth, Australia.

Furthermore, the presence of Russians did generate cultural synergy and adaptation with the numerically dominant Chinese population. Queen's Café, presently classified as a Western cuisine restaurant, is known for its origins as a place where diners could eat Russian-style food modified to appeal to non-Russian Western and Chinese clientele.[53] The original restaurant was founded in 1952 and presently a group of four branches is now owned by Susanna Tsang, the daughter-in-law of founder Mischa Yu, Queen's Café is well known for its version of borscht, or literally Russian soup.107F[54] Establishments that maintained more authentic cooking practices were the Cherikoff Bakery and Chantecler Restaurant on 174–176 Nathan Road in Tsim Sha Tsui near St. Andrew's Church and later another branch was opened on the Prince Edward district of Kowloon.

Russians in Hong Kong also became part of a diverse population that was mostly transient. As exemplified by the paragliding pilot Aleksandr Kuzminskii in 1912 mentioned earlier in this chapter, the exoticism and novelty associated with Russians was part of the region's allure and mystique. Although individual Russians are not commonly remembered in popular histories of Hong Kong, it is a usual part of the "Hong Kong story" that the region was a place for Russian sojourners. Ivan [Aleksandrovich] Goncharov (1812–1891) came to the city as part of his trip on a schooner named *Pallada* in 1853. The *Pallada*'s ultimate destination was Japan, but Goncharov published a comprehensive travelogue entitled *The Frigate Pallada* including letters he wrote from all the stops on the journey starting in Kronstadt, a naval base near St. Petersburg, and circling the African continent via the Cape of Good Hope, and to several points in Asia including Hong Kong, Singapore, Shanghai, and Manila.[55] Goncharov had seen Chinese people in Singapore and deemed them "unattractive" and not "manly or hearty."109F[56] He was not impressed by what he saw of Chinese traders, even a wealthy merchant named "Wampoa" who acted as a generous host to Goncharov and his companions when they visited his luxurious home. In Hong Kong, Goncharov described the Chinese and European quarters with less overt disdain for their inhabitants. He noted the differences in physical appearance and behavior of Chinese people according to social class, and concluded that unlike the Singaporean Chinese, some Chinese women in Hong Kong were "not at all bad to look at."110F[57] As Edyta M. Bojanowska has argued, the significance of such observations lies in their influence over Russian imaginations about China, Asia more broadly, and the status of Russians in the nineteenth century world order. Goncharov did not speak of "globalization" as we understand it in the twenty-first century, but in Bojanowska's lens, the comparisons between Asia and Europe, and more specifically Russia and its imperial contemporaries, articulate a global sensibility.11F[58]

Anton [Pavlovich] Chekhov (1860–1904) also visited Hong Kong in 1890. The first foreign port he had visited, Hong Kong left a deep impression on Chekhov.112F[59] He did not record many observations about his stay, but he did criticize other Russians traveling with him for accusing the English of abusing the "natives." His dry response to what he considered as toothless denunciation was, as translated by Constance Garnett, "Yes, the English exploit the Chinese, the Sepoys, the Hindoos, but they do give them roads, aqueducts, museums, Christianity, and what do you give them?"113F[60] He also recalls the view from Victoria Peak (Mount Austin) in Hong Kong and compares it favorably to the landscape he encounters when he visits the Monastery of St. Martini in Naples during the following year.1[61]

Perceptions that Russians were not fully integrated into Hong Kong society may have been a chicken-and-egg factor in the migration out of the region that decimated the resident Russian population. As described by Pio-Ulski Langley, Russians in Hong Kong dealt with their status as members of a minority group, by nationality (national origin, if officially stateless) and ethnicity. For some, religious life helped them sustain their social and cultural identities. For others, assimilation into their neighborhoods, schools, and workplaces meant becoming "more British" and conversely, "less Russian," a shift that helped them prepare for the next step of migration to another homeland with a predominantly English-speaking population. Some Russians and other Slavic peoples also sought to improve their social standing, and also prepare for migration, by Anglicizing their surnames and adopting British–English cultural norms.

Our understanding of both the ROC congregations led by Father Uspensky and Father Wen, and about Russians in Hong Kong more generally, is constrained by the relative dearth of sources and limited scholarly interest in these topics. The Hong Kong PRO contains thousands of records that pertain to properties and businesses associated with Russians, but there is very little non-economic data, particularly about individuals' daily lives.[62] About the Russian Orthodox community, the scarcity of evidence resulted from the literal dispersion of sources. Some documents were taken out of Hong Kong by departing members of Church of Saints Peter and Paul and the Church of the Holy Resurrection when they migrated to other places. Others were most likely destroyed or lost after church operations suspended. Reconstructing a comprehensive history of the community will require more rigorous triangulation of what few textual sources survive. Reliance on oral histories, which have revealed some aspects, mainly in the general media, as cited in the examples earlier, will be less productive in future research because persons with first-hand experiences are now elderly or deceased, and individuals who could give second-hand accounts are difficult to trace because they do not have any personal connections to Hong Kong. Another major challenge in elucidating how the presence of the Russian Orthodox community affected social life in Hong Kong is that studies of the development of Christianity in Hong Kong during this period largely focus on the establishment and expansion of churches for Chinese congregations and the inclusion of Chinese persons in churches operating in English and other non-Chinese languages. In his seminal history of Christian churches in Hong Kong published in 1941, Pastor Liu Yüeh-sheng [Lin Yuesheng] (1893–1960) concentrated on churches serving ethnic Chinese believers, but also included some profiles of churches like St. Andrew's Church, described in Chinese as "St. Andrew's Church for westerners." The two-page description of this church provides many basic details about the physical church, leadership, and milestone dates in its history since the congregation was founded in 1899 such as the dedication of the church edifice on October 10, 1906.115F[63] However, the presence of the Russian Orthodox community is not mentioned at all. The absence of this detail reflects the general bias of this text toward Protestant churches, but also reflects how Russian Orthodox believers existed at the margins of both Hong Kong society at large and within the Christian community.

It is also important to note that the interlude in the history of the Russian Orthodox community in Hong Kong from 1970s to the late 1990s is representative but by comparison, less dramatic than the interruption of Orthodox practice in mainland China from the 1950s to the 1990s. Yue Feng argues that 5,587 Chinese had converted to Christianity from 1715 to 1956 through the efforts of 20 successive missions.[64] As described in chapter 1, after the last mission was discontinued in 1956, the PRC government established the

Chinese Autonomous Orthodox Church which was supposed to be a fully indigenous institution and that was not permitted to be governed by the Moscow Patriarchate and other non-Chinese authorities. The dioceses of Beijing, Tianjin, Shanghai, Harbin, and Xinjiang, which were established in the late 1950s, have regulated Orthodox faith and practice until the present day. Although not under political pressure to change its doctrines and practices, as in the PRC, the Russian Orthodox community in Taiwan also went through the gradual diminishing of members from 1945 to 1970. The Taipei parish was suspended in the 1970s because it was deemed to be insubstantially active for 50 years. If new sources are found in the future, evidence about the Hong Kong churches can also substantiate the shared history of Russian Orthodoxy in Greater China during this period.

THE POST-1997 ERA

The revival of the Hong Kong community in the 1990s should be set in the context of the political transition from the USSR to the Russian Federation starting in 1991 and the concomitant changes in policies about religion. The USSR government, like the PRC center, espoused the principle that religion would become insignificant and according to Philip Walters, "ultimately disappear" in a Marxist–Leninist society.[65] As Sabrina Ramet, among other scholars, has discussed, history took a different turn and the reconciliation of relations between the Soviet then Russian state and religious groups occurred in phases and as related to the eventual establishment of the OPASPP, entailed the resumption of not only religious services but also operations such as the publication of religious texts and charity work.[66]

Father Pozdnyaev first visited the PRC in 1994 at the invitation of one of his godsons, a Chinese man living in Moscow.[67] In 1996, with the blessing of then-Metropolitan (now Patriarch) Kirill, Father Pozdnyaev was a member of an international delegation to the Russian embassy in Beijing and gained the support of the Russian Ambassador the PRC, I.A. (Igor Alekseevich) Rogachev (1932–2012), to revive the mission in Hong Kong, which would also be in line with the resumption of Orthodox religious services in mainland China by Moscow Patriarchate clergy after a forty-year hiatus due to political and diplomatic restrictions. After Metropolitan Kirill visited Hong Kong in November 2001 and heard the request of Russian-speaking Orthodox Christian believers who wanted to re-establish a congregation headed by a Moscow Patriarchate-selected priest, he appointed Father Pozdnyaev as the pastor.126F[68] Father Pozdnyaev arrived in Hong Kong in 2003 to assume this position. For the first year of his tenure and residence, he performed services at the Saint Luke Orthodox Cathedral parish of the Orthodox Metropolitanate of Hong Kong and South East Asia (OMHKSEA), with the permission of rector Metropolitan Nikitas (Lulias). In summer 2004, Father Pozdnyaev blessed the Russian Orthodox Church premises situated at 4–6 Hennessy Road, Wanchai, which was officially registered as the Orthodox Brotherhood of Apostles Saints Peter and Paul (OPASPP).[69]

The Wanchai Church became the base to rebuild the community in several ways. Father Pozdnyaev added elements of Chinese design to the church which was within an office building. He established church-to-church relations with the OMHKSEA congregation. In doing so, he confirmed that the OPASPP as an entity that was separate from the OMHKSEA, and that distinction has been maintained until the present day. Metropolitan Nikitas visited the OPASPP Church in October 2005 to act as co-celebrant with Father Pozdnyaev of an infant baptism. In 2006, Father Pozdnyaev, acting as vice-president, cofounded the Orthodox Fellowship of All Saints of China (OFASC) in the United States with Nelson Mitrophan Chin and commenced activities of activities of the Fellowship's Hong Kong branch. The OFASC developed a trilingual website, in English, Chinese, and Russian, to serve Chinese believers throughout the world.[70] The following year, the parish established the RLC to teach Russian as both a foreign language for non-native learners and as a native language for children and youth. Father Pozdnyaev and Sergey (also known as Sergio) Min, a layperson, registered the RLC as a company to hire teachers and manage the school as a for-profit institution. In January 2008, Father Igor Filyanovsky, rector of the Parish of the Holy Trinity of Melbourne, brought the icon of Apostles Peter and Paul that had belonged to the church led by Father Uspensky to Hong Kong and returned it to the Hong Kong congregation. On October 6, 2008, the Parish of Saints Peter and Paul was officially re-established by the decision of the Moscow Patriarchate. In the capacity of member of the Department for External Church Relations (DECR) of Russian Orthodox Church, Father Pozdnyaev was formally appointed as rector of the parish.[71]

More changes occurred in the decade following the parish's re-establishment. The parish church moved in August 2010 to a building on 2–12 Queen's Road West in the Sheung Wan district, holding the first official service in September 2010, and to its current location on 32–36 Des Voeux Road in July 2016.[72] Owning the remodeled and custom-designed premise and having enough space so that the RLC does not have to use the church's worship space has meant that the OPASPP can hold daily services instead of only on some days of the week when the church and RLC had to share space according to a common schedule. In 2013, the OPASPP continued its physical expansion by leasing a property on Lantau Island as a residence for visiting priests and pilgrims. Acquiring this space was also vital for the establishment of a physical plant for the China Orthodox Press in 2014.

Several milestone events of the OPASPP are also significant for the ROC in China. In 2007, the Act of Canonical Communion restored unity between the Moscow Patriarchate and ROCOR.[73] This decision is monumental because it has meant that clergy's and congregations' affiliations do not preclude interaction between them. As discussed earlier in this chapter, this difference affected the churches led by Father Uspensky and Father Wen. Another monumental event was the 300th anniversary of the founding of the first Russian Ecclesiastical Mission in China in 2012. The OPASPP co-organized liturgical services, lectures, and academic discussions to celebrate this milestone with the Institute of Sino-Christian Studies and the Chinese University of Hong Kong. Bishop Ephraim of Bikin (Roman Prosyanok), provost of the Khabarovsk Theological Seminary, was the official leader of these celebrations. Bishop Ephraim was the first bishop to perform services in the OPASPP Church. These events also commemorated the settlement of Albazinians in Beijing under the spiritual guidance of Father Maxim Leontiev (Maksim Leont'ev) in 1712. The OPASPP celebration on December 7, 2012 was especially momentous because among the visiting clergy from New Zealand, Taipei, Moscow, Archpriest Michael Li from Australia was the first ethnic Chinese priest to lead a service in the church.[74] Two years later, the OPASPP celebrated the ordination of Father Anatoly Kung (Kung Cheung Ming), one of less than ten Chinese clergy in the Greater China area. Another major event for both the OPASPP and the ROC in China was the special liturgical service to celebrate the parish's move to the current location, held on October 14, 2016. The OPASPP clergy co-officiated the service with the rector of the Dormition of the Most Holy Theotokos Church in Beijing, rector of the Taiwan Orthodox Church, and monastic representatives from France and Finland.[75] The service was performed with segments in different languages, following the church's customs. Father Pozdnyaev used English for some segments of the service, including the blessings preceding the Communion, Slavonic for most steps, and made announcements in modern Russian to deliver announcements.[76] Father Kung used Mandarin when chanting and acting as principal officiant. Two Chinese readers recited the Profession of Faith in Cantonese. The consecration and pronouncements immediately and after Communion were in English, and the ending blessing was delivered in Slavonic.

The current OPASPP Church in Sheung Wan is a place that would be recognizable as an Orthodox Church to believers from all parts of the world and simultaneously reflects the church's site in China. The design of the church, led by Father Pozdnyaev, was based on the principle that it should be a space that welcomes believers of all backgrounds, and in addition to serving the fundamental purpose of worship, should also be a place where parishioners are comfortable and in which they take pride. The iconostasis, as seen in figure 2.2, was rendered in a different style than the one in figure 2.1 and

Figure 2.2 Iconostasis of the Church in Sheung Wan.
Source: Permission granted by the Saint Apostles Peter and Paul Orthodox Church in Hong Kong.

reflects the esthetics of the church as a whole as a new and lasting space for the parish.

The church's design also reflects the incorporation of many functions carried out under the auspices of the OPASPP. The church and RLC share a foyer through which every person enters. Every inch of space on the property, which occupies one floor of the building, serves a practical purpose as well as an esthetic and religious one. A visitor to these premises can meet church staff in offices, attend liturgical services, and socialize with other members of the community. The relatively compact space facilitates and encourages the spiritual and secular functions of the parish to be conducted in tandem. While considered as the most pragmatic arrangement, the current church/office/classroom/meeting room configuration is also crucial tool in the parish's outreach, as will be seen in the next two chapters, because the RLC and the COP, as organizations affiliated with the OPASPP, are literally housed together with the church and also share its mission of disseminating knowledge about Russian culture and society in Hong Kong and expanding a community based on faith by situating it fully in Hong Kong life and through publications in hard copy and digital versions, to other places in Greater China, East Asia, and around the world.

NOTES

1. Hong Kong Public Records Office, Carl Smith Collection, 177461.

2. Regarding Christianity in colonial Hong Kong and the comparison with present-day institutions and practices, see Lida V. Nedilsky, *Converts to Civil Society: Christianity and Political Culture in Contemporary Hong Kong* (Waco, TX: Baylor University Press, 2014), 36–39.

3. Literature in both English and Chinese about Hong Kong's history includes abundant publications by both professional and avocational historians. For the English-language reader, we suggest these comprehensive works about Hong Kong's modern history to introduce and compare both the colonial and postcolonial periods: John M. Carroll, *A Concise History of Hong Kong* (Lanham, MD: Rowman & Littlefield, 2007) and Steve Tsang, *A Modern History of Hong Kong: 1841–1997* (London: I.B. Tauris, 2003). Among the many works in Chinese, see Siu Kwok Kin, *Xianggang lishi yanjiu* [Study of the history of Hong Kong] (Hong Kong: Xian zhao shushi, 2004) and Tang Ka Jau et al., eds., *Xianggang lishi tanjiu* [Exploring the history of Hong Kong] (Hong Kong: Xianggang shixue hui, 2011).

4. Bruce Shepherd, *A Hand-book to Hongkong: Being A Popular Guide to the Various Places of Interest in the Colony, for the Use of Tourists* (Hongkong [Hong Kong]: Kelly & Walsh, 1893), 79–80.

5. William Legge, *A Guide to Hongkong with some Remarks upon Macao and Canton* (Hong Kong: Walter W. Brewer, 1893), 9, and Carl Crow, *The Travelers' Handbook for China (including Hong Kong)*, 3rd ed. (New York: Dodd, Mead & Co.; Shanghai: Carl Crow, 1921), 289. Not so evident in these books is that these places of worship were built over time rather than being immediately established and operational. Work on the Hongkong Colonial Chapel started in March 1846, was opened for services in March 1849, and it became St. John's Cathedral in 1852. The first Roman Catholic church was consecrated in 1842 and then the cathedral was built in the 1880s. See Solomon Bard, *Voices from the Past: Hong Kong 1842–1918* (Hong Kong: Hong Kong University Press, 2002), 20.

6. See Vicky Lee, *Being Eurasian: Memories Across Racial Divides* (Hong Kong: Hong Kong University Press, 2004), Emma Jinhua Teng, *Eurasian: Mixed Identities in the United States, China, and Hong Kong 1842–1943* (Berkeley: University of California Press, 2013), and Catherine Ladds, "Eurasians in Treaty-port China: Journeys across Racial and Imperial Frontiers," in Jacqueline Leckie, Angela McCarthy, Angela Wanhalla, eds., *Migrant Cross-Cultural Encounters in Asia and the Pacific* (Abingdon: Routledge, 2016), 19–35.

7. About this period in the ROC's history, see Daniela Kalkandjieva, *The Russian Orthodox Church, 1917–1948: Decline to Resurrection* (London: Routledge, 2014).

8. Jane Ellis, *The Russian Orthodox Church: A Contemporary History* (Bloomington and Indianapolis: Indiana University Press, 1986), 3–5.

9. Ellis, *The Russian Orthodox Church*, 125.

10. These churches include the Dormition of the Most Holy Theotokos Church in Beijing, St. Nicholas Church in Tianjin, the Cathedral of the Icon of the Mother of God "Surety of Sinners" in Shanghai, the Church of the Theophany in Shanghai, and several churches in Harbin including the St. Nicholas Church, Church of the Holy Annunciation, Church of the Holy Iveron Icon, St. Sophia Cathedral, St. Aleksejev Church, Protection (Pokrov) of the Theotokos Church, and Church of the Dormition.

For a concise history of these churches from 1900 to 1986, see Otdel vneshnikh tserkovnykh sviazei Moskovskogo patriarkhata [External Liaison Office of the Moscow Patriarchate], *Pravoslavie v Kitae* [Eastern Orthodox Christianity in China] (Moscow: Moscow Patriarchate, 2010).

11. All three organizations are still active. See (Hong Kong) Confucian Academy, "Kongjiao xueyuan" [Confucian Academy], accessed July 7, 2018. http://confucianacademy.com, Hong Kong Buddhist Association, "Xianggang Fojiao lianhehui" [The Hong Kong Buddhist Association], accessed July 7, 2018, http://www.hkbuddhist.org/zh, Hong Kong Taoist Association, "Xianggang Daojiao lianhehui" [Hong Kong Taoist Association], accessed July 7, 2018, http://www.hktaoist.org.hk.

12. Both of these organizations are currently active. Hong Kong Chinese Christian Churches Union, "Xianggang Huaren Jidujiao lianhui" [The Hong Kong Chinese Christian Churches Union], accessed July 9, 2018, http://www.hkcccu.org.hk, and Hong Kong Christian Council, "Xianggang Jidujiao xiejinhui" [Hong Kong Christian Council], accessed July 9, 2018, http://www.hkcc.org.hk.

13. The Hong Kong diocese formally belongs to the Archidiocese of Guangzhou but is autonomous within the bounds of the Hong Kong Special Administrative Region (HKSAR).

14. Dittmar Schorkowitz, "The Orthodox Church, Lamaism, and Shamanism among the Buriats and Kalmyks, 1825–1925," in *Of Religion and Empire: Missions, Conversion, and Tolerance in Tsarist Russia*, eds. Robert P. Geraci, and Michael Khodarkovsky (Ithaca, NY: Cornell University Press, 2001), 201–25.

15. Nina Federova, *The Family* (Boston: Little, Brown, and Company, 1940). Antonina Riasanovsky had two sons. One was the acclaimed historian of Russia, Nicholas V. Riasanovsky (1923–2011).

16. Tatiana Erohina, *Growing Up Russian in China* (Bloomington, IN: iUniverse, 2011).

17. Ibid., chapter 10, 86–88.

18. See Hong Kong History Museum, "Secrets of the Russian Monarchs: Nicholas II's Visit to Hong Kong," accessed June 16, 2017, http://hk.history.museum/documents/54401/2823302/Nicholas+II+Visit+to+Hong+Kong.pdf. Nicholas II's visit was one subtopic of the Hong Kong History Museum's "Treasures from Tsarskoye Selo, Residence of the Russian Monarchs" exhibition held from October 29, 2014 to March 16, 2015.

19. Joseph Ting Sun-pao and Lo Shuk-ying, *Fei Wo zuyi: Zhanqian Xianggang de waiji zuqun* [Not of my kind: foreign communities in Hong Kong before World War Two] (Hong Kong: Joint Publishing, 2014), 131.

20. Lawrence K. K. Ho and Chu Yiu Kong, *Xianggang jingcha: lishi jianzheng yu zhifa shengya* [The Hong Kong police: witnesses to history and careers in law enforcement] (Hong Kong: Joint Publishing, 2011), 53–55, and Pao and Lo, *Fei Wo zuyi*, 137.

21. Businesses bearing the names and traditions of these establishments still exist and operate in Hong Kong today.

22. Recent publications include Stuart Heaver, "How the White Russian Refugee Crisis Unfolded in China a Century Ago, and the Lucky Ones Who Made It to Hong

Kong," *South China Morning Post*, May 7, 2017, accessed May 17, 2017, http://www.scmp.com/magazines/post-magazine/long-reads/article/2092988/how-white-russian-refugee-crisis-unfolded-china, and Christopher DeWolf, "Why do Hong Kong Restaurants Serve Borscht? The Overlooked History of Russian Hong Kong," *Zolima Citymag*, October 4, 2017, accessed December 10, 2017, https://zolimacitymag.com/why-do-hong-kong-restaurants-serve-borscht-the-overlooked-history-of-russian-hong-kong.

23. Father Uspensky was an expert in Northeast Asian languages. He studied Chinese, Mongolian, and Korean at the Lazarev Institute of Oriental Languages in Vladivostok. For a complete hagiographical account of his life and achievements, see Orthodox Parish of Apostles Saints Peter and Paul (Moscow Patriarchate), *Saint Apostles Peter & Paul Orthodox Church in Hong Kong (Moscow Patriarchate)* (Hong Kong: China Orthodox Press, 2016), 34–51.

Also note that Bishop Viktor [Svyatin] became an archbishop in 1938, as cited in other references to him in this chapter.

24. Interestingly, the St. Andrew's Church website only mentions the relationship with the Russian Orthodox community on its Historical Milestones webpage referring to a 1955 fundraising concert featuring a Russian Orthodox choir. See St. Andrew's Church Kowloon, Hong Kong, "Our History," accessed September 8, 2017, http://standrews.monkpreview2.com/about-us/our-history.

25. See Dionisy Pozdnyaev, "Orthodox Christianity in Hong Kong," appx. 2 in *Pravoslavie v Kitae (1900–1997)* [Orthodox Christianity in China (1900–1997)] (Moscow: Izd. Sviato-Vladimirskogo Bratstva, 1998), accessed June 28, 2017, http://www.orthodox.cn/localchurch/pozdnyaev/index_ru.html.

26. In the following years, other clergy took over responsibilities for the churches outside of Hong Kong. On March 17, 1935, Priest Yevgeny Lutchev (n.d.–ca.1938) was appointed rector of the Church in Guangzhou. Nearly a year later, on February 7, 1936, Archpriest Mikhail Yerokhin (n.d.–1992) was appointed rector for the Manila parish, and in Amoy (Xiamen), a prayer house dedicated to St. Nicholas the Miracle Worker (270–343) was consecrated by Father Uspensky in April 1937. Congregations of these churches developed according to local social and cultural conditions.

27. Michael B. Share describes him as the "center" of the community. *Where Empires Collided: Russian and Soviet Relations with Hong Kong, Taiwan, and Macao* (Hong Kong: Chinese University Press, 2007), 93.

28. Few documentary records about the Hong Kong deanery and the Church of Saints Peter and Paul survive from the 1930s. For the 1939 *Charter of the Orthodox church communities of the cities of South China and the Philippine Islands* ratified in Shanghai, one of the few sources, see *Ustav Tserkovnykh pravoslavnykh obshchin gorodov Iuzhnogo Kitaia i filippinskikh ostrovov* [Charter of the Orthodox church communities of the cities of South China and the Philippine Islands] (Shanghai, 1939).

29. Schedules of services were published in newspapers. See *Hong Kong Daily Press (1938)*, "Russian Orthodox Church," July 2 (1938): 3.

30. Documents about church construction were lost after the war, when many members of the planning association left Hong Kong. Therefore, the actual state of

readiness for erecting a church building and the exact reasons, whether financial, political, or purely logistical, are subject to speculation until material evidence can be recovered.

31. The map is part of the Hong Kong government archives on land, but is not a public document.

32. 1945 was also an important year for the community because Bishop John of Shanghai (later known as St. John of Shanghai and San Francisco) officiated a service at St. Andrew's Church during his visit to Hong Kong.

33. The dimensions of the Russian Orthodox community in Asia also changed during the late 1940s and 1950s. The cathedral in Manila was severely damaged during a bombing by Japanese forces in 1945, which hampered religious and community operations there.

34. This difference of opinion may have partially stemmed from the disparate backgrounds of the people involved. Some congregants were Russians working for British companies, including some who gained British nationality. They and other parishioners supported the decision to become part of the Moscow Patriarchate. See OPASPP, *Saint Apostles Peter & Paul*, 10.

35. Father Uspensky attempted to consult with Archbishop Viktor in September 1955 about the problem of affiliation, but never received a clear response. The lack of complete communication is considered as one reason the Hong Kong deanery did not join the Chinese Autonomous Orthodox Church.

36. There are no known sources that provide the name of the French national.

37. Orthodox Fellowship for All Saints of China, "In Memoriam: Protopresbyter Elias Wen," accessed May 18, 2017, http://www.orthodox.cn/localchurch/shanghai/eliaswen_en.htm.

38. See Orthodox Parish of Apostles Saints Peter and Paul (Moscow Patriarchate), "Archpriest Dmitry Uspensky," accessed April 28, 2017, https://orthodoxy.hk/parish/archpriest_dimitry_uspensky.

39. Michael B. Share has stressed Father Uspensky's anti-communist attitudes and his expression thereof as a clergyman based outside of the USSR. See *Where Empires Collided*, 241.

40. About the Shanghai Chinese Orthodox Association, see Shanghai City Gazetteer Office (Shanghai shi difang zhi bangongshi), "Di'er jie Dongzhengjiao" [Section 2: Eastern Orthodox Christianity], accessed February 20, 2017, www.shtong.gov.cn/node2/node2247/node79044/node79333/node79336/userobject1ai103744.html.

41. "Archbishop John, Head of Orthodox Church in China, Resettlement Plans," *South China Morning Post*, July 24, 1949.

42. Chan subsequently transferred the rights to the Electro Enterprises and Advertising Company on September 23, 1974. No further information is readily available about Chan and Li's personal identities. Regarding these transactions, see Indenture between Lai Wai Suen and the Colony of Hong Kong, concerning the Lease of New Kowloon Inland Lot No. 725 (commencing 1st day of July 1898), registered Vol: CJX. Fol:53, prepared by the Land Office (Hong Kong, 5 November 1930), printed at Noronha & Co. Hong Kong; Indenture of Assignment between

Lai Wai Suen (the Vendor) and Chan Bing Yim (the Purchaser), concerning New Kowloon Inland Lot No. 725 (No.12 Essex Crescent), instrumented on 25 April 1962, registered as Memorial No. 367371, the Land Office of the Colony of Hong Kong (Hong Kong, 12 May 1962); Indenture of Assignment between Chan Bing Yim (the Vendor) and Electro Enterprises and Advertising Company Limited (the Purchaser), concerning New Kowloon Inland Lot No. 725 (No.12 Essex Crescent), instrumented on 23 September 1974, registered as Memorial No. 1113283, the Land Office of the Colony of Hong Kong (Hong Kong, 18 October 1974).

43. About the February 1968 agreement that Father Uspensky would not formally retire as the church's pastor, see OPASPP, *Saint Apostles Peter & Paul*, 14.

44. See "Nekrolog (Obituary)," *Zhurnal Moskovskoi Patriarkhii* (Journal of the Moscow Patriarchate) (1970, no. 5), 48.

45. Robert Bickers, *Britain in China: Community, Culture and Colonialism 1900–1949* (Manchester: Manchester University Press, 1999), 72. Bickers notes that some Russians decided to improve their political standing by assuming Chinese citizenship, especially in the 1930s.

46. Bickers, *Britain in China*, 99.

47. Carl Smith Collection, 177469–70.

48. About the Goldens, see Carl Smith Collection, 103445 and Niculau Turin, Carl Smith Collection, 148373 and 148375. Turin's first given name is unusual, so it is possible that he was called Nicolau or Nicula, so both versions of this name are given in the glossary.

49. For the Belanovsky memorial service, see Carl Smith Collection, 081199 and 081201, and the Vaganoff requiem mass, see Carl Smith Collection, 177467–8. The burial service for Tatiana Belanovsky was held on May 17, 1950 at St. John's Cathedral after her death at age 61. Note that the handwriting of the record about the Vaganoff requiem mass is very unclear, so "Vaganoff" is the most likely but not absolutely verifiable surname of the deceased.

50. See Carl Smith Collection, 148857–8 and 148865.

51. Carl Smith Collection, 1488865.

52. DeWolf, "Why Do Hong Kong Restaurants Serve Borscht?" and Nona Pio-Ulski Langley, "Pio-Ulski," accessed January 20, 2018, https://pio-ulski.com.

53. Sometimes it is known as a Russian Western restaurant, see OpenRice, "Queen's Cafe," accessed October 8, 2017, https://www.openrice.com/en/hongkong/r-queens-cafe-wan-chai-russian-r152809. This restaurant also belongs to the broader category of "soy sauce Western" restaurants. For a definition of "soy sauce Western," see Andrea Lo, "East Meets West: Best Soy Sauce Western in Hong Kong," *Ovolo Hotels*, accessed August 29, 2017, https://www.ovolohotels.com/east-meets-west-best-soy-sauce-western-hong-kong.

54. Tsang is the widow of Mischa Yu's only son, Stanley Yu. She now operates the restaurants with her three sons.

55. See chapter 7 of the book, first published in a complete edition in 1858 after serial publication from 1855 to 1857. Ivan Aleksandrovich Goncharov, *Fregate Pallada* [The Frigate Pallada] (St. Petersburg, 1858). For an English version, see *The Frigate Pallada*, trans. Klaus Goetze (New York: St. Martin's Press, 1987).

56. See Goetze translation of *The Frigate Pallada*, 213–14.

57. Goetze, trans., *The Frigate Pallada*, 243.

58. Edyta M. Bojanowska, *A World of Empires: The Russian Voyage of the Frigate Pallada* (Cambridge, MA: Belknap Press of Harvard University Press, 2018), 21.

59. See D. Kapustin, "Gonkong—pervyi port zagranichnogo puteshestviia Chekhova" [Hong Kong—the first port abroad in Chekhov's travels], *Problemy Dal'nego Vostoka*, no. 3 (2009): 155–67.

60. Anton Pavlovich Chekhov, *Letters of Anton Tchehov to his Family and Friends*, trans. Constance Garnett (London: Chatoo & Windus, 1920), 218–19.

61. Chekhov, *Letters of Anton Tchehov*, 245.

62. For a general description of the PRO as a resource for Christianity in Hong Kong, see Tiedemann, ed., *Handbook of Christianity, Volume Two*, 8.

63. Liu Yüeh-sheng [Liu Yuesheng], *Xianggang Jidujiaohui shi* [The history of Christian churches in Hong Kong] (Hong Kong: Xianggang Jidujiao lianhui, 1941), 130–31. Liu was not the only observer to overlook, either deliberately or by lack of knowledge, the presence of Russian Orthodox Christians. Earl Herbert Cressy did not include any citations of Orthodox churches in his two studies of Hong Kong's Christian churches conducted in the 1950s. See Earl Herbert Cressy, *City Churches in Hong Kong: With a Supplementary Survey of All Churches in the Colony* (Hong Kong: Earl Herbert Cressy, 1956), and Earl Herbert Cressy, *Urban Church Growth in Hong Kong 1955–1958: Second Hong Kong Study*, self-published (Hong Kong: Earl Herbert Cressy, 1960). Loren E. Noren also did not include any references to Orthodox communities in his study which was contemporaneous to Cressy's work. See Loren E. Noren, *Urban Church Growth in Hong Kong 1958–1962: Third Hong Kong Study* (Hong Kong: s.n., 1963). The dominant inclination in academic studies of religion in Hong Kong toward mainline Protestant Christianity is also evident in bibliographies like Stephen Lau and Lewis Choi, eds., *Literature on Chinese Christianity and Society since the Inception of the People's Republic of China: An index of writings located in Hong Kong*, 2 vols. (Hong Kong: sn, 1996). The Chinese names of Lau and Choi are not cited in extant sources.

64. Yue, *Dongzheng jiao shi*, 308–09.

65. Philip Walters, "A Survey of Soviet Religious Policy," in *Religious Policy in the Soviet Union*, ed. Sabrina Petra Ramet (Cambridge: Cambridge University Press, 1992), 4.

66. Sabrina Petra Ramet, "Religious Policy in the Era of Gorbachev," in *Religious Policy in the Soviet Union*, ed. Sabrina Petra Ramet (Cambridge: Cambridge University Press, 1992), 33–39.

67. This visit to mainland China included activities and tours in Beijing and Tianjin. Father Pozdnyaev's godson would prefer to remain anonymous.

68. See Khabarovsk Pravoslavnyi [Khabarovsk Orthodox], "V Kitae mnogie gotovy byli by priniat' Pravoslavie" [In China many would be willing to accept Orthodoxy], last modified September 30, 2010, accessed February 9, 2018, http://pravostok.ru/blog/v-kitae-mnogie-gotovi-bili-bi-prinyat-pravoslavie.

69. Father Pozdnyaev and Sergei Min registered the church as a legal organization.

70. See "Orthodox Fellowship of All Saints of China," accessed August 8, 2017, http://www.orthodox.cn/ofasc.

71. The DECR has its own official website. See Department for External Church Relations (DECR), "Department for External Church Relations, Moscow Patriarchate," www.mospat.ru. The website may be read in Russian, English, Greek, French Italian, and Spanish.

72. Many addresses in Hong Kong combine multiple property numbers, particularly for large commercial complexes and residential buildings.

73. For an official English translation of the Act, see "Act of Canonical Communion, " The Synod of Bishops of the Russian Orthodox Church Outside of Russian, accessed March 2021, https://web.archive.org/web/20070614175937/http://www.russianorthodoxchurch.ws/synod/engdocuments/enmat_akt.html.

74. John Peck, "300 Years of Orthodox Christianity in China," accessed May 19, 2017, https://journeytoorthodoxy.com/2013/02/300-years-of-orthodoxy-in-china/.

75. The Dormition of the Most Holy Theotokos Church in Beijing, Russian Orthodox Church Moscow Patriarchate, accessed October 28, 2017, http://orthodoxbj.com/en.

76. The term "Slavonic" in this book denotes the language often known as "Church Slavonic."

Chapter 3

The Russian Language Center

A SKETCH OF RUSSIAN LIFE IN HONG KONG

"I am Dasha. I am six years old. I love my school in Hong Kong. And I love my friends in my school (*Ia Dasha, mne 6 let. Ia liubliu moiu shkolu v Gongonge. Takzhe ia liubliu moikh podruzhek v moei shkola*)."[1] This is the opening sentence of Dasha's essay about her life in Hong Kong, one of the stories included in *ABC of Hong Kong* (*Azbuka Gonkonga*), a children's book project which was organized and presented by the Russian Language Center (RLC) on October 1, 2017. A former student at the RLC, Dasha lived in Hong Kong for two years before her family moved away. Like many children from Russian-speaking families in Hong Kong, she spent an important part of her childhood in the city, and her memory of learning the Russian language and making friends at the center is preserved as a piece of the RLC's history and as an example of student work that can be used as teaching material at the school.

The *ABC of Hong Kong* project was the brainchild of Anastasia Kraeva, teacher and the coordinator of the "Russian for Kids in Hong Kong" program at the RLC. Kraeva and her colleagues launched the project in early March 2017 to collect not only children's memories but also their impressions and interpretations of life in the city. Each child's writing is associated with a letter of the Russian alphabet, such as "Г" (g) for "Гонконг" (Gonkong/Hong Kong). Compiled according to the two guiding principles of being specific to Hong Kong and being written only in Russian, the book was designed to be the first Russian-language book for children in Hong Kong. It is groundbreaking not only because it is the first publication of this kind, but also because it teaches children the Russian language using materials related to Hong Kong's local setting, such as pictures of indigenous animals and plants, unique architecture, and landscapes in Hong Kong. The book also includes selected drawings and essays on various topics about the city's appearance and about Russian life in the city. Children who studied at the RLC from 2007 to 2017 contributed to the book's content. The book project was also part of a long-term experiment by the center to create a series of educational materials from basic to advanced levels for children of different ages learning Russian in Hong Kong.

This activity exemplifies how the RLC has tailored its operations as a private-sector language school to promote the study and use of the Russian language in Hong Kong.[2] In addition to teaching the language and introducing Russian culture in its children's classes, the RLC welcomes both youth and adult students to participate in the Russian cultural events that it organizes both as social occasions for the Russian-speaking community and to attract people who do not have personal connections to Russia to learn more about Russia's past and present. The RLC's curriculum for children typifies the school's general efforts to pursue inculturation, an approach that includes incorporating elements of Hong Kong's unique culture into classes and teaching Russian as both a first and a second language to accommodate students from households in which Russian is the primary language as well as those who have just one Russian-speaking parent. The RLC's courses for children are also important because they stress language rather than religion as the principal marker of Russian heritage and identity in Hong Kong.

This chapter discusses how the RLC, by operating successful programs for adults and children, has contributed to the mission of the OPASPP as an institution promoting awareness and interest in Russian culture. The original purpose of the RLC was to teach classes for adults interested in learning Russian for business, tourism, and personal relationships. The school fills a niche in the Hong Kong language education market because Russian language is not regularly taught in Hong Kong schools, excepting some courses given at irregular intervals at Lingnan University, Chinese University of Hong Kong (CUHK), and HKU Space, the community college of the University of Hong Kong (HKU), and since late 2019, as standard courses in the School of Modern Languages and Cultures of HKU. The only direct competitor for students seeking private tuition in Russian language at present is the Russian Culture Association (RCA). The RCA targets individuals who want to learn Russian by Chinese as the medium of instruction. Its webpage gives information about course schedules and fees only in Chinese.[3] The two schools are also different because the RCA only offers instruction for adults, whereas the RLC curriculum includes courses for young students, from toddlers to primary and secondary school students. The "Russian for Kids" program consists of language classes held at the school campus and non-language-centered activities organized by RLC teachers such as Art Jammin on Lamma Island. The following three sections examine how the RLC has developed into a social and cultural institution that functions independently of the church while sharing the objective of fostering Sino-Russian relations through the dissemination of knowledge about Russian culture and society, and serves both adult students who are learning Russian as a foreign language and promotes emotional attachment and a sense of community for both children who study Russian as a heritage language and those who study it as a foreign language.

THE RLC AND THE OPASPP

Culture rather than religion as the emphasis for educating students of both Russian and non-Russian background as the main mission of the school reflects how the RLC has changed during its twelve-year history. During the first few years following the RLC's establishment, the missions of the center and the OPASPP were more closely integrated. Although mastery of the Russian language was the primary objective of RLC courses, supporting the work of the church and attracting believers to join the church were explicit purposes of the center. As described in chapter 2, Father Pozdnyaev and Sergio Min, a parish member, established the RLC in 2007 as a private company. According to Father Pozdnyaev, the initial motivation behind the RLC was the desire to develop an additional source of income for the church. In his words, the business model was "to earn money through teaching of the Russian language to those people here in Hong Kong who have certain needs."[4] In addition to covering some of the church's rental expenses and operating costs, the RLC serves as the legal sponsor for staff who work for both the church and the school, such as translators for the China Orthodox Press (COP) and choir teachers.

However, from the beginning, the RLC's founders saw a professional attitude to language studies as a key feature of the center. Consequently, Father Pozdnyaev hired professional teachers from the Russian Federation who not only are native speakers but also had formal credentials in teaching Russian as either a foreign or a native language. Moreover, most of the RLC teachers are Orthodox Christians and members of the OPASPP parish. While being an Orthodox Christian is not a formal prerequisite for employment, Father Pozdnyaev believes that "it is more suitable [for teachers who are Orthodox] to work together."[5] Since RLC teachers do help the OPASPP organize activities, their knowledge of Orthodox faith and tradition is considered advantageous for this kind of work.[6] Irina Ustyugova, the longest-serving teacher, is the wife of Father Anton Serafimovich and therefore a matushka (priest's wife) to OPASPP parishioners. Irina Ustyugova's employment and dedication to the RLC was the catalyst for Father Serafimovich to transfer to Hong Kong and join the OPASPP as a member of the clergy. Other long-time teachers, including Anastasia Kraeva and Tatiana S. Pugacheva, are also Orthodox Christians. These three teachers are open to discussing the tenets of the faith if students, and, in the case of children and youth, their parents, ask about them. They also encourage RLC students to participate voluntarily in church-organized activities such as receiving choral training and performing in holiday plays. But in other aspects, the teaching staff embraces the mission that the RLC is principally an outreach platform for Russian language and culture and shares the same priorities of language proficiency and cultural awareness as other private language schools in Hong Kong.

Even as a non-religious institution, the RLC has maintained close, mutually dependent connections with the OPASPP since its establishment. Classes and administrative work have always taken place in physical space shared with the church. The RLC, previously located in the Sincere Insurance Building on Hennessy Road in Wan Chai from August 2007 to August 2010 and then in the Arion Commercial Center on Queen's Road West in Sheung Wan from September 2010 to July 2016, and together with the church, moved in July 2016 to the Kingdom Power Commercial Building in Sheung Wan, where it continues to share space with the OPASPP. The new Sheung Wan site functions as the base for most of the RLC's regular language programs and cultural events, but the RLC has expanded the physical scope of its operations so that many outdoor children's activities held in various additional locations throughout Hong Kong, including Sai Kung, Clearwater Bay, Mid-Levels, and Lamma Island. In 2017, the RLC also opened a new program for adult education in Jordan, Kowloon. Although only some of the courses take place at the Jordan location, it marks a new step for the RLC, which is branching out from Hong Kong Island as it seeks to increase its market share in Russian language education. A RLC poster (figure 3.1) also illustrates the outreach to Russian speakers who want to study English, Chinese, and French at the RLC, which offers courses in these languages taught in Russian.

As introduced in chapter 2, the church and the RLC now share space for their functions but they are physically more separate in the current configuration of the Sheung Wan facilities. In contrast to the previous site in the Arion Commercial Center, where the RLC classrooms were separated from one another by movable partitions inside the main church chamber, the current location provides the RLC with a separate entrance to the premises it shares with the church. Its new space includes bigger classrooms and better-equipped public facilities, such as office, bathrooms, and pantry, than were available at the old site, and it also allows the RLC to have its own small library of Russian novels, memoirs, children's books, DVDs and CDs of Russian movies and music, as well as a display board for all kinds of program

Figure 3.1 Poster for the Russian Language Center.
Source: Permission granted by the Saint Apostles Peter & Paul Orthodox Church in Hong Kong and the Russian Language Center, Hong Kong.

advertisements, posters, and children's artwork. However, co-sharing space is still integral to the work of both the RLC and the church. Father Pozdnyaev, as both the head of the parish and one of the RLC directors, shares the office with teachers; a sliding door next to his desk connects the RLC with the church chamber. The RLC is open regularly on Hong Kong's official public holidays to host members of the congregation, visitors, and participants in religious events. By sharing its facilities with the church, it makes a larger venue available for the latter's use.

The delineation of the RLC's mission from that of the church, even though the two bodies coexist in the same space, is also evident in the RLC's greater network of partner institutions. The OPASPP is still one of the RLC's official partners, but the RLC also works closely with the International Association of Teachers of Russian Language and Literature (also known by the abbreviation of its Russian name, MAPRYAL),[7] the Russian Consulate General in Hong Kong, the Russian Club in Hong Kong, the Russian Business Club (Hong Kong), From Russia with Art, and the Russian Bazaar. The RLC has also developed several partnerships with Russian social and cultural organizations based in Hong Kong to organize events such as From Russia with Art, the Russian Bazaar, and the Russian Cultural Week. From Russia with Art, founded by an independent nonprofit organization called Artisia Limited in 2014, is an annual cultural event aimed at promoting classical and contemporary Russian arts among the Hong Kong public.[8] The Russian Bazaar is similarly an annual event organized personally by teachers of the RLC to introduce Russian or Russian-inspired folk artists, crafts, and food on various occasions.[9] Collaborating with the Russian consulate-general of Hong Kong and local businesses like Russian online grocery vendors and restaurants, the RLC held the first Russian Cultural Week in October 2017. During this event, participants could see and learn visual art in Russian-style art schools, learn how to cook Russian cuisine, hear Russian music, and join tours to see the graves of Russian persons buried in the Hong Kong Cemetery like Nicholas Belanovsky (1889–1977), the architect of Shanghai's Cathedral of the Icon of the Mother of God "Surety of Sinners," and the artist George V. Smirnov (1903–1947) who was well-known in Macau.[10]

The Russkiy Mir Foundation, a joint enterprise of the Russian government and civil organizations, was also a significant partner, providing financial support to the RLC from its founding in 2007 until 2011. The RLC fulfilled its responsibilities as a grant recipient by structuring its curriculum according to the three aspects of the foundation's mission: promoting the Russian language, encouraging appreciation for Russian culture, and nurturing bonds among members of the Russian community in Hong Kong through cultural and social programs.[11] The Russkiy Mir grant was also beneficial to the church community because children of OPASPP parishioners received tuition waivers for the RLC's Russian language, literature, and history courses through this source from 2008 to the end of the funding period.

EXPANDING PROFESSIONAL AND CULTURAL HORIZONS FOR ADULT LEARNERS

Students in the adult courses are people from diverse cultural backgrounds who are currently studying or working in Hong Kong. They have different reasons for studying Russian language and culture. According to RLC teacher Tatiana S. Pugacheva, most of the adult students are learning

Russian to be able to communicate when traveling and conducting business in a Russian-speaking country. Other students want to be familiar with the language because they have been admitted to Russian universities for short-term exchange programs (studying in English or other languages) or would like to travel for leisure in Russian-speaking countries. For a few students, personal connections to Russian language and culture, such as romantic relationships with Russian partners, are the motivation to develop competency in Russian.[12] None of these students identify as members of ethnic Russian or Russian-speaking families.

With teachers keeping this fact in mind, religion is mentioned and introduced in courses for adults, youth, and children, but not imposed, as part of Russian culture and as the root of the Russian language. Irina Ustyugova notes that from time to time, adult RLC students become interested in church services and events, as the school and the church are physical neighbors and RLC teachers are always open to inquiries and discussion about spirituality and religious practices. The synergy of religion and language education is embodied in the culture-focused curriculum. In Ustyugova's words, "As teachers, we keep students aware of all the holidays about our traditions, just because Christianity is a huge part of our culture; our [Russian] culture is Christian."[13] This awareness can also be seen in the logo of the RLC, which is on figure 3.1 and signals Russian identity in the signature colors of the national flag but contains only a nuanced connection to Orthodox Christianity. The logo's image is a *koch*, a traditional small Russian boat used in icy waters, carrying a Byzantine onion dome typical of northern Russia. In Ustyugova's view, the idea behind the design is to refrain from "announcing" the religion explicitly.[14] Through such positioning, the RLC has sought to serve more of a secular function by focusing actively on various aspects of language and culture related to the Russian-speaking community but are not exclusively associated with Orthodox Christianity.

The curriculum, teaching–learning style, and student composition of the adult programs moreover reflect the RLC's international, secular approach to language education. RLC adult course curricula are based on the European Council's Common European Framework of Reference for Languages (CEFR), as well as the Russian Federation's standards for proficiency in Russian as a foreign language.[15] Class organization is based on graded levels ranging from basic to intermediate communicative competence. Current RLC courses cover the first three (A1, A2, and B1) of the six official Levels of Competence in Russian as a Foreign Language.[16] A new round of the elementary course (A1) is usually offered starting in April or May each year. Students who achieve level B1, which normally takes three years of weekly two-hour lessons, and who want to achieve further proficiency can study with teachers in one-on-one classes or form advanced classes in small groups.

Students at all levels are encouraged to speak aloud to their teachers and classmates, creating an intimate and interactive atmosphere for learning. Full immersion in Russian is encouraged from the first year of learning, as seen in the choice of *Russkii Iazyk: 5 Elementov* (Russian Language: 5 Elements) as the elementary course textbook, rather than a bilingual textbook.[17] All RLC teachers also use English to clarify and supplement their instructions and guidance to students as given in Russian.

Adult students have joined the RLC classes for various reasons. One student, Wan Tsz Ming, started his studies at the RLC in March 2016.[18] He likes Russian literature and classical music, has friends from Russian and Kazakhstan, and participates in Eastern European cultural events. Wan joined a summer internship program in Moscow "Russia Beyond the Headlines" and has traveled to Russian cities. Since he has considered applying to universities in Moscow for graduate study, Wan started learning Russian at the RCA because of the inexpensive cost of tuition and because classes are conducted in Cantonese which is his native language. However, he subsequently decided to take classes at the RLC because of the instructors' "dynamic teaching style" and the opportunities to engage in cultural activities like the Book Café, a group organized by Irina Ustyugova that meets occasionally to discuss a work of Russian literature.[19] Wan believes that it is not easy to promote Russian culture in Hong Kong because it is "less fancy" than cultures of Western European countries like France and Germany, and because HKC hold negative stereotypes about "Russia" because the USSR is a former Communist country. He thinks of OPASPP clergy as friendly and accommodating of Russian language learners, but he has not participated in church activities besides Maslenitsa (Cheesefare Sunday).

Ingrid Chow also started learning Russian through the RCA courses, beginning in 2010. She then joined classes at the RLC in 2013 because qualified students could study for free and then for half of the regular tuition price because of Russkiy Mir Foundation sponsorship. After she finished the A1, A2 and B1 level courses, she joined the reading program led by Tatiana Pugacheva.[20] The reading course was one of the special courses designed for intermediate and advanced level students. Chow has attended many cultural events organized by the RLC and was aware of the relationship between the RLC and the OPASPP. When she first visited the RLC, she wondered if she must wear a head scarf to enter the RLC since the center was inside the church chamber.[21] She also recalls hearing people singing hymns and sometimes worried if she might disturb church-related items in the Wanchai Church. In the current RLC site, which is adjacent to the church chamber, she feels the presence of the church less directly, though she always understood the RLC was administered by the church. In both Chow and Wan's experiences, interest in Russian culture was a significant reason to study Russian language, and the RLC has been a school both independent and also related to the church.

RUSSIAN FOR CHILDREN AND YOUTH: BUILDING CONNECTIONS BETWEEN LANGUAGE AND PERSONAL IDENTITY

In addition to teaching Russian as a non-native language to adults, the RLC provides language instruction to younger students, from preschool-aged children to teenagers. "Russian for Kids," advertised and promoted primarily in Russian, targets specifically, though not exclusively, children from Russian-speaking families. Father Pozdnyaev has described "Russian for Kids" as the "second stream" of the RLC to develop a full-scale language program to teach Russian as a native language.[22] The children's program was officially launched in 2011, four years after the opening of the RLC, in response to requests from parish members with children. These parents asked the RLC to start classes for children and youth because of the limited options for Russian language education in Hong Kong. There is currently no Russian international school in Hong Kong, and other private language schools do not offer Russian courses for minors. In-home education by parents is also not a viable option for many of the families involved with the children's program, because they are both multicultural and international, in the sense that one or both of the parents left a Russian-speaking country at an early age and grew up developing proficiency in languages other than Russian. Moreover, most of the families have one Russian-speaking parent and one non-Russian-speaking parent, so Russian is not the primary language used within the home. The Russian-speaking parents (typically mothers) cannot teach Russian systematically to their children, but they do wish that their children be able to speak Russian while receiving their formal educations in English-medium, Chinese-medium, or bilingual schools, to be immersed in Russian culture beyond their own families, and to feel connected to the Russian-speaking community in Hong Kong. They aspire for their children to identify as Russian, even though they are growing up in Hong Kong and hold other cultural and ethnic identities related to their non-Russian parents.

Whereas the adult education courses, particularly for first-year students, entail the use of both English and Russian to facilitate learning, RLC teachers clearly and consistently apply the principle of teaching Russian as the subject while also using it as the medium of instruction in all "Russian for Kids" courses. These courses were developed starting in 2014, after Anastasia Kraeva, a specialist in early childhood education, was hired as a teacher. Kraeva coordinated the design and inauguration of courses based on a comprehensive system of preschool and early-school children's development: playgroups focused on games for children between one and five years of age, and group classes to develop speech and basic literacy skills for children between five and seven. In view of the importance of encouraging children's linguistic development according to their age and ability, each of the two categories comprises a variety of types of classes. For example, two different toddler playgroup sessions were offered in December 2016. The "Parent & Child Playgroup" was aimed at toddlers of one to one-and-a-half years of age and involved bolstering interaction between parents and children. The "Learn & Play Group" for toddlers around age two focused on interaction between children.

Anna Rayton, a Russian mother who had been living in Hong Kong for ten years and was a parent of children attending classes at the RLC for four years as of June 2017, witnessed the growth and development of the school with a growing body of young students and an increasing number of activities and events. She recalled an informal group in 2009 called "Ladushki" (named after a Russian children's song) for mothers and children up to seven years old. Elena Loktionova-Mccaffrey, a former lecturer at the University of Hong Kong, and later Natalia Bezverkha acted as the event planner and director of Ladushki, leading the group in regular meetings that were held on Wednesday nights at the group members' homes on a rotating basis. The structure of these meetings was like that of a playdate: mothers conversed and enjoyed refreshments while their children played together. The regular meetings of Ladushki ceased in 2015. Ladushki members now meet only to hold parties for holidays such as Christmas and sometimes for picnics. According to Rayton, the group was affected by how the members changed.[23] The Russians who joined Ladushki when it first began had substantial resources; they could host events in their own homes and afford transportation costs to visit other members' homes. Ladushki was also probably more important to its initial members because the Russian community in Hong Kong was small at the time. Subsequently, the group was joined by new members who did not have enough space in their homes to invite guests and who lived far away from each other. But there is continuing discussion among current members about reinstating the group's former practice of meeting on a weekly basis.

For school-age children, the RLC offers courses in two categories: group classes to develop reading and writing skills for children between seven and ten, and comprehensive (reading–writing–speaking–listening) classes in Russian language and literature for teenagers from ten to sixteen years of age. At the more advanced levels, students can receive one-on-one instruction, and sometimes Anastasia Kraeva, as the lead teacher of the children's program, visits students' homes to teach them. Making full use of her expertise in early childhood education and her experience in working with Russian communities overseas, Kraeva is now fully in charge of the "Russian for Kids" program and works with Irina Ustyugova to design and organize various activities.

As with the adult courses, children and youth classes are held throughout the week, usually with playgroups scheduled in the morning and hourly sessions for school-age students between three and six o'clock in the afternoon. Each class is relatively small, with up to ten students. To mark student progress and give students an incentive to study hard, the RLC celebrates its students' achievements in May as part of its annual spring graduation festival. Since September 2017, the center has expanded its curriculum to offer a dedicated course for bilingual children on Thursdays, led by Anoush Davies, an experienced teacher of Russian language for children as well as a parent in an international family. The course is aimed at students who have one Russian parent and understand the language to a certain degree but generally do not speak Russian at home. All classes follow the Hong Kong school year, running from September to June. In July and August for most years, the "Russian for Kids" program is suspended for summer break, because most students leave Hong Kong to go on family vacations, and RLC teachers also choose to return to their home countries to visit family and friends.

RLC teachers also promote full immersion in Russian communication for all the children's courses by encouraging students to play, draw, sing, read, work on handicrafts, perform drama, and make friends using the Russian language. Some students also join the OPASPP's children's choir, Carousel, which was formed in 2015 and conducts regular classes for children aged six and older on Saturdays. In addition to music training, children have the option of taking acting lessons for music plays on Orthodox holidays, including Easter and Christmas. In addition to performing for church audiences, the children's choir is actively involved in activities organized by the RLC such as Russian Songs Night. Using various teaching media, the RLC aims to provide children with a friendly and enjoyable environment and to convince them that the language program is both entertaining and educational. The curriculum is furthermore designed according to the principle that the learning environment is the program's core element, because when placed in an appropriate language environment, children can master the language naturally, without tension. This approach is particularly helpful since the majority of the center's students would be considered by standard pedagogical criteria as low-proficiency heritage speakers.[24]

Cultivating the right environment for language learning and building a community is evident in how the younger students of RLC join because their parents share the same aim of teaching them language through culture. Liudmila Popova learned about the RLC through Anna Rayton. She enrolled her son in the choir to learn how to sing in Russian and in art classes taught in Russian.[25] Popova was grateful that Svetlana Kremneva,[26] the director of the church choir and teacher of the children's choir, was a professional and caring teacher who taught responsibility, and self-discipline to the children during choir rehearsals, espousing the traditional roles played by a Russian grandmother. Popova thinks that the music and art courses are especially important for her son because although she and her husband are Russian-speaking, they maintain busy full-time careers, and have little time to teach him Russian. With their domestic helper acting as his primary caretaker, her son is primarily exposed to English. At the RLC, he is fully immersed into the Russian-language environment and enriches his vocabulary. She hopes that her son will become proficient by taking language courses consistently, which she considers to be essential because of his heritage.

During holiday seasons, the RLC also hosts creative workshops for children to explore their interests, such as "Winter Branches" (*Zimnie vetki*) in December 2016 that taught children how to decorate a Russian Christmas tree and set up a New Year table in accordance with Slavic tradition. During school breaks, the RLC offers short-term intensive programs that feature Russian cultural themes and are usually designed to incorporate content from films. For instance, in the 2016 winter intensive course, children watched the film *The Snow Queen* (*Snezhnaia koroleva*) and discussed the different characters in the fairy tale. In another intensive course, "Finest, the Brave Falcon" (*Finist-iasnyi sokol*), which took place April 3 to 7, 2017, student engaged in a variety of learning tasks and cultural activities over three consecutive days based on the 1976 fantasy adventure film of the same name, including workshops on making traditional costumes, preparing and sharing food, and music performance.

The RLC provides even more opportunities for young students and members of the public to learn about Russian culture by organizing several annual events. Among these, the Russian Language Day is often regarded as the most important cultural festival for RLC students and their families because it started in 2008. Unlike the United Nations Russian Language Day, which was established on the birthday of the renown poet Alexander S. Pushkin (1799–1837) on June 6, 2010, the RLC's Russian Language Day follows the church's Julian calendar and coincides with the Slavic Literature and Culture Day on May 24. Similar in design to the center's other events, the Russian Language Day revolves around a Russian theme, featuring either a famous historical figure, a form of art, or a custom in the Russian tradition. This celebration is also combined with the graduation festivities (*vypusknoi*) for students completing RLC courses, for which the RLC staff organizes a series of cultural events spanning several months and including competitions, art performances, and prize presentations. The whole event, therefore, starts as early as March and continues through June, satisfying multiple goals:

assessing the students' performance and celebrating their achievements during the past year, promoting the Russian language, showcasing the richness of Russian and more broadly Slavic cultures, and providing a friendly and relaxing atmosphere for social gatherings of Russian families and friends. Often, the final event of the celebration is supported by the members of the Russian-speaking community in Hong Kong, including the Orthodox Church, the Russian Consulate General, and the Russian Club in Hong Kong.

To boost awareness of the children's program in the local educational market and to attract more students of non-Russian background to study and appreciate Russian language and culture, the RLC promotes itself actively. It participated in the International Day at Hong Kong Yew Chung International School and demonstrated how interesting Russian class can be when the language is learned through watching animations such as *Masha and the Bear* (*Masha i Medved*). But RLC teachers acknowledge that broadening the pool of students involved in "Russian for Kids" also runs the risk of compromising the program's mission of providing heritage language education and therefore compel the RLC to focus more on bilingual or Russian as a foreign language education in the programs for children and youth.[27]

Moreover, the RLC's inclusion of students irrespective of religious background does not entirely mitigate concerns about the incorporation of religious elements in its classes, especially for non-Orthodox Christian families. In line with the RLC's general principle of openness to students of all religious backgrounds, the children's curriculum affirms respect for the secular dimension of Hong Kong society. Only topics that are intelligible to the Hong Kong students in her classes, such as Russian cultural practices around the Orthodox holidays of Easter and Christmas, are introduced to students. Focusing on these topics show the differences between Russian and Hong Kong traditions of celebrating these holidays, thus offering varied opportunities for children to play and enjoy the language in practice. Although some non-Russian families do become interested in learning about Orthodox Christianity, the choice of accepting the religion is entirely voluntary. As members of the parish themselves, many RLC teachers are receptive to sharing information about the faith if students and their families want to know more about Orthodox Christianity. In addition, Kraeva reported that Russian parents from five families had asked her to give individual lessons to their children about the Russian Orthodox Church and to explain the differences between the Orthodox Church and other Christian denominations. Since many of the parents left the Soviet Union, the Russian Federation, or former Soviet Union states at an early age, they are often not familiar with these topics themselves, and they consequently approach the RLC for help. In such circumstances, Kraeva "opens [her] heart" and answers their questions.[28]

Religion becomes less controversial when students' families work with the RLC to address any potentially sensitive issues, and religious elements are accepted as elements of the children's language and cultural education. As an example, Irina Ustyugova shared an experience with a Jewish family. Being nonreligious themselves, the parents were rather concerned about God being a constant theme in their child's lessons. Ustyugova reassured them that the priority was mastery of the language.[29] After a few years of classes at the RLC, the child volunteered to participate in the Christmas pageant by playing an angel, and the parents no longer saw it as a problem because their child enjoyed preparing, rehearsing, and performing the play with friends. They also understood that for their child, the Christmas performance was not about religion, but about learning and practicing the Russian language in an interesting way.

The ongoing priority on exposing students to Russian culture, rather than on religion and culture as symbiotic and essential elements of "Russian identity," in the RLC's Russian language classes for children reflects three factors. First, as discussed in previous chapters, Hong Kong's Russian population has changed greatly in size and composition during the past two decades, particularly from the "original diaspora" that formed nearly a century ago in the 1910s and 1920s. The second factor is the Hong Kong Russian Orthodox Church's shift from its original mission of serving a primarily Russian population to now welcoming more non-Russian members. Affecting both factors is the third variable that after 1997, Hong Kong is being integrated incrementally in the PRC as a regular Chinese city rather than a British-governed cosmopolis. Russians form one of many minority groups that face challenges due to the use of Chinese as the primary medium of politics, business, and education, and because social and cultural norms are dictated by the Chinese majority.

The first factor—demographic shifts in the size and composition of the Russian-speaking population in Hong Kong—is evident in data compiled by the Hong Kong Government Census and Statistics Department. This government agency conducts comprehensive censuses and by-censuses and produces reports on specific demographic variables. It also publishes updated estimates every year between the full-scale censuses. Ethnicity and language use are two of the variables measured for both "mobile residents" and "usual residents."[30] However, for ethnicity, "Russian" is not a discrete category. Instead, people who belong to the Russian community (including non-Russian persons) may fall into the categories of "White," "Others," or "Other Asian" (for Central Asians native to parts of the former Soviet Union).

Therefore, the demographic shift can be approximated by indirect means, such as the number of people in Hong Kong who claim "Russian identity" in a broad and largely emic sense. Persons who identify as Russian, based on observations at the RLC, include those who have one Russian parent and one non-Russian parent, those who are Russian-speaking or Russian cultural natives but do not consider themselves "ethnic Russian," and those who were born in the Soviet Union or the Russian Federation but lived extensively in other countries before coming to Hong Kong. These people are just as "Russian" as those who have two Russian parents, use Russian as their sole native language, and came to Hong Kong directly from Russia. These parameters to define who is "Russian" is based on the conventions of recent scholarship on contemporary Russian language and Russian identity. S. V. Ryazantsev, for example, argues that Russian language is the "main unifying sign" (*osnovnym ob"ediniaiushchimi priznakom*) and the "real social instrument" (*real'nyi sotsial'nyi instrument*) for Russian nationals and citizens of former Soviet Union countries, and he thus justifies the term "Russian-speaking communities" as being more accurate than the concept of a "Russian diaspora."[31]

The RLC's emphasis on developing a culturally defined social community engenders a welcoming, or at least non-controversial, point of contact for many people who identify as Russian or as Russian-speaking. Families that may otherwise self-exclude themselves from OPASPP services because only one of two parents in the family is Russian (and an Orthodox believer) can still find ways to build connections within the Russian-speaking community. Since there is no international school in Hong Kong based on the Russian Federation's standard curriculum for primary and secondary education, as for the United States, Canada, Germany, and Singapore, among other countries, the RLC gives students some exposure to Russian-style pedagogy much like the Scuola Italiana Manzoni does for youth from Italian expatriate families in Hong Kong.[32] RLC playgroups for children up to seven years old also provide vital emotional and social resources for mostly mothers to form friendships with other Russian-speaking persons, which may be the exception than the norm because they are mainly integrated into workplaces and residential communities where they are the only Russian or Russophone members.[33]

Studying Russian language at the RLC also helps some Hong Kong Chinese people, including those interested in converting to Orthodox Christianity and joining the OPASPP parish, develop a more authentic understanding of contemporary Russian society and culture. RLC activities like discussions of Russian literary classics, showings of Russian films, and events like the aforementioned Russian Song Night and the Slavonic Literature and Culture Day attract both Orthodox and non-Orthodox participants. The RLC also plays a vital role in helping OPASPP parishioners who want to study Russian as a foreign language. Although the full tuition waivers for children subsidized by the Russkiy Mir Foundation are no longer granted, adult members of the OPASPP can apply to receive need-based tuition waivers if they want to take RLC courses. The direct benefit to the church is that these students can be more fully incorporated in social activities and comprehend more of the liturgical service conducted in Slavonic.

The second significant factor is the Hong Kong Russian Orthodox community's changing purpose. As introduced in chapters 1 and 2, in the early twentieth century, many people left Russia to flee from the Russian Revolution and other catalysts of political and social instability. The Russians who came to Hong Kong included merchants, professionals, unemployed women, and children. After World War II and toward the end of the British colonial period, many Russians chose to leave Hong Kong and migrate to other countries such as Australia and the United States. Church services and Russian Orthodox community activities were effectively suspended from the mid-1970s to 2001. After Father Pozdnyaev reestablished the Russian Orthodox parish in 2003, the OPASPP became an important religious and spiritual home for Russians in Hong Kong.

In response to the small and transient population of ethnic Russian believers in the region, Father Pozdnyaev has also promoted the adaptation of the church's operations and services to serve non-Russian believers, which will be discussed further in chapters 4 and 5. He has welcomed converts, especially Hong Kong natives of Chinese ethnicity, and has sponsored the translation and publication of religious and cultural texts in Chinese. OPASPP ritual services are sometimes conducted in various combinations of two or three different languages, using Russian, English, Cantonese, and Mandarin. Visitors, such as tourists from mainland China, are welcome to visit and learn more about the church.

The parish's present focus on making the church and the faith more accessible to the Hong Kong public and mainland Chinese visitors can be attributed to the third factor: Hong Kong's being a Chinese-dominated multicultural society. Situated on the southeast tip of the PRC, Hong Kong is known as "Asia's Global City."[34] Residents and visitors can taste cuisines from other parts of China, Asia, Europe, Africa, and the Americas. The world's major religions are all practiced and legally tolerated within Hong Kong's territory. Daily conversations occur in a multitude of languages. People in Hong Kong can also learn a wide variety of languages thanks to the presence of institutions sponsored by foreign governments, such as the British Council and the Goethe Institut, and non-official organizations, such as the Alliance Française de Hong Kong and the Japanese Club of Hong Kong.

The RLC has played a pivotal role in making Hong Kong and its connection to Russia increasingly important topics in the life of the local Russian community. For example, in 2010, the festival was celebrated with traditional Russian folk dances joined by both children and parents and a Russian Fair selling various Russian products. Prior to that the event, the RLC organized contests for portrait photography, essay-writing on the theme of "Reading Chekhov," and literary translation, all dedicated to the 150th anniversary of Anton Chekhov's death. In 2011, the Language Day event featured Russian fairy tales and folk legends. In the photography contest for that year, entitled "Russian Traces in Hong Kong," participants were invited to submit photographs capturing intriguing aspects of Russian culture, language, or way of life in Hong Kong. In 2012, many prominent members of the Russian community in Hong Kong joined the climax of the fifth Russian Language Day with Vladimir A. Kalinin, then Russian consul-general in Hong Kong, delivering a speech at the reception. That year, in addition to hosting a screening of the film *Moscow, I love you!* (Moskva, ya lyublyu tebya!), the RLC organized an annual Russian charity market to support the Russian association Volunteers to Help Orphans (Volontery v pomoshch' detiam-sirotam) and raised funds by selling homemade deli foods and books to support the project "Children in Need" (Deti v bede).[35]

As explained throughout this chapter, the RLC's regular curricular and special holiday activities involve various cultural elements, but they always stress the acquisition of Russian language naturally and frequently over the inculcation of cultural values, especially religious ones. As Anastasia Kraeva explained, the teachers' main role is to lay the developmental foundation for language acquisition, to prevent students from confusing the grammar rules of two or more languages, and to help them overcome the stage of understanding but not being able to speak the language that is experienced by most bilingual or multilingual children.[36] The idea and image of the Russian language that Kraeva tries to present in her teaching is that Russian is a "happy" language, and that it is useful for playing and making friends. She hopes to promote a safe and stimulating learning environment in which each class serves as a "small paradise" for children to talk and engage with each other.[37] In this way, children will appreciate the language as a medium of both knowledge acquisition and entertainment. Previous studies have shown that associating a language with fun cultivates "language loyalty," or positive emotional attachment to the language.[38] The principle that "culture comes second" is also important because children cannot understand abstract themes like adult learners can. From time to time, however, some children express curiosity about Russia and ask further questions about Slavic culture and tradition, which Kraeva sees as their moment to approach to the "Russian soul," hence to arouse their Russian identity.

In addition to treating the Russian language as both the subject and the medium of instruction, another major characteristic of "Russian for Kids" in the RLC is its active effort to incorporate parents in the learning environment and learning process of their children. This practice is particularly prominent in Kraeva's playgroup for toddlers. The RLC currently hosts three weekly playgroups, with each session lasting one and a half hours. There are seven to ten toddlers in each group, and all are accompanied by at least one parent or a domestic helper. In most cases the accompanying adult is the child's mother who is a Russian speaker herself.

During one Russian playgroup for toddlers ranging in age from one to one and a half on Tuesday, May 29, 2017, Anastasia Kraeva introduced various games and activities for children and their parents to participate together, including singing nursery rhymes, talking with puppets, naming colors, and playing with paints. She used Russian as the medium of instruction and required all participants to communicate in Russian during the activities to develop the children's physical, cognitive, psychological, and social abilities. Although some of the toddlers were not yet speaking or were able to use only very basic phrases, such as "hello" (*privet*) or "there" (*vot*), Kraeva considered it essential to form an attachment to the Russian language in a comfortable and entertaining environment.

For parents, the playgroups serve as social venues as well. They play and learn with their children, and they meet people who share their concern of raising children in a multilingual society. Before and after each class, the parents discuss their children's development, exchange experiences, and socialize with each other in Russian. More importantly, they see this program, and the RLC, as a place to strengthen family bonds. As many families need to speak languages other than Russian within the household and in their workplaces and schools, the RLC represents their only hope to secure formal instruction in Russian for their children. Some parents who want to create more opportunities for their children to grow up with Russian arrange private playgroups during holidays and invite Anastasia Kraeva to organize the activities. Playgroup parents appreciate the role the RLC plays in demonstrating the vitality of the Russian language, associating the language with the family, and improving the linguistic abilities of their children. Regular socializing among parents also takes place during Russian language courses for older children. Parents drop off school-aged children at the RLC for a one-hour session after school. While the children are in class, parents often gather and socialize in a nearby café. As Tatiana Pugacheva described it, "Our center is an island where parents come for rest. And mothers have their own club."[39]

Another aspect of the RLC's children's program that engenders social interaction is the series of extracurricular activities that take place outside of the school premises. Several full-time RLC teachers and their families live on Lamma Island, which is about six miles (ten kilometers) away from downtown Hong Kong and reachable from the Central district via a thirty-minute ferry ride. The outlying site offers a geographic advantage for regular Sunday activities: children and their parents can relax in the island's natural environment while exploring themes of Russian culture under the guidance of the teachers. For example, during the play *Old Russian Life* (*Drevnerusskaia zhizn'*) performed on November 2, 2014, children learned about Russian folk culture and the history of the Rurik Dynasty (862–1610) by role-playing as ancient Slavic heroes, making Russian handicrafts, and dancing to traditional songs about the defense of Russian land in the time of Vladimir the Great (Vladimir Sviatoslavich 980–1015). During a family event entitled "I Understand the World" (*Ia poznaiu mir*), held on February 19, 2017, student families went on hiking on the island while playing, singing, and performing various tasks along the way. During the Family Art Picnic (*Cemeinyi art-piknik*) hosted on March 19, 2017, children and their parents enjoyed an afternoon of drawing pictures of the island's landscape and eating picnic lunches on the beach.

Exposure to Hong Kong's natural environment, which increases students' interest in Hong Kong as a place, is also a channel to deepen students' social attachment to the region. During the 2017–18 academic year, RLC focused on discussing and representing the relationship between the Russian-speaking community and Hong Kong society. RLC students, such as Dasha, quoted in the beginning of this article, were asked to paint a Russian word or to write stories associated with their daily lives in Hong Kong for the *ABC of Hong Kong* book project and competition. Meanwhile, their parents were invited to participate in a photo contest on the topic of their children learning Russian in Hong Kong. The festival took place on May 7, 2017, in the Steam Studio, Sheung Wan. RLC teachers, with around thirty families and their friends, participated in the event. The event was celebrated with a musical performance by the children's choir Carousel, an art exhibition, and the presentation of prizes for the best students of the year and the most creative families. The event received wide attention. The Coordination Council of Russian Compatriots in China reported it as a "family holiday" (*semeinyi prazdnik*) and praised the RLC for providing exemplary Russian language education in Hong Kong.[40]

With the Russian Federation and the Russophone countries of Central Asia becoming increasingly open to international markets, learning Russian offers more advantages than ever. Nevertheless, the overall opportunities for exposure to Russian language and culture in Hong Kong are still limited. With an understanding of its students' diverse needs, the RLC not only functions as a professional language institution but also actively facilitates cultural exchange through regular and one-time cultural activities. Although the RLC has always been associated with the OPASPP, it maintains a relatively high level of autonomy in its operations, a secular identity, and nonreligious priorities for two major reasons. The first reason is that the RLC staff aims to teach Russian as a foreign language and to boost awareness of Slavic culture among non-ethnic Russian people in Hong Kong by offering language modules at different levels together with various theme-based classes, interest groups, and workshops. Second, the RLC teaching staff regard it as equally important to serve the Russian-speaking community in Hong Kong, to recreate elements of a Russian childhood for their own children who are growing up as expatriates, to help ethnic Russian or Russian-speaking families maintain Russian customs, and to provide varied opportunities to build a close-knit cultural community that brings the geographically distant Russia closer.

The success of the RLC as both a language and a cultural center is largely attributable to the efforts of an enthusiastic and productive teaching team. Previous and present instructors have cultivated close friendships with one another during and after their employment with the RLC, which helps the teaching staff deal with the difficulties of working under intense time and resource pressure. Being overseas Russians and Russophones themselves, they work cohesively with a clear awareness of and strong commitment to the role the RLC plays in Hong Kong society, and they value highly the intangible rewards of promoting Russian language and culture. Due to frequent interaction and easy management, the team members cooperate smoothly for various occasions and invest extra time to perfect their projects. Another distinguishing feature of the RLC is its high level of flexibility. The school grants each teacher the opportunity to design and launch new programs aimed at teaching and promoting various aspects of Russian language and culture according to their knowledge, specialties, and available resources at the time. The RLC is therefore able to adjust dynamically to meet the changing needs and expectations of the market, and it can also join freely in various events hosted by other Russian organizations to extend its influence and reach out to new audiences.

One such initiative that has sustained and developed in the recent three years has been related to bilingual education. In December 2016, the RLC organized series of seminars, titled "One Child, Two Languages" (*Odin rebenok-dva iazyka*), dedicated to the issue of bilingualism and the acquisition of Russian language by children in Hong Kong. The seminars featured discussion of critical issues in language education, such as the benefits of being bilingual from both psychological and practical perspectives, the problems faced by children in processing several foreign languages, and the ways in which parents can support and help their children in different situations. Anastasia Kraeva and Irina Ustyugova led the seminars and invited specialists as guest speakers. Natalia Koval, a speech-language pathologist and an experienced kindergarten teacher, shared her experience in training bilingual children. Anna Petrova, a neurolinguistics specialist in the Faculty of Education at the University of Hong Kong, presented her research on how children can process and acquire diverse language abilities in multilingual environments. Parents actively joined in the discussion, sharing their experiences and concerns with the teachers and the guest speakers. Later, video clips of guest lectures were uploaded on the RLC's Facebook page at the request of participants as well as people who could not attend the seminars. Conversations between parents and teachers on the topic of teaching Russian as a native language still take place on a regular basis, with the RLC playing a key role in helping children to communicate, play, and engage in the Russian language during classes and within their families.

Proving that Russian can be a useful language in Hong Kong is especially crucial to the RLC's mission because many students do not use Russian at home or as a primary language of socialization. Although the "Russian for Kids" program was originally designed for students who belong to Hong Kong's Russian-speaking population by virtue of their ethnicity or their parents' identities as native users of the Russian language,[41] there are also local and international children who join the RLC and wish to learn Russian as a foreign language, much as other children choose to learn French or Italian. Anastasia Kraeva gave the example of a Cantonese child who had happened to watch Russian cartoons and had started to pick up some simple Russian words before his parents looked for a way in which he could learn Russian systematically. In view of the limited educational resources for the Russian language in Hong Kong, the RLC was the family's best option. Such children are welcomed equally and granted the same attention as heritage students during classes. According to Kraeva, making language study a "happy and interesting experience" for such students is imperative. She admitted that sometimes non-heritage students perform even better than the children from Russian families, because the former truly enjoy the language and are more self-motivated.

However, the RLC also faces the obstacles associated with the reality that Russian is hardly a language of daily necessity in Hong Kong. Although many people attend the adult courses for work-related reasons, continuing enrollment remains a challenge because for many students Russian is a very difficult language to learn. Adult students who enroll in RLC courses for more than two years tend to be those who have strong personal connections with Russia or Russians, particularly by having a Russian spouse. Similarly, families who send their children to the RLC may not always prioritize learning Russian, since Russian is often not the main mode of communication in the household. Some parents see the language classes more as an extracurricular activity, like studying music or art, than a rigorous academic subject. The RLC has adapted to these limitations by continually developing new programs and ways to help learners of diverse backgrounds achieve their own goals as well as those of the school's mission as a private institution providing exposure to both Russian language and culture.

Just as the RLC contributes to Sino-Russian relations by helping ethnic Chinese and other non-Russian students understand Russia and ethnic

Russian students develop their social and cultural identities while living in a Chinese society, the China Orthodox Press, which is affiliated but formally independent from the OPASPP, disseminates knowledge about Orthodox Christianity as a faith and as lived through culture to Sinophone readers, as will be discussed in the next chapter in relation to Hong Kong's Russian Orthodox community as an important source of information about Christianity in China.

NOTES

1. Russian Language Center in Hong Kong, "Kusochki Azbuki" [A piece of the ABC], Facebook, September 1, 2017, https://www.facebook.com/rlchk/photos/gm.115171819182981/1660583110679782/.

2. The RLC's geographic location and cultural context of the host society also makes it unique as a subject of scholarship because most research on Russian language education focuses on North America, Western Europe, and on Russian Jews in Israel. See Lara Ryazanova-Clarke, ed., *The Russian Language Outside the Nation* (Edinburgh: Edinburgh University Press, 2014), especially 204–22.

3. Russian Culture Association, "Courses," accessed October 10, 2017, http://www.russian-hk.org/courses.html. In the past, more schools offered courses to meet demand for Russian language instruction. See Brian Yeung, "'Da' to the Language," *South China Morning Post*, November 26, 2013, 16.

4. Dionisy Pozdnyaev, interview, June 15, 2017, OPASPP offices, Sheung Wan, Hong Kong.

5. Dionisy Pozdnyaev, interview, June 15, 2017.

6. Kira Pozdnyaeva, wife of Father Pozdnyaev, has been the director of the RLC since 2018. She oversees the daily operations and special events of the RLC. Irina Ustyugova, who joined the RLC in 2009, is the longest-serving teacher and acts as the administrator for daily operations. She is the main editor and contributor to the RLC Facebook page and Facebook group "Learning Russian in Hong Kong." Ustyugova and Tatiana Pugacheva teach most of the Russian courses for adults. Tatiana S. Pugacheva returned to Russia in summer 2018. Anastasia Kraeva is the specialist in early childhood education and acts as both curriculum coordinator and teacher for the children and youth courses. Nadezhda Sperantova is a teacher at the most recently established Kowloon site. Other teachers have joined the Sheung Wan campus staff including Anoush Georgievna Davis who teaches courses for bilingual children and Leonid Patorsky who teaches adult courses. Former teachers include Dmitry Ivanov. The RLC also employs part-time teachers for courses in languages other than Russian such as English and French.

7. "MAPYRAL," accessed September 25, 2017, https://ru.mapryal.org/internationalassociation-of-teachers-of-russian-language-and-literature-mapryal.

8. The now-discontinued "Russia with Art" website, last accessed by the authors on October 17, 2017, was https://www.frwa.asia.

9. See "Russian Bazaar (Facebook page)," accessed May 5, 2018, https://www.facebook.com/russianbazaarhk.

10. For a biographical profile of Belanovsky, see Gwulo.com, "Nicholas BELANOVSKY [1889–1997]," subm. by Dmitry Belanovsky on September 11, 2011, 01:34, https://gwulo.com/node/9220, and for Smirnov, see "SMIRNOV Iurii (Georgii) Vital'evich," accessed June 4, 2018, http://www.artrz.ru/menu/1804657343/1804871053.html.

11. On the Russkiy Mir Foundation, see the foundation's website at http://russkiymir.ru/, accessed May 31, 2017.

12. Tatiana Pugacheva, interview, May 28, 2016, Sheung Wan, Hong Kong.

13. Irina Ustyugova, interview, May 31, 2017, Sheung Wan, Hong Kong.

14. Ibid.

15. For CEFR, see Council of Europe (European Council), "Common European Framework of Reference for Languages: Learning, Teaching, Assessment (CEFR)," accessed January 16, 2017, https://www.coe.int/en/web/common-european-framework-reference-languages. For the Russian Federation standards for Russian proficiency as represented in the Test of Russian as a Foreign Language (TORFL), see "Training and Testing Language Language Center for Foreigners," accessed November 28, 2017, http://russian-test.com/eng/center/about_the_center.html.

16. Ministry of Education and Science of the Russian Federation, "Level of Competence in Russian as a Foreign Language," accessed May 12, 2017, http://en.russia.edu.ru/russian/levels.

17. About the textbook series for RLC classes, see Tat'iana L. Esmantova, *Russkii iazyk: 5 elementov* [Russian language: 5 elements], 4th ed., 4 vols. (St. Petersburg: Zlatoust, 2014). For comparable Russian language and culture textbooks that use Chinese as the primary medium of instruction, see He Hongmei, Ma Buning, and Li Qinghua, eds., *Quanxin daxue Eyu zonghe jiaocheng* [The new comprehensive course of Russian language for university], 12 vols (Beijing: Gaodeng chubanshe, 2009); Wang Yingjia, ed., *Eluosi sehui yu wenhua* [Russian society and culture] (Wuhan: Wuhan daxue chubanshe, 2001); Ma Fuzhen, ed., *Eluosi guoqing yu wenhua / Stranovedenie i Kul'tura Rossii* [National studies and culture of Russia] (Harbin: Harbin gongye daxue chubanshe, 2008); Lu Su, ed., *Eyu shangwu xinhan jiaocheng / Kommercheskaia korrespondentsiia na russkom iazyke* [Commercial correspondence in Russian language] (Beijing: Beijing daxue chubanshe, 2016).

18. Wan is the person's surname.

19. Wan Tsz Ming, interview, April 22, 2017, Sheung Wan, Hong Kong.

20. A1, A2, and B2 are levels of competency according to the CEFR scheme of assessment.

21. Ingrid Chow, interview, April 29, 2017, Sheung Wan, Hong Kong.

22. Dionisy Pozdnyaev, interview, June 15, 2017.

23. Anna Rayton, interview, June 24, 2017, Sheung Wan, Hong Kong.

24. For a similar case of "low-proficiency heritage speakers" at the university level in the United States, see Alla Smyslova, Low-proficiency Heritage Speakers of Russian: Their Interlanguage System as a Basis for Fast Language (Re)building,"

in *Russian Language Studies in North America: New Perspectives from Theoretical and Applied Linguistics*, ed. Veronika Makarova (London: Anthem Press, 2012), 161–92.

25. Liudmila Popova, interview, June 24, 2017, Sheung Wan, Hong Kong.

26. Svetlana Kremneva and her family left Hong Kong in 2018.

27. On heritage language education, see Maria Polinsky, "Heritage Language Narratives," in *Heritage Language Education: A New Field Emerging*, eds. Donna M. Brinton, Olga Kagan, and Susan Bauckus (New York: Routledge, 2008), 149–64.

28. Anastasia Kraeva, interview, May 31, 2017, Sheung Wan, Hong Kong.

29. Irina Ustyugova, interview, May 31, 2017.

30. Only permanent Hong Kong residents are counted as "usual residents" or "mobile residents." The former are persons who live in Hong Kong, traveling elsewhere only for brief periods of time for work or leisure; the latter are persons who have been living in Hong Kong for only one to three months in the six-month period preceding a demographic survey.

31. S. V. Ryazantsev, "Emigranty iz Rossii: Russkaia diaspora ili russkogovoriashchie sobshchestva?" [Emigrants from Russia: Russian diaspora abroad or Russian-speaking communities?], *Sotsiologicheskie Issledovaniya* 12 (2016): 93.

32. See "Scuola Italiana Manzoni," accessed July 6, 2017, http://www.manzoni.edu.hk/index.php/2011-09-09-04-09-55.

33. As described earlier in the chapter, the first playgroup for Russian mothers and children began in 2009, with meetings taking place at participants' homes on a rotating basis. Now playgroup classes are held at the RLC. Anna Rayton, interview, June 24, 2017.

34. On the "Asia's World City" brand, Brand Hong Kong, "Brand Hong Kong," and Hong Kong [Special Administrative Region] Government, "Asia's World City," accessed September 9, 2017, http://www.info.gov.hk/info/sar5/easia.htm.

35. "Volontery v pomoshch' detiam-sirotam" [Volunteers to help orphans], accessed September 14, 2017, https://www.otkazniki.ru.

36. Anastasia Kraeva, interview, May 31, 2017.

37. Ibid.

38. About the concept of language loyalty, as developed by Joshua Fishman, and applied to various linguistic communities, see Ofelia García, Rakhmiel Peltz, and Harold F. Schiffman with Gella Schweid Fishman, *Language Loyalty, Continuity and Change: Joshua A. Fishman's Contributions to International Sociolinguistics* (Clevedon: Multilingual Matters, 2006).

39. Tatiana Pugacheva, interview, June 10, 2017, Sheung Wan, Hong Kong.

40. Larisa Zhebokritskaia, "Prazdnik russkogo iazyka v Gonkonge" [Russian Language Day in Hong Kong], *Koordinatsionnyi Sovet Sootechestvennikov v Kitae* [The Coordination Council of Compatriots in China], accessed May 15, 2017, http://www.russianchina.org/news/2017/05/15/8158#more-8158.

41. For interpretations of "Russian-speaking population," which is a common concept in describing the diaspora, see David D. Laitin, *The Russian-speaking Populations in the Near Abroad* (Ithaca, NY: Cornell University Press, 1998).

Chapter 4

The China Orthodox Press

By virtue of its name, the China Orthodox Press (COP) is more evidently related to Orthodox Christianity than the Russian Language Center (RLC). However, like the RLC, the COP is both an arm of the OPASPP and an independent entity with its own significance for the Russian Orthodox community of not only Hong Kong but also of Greater China. A visitor to the COP website, which is available in English, Russian, and Chinese, can learn about the many books, CDs, and other media that the press distributes worldwide. However less obvious, until one opens the cover of a book or checks the credits for a nontextual publication, is that the full operations of the press began in 2014 but that much of the content has been produced through the parish's in-house translation program since 1998. Translators and editors affiliated with the OPASPP have rendered translations of liturgical texts, theological literature, and works of other genres from the original versions in Church Slavonic, Russian, and other languages. The primary direction of translation is from these languages into Chinese. The purpose of such translations is to facilitate worship and comprehension of spiritual concepts and Orthodox Christian cultural values by Chinese-language natives. Since the original and target languages are linguistically distant, the translation process is especially complex, often involving consultation of versions previously translated into various languages such as a Greek to Russian to Chinese translation.

This chapter analyzes how the COP, through production and distribution, provides knowledge about Orthodox Christian belief and life to believers and interested nonbeliever readers in Greater China and Sinophone communities in other areas of the world. The primary focus will be on how the COP generates a literary bridge between the historical languages of Orthodox Christianity to Chinese. In doing so, it follows in the footsteps of predecessors based in mainland China since the eighteenth century.[1] The COP has produced and acted as a partner with other presses on many publications. We will examine why the COP's work is important by starting with a concise discussion of ROC mission-based translation and publication. Then the following three sections will introduce and discuss the features of representative publications from three categories: (1) histories of the community, (2) practice of Orthodox Christian worship and life, (3) culture, beliefs, and values of Orthodox Christianity. All three of these sections will highlight how the COP plays important roles for connecting the Hong Kong ROC community to the ROC as a global faith organization and for expanding access to information about Orthodox Christianity by producing both Traditional Chinese and Simplified Chinese, as well as bilingual and multilingual publications, which distinguish it from other publishers supplying for the same genres in Taiwan and the PRC mainland.

TRANSLATION AND PUBLICATION IN MISSION WORK

From the first Beijing mission in 1715, the ROC acted as a conduit of knowledge between the Romanov and Qing empires. Translation was the means of linguistic and cultural exchange permitted officially by both the Russian and Chinese imperial governments.[2] ROC missionaries also utilized translation as a means of studying not only Chinese language but also characteristics of Chinese governance and society. Missions published Chinese–Russian lexicons, books to instruct Russian students in the Chinese language, and translations of Chinese philosophy and literature. Missionaries developed sufficient proficiency in Chinese to translate and modify essential theological manuals like the 1810 version of the *Institutio Ad Fidem Christi* (Conversations with Angels), originally a seventeenth-century Jesuit work, and revised substantially by Archimandrite Iakinf (Nikita Yakovlevich Bichurin) (1777–1853), head of the ninth Beijing mission from 1807 to 1821.[3]

Archimandrite Grigorii Karpov (1814–1882), priest of the twelfth Beijing mission and chief of the fourteenth mission, and later canonized as St. Gurii of Taurida, is one of the most significant personalities in the narrative of translation as a form of missiology. From 1856 to 1874, he applied his exceptional expertise in Chinese language and culture to setting the full foundation for subsequent missions by completing translations of major theological texts. He influenced not only the spread of the faith in China but also in Japan. Japanese believers absorbed the spiritual and cultural dimensions of Orthodox Christianity by reading his 1860 translation of *The Orthodox Mirror* (Ch. *Dongjiao zongjian*), which is a translation of *The Mirror of Orthodox Confession* written by St. Dmitry of Rostov (1651–1709). Karpov was prolific during his tenure in China, producing definitive translations of the New Testament in 1864 and Book of Psalms in 1879 as well as many texts about Orthodox belief and church history. Publication flourished after the Qing government lifted restrictions on proselytization in 1880. Under Archimandrite Innocent's leadership, more publications about basic theology and ritual broadened the base of knowledge about Orthodox Christianity in Chinese.

Starting in the twentieth century, textual transmission also took the form of periodicals. German Sinologist Rudolf Löwenthal (1904–1996), based at Yenching University from 1934 to 1947, summarized the extant periodicals from 1900 to 1940 in a book about Christian presses in China.[4] Gathering information from sources in Peiping (also known as Beiping, and now as Beijing) and Harbin, Löwenthal identified 10 Russian-language Christian journals, 7 published in Harbin. Out of these journals, 4 were specifically Russian Orthodox. The two Beijing-based journals were *Chinese Good News* or *Chinese Good Tidings*, which had originally been called *The News of the Brotherhood of the Orthodox Church in China*, that concentrated on religious topics,[5] and the short-lived *The Path of Youth* published by the Peiping (Beijing) mission that featured anti-Communist messages to Russian emigrant readers for two issues. Other Orthodox publications that circulated in China during the late 1920s and 1930s were a Shanghai-based *Church Bulletin*, published on Sundays starting in 1928, and *Sower* in Harbin from October 1920 for 82 monthly issues.[6] Although the majority of Russian Orthodox publications started in Harbin from 1920 onward, only one, *Heavenly Bread* was still functional as a monthly publication founded by the Our Mother of Kazan monastery in 1926. *Heavenly Bread* provided news about the ROC, including official announcements, and articles on religious topics, including about Orthodox theology.[7]

In the past and into the present, all ROC missions and presses have faced similar obstacles in creating publications that make sense to their intended audiences. Accurate and linguistically sophisticated translation is vital for communication of abstract ideas. Complicating the act of translation between Russian and Chinese has been the profound differences between the languages, which are not related in any way but the cross-borrowing of loan words. In particular, Church Slavonic does not have an exact equivalent in Chinese. In sound, as spoken in liturgical services, it is a distinct medium of spiritual communication and expression. In writing, its representation in the Cyrillic alphabet enables a polyethnic group of believers, who may be more proficient in speaking languages other than Russian, to share a common understanding of ideas expressed through one script.[8]

Further complicating translation work is the conversion of Orthodox Christian theology into comprehensible terms of spirituality and philosophy for Chinese readers. Like Buddhism and Islam, Orthodox Christianity is considered a foreign religion in China not only because of its origins but also because its conceptual roots are not in the life patterns and beliefs about humanity that evolved from the first discernibly Chinese societies. What is "Chinese" itself is subject to great variation in interpretation before the twentieth century, and certainly during the lifetime of Confucius (551–479 BCE) and other thinkers who developed the texts known as classics. Religions with tenets that differ from the humanism in what is now called Ruist thought (or more commonly understood as Confucianism) has been subject to official and popular censure throughout Chinese history, often on the basis that they do not fit Chinese "indigenous" (another inherently contentious term) norms of thought and behavior. Whether Orthodox Christianity as a religion can be compatible with Chinese state and society is still debatable today. Although Christianity has taken different forms since the 1980s as economic liberalization has led to major social and cultural shifts, as discussed in earlier chapters, the PRC government remains wary of religious activity and spiritual beliefs that are deemed to be in conflict with the state's official preference for atheism.

Like preceding missions in China, the OPASPP plays an important role in bridging the cultural and linguistic gap for Chinese believers and Chinese-language readers who want to learn about Orthodox Christian faith and life by making religious texts available in Chinese. Besides the fundamental differences between Russian and other original languages and Chinese, translation into Chinese is difficult because there are multiple forms and scripts in use for written Chinese language. For authenticity, or parity in literary styles, Classical Chinese may be considered as the most appropriate equivalent of Greek, Latin, and Church Slavonic. However, only some native readers of Chinese are completely proficient in reading classical Chinese. For this reason, Chinese vernacular languages, particularly modern standard Mandarin, are used for texts that introduce the tenets of faith, including the Bible, and customs of Orthodox Christian culture. Another key variable in rendering Chinese-language translation is script. Most Chinese native users in the present day prefer Simplified Chinese characters, including Chinese in the PRC, Singapore, and the global diaspora. Traditional Chinese characters are used in Hong Kong, Taiwan, and in other Chinese-language communities. Since Mainland Chinese readers are the primary target audience for many COP publications, the Chinese translations of these texts follows Mainland Chinese grammar conventions. If there are no synonymous words exist in Modern Written Chinese for a term, translators have created new vocabulary, borrowing and adapting from Chinese versions of Protestant and Roman Catholic texts if deemed appropriate and close enough in meaning to the original Orthodox term. The translated texts also reflect similarities with Japanese and English-language editions, particularly in the choice of vocabulary for translations in these languages.

The COP has been a small but prolific enterprise since it was co-established with the OPASPP, managing both translation and production in Hong Kong. Roman Kremnev played an essential role in the printing and distribution of all publications until he and his family migrated out of Hong Kong in late 2018. Formerly a director of programs for state television and church television in what is now the Russian Federation, Kremnev started to visit Hong Kong in 2012 for major holidays, then moved to the territory in 2014 to assume his position with the COP. Kremnev does not read Chinese so he worked with Lin Sen, who worked as the principal translator from 2014 to 2017, on proofreading and handles most of the typesetting based on his familiarity with the text through that process.[9] He also collaborated with his son on text layout and consulted with Father Anton Serafimovich about technological issues. Kremnev supervised all stages of printing at the OPASPP's Lamma Island facility.[10] He considered the working environment to be comfortable and interesting because he used Russian for most functions but was also exposed to other languages that are spoken in the church such as Cantonese and Mandarin.[11]

With very few staff members and a small physical plant, the OPASPP and COP has nevertheless maintained a steady and remarkable pattern of growth, publishing at least two new works since 2006, as seen in table 4.1. Especially notable is that some are produced in both Traditional Chinese and Simplified Chinese versions, which expand the market for the given publication. The OPASPP helps to promote these publications through the Orthodox Bookstore and Library website, which sells books about liturgy, theology, church history, and current affairs of the ROC at large and in China and Hong Kong in English, Chinese, Russian, and Korean, as well as audiovisual media and supplies for worship such as incense. All COP publications are available through this website.[12] The Orthodox Bookstore and Library website, which is viewable and searchable in English, Russian, Simplified Chinese, and Traditional Chinese, connects the intellectual enterprise of making knowledge about the spiritual, social, and cultural dimensions of Orthodox Christianity accessible to Sinophone readers to the commercial business of selling hard and digital copies of publications to support the work of the COP and the OPASPP. As will be discussed in all of the following sections, the OPASPP and the COP are also contributing to a broader endeavor of disseminating information about Orthodox Christianity in which the OMHKSEA and Orthodox publishers in Taiwan (Republic of China) are also involved.

Table 4.1 Number of Publications in Traditional Chinese and Simplified Chinese Scripts, 1998 and 2005–2016

Year	Traditional Chinese	Simplified Chinese
1998	2 (including 1 DVD)	2 (including 1 DVD)
2005	0	1
2006	0	5
2007	2	2
2009	2	5
2010	1	7
2011	1	1
2012	4	1
2013	3	0
2014	12	3
2015	13	6
2016	10	1

ABOUT THE COMMUNITY AND RELIGIOUS IDENTITY

COP publications that describe the history about the ROC, and particularly how it has existed and developed in China, demonstrate how the OPASPP is part of wider regional and international communities of the ROC and the Orthodox world.[13] Narratives about how the ROC has developed in China places significant personalities and places in context. Record-keeping also serves the purpose of self-reflection that gives momentum to missionary work. A historical precedent that is also evident in how the Russian Orthodox community in Hong Kong evolved, as discussed in chapter 2, is the contemplation of Archimandrite Innocent who wrote in 1916 about the China mission as developing in three phases. He considered the first period, from the death of Father Maksim Leont'ev as a "preparative" stage of establishing institutions and formulating strategies for proselytization.[14] Leont'ev's twenty-year tenure, during which the first chapel was consecrated in the Manchu district of the imperial capital, is implied to be a "phase zero." During the second period, from 1860 to 1902, the mission is described as having matured into political and religious subsections. Innocent credits the 1858 Treaty of Tianjin as a turning point in the mission's history because foreign missionaries gained more stability with the right of abode in China. Unsurprisingly, Innocent deems the third phase, starting in 1902, as the most successful one, as measured in the number of Chinese converts, 5,587 as of 1915, and the breadth of the mission's activities as a religious, educational, and media-producing organization.[15] This framework, which stresses how the ROC adapted and grew in China, is significant for two reasons. Media, education, and religion are still intertwined in the web-based and hard-copy publications that the COP and its partners produce, which commemorate and reinforce awareness of the Church's roots and milestones. Innocent's history-based conception also affirms that the ROC can be a relevant institution in predominantly Chinese societies. Sharing history is furthermore a part of a communal identity that both believers in China can embrace, and that believers outside of China can understand. With elements such as full color photographs and bilingual text, these autochthonous histories are interesting and accessible to general readers as well.

Engendering the sense that the ROC is an institution of historical importance in China and a vital part of the Orthodox Christian world is communicated in publications such as the translation of *A Pocket Church History for Orthodox Christians*. Written by Father Hieromonk Aidan (Keller) and published in 1994 by St. Hilarion Press, the COP published in the Chinese-language translation by Peter Lu entitled *Zhengjiao Jidutu de jiaohui lüeshi* (A concise history of the church for Orthodox Christians) in 2016.[16] The inclusion of some English-language terms in parenthetical translations suggests that the translation was rendered under the assumption that readers will be better able to understand some of the vocabulary by comparing the Chinese and English terms. This feature of the book also implies that this book targets an audience of readers with adequate education to reach high proficiency in English, which is now likely in not only Hong Kong but mainland China and other Sinophone societies.

Works about the history of the ROC in China vary in scope and purpose. The bilingual Russian–Chinese publication *Pravoslavie v Kitae / Dongzhengjiao zai Zhongguo* (Eastern Orthodox Christianity in China), compiled and published by the Moscow Patriarchate, describes the history of the ROC in China from 1651 to the present through the lens of the ROC center.[17] It contains many high-resolution replications of church documents and color photographs of notable church leaders and laymen. Not available for acquisition by the public, it conveys the official narrative of the ROC in China for a select audience. By comparison, the Chinese translations of Victor Selivanovsky's *Orthodoxy in China* and Father Dionisy Pozdynyaev's *Orthodox Christianity in the People's Republic of China* are available for purchase and describe general historical details as interpreted through their individual authors' perspectives and experiences.[18] The latter, published in 2015, summarizes Father Pozdnyaev's own views on the then–current condition of the Orthodox Church in China reflects both optimistic and critical perspectives. Pozdnyaev introduces how the Chinese Autonomous Orthodox Church evolved from the political agenda of full state control over religious belief and practice. Written to be accessible for both Orthodox community members and non-Orthodox lay readers, the booklet delivers a measured polemic that Orthodox Christianity in Mainland China can thrive, despite political strictures. Pozdnyaev expresses hope about the potential development of the Orthodox Church in the open revival of Chinese Christianity in the late twentieth and twenty-first centuries while being critical of chronic problems such as disagreements between Chinese church leaders, reliance on foreign assistance to satisfy basic needs such as the supply of religious texts, and the overall declining number of believers. Another important feature of this book is that it is bilingual, with English "verso" and Chinese "recto." Some terms in the Chinese translation are coupled with English terms such as "multitudinous congregation" for "*xuduo Eluosi jiaohui de zuzhi*,"[19] and also with Russian terms, for proper nouns like the Mother of God of Tabyn icon (Tabynskii obraz Bozhiei Materi), that is translated into Chinese as "*Shengmu shengxiang*."[20] Another text which combines religious and cultural knowledge through the ROC in China's history is the 2016 *Chushi Dongzhengjiao (Introduction to Orthodox Christianity)*, a guide to the religion for Chinese people living in Russia based on the writings of Metropolitan Hilarion of Volokolamsk, educates its readers through simple descriptions of the faith's tenets and history.[21] Divided into eight chapters, this book provides a concise history of the Orthodox Church (20–27), the Russian Orthodox Church (30–49), Orthodox Christianity in China (52–99), and then explains religious principles and cultural views (102–119) including about religion, architecture and family, a whole chapter on morals (*daode*) (chapter 6, 122–39), one about Church teachings, holy mysteries, and rituals (142–211), and concludes with explanations of how Orthodox Christianity differs from other Christian sects. This book is visually appealing and accessible to a wide audience. All the photographs are color prints, and each subsection of a chapter is one to five pages long. There are some scriptural citations but no overt references to conversion. Moreover, the book explicitly portrays Sino-Russian political as well as religious relations in a positive light. State leaders like Vladimir Putin and Xi Jinping, are portrayed in some photographs. Chinese believers look proud and content. Russian church leaders and clergy are portrayed as dignified and benevolent. A significantly absent detail, however, is any mention of Orthodox Christian communities in Guangdong Province and Hong Kong.

The OPASPP and COP have also demonstrated how Hong Kong is part of the community formed by the ROC in China through publications such as a 132-page soft bound book published in 2012 to celebrate the 300th anniversary of the Russian Ecclesiastical Mission to China. This book has Russian and Chinese titles on the front cover and an English title on the back cover. It features many color photographs of Hong Kong's urban landscape, landmarks such as the Star Ferry terminal and the International Finance Centre (IFC) building, the OPASPP church, lectures given by OPASPP clergy at the Chinese University of Hong Kong (CUHK).[22] The OPASPP's own history and Hong Kong are the central topics of *Orthodox Church of Apostles Saints Peter and Paul in Hong Kong* published by the COP in 2016. This

99-page book also roots the OPASPP's social and cultural identity in Father Uspensky's mission.[23] The Russian–Traditional Chinese version of the book has a Russian title in red rendered vertically with the Traditional Chinese title in black rendered horizontally (top to bottom).[24] The English–Simplified Chinese version has an English title in red printed vertically on top of a Simplified Chinese title formatted horizontally like the Traditional Chinese version. Similarly, within the book, the Chinese text in the book is in red and the Russian/English text is in black.[25] The content of the two version is the same. The first section is about the history of the parish, the second section about Father Uspensky, the third section about the treasures of the parish such as the Icon of St. John Maximovitch, the fourth section about the church cemetery in Happy Valley, and the fifth section about the activities of the parish such as translation and publication, RLC, church music.

A more personalized history of the OPASPP is found in Father Pozdnyaev's diaries for 2016 and 2017 which were published in separate Chinese and Russian volumes per season. The Chinese versions were entitled *Xianggang shouzha* (Hong Kong handbook) and the Russian versions, *Gonkongskaia Tetrad'* (Hong Kong notebook).[26] These books include many photographs of priests, parishioners, and objects like holiday foods. Each booklet is very brief, the shortest is 56 and the longest in 105 pages. The Chinese and Russian versions of each volume have different outer covers, but the common theme of the cover design is a flower representing the season on the left side and the domes of a church on the right side. The Table of Contents for the Chinese versions of the spring 2016, summer 2016, autumn 2016, and winter 2017 volumes list entries by the featured dates, but the only equivalent Table of Contents in a Russian version is for the spring 2016 one. Other elements of formatting in the two versions of each volume, such as use of font and color and the size of images, vary but the written content and images are the same. Each volume describes facets of the routine church operations and significant events such as the design of the altar for the current church and the installation of the altar.[27] Father Pozdnyaev comments on the growth of the parish community,[28] and how the parish is involved in community events such as a performance of the church choir on March 7, 2016 at the Romanov Ball to raise money for the hospice for children in Moscow.[29] These texts serve as repositories of what were very recent memories when they were written, such as the procession of the Cross for the church's patron saint day on July 12, 2016,[30] and the Blessing of the South China Sea held on January 19, 2017,[31] and reminders of the community's history such as photograph of the young Father Uspensky,[32] and a document from the "Orthodox Church Community of Hong Kong" written in Russian when the Committee was based on 164 Nathan Road and the obscured right-hand side of the document letterhead shows the relationship with St. Andrew Church.[33] Although the COP discontinued publishing them after the two-year series because there was no full-time translator available to oversee the translation of Father Pozdnyaev's Russian-language text into Chinese, the living history of the parish has been recorded in the "Messenger of the Orthodox Parish of Apostles Saints Peter and Paul in Hong Kong" bulletin published on a monthly basis starting in September 2016 after the parish's move into the current church. This pamphlet provides information about the achievements of the parish, services, upcoming events, projects such as Sunday School and theology classes, church finances and donations. One version of each edition is in English and traditional Chinese (one side of sheet for each language) and one version is in Russian and simplified Chinese. The subtitle of the bulletin, "An insight into the daily life of our Hong Kong parish," emphasizes both the present and the cumulative experiences of this community.

RELIGIOUS PRACTICE

Monolingual, bilingual, and multilingual texts for religious practice, including those that educate readers about cultural attributes of Orthodox Christian life, form another major category of the COP's publications. Books for church services teach believers how to participate in organized worship.[34] Other texts about prayer and holidays are useful for religious activities conducted by individuals, families, and groups within and outside of church settings. Converts to Orthodox Christianity, especially Hong Kong and Mainland-born Chinese who have no exposure to Russian culture through formal education or family background, can read about customs in a familiar language and as will be discussed, with illustrations and images that emphasize the compatibility of the faith with the social environment in which they live. These texts perform a similar function to those for Anglophone readers such as *Welcome to the Orthodox Church: An Introduction to Eastern Christianity* by Frederica Mathewes-Green, who converted with her family in 1993 and whose husband is a pastor for a church in Baltimore, Maryland.[35] As a priest's wife, Mathewes-Green wrote about her own experiences and guides readers through theology, and the material culture of the Church, and how to participate in church services, life events like weddings and funerals, and even the coffee hour after worship. Likewise, the books for Sinophone readers conveys information that people who are born and raised in Orthodox Christian families, such as the meaning of church architecture, symbols (how to cross oneself), and the roles of the clergy may take for granted.

In this section, we will focus on the format of texts that are intended for use by believers in the OPASPP community and other Sinophones in the Russian Orthodox world. The positioning of written content in different languages and inclusion of illustrations are vital aspects of these publications because like the histories discussed in the previous section, they engender the sense of how worship in Chinese, Church Slavonic, and English are connected to the same tradition and source of spiritual origin.[36] Examples will be given for each of the following subcategories of publications about religious practice: manuals for church services, lexicons and calendars, and music scores. Analysis of these examples will be principally organized by features of their impagination, or how content is arranged on a page or spread as a purposeful means of communication.[37] Manuals for church services are important for all participants because they explain the exact steps and purposes of each type of service. Some books are general references, such as the Chinese translation of Bishop Alexander Mileant's *Orthodox Christianity*.[38] Others are specifically oriented for new converts, such as the translation of Father Alexander Torik's *Churching: For Beginners to Church Life*.[39] The COP has also published Father Pozdnyaev's own book describing general information about services and general expectations for behavior in a church.[40] References such as lexicons and calendars are useful for believers of various backgrounds by providing information in translation. The OPASPP and the Krutitisky Foundation collaborated on the production of a Russian–Chinese dictionary of Orthodox vocabulary which was published in Moscow. The entries are organized by Russian alphabetic order. Each entry consists of a Russian lexeme in bold as the first item of information on each vertical row followed by corresponding traditional Chinese characters and their transcriptions in Hanyu Pinyin with tone markers. Some entries in the dictionary include supplementary details in Russian and Chinese italicized text.[41] Calendars in Traditional Chinese and Simplified Chinese published by the COP will be discussed as representative examples of how knowledge is more accessible because of the linguistic and cultural translation that they embody. Music scores are important publications for religious practice because singing is an essential form of Orthodox Christian worship. The OPASPP and COP have enriched the corpus of church music by translating traditional hymns and by commissioning new works for services.

Translations of texts that are more prevalent in Russian and English into Chinese deliver both essential access to information and like the Chinese-language and bilingual histories of the Church discussed in the previous section, connect the users to religious practice and life in an immediate sense without linguistic barriers. The COP-produced liturgical calendars reflect experimentation with different media and suggest that the press and the OPASPP have been conscious of making these resources "user-friendly." Liturgical calendars are applicable worldwide and are published both in the Russian Federation by the Moscow Patriarchate and by individual branches of the ROC.[42] The COP has published calendars in a handbook format, in one-page laminated format, and most recently, a mobile application (app) version.[43]

The calendar handbooks, such as the ones published in 2006 and 2007, give practical information about dates in both Julian and Gregorian calendars, and for each daily entry, a concise explanation of the saint(s) commemorated, Bible verses to be recited on that day, and guidelines about fasting regulations.[44] How this information is presented in the handbooks is significant because of the small differences between the two versions.[45]

The front outer cover of the 2006 handbook bears the Chinese title and below it, a photograph of a scene with beggars outside of a church. The physical features of the people and the church depicted in the scene suggest that it is set in Russia. The verso of the cover features a photograph of Patriarch Alexei and his blessing of the publication and on the recto facing it, the Apostles Creed in a calligraphic version of black text set on a red background with a printed version in Simplified Chinese characters. The main content of the handbook is divided into a section for each month, which starts with an evocative image of a holy figure to the left of a brief description of the month. The end of the handbook consists of supplementary content such as a three-column comparison of the contents of the Orthodox Bible, Roman Catholic Bible, and Protestant Bible, frequently recited prayers, and regulations about fasting, and Chinese-style illustrations.[46] The 2007 handbook varies from the 2006 publication in format and content. The title on the front outer cover is the same, but the image with it is of three saints instead of the beggars by the church. The Patriarch's approval on the verso of the cover and the Apostles Creed on the facing recto are likewise the same, but there is an unlabeled image of holy figures which resemble Christ the King with the Apostles in this part which was not in the 2006 handbook. The next page before the main content organized by month and date gives a description of St. Polycarp (69–155), a martyred bishop of Smyrna.[47] Also unlike the 2006 version is that there is no image to start each monthly section and the description of each month is briefer. Furthermore, in the back matter for the 2007 handbook, the comparison of Orthodox, Roman Catholic, and Protestant Bibles is not organized by columns but by Bible chapters that are numbered separately for the Old and New Testaments. Each entry by chapter is organized from left to right with the number, Orthodox name, and Roman Catholic and Protestant versions separated by a slash mark in parentheses ("C/P") or for some, that there is no equivalent in one or both the Roman Catholic and Protestant Bibles. This section ends with a total count of the Orthodox Old Testament consisting of 27 chapters and the Orthodox New Testament consisting of 77 chapters but does not give equivalent figures for the Roman Catholic and Protestant Bibles.[48] The other appendix materials include common prayers and an explanation of fasting customs, like the 2006 handbook.[49] The last unnumbered pages of the handbook are the St. John Maximovitch image taking up one whole page (recto) and his biography (verso), and an image of the "Icon of the Ark of Salvation" that was made in 1817 and is in the Mt. Athos Holy Monastery of Zografos.

The differences between the 2006 and 2007 handbooks suggest that they are meant to be distinct and to introduce different content to the users instead of just presenting the most basic details of the calendar. Since the handbook should be consulted frequently, if not on a daily basis, the user can absorb the knowledge about the saints and the organization of the Bible through regular exposure. As seen in figure 4.1, the format of the entries for each date is also significant in how they help the reader process the given information. In the 2006 handbook, each page is divided into separate sections for each day organized in rows which are split into two columns. The left column is in red with the liturgical date and the right column in yellow with the Gregorian calendar date and the day of the week (Monday, Tuesday). Each section provides information about prayers, saints, and services associated with that day, but the organization of this content is not clearly delineated by headings or other indicators that separate the details into types or categories. In the 2007 handbook, instead of headings in both yellow and red, with colors differentiating the two columns for each day, headings are alternately in red and yellow. The heading for each day is more concise, formatted as "the liturgical calendar

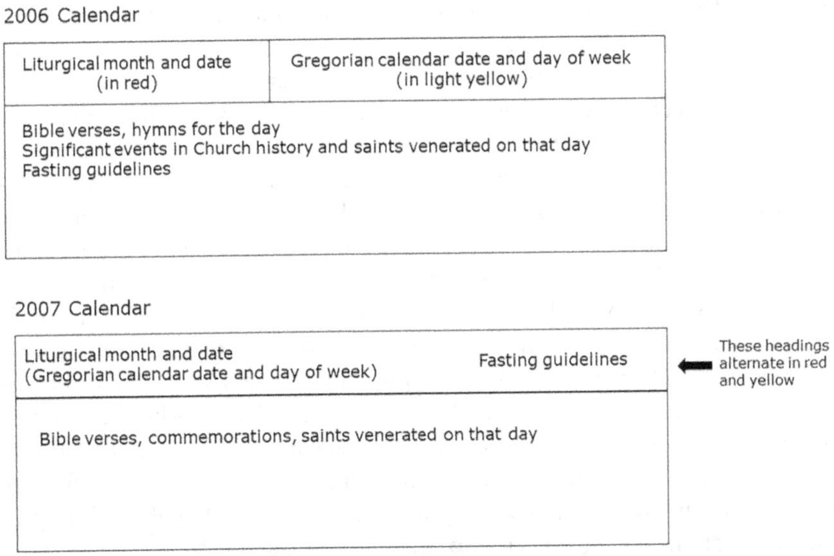

2006 Calendar

Liturgical month and date (in red)	Gregorian calendar date and day of week (in light yellow)
Bible verses, hymns for the day Significant events in Church history and saints venerated on that day Fasting guidelines	

2007 Calendar

Liturgical month and date (Gregorian calendar date and day of week)	Fasting guidelines
Bible verses, commemorations, saints venerated on that day	

⬅ These headings alternate in red and yellow

Figure 4.1 Comparison of the Format of the 2006 and 2007 Liturgical Calendars.
Source: Illustration by Eugenia Kim and Loretta Kim.

date (Gregorian date and days of week in parentheses)," rather than the dates divided into two columns in the 2006 edition. Content of each day-related entry is also more concise, such as details about regulations for fasting such as whether "all can be eaten" (*yi qi ke shi*) or about the kinds of food that can be eaten such as "wine and oil may be consumed" (*jiu you ke shi*) included on the right-hand side of the row with the dates rather than under the heading. The type of information in each daily entry is also more discernible at first glance in the 2007 handbook than in the 2006 version because the content is divided by some subheadings marked with colons on rows above the relevant details.

The one-page Simplified Chinese calendars have varied in design while serving the same function of advising users about services, prayers, and fasting as the handbooks. For example, the 2015 calendar gives the full yearly calendar based on the Gregorian system in the upper left-hand corner in a grid with monthly calendars formatted in a grid style consisting of seven columns and five rows for each month starting with Sunday (the character for *ri* in the column heading) rather than Monday (*yi*) which is common for the Hong Kong calendar, as replicated in figure 4.2. Below this calendar is an image of priests officiating a service. The people participating in the service are wearing clothing common to Southern China during the Qing dynasty and the men are wearing their hair in queues. Dates for the twelve major holidays and fasting periods of the year are listed on the right-hand side. The numerical calendar is also marked to indicate on which dates fasting must be practiced. Dates are highlighted in different colors such as green for fruits and vegetables, periwinkle for when fish can be eaten, pink for non-fasting weeks, and orange for the week when no meat can be eaten.[50]

Other publications reflect the consideration of not only how to organize the content in a single language, as seen in the handbook format and one-page calendars, but also the choice of Chinese language and how it affects the utility of the content. The COP and the OPASPP have created publications in Traditional Chinese that are most suitable for Hong Kong and Taiwan, since that type of script is the primary means of written communication in both regions. However, with the increasingly significant presence of persons in Hong Kong who use Simplified Chinese as a principal or sole form of written Chinese, COP publications in Simplified Chinese such as the calendars serve both users in Hong Kong and in the PRC mainland.[51] Although content rendered in Traditional Chinese and Simplified Chinese is especially versatile because it can be pronounced orally according to an individual's preference for a particular Chinese spoken language, some of the COP publications provide annotations that are specific to Mandarin or Cantonese.

One such example is the collection of pieces based on the eight church modes by Russian composed Nina Starostina published in 2017. The outer

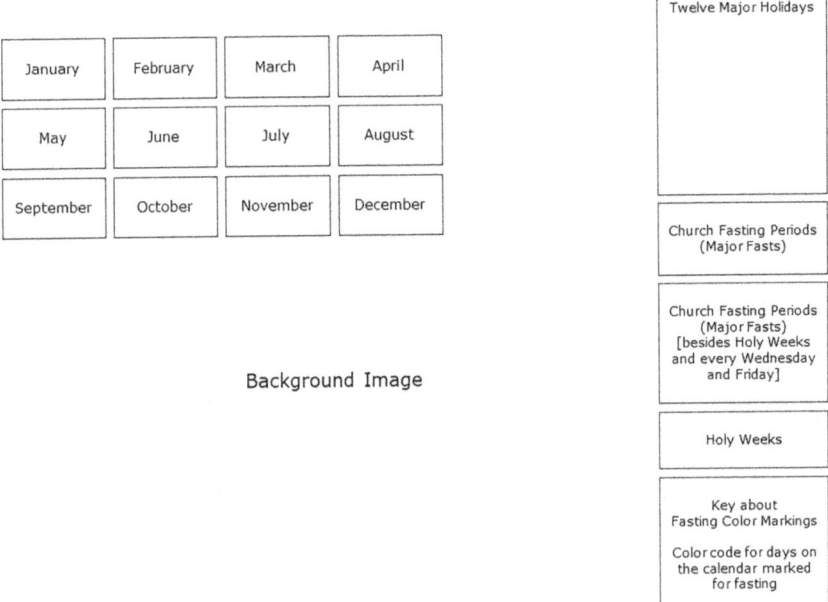

Figure 4.2 Format of the 2015 Simplified Chinese Calendar.
Source: Illustration by Eugenia Kim and Loretta Kim.

front cover of the book gives only the Chinese title and Starostina's name as transcribed in Chinese characters, as well as an image of female Chinese musicians dressed in late imperial Chinese fashion. The first page gives brief explanations of the eight church modes in italicized traditional Chinese and in Russian.[52] The main content of the book is arranged with two pages, or one spread, for each mode. Each page notes the mode in red in larger font with the subtitle, such as "minor praise" or "supplementary praise" in black. The score for singing includes lyrics in Traditional Chinese with modern standard Mandarin transcription in Hanyu Pinyin below as seen in figure 4.3.

This combination of Traditional Chinese and Mandarin annotation can be compared with the annotation of Chinese in a 2015 publication of vespers.[53] This text is entirely in Traditional Chinese except for titles, which are given in Chinese and in Russian. Some of the terms in this text are annotated in parentheses containing Hanyu Pinyin transcriptions with tone markers, the Zhuyin Fuhao transcriptions with tone markers, both indicating pronunciation in Mandarin, and with Jyutping Romanization transcriptions with tone numbers and alternative Chinese characters, preceded by the character *yin* (sound), for some Chinese characters which represent and help a reader with the pronunciation of the term in Cantonese. The Hanyu Pinyin, Zhuyin Fuhao, and

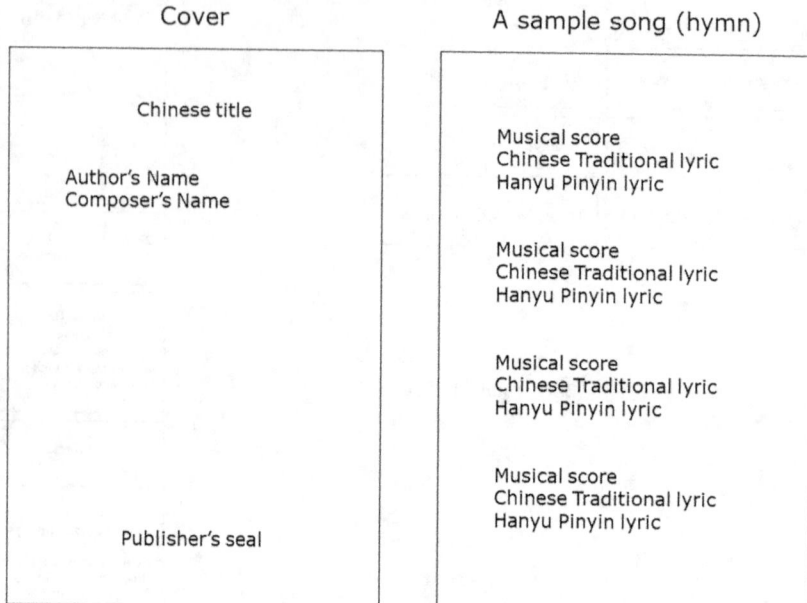

Figure 4.3 Format of the *Eight Church Modes* Book.
Source: Illustration by Eugenia Kim and Loretta Kim.

Jyutping are separated by slash marks. The inclusion of these details about pronunciation enhances the accessibility of this text to users who speak either Mandarin or Cantonese, or who want to know and compare the pronunciation in both languages.

Formatting Chinese text to optimize comprehension through the use of color and font size is also a key feature in publications such as the 2015 Chinese translation of the Divine Liturgy of St. John Chrysostom with a section of choral sheet music composed by Nina Starostina following the service text.[54] The lines recited by the congregation are in larger font than those recited by the officiants. Some text for the officiants such as prayers is in blue rather than in black as for the congregation. These visual cues are not atypical for religious service materials but can be considered as more useful for participants who may not be as familiar with the proceedings or may be following the service in Chinese while the officiants are using Church Slavonic or a combination of Chinese and Church Slavonic, which is a common occurrence for services in the OPASPP church.[55]

The Divine Liturgy of St. John Chrysostom has also been published in bilingual versions by the COP, which reflect how two languages are represented together in a text. The earliest bilingual version was published in 2013, pairing Church Slavonic and English.[56] The COP then published two other versions in 2014, one with Church Slavonic and Traditional Chinese, and the other with English and Traditional Chinese.[57] In both 2014 publications, Traditional Chinese text is arranged on the recto of the page and the other language, Church Slavonic or English, is on the verso. This format makes both languages accessible if the book is open so that a full spread, consisting of two pages, is visible. It is also possible to use the book by just focusing on one language if only the rectos or versos are read. The alignment of languages in this way is different from the 2013 Church Slavonic–English version in which each page is divided into two columns with Church Slavonic on the left-hand column and English on the right-hand one, as seen in figure 4.4. This columnar formatting also keeps the two languages visible, but the user must read each page, recto and verso, in order.

Another example of a bilingual text that fits users worshipping in different languages is the Church Slavonic–Simplified Chinese prayer book with Russian and Chinese titles and a Russian Orthodox cross on the outer cover.[58] The first verso page has Russian and Chinese references to the OPASPP and that the book was published in 2005 with contributions from the Moscow Patriarchate Krutitsy Metochion Foundation. The second verso only has the Chinese-language statement that Patriarch Alexei permitted the publication. The Table of Contents is organized with Russian on top of Chinese and

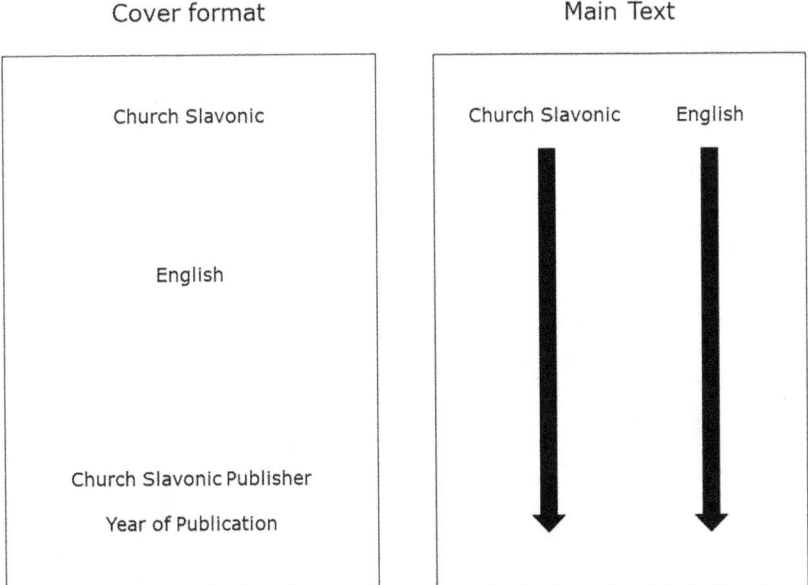

Figure 4.4 Format of the *Divine Liturgy of Saint John Chrysostom* Service Book.
Source: Illustration by Eugenia Kim and Loretta Kim.

divided into three parts: Morning Prayers, Evening Prayers, and Sacraments (Divine Liturgy) in Honor of St. John Chrysostom.[59] Each section consists of Church Slavonic text on the verso and Simplified Chinese text on the recto of pages, as seen in figure 4.5. The final page of the book lists the twelve major holidays of the liturgical year with Russian on the left-hand side and Chinese on the right-hand side, with dates in both languages provided according to both liturgical and Gregorian calendars.

The COP also published another prayer book with a different title, *An Orthodox Prayer Book* (*Zhengjiao qidao shu*), and content in Traditional Chinese in 2013,[60] and in Simplified Chinese in 2016.[61] These books have sections about morning prayers, daytime prayers, and evening prayers, and odes to Jesus Christ, the Virgin Mary, saints, and instructions for what to do before and after receiving Communion, when to make certain body movements such as the sign of the cross, and the Paschal Hours.[62] Both versions are available for sale on the Orthodox Bookstore and Library website as printed books and as Portable Document Format (PDF) files that can be read online or downloaded. These texts are only in Chinese and do not demonstrate how the context is matched with the Church Slavonic version, so they are more useful for worship only in Chinese or for reference to the content focusing on the meaning rather than on the translation or coordination of recitation in worship.[63]

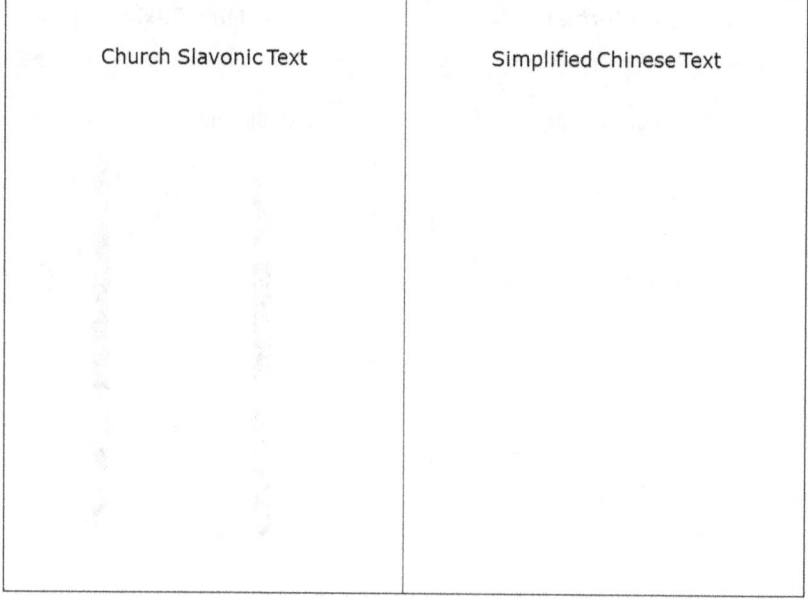

Figure 4.5 Format of the Prayer Book.
Source: Illustration by Eugenia Kim and Loretta Kim

How to bring the two languages together in a bilingual text has varied in COP publications. Some are arranged similarly to the Divine Liturgy of St. John Chrysostom and the 2005 prayer book with one language on the verso and another language on the recto.[64] Other publications combine two monolingual versions into one volume in a back-to-back format (one language in the front section, another in the back section). For the Service of the Holy Protomartyrs of China, Slain during the Boxer Rebellion held in 2015, the COP produced two volumes. One was the English text in the front section and the Traditional Chinese text in the back section.[65] The other volume was arranged with Russian text on the verso and Traditional Chinese on the recto.[66] Both books have the same image of an Orthodox church line drawing. The first book has the English title on top and the Chinese title on the bottom of the front cover. The other book has the Russian title on the top and the Chinese title on the bottom. The Chinese title is slightly different from the Russian and English ones. It means "praise for the feast day of the 222 martyrs in China," not indicating that the honored persons were killed during the Boxer Rebellion.

The COP has also published some trilingual texts such as the service book for the Thanksgiving Service held to commemorate the 300th anniversary of the Russian Ecclesiastical Mission in China.[67] This book has a green wraparound cover. As seen in figure 4.6, the OPASPP logo is on top of the front cover. Also on this cover are the Russian title in the middle with the English title below it and an orange box on the bottom with the detail that this service commemorates the 300th anniversary of the Russian Ecclesiastical Mission in China. The orange box text is similarly arranged as the titles with Russian on top of English. The Chinese title appears only on the back cover, without the titles in either of the other two languages. The first page of the book, opened from left to right, includes the name of the OPASPP in Russian, English, Chinese with the year in a vertical format. On the first full spread, the Russian and English titles of the book are on the verso, and the Traditional Chinese title, written vertically, is on the recto.

Each spread is divided into three parts by language. The Russian and English versions of the service are laid out as parallel text on the *verso* and the Traditional Chinese version is on the *recto*. This book's layout is aligned clearly so that a person could follow the service in all three languages in three different scripts. This arrangement reflects the actual circumstances of the service in which participants had different needs for languages in which they could understand and join the proceedings. This book is also significant as a text of eventual historical value because it records the translation and interpretation of the service which could be useful for adaptation to other events in which all three languages must be employed.

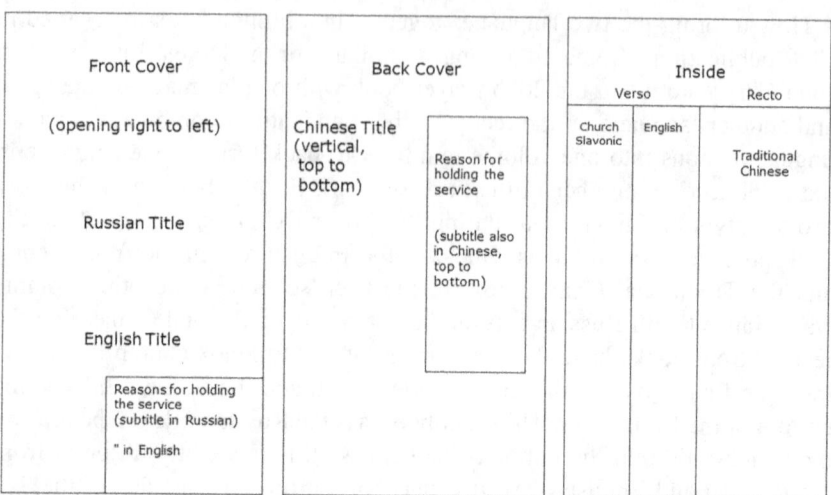

Figure 4.6 Format of the *300th Anniversary of the Russian Ecclesiastical Mission Service Book*.
Source: Illustration by Eugenia Kim and Loretta Kim.

RELIGIOUS CULTURE AND BELIEF

Transmitting knowledge about the cultural values and beliefs of Orthodox Christianity also extends beyond worship and to the realm of spiritual cultivation by individuals through reading about communal life and theological questions. Some books about worship include explicit references to Orthodox tradition and lived experience such as the 2016 COP reprint of the Chinese translation of the Psaltirion (or psalter, compilation of psalms) rendered by the Russian Ecclesiastical Mission in 1879.[68] Divided into 20 kathismas (sections) and titled in Chinese as *Sheng yong jing* (*Holy Scriptures, Sviashchennoe pisanie*), the COP reproduction is in very large print and suitable for use in liturgical services. The front cover identifies it clearly as a publication of the Capital Eastern Orthodox North Hostel in the "Year of our Lord's birth 1879" (*shangdi jiangsheng yi qian ba bai qi shi jiu nian*).

Other materials created by the OPASPP and published by the COP, which are particularly helpful for persons who have just joined the faith or are interested in doing so, also connect the readers to the Orthodox Christian world, emphasizing the importance of both ritual and also about mindset. Among these texts are two Russian–Traditional Chinese bilingual publications released in 2014, the first about how to prepare for the sacrament of Communion and the other about the first time one engages in the sacrament of Confession.[69] Both books have a different layout from those for services as described in the previous section. The content is laid out with Chinese on the verso and Russian on the recto of the pages and were translated from Russian to Chinese by Father Anatoly Kung, who also translated a book about the ritual and meaning of baptism.[70] Texts about fundamental aspects of the faith such as the Orthodox interpretation of who was Jesus Christ and how to pray have also been important publications of the COP.[71] The 2015 Traditional Chinese translation of the book by Father Daniel Sysoev (1974–2009) about how to pray is meaningful not only for the content but also the author's untimely death as a victim of murder.[72] The subjects of what prayers mean and why they are conducted in church is also covered in the Taiwan-published translation of then-Archbishop Hilarion (Alfeyev)'s television programs broadcast in spring 1999 called "On Prayer."[73] The OPASPP has published writings by now-Metropolitan Hilarion about Orthodox theology,[74] which contribute to the genre of introductions to Orthodox beliefs that include translations into Chinese and original works in Chinese. Representative of the former is the Chinese-language version of *The Orthodox Church: Its Faith, Worship, and Life* (*Zhengjiao de jingshen yu lingxing*) published in 2002.[75] Translated by Father Stephen Avramides (d. 2013), this work about Father Antonios Alevisopoulos (1931–1996), introduces the tenets of the faith, including abstract concepts such as truth and salvation, and also explains practices such as holy sacraments and saints. This book helps readers understand how Orthodox Christians can engage in moral and spiritual cultivation. Among texts originally written in Chinese are a basic guide to liturgy authored by Father Li Liang and published by the Taiwan Orthodox Church (OMHKSEA) in 2007.[76]

Faith as expressed in the practice and mindset of worship is taught at multiple levels and for different target audiences. Useful as a guide to daily life and customary practice as an Orthodox Christian, and like the calendars, situating Orthodoxy in a distinctly Chinese setting, is the COP Traditional Chinese publication of the translation of a book written about an Orthodox family and how they observe Orthodox precepts in their home and community. Published in 2012 as part of the 300th anniversary of Orthodoxy in China, the book is titled *Mingtian shi libai ri: jieshi shengfeng li de gushi* (Tomorrow is Sunday: a story explaining the sacraments). Written by Galatea Grigoriadou Soureli in Greek, and translated by Ivan Shchelokov from Russian to Chinese, the book features a young boy and his family members who all have Slavic church names like Aleksandr and Sofia.[77] The adult female and older girl characters wear head scarves. All the people are Chinese. The hand-drawn illustrations by Julia Naumova include many images of Jesus Christ and icons. This book was modified from its original version to show features of Russian Orthodox culture. It is marketed as a book for children, but it depicts how both adults and children perform Orthodox customs.[78]

The COP has also developed a wide selection of publications for readers interested in historical texts and more advanced theological studies. Some of these books were published as volumes of the Chinese Orthodox Church Library series. An early publication in this series is the 2006 Simplified Chinese edition of *Chanhui zhinan: da zhai qijian shenfu guanyu chanhui de xunhui* (Guide to repentance: a priest's exegesis on repentance during major fasts).[79] This book is a compilation of lectures by Archimandrite Ioann (Krestiankin) (1910–2006) about confession and repentance given at the Pskov-Caves Monastery (Pskovo-Pechersky Dormition Monastery) originally entitled *Opyt postroeniia ispovedi* (Experiences of constructing confessions). The translator is a native of Sichuan province named Wen Jian, who also identifies herself by a church name, Helena. The publisher is identified as the Saint (Apostles) Peter and Paul Church of Hong Kong (Ch. *Xianggang Sheng Bide Sheng Baoluo tang*) rather than the OPASPP, reflecting that the OPASPP was not yet a publishing entity.

Another book in the series, *Zhengjiao dui danshen nü de jingli* (Orthodox veneration of the Theotokos) was published the following year in 2007.[80] The original work was written by John Maximovitch, who had been the bishop of Shanghai as introduced in chapter 1 and later Archbishop of China as a leader of the ROCOR. After his death, he was canonized as St. John of Shanghai and San Francisco. First published in 1978 as *The Orthodox Veneration of the Mother of God*, the 2007 version was the first in Simplified Chinese and prefaced by an introduction by the Hieromonk Damascene, a Serbian Orthodox clergy and author of theological works, explaining why proper understanding of the Virgin Mary is essential for Orthodox worship.[81]

These books are representative of two areas in which the COP has enhanced the Chinese-language corpus and marketplace of Orthodox Christianity. The first is of spiritual cultivation through the examples of saints and the material culture of iconography. The second is of the moral foundation that Orthodox Christian believers are encouraged to embrace and apply to their own lives. These themes are especially important because they connect readers to Orthodox Christianity as a lived experience rather than just theology or more broadly, philosophy, which has been the primary focus of relevant publications in the PRC mainland.[82]

Lives of saints and other holy figures has been a key category of COP publications ranging from the 2007 translation of St. John of Shanghai and San Francisco's work on the Virgin Mary, the 2014 translated biography of St. Mary of Egypt (344–421) written by St. Sophronius of Jerusalem (560–638) and illustrated by RLC teacher Anastasia Kraeva,[83] and the 2015 translation of Bishop Alexander Mileant's biography of St. John of Shanghai and San Francisco.[84] The format of these translated works are significant as the content because they reflect collaborations between the OPASPP and other Orthodox Christian organizations, and for some books, multiple layers of translation. A concise introduction to reading the *Synaxarion* (collected hagiographies about the lives of saints) published in 2007 in Simplified Chinese exemplifies the curation of texts.[85] This publication is a small Greek book with two color photographs of the two authors St. Nikolaj Velimirović (1881–1956) and St. Justin Popović (1894–1979) followed by their exegeses about the *Synaxarion*. This book is credited to the two saints as authors and in doing so, places the emphasis on the direct transmission of thought from these thinkers to the readers. Another representative publication about saints resulted from the collaboration of the OPASPP and the Chinese Patriarchal Metochion, a unit of the Moscow Patriarchate's Department of External Church Relations that acts as a liaison body with the Chinese Autonomous Orthodox Church. One text produced in simplified characters is a joint publication of the OPASPP and the Printed in 2016, the Simplified Chinese book is a translation of teachings by St. Nectarios of Aegina (1846–1920) (Aiyina dao de sheng zhujiao Nieketali), *Tongwang xingfu zhi lu* (St. Nectarios of Aegina: On the road to happiness) with the Russian title, *Put' k schast'iu*.[86] This book teaches readers about the life and beliefs of St. Nectarios, an important thinker in Eastern Orthodox Christianity, and includes Chinese translations of the Ten Commandments and the Lord's Prayer, which are printed on the final pages.

Some texts about and written by saints and other persons of exceptional holiness have also linked Sinophone readers back to the Russian language and the Russian setting. The COP's 2015 publication about St. Symeon the New Theologian (949–1022) involved multiple translators and editors.[87] Father Seraphim Rose performed the translation from Russian to English. Chu Guo completed the translation from Father Rose's English version to Chinese. "Yifan" and Ambrose Lin (Lin Sen) edited and proofread Chu's Chinese version.[88] In the following year, the COP published the translation of Peter France's *Elders of Optina* which is translated into Chinese as "Elders of Russia, hermits in the forest."[89] This book introduces readers to the practice of religious hermitage, Mt. Athos, and the Hermitage of Optina and two of the elders, Macarius (1788–1860) and St. Ambrose (1812–1891). Some key terms are given with English equivalents in parentheses, and color illustrations of the elders and the places in the book enhance the reader's understanding of what they looked like.[90]

Icons and iconography are other topics that bring the material culture and the spirituality of Orthodox Christianity together in print. The COP Simplified Chinese publication in 2010 of a book about the history and meaning of icons fills a niche in the literature about iconography with translations and academic expositions produced in Taiwan and the PRC mainland. It gives both English and Chinese explanations of what icons are and what their components and colors mean.[91] Likewise, practical knowledge about appreciating and revering icons is conveyed in a 2006 Traditional Chinese translation of a well-known book and a 2014 book by an ethnic Chinese author, Pelagia Yu, about Byzantine iconography focusing on the life of Jesus, both produced by the Orthodox Church of Taiwan.[92] The former is the translation of a book written by the nuns of the Abbey of St. John in Müstair, Switzerland which is known in English translation as *What Do You Know About Icons*?[93] The book explains the artistic and spiritual elements of icons, and was published as *Nin dui shengxianghua you he lijie?* (a direct translation of the book's original title) in 2006.[94] The Chinese translation, like other versions, includes a section on theological questions and answers (*shenxue wen da*), prayer for icons, and a bibliography with most sources in English.[95] In 2012, Xu Fenglin published a history of Orthodox icons through the Peking University Press as an academic monograph about the cultural significance of icons.[96]

Ethics and morality are the topics of another area in which the COP and also publishers in Taiwan have broken more ground than the PRC mainland. Decisions about personal behavior such as whether to marry is explicated in texts like *Hunyin zhi huihuang* (with the English co-title *The Splendor of the Marriage in the Orthodox Church*), authored by Yu Juan.[97] The first page of the book has another subtitle for the book *Hunyin zhi mei zai Dongzhengjiao*, translated as *The Beauty of Marriage in the Orthodox Church*. This text provides extensive descriptions of the Orthodox marriage ceremony and photographs of mainly Asian brides and non-Asian grooms participating in the rituals. The OPASPP has also published a book about the virtues of Christian marriage. A 2014 translation of Bishop Alexander (Mileant)'s treatise about marriage in Simplified Chinese discusses the moral value of choosing marriage over celibacy or "free love" as an Orthodox Christian.[98] Other books prepare believers for death such as the 2015 COP Simplified Chinese book about the end of a Christian life,[99] and the 2012 translation of Aleksei Osipov's work about the eternal soul published by Taosheng Publishing House under the supervision of Father Pozdnyaev as chief editor.[100]

Orthodox beliefs as reflected in the tenets of the faith and related to worship and to the study of theology are furthermore communicated in books such as Father Kung's original translation of Archpriest Oleg Davydenkov's *Katikhizis: Vvedenie v dogmaticheskoe bogoslovie* (Catechism: introduction to dogmatic theology).[101] The Chinese version, entitled *Zhengjiao jiaoli wenda: Oliege Daweijie'enkefu da shenfu* (Questions and answers about Orthodox Theology: Archpriest Oleg Davydenkov) introduces the thought of Davydenkov, a professor at St. Tikhon's Orthodox University of Humanities, and the importance of studying the catechism.[102] This Chinese version, with a captivating color image of the Bible and a cross near water, includes Greek terms and Russian-language citations so that readers can refer to original concepts and sources. The basic notion of faith is also analyzed in the translation of *How We Believe* by Archbishop Pavel of Karelia and All Finland

(1914–1988), with more comprehensible Chinese title that can be translated into English as "How do Orthodox followers believe in their faith."[103] The Russian–Chinese bilingual version published by the COP in 2015 is divided into two parts. The front to back in standard modern reading style is the original Russian version and one blank page separates it from the Chinese translation which is formatted in Asian style (read back to front) and with the Traditional Chinese text arranged in vertical lines read right to left in the traditional Chinese pagination style.[104] The "two books in one" format preserves the authenticity of the original text and gives Sinophone readers the experience of reading in a familiar format.

Scholars and publishers in the PRC mainland have concentrated more on Orthodox theology as a philosophy, which is most likely influenced by the reality that discourse about foreign religious thought is subject to political constraints. Conveying the tenets of Orthodox Christianity is therefore sensitive as an intellectual as well as social project. Zhang Baichun, a professor of philosophy and sociology at Beijing Normal University who earned a doctoral degree from St. Petersburg University, contends with this hardship in his ongoing work as a nonbeliever who analyses Orthodox Christianity as a type of philosophy. An expert on the thought of philosopher Nikolai Berdyaev (1874–1948), Zhang participates in dialogues about Orthodox Christianity and Orthodox institutions in China throughout the world. He emphasizes his strength as an objective examiner of Orthodox Christianity as a social and psychological phenomenon in his work, such as the 2001 monograph *Dangdai Dongzheng jiao shenxue* (Contemporary theology of the Orthodox Churches) and a 2011 monograph *Feng suizhe yisi chui: Bie'erjiayefu zongjiao zhexue yanjiu* (As the wind blows: Berdyaev's research on religion and philosophy).[105] Zhang's research and publications differ expressly from missionary produced texts in the eighteenth through early twentieth centuries, but the underlying aim of translating not only the language but also embedded cultural elements of Russian Orthodox Christianity into Chinese is a common thread that links them.

Translation has been a critical way in which knowledge of Orthodox theology has been disseminated in the PRC mainland such as the summary of church doctrine by Father Sergei Nikolaevich Bulgakov (1871–1944) published by the Commercial Press in Beijing in 2005.[106] This book has a Russian–Chinese bilingual index that facilitates comparison between the terms in both languages. However, the COP has taken a more prominent role in contributing translations to the marketplace such as the translation of lectures delivered by Sergei Khoruzhiy (1941–2020)'s at Beijing Normal University from July 29 to July 3, 2009. Khoruzhiy was a professor at various institutions, including the Russian Academy of Sciences and the Russian Academy of Natural Sciences.[107] These works are similar to the translations of Metropolitan John Zizioulas' lectures on Christian dogmatics published in Taiwan.[108] The bilingual English–Chinese Table of Contents about the lectures given at the Thessaloniki University's School of Theology, during the academic year from 1984 to 1985 is useful for the reader to navigate the content about dogma and the cognizance of faith. Advanced theological studies have also been published by the OPASPP such as a book translated into Chinese with the title as "Truth and communication" (*Zhenli yu jiaoliu*) which gives very complex explanations of the "ecclesiology of personality" (*ren'ge de jiaohuixue*) as well as the main question of how the church fathers dealt with the issue of "truth."[109]

The OPASPP and COP have been instrumental in not only producing translated texts about subjects related to the beliefs and practices of Orthodox Christianity but also transmitting them to audiences that encompass both readers within and outside of the Orthodox world. In 2009 and 2010, the OPASPP collaborated with the OFASC as joint publishers of a *Missionary Leaflets* series.[110] Each of these publications combined English and Chinese versions into one volume with the English section opening front to back, and the Chinese section opening back to front with Simplified Chinese written vertically.[111] The theme of each volume is different, but cites Bible verses and encourages the reader to think about how spirituality should influence personal growth in ways that are not exclusive to Orthodox Christianity. Another example of collaboration and outreach to a broader readership is the Traditional Chinese translation of Clark Carlton's book about what Protestant Christians should know about Orthodoxy. Produced in 2013 with Taosheng Publishing House in commemoration of the 80th anniversary of Orthodox Christianity in Hong Kong, this book includes a glossary table with the Chinese equivalents of names of non-Chinese people and places on the left-hand side of the pages with the original English terms on the right-hand sides,[112] and a list of names of apostles and other biblical figures in English on the left column and then three columns to the right of it with equivalents in Chinese romanization common in Protestant, Orthodox, and Roman Catholic usage.[113] Another appendix section gives a similar comparison of the chapters of the Protestant, Orthodox, and Roman Catholic Bibles, like the 2007 calendar handbook discussed earlier in this chapter.[114] The opposite approach of applying an Orthodox perspective on non-Orthodox Christianity has also been represented in the 2009 Simplified Chinese translation of *Sola Scriptura: An Orthodox Analysis of the Cornerstone of Reformation Theology*, by Father John Whiteford who converted from to the Church of the Nazarene denomination to Orthodox Christianity, published in collaboration with the OFASC.[115]

Production of translated and original publications for the past two decades that facilitate worship in Chinese and spiritual cultivation is a crucial way which the OPASPP has acted as a bridge between the international ROC community and readers in both the PRC mainland and Hong Kong, as well as other Sinophone communities around the world. Since the main goal of generating a corpus of literature has been to disseminate knowledge about Orthodox Christian beliefs and practices, the OPASPP has increased access to the COP publications by creating digital versions as well as print versions for many of them and making several of these digital texts available free of charge. Also, to communicate most effectively in the medium of translation, editors and translators for the COP, including Father Pozdnyaev and Father Kung who have assumed both roles, continually discuss how fundamental concepts of Orthodox theology and worship can be adequately and appropriately translated into Chinese.[116] Another prime concern of the OPASPP and the COP has been expanding the target audience of the publications. The COP has thus far pursued a diverse publication agenda. Some of its outputs are primarily works of general reference. Others contribute to academic debates about Orthodox Christianity in China and Asia. All of these works reinforce the OPASPP's endeavor to continue the critical component of Orthodox missiology in China by learning about the host society through translation and presenting information about the Church in an approachable way to attract new believers who may otherwise not be able to comprehend seminal texts in Russian or even their English-language translations.[117] Similarly, how the OPASPP has created a community that adapts Russian culture and Orthodox Christian life to the particular social and cultural characteristics of Hong Kong is the subject of the next chapter.

NOTES

1. For an extensive list of major publications from 1810 to 1900, see Tiedemann, ed., *Handbook of Christianity, Volume Two*, 194–206.

2. For a study of the broader significance of writing for the development of Russian culture and civilization, see Simon Franklin, *Writing, Society and Culture in Early Rus, c.950–1300* (Cambridge and New York: Cambridge University Press, 2002).

3. The 1810 version combined the original version by Francesco Brancati (1607–1671) with a section from the work of Andre-Jean Lubelli (1610–1683) who were both Jesuits.

4. Rudolf Löwenthal, *The Religious Periodical Press in China* (Peking [Beijing]: Synodal Commission in China, 1940).

5. Originally published in Harbin from 1904, the journal changed names in 1907 and publication location to Beijing. See Lomanov, "Russian Orthodox Church (Republican China)," 555.

6. Löwenthal notes that individual issues of the *Church Bulletin* were identified with pictures of saints on the upper part of each page rather than with the publication title. See *Religious Periodical Press*, 271.

7. Löwenthal, *Religious Periodical Press*, 272.

8. The Cyrillic alphabet is especially sacred because it was introduced by Saint Stephen of Perm (1340–1396). April 26 is therefore celebrated as both the day honoring this saint and as Old Permic Alphabet Day.

9. Lin Sen, a native of Hechuan (Chongqing) in Sichuan province, was hired as a staff member of the RLC to perform translations of text chosen by Father Pozdnyaev. Lin is a graduate of the Russian department of the Beijing Foreign Studies University. Mentored and baptized by Father Pozdnyaev, Lin visited Hong Kong during every Easter season as a guest of the church and toured holy sites in Greece as part of an OPASPP-sponsored trip. Bishop Ephraim of Bikin endorsed Lin's appointment in 2014 as a translator of religious texts. Lin was responsible for translating Slavonic and modern Russian texts into Chinese until he resigned in 2017. Other translators have produced content for the COP publications, including Father Kung who oversees large-scale projects such as the translation and editing of the *Book of Services of the Twelve Feasts* (Ch. *Shi'er jieri zhanli liyi wenben*, Ru. *Liturgicheskie teksty dvenadtsati prazdnikov*).

10. The China Orthodox Press does not have a store or a separate office from the parish offices. Part of the Lamma Island hostel for visiting clergy is used as the physical home for the printing equipment. The church maintains a collection of printed materials in a bookcase display area adjoining the sanctuary. Interested persons can browse through the texts and purchase them by paying at the church's office.

11. Roman Kremnev, interview, July 6, 2017.

12. Orthodox Parish of Apostles Saints Peter and Paul (Moscow Patriarchate) (OPASPP), "Orthodox Christianity Bookstore and Library," accessed September 10, 2017, http://www.orthodoxbookshop.asia/catalogue.

13. The COP has also published works that are about the origins and evolution of Christianity. One example, which was published during the first year of the press' operations, is a bilingual version of Archimandrite Cyril Hovorun's lectures given in China during 2013 discussing the three phases of Nestorianism: theological identity, political identity, and cultural identity. The half of the book that is read front to back is in English. The second half, which is read back to front is in Traditional Chinese. A table of contents in Chinese is interspersed between the two halves. The lectures were translated by Anna Chan and edited by Lin Sen. See Cyril Hovorun/Xiushi da siji Jili'er boshi (Guowolong) [Archimandrite Dr. Cyril (Hovorun)], *From Antioch to Xi'an: an Evolution of "Nestorianism"/You Antia dao Xi'an: Niesituoli pai de yanbian* (Hong Kong: China Orthodox Press, 2014).

14. Innocent, "The Russian Orthodox Mission in China," 679.

15. Ibid., 685.

16. The original version is Adrian Keller, *A Pocket Church History for Orthodox Christians* (Austin, TX: St. Hilarion Press, 1994). The translated version is [Xiushi siji] Aidan (Kaile) [Father Hieromonk Adrian (Keller)], *Zhengjiao jidutu de jiaohui lüeshi* [A concise history of the Church for Orthodox believers], trans. Peter Lu

(Hong Kong: China Orthodox Press, 2016). Regarding Aidan Keller, see "Hieromonk Aidan (Keller)/Ieromonakh Aidanii (Keller)," ROCOR Parish and Clergy Directory, Russian Orthodox Church Outside of Russia (website), last modified January 31, 2012, http://directory.stinnocentpress.com/viewclergy.cgi?Uid=470&lang=en. Other general histories about Orthodox Christianity include the translations of Aristeides Papadakis and John Meyendorff's work on the early history of the Christian Church by the Taiwan Orthodox Church and Nikolai Mikhailovich Nikol'skii's history of the ROC. For the original texts, see Aristeides Papadakis (with John Meyendorff), *The Christian East and the Rise of the Papacy: The Church AD 1071–1453* (New York: St Vladimir's Seminary Press, 1994) and Nikolai Mikhailovich Nikol'skii, *Istoriia russkoi tserkvi* [History of the Russian Church] (Moscow: Politicheskaia literatura, 1988). For the translated works, see Yalisidilisi Babalaqisi boshi [Dr. Aristeides Papadakis], *Jiaohui lishi* [History of the Church] (Xindian: Taiwan jidu zhengjiaohui, 2006), and Ni Mi Nikelisiji [Nikolay Mikhaylovich Nikolsky], *Eguo jiaohui shi* [History of the Russian Church], trans. Ding Shichao, Yuan Yibo, and Du Like, ed. Ding Shichao (Beijing: Shangwu yinshuguan, 2000).

17. Otdel vneshnikh tserkovnykh sviazei Moskovskogo patriarkhata, *Pravoslavie v Kitae*.

18. See Xieliwanuofusiji [Selivanovsky, V.], *Dongzhengjiao hui zai Zhonghuo* [The Orthodox Church in China], trans. Gao Yongsheng, ed. Ambrose Lam (Lin Sen) (Hong Kong: China Orthodox Press, 2014), based on the original Russian text, Victor Selivanovsky, *Pravoslavie v Kitae: Sbornik materialov vystavki* [Orthodoxy in China: collection of exhibition materials] (Blagoveshchensk: Missionerskii otdel Blagoveshchenskoi eparkhii RPTs, 2013) and the English translation, Victor Selivanovsky, *Orthodoxy in China*, ed. Eric S. Peterson, trans. Olga V. Trubetskoy (California: CreateSpace Independent Publishing Platform, 2015). Father Pozdynyaev's history was originally released in 2010 and republished in 2015. See Dionisy Pozdynyaev, *Zhongguo dalu Zhengjiaohui zai zizhi kuangjia xia jiaohui shengming de fuhuo* [Orthodox Christianity in the People's Republic of China: revival of church life within the framework of an autonomous church], trans. Sun Yue (Hong Kong: China Orthodox Press, 2015). The COP also distributes books about ROC history in China by other producers such as Tatiana Manakova, *Krasnaia Fanza Rossiiskogo Posol'stva v Pekine: Ostrovok Pravoslaviia v Kitae* [Red fangzi of the Russian embassy in Beijing: An islet of Orthodoxy in China] (Beijing and Moscow: n.p., 2007). The back cover of this book gives a summary in English on the left and Simplified Chinese on the right. The book's title is translated into Chinese, and the author's name is transliterated by Chinese characters.

19. *Zhongguo dalu Zhengjiaohui*, 3.

20. Ibid., 31.

21. Waluokelamusike du zhujiao Yilaliyong [Metropolitan of Volokolamsk Hilarion], et al., *Chushi Dongzheng jiao: Gei juzhu zai Eluosi de Zhongguoren* [Introduction to Orthodox Christianity: for Chinese living in Russia] (Moscow: Eluosi Dongzheng jiaohui Mosike zongzhujiao bangongting chubanshe, 2016 / Hong Kong: China Orthodox Press, 2016). The title of the book is in Traditional Chinese, but the content is in Simplified Chinese. This publication does not indicate

whether it is a direct translation of another book or based on particular source texts. Metropolitan Hilarion is the author of many works on Orthodox Christianity, including Ilarion, *Pravoslavie* [Orthodoxy] (Moscow: Sretenskogo monastyria, 2008).

22. Orthodox Parish of Apostles Saints Peter and Paul (Moscow Patriarchate) (OPASPP), *Prazdnovanie 300-letiia Rossiiskoi Dukhovnoi Missii v Kitai* [300th Anniversary of the Russian Ecclesiastical Mission to China] (Hong Kong: China Orthodox Press, 2012).

23. Orthodox Parish of Apostles Saints Peter and Paul (Moscow Patriarchate) (OPASPP), *Saint Apostles Peter & Paul Orthodox Church in Hong Kong / Xianggang Sheng Bide Sheng Baoluo jiaotang* (Hong Kong: China Orthodox Press, 2016), available in hard copy and online, accessed January 15, 2017, http://www.orthodoxbookshop.asia/catalogue/orthodox-church-of-apostles-saints-peter-and-paul-in-hong-kong_319 and *Pravoslavnyi khram Pervoverkhovnykh Apostolov Petra i Pavla v Gonkonge* / Xianggang Sheng Bide Sheng Baoluo jiaotang [Orthodox Church of Apostles Saints Peter and Paul in Hong Kong] (Hong Kong: China Orthodox Press, 2016), available in hard copy and online, accessed January 2, 2021, http://www.orthodoxbookshop.asia/catalogue/orthodox-church-of-apostles-saints-peter-and-paul-in-hong-kong_273/. This history does not mention Father Wen and his congregation.

24. The top to bottom positioning of the Chinese script follows the original formatting of written Chinese which is still used for some books and for newspapers and magazines.

25. The use of color to differentiate text by language is interesting because red ink has traditionally been subject to limited use in Chinese culture.

26. Dionisy Pozdynyaev, *Xianggang shouzha: 2016 xia* [Hong Kong handbook: summer 2016] (Hong Kong: China Orthodox Press, 2016) and Dionisy Pozdynyaev, *Gonkongskaia Tetrad'. Zima 2016–2017* [Hong Kong notebook: winter 2016–2017] (Hong Kong: China Orthodox Press, 2017).

27. About the design of the altar see Dionisy Pozdynyaev, *Gonkongskaia Tetrad'. Vesna 2016* [Hong Kong's diary spring 2016] (Hong Kong: China Orthodox Press, 2016), 15, and Dionisy Pozdynyaev, *Xianggang shouzha 2016 chun* [Hong Kong's diary spring 2016], trans. Lin Sen (Hong Kong: China Orthodox Press, 2017), 15. About the installation of the altar, see Dionisy Pozdynyaev, *Gonkongskaia Tetrad'. Osen' 2016* [Hong Kong's diary autumn 2016] (Hong Kong: China Orthodox Press, 2016), 51, and Dionisy Pozdynyaev, *Xianggang shouzha 2016 qiu* [Hong Kong's diary autumn 2016], trans. Lin Sen (Hong Kong: China Orthodox Press, 2017), 47.

28. For example, for group photos of new Hong Kong (Chinese) members of the parish, see *Gonkongskaia Tetrad'. Osen' 2016*, 24–25, and *Xianggang shouzha 2016 qiu*, 23.

29. *Gonkongskaia Tetrad'. Vesna 2016*, 37, and *Xianggang shouzha 2016 chun*, 37.

30. Dionisy Pozdynyaev, *Gonkongskaia Tetrad'. Leto 2016* [Hong Kong diary's summer 2016] (Hong Kong: China Orthodox Press, 2016), 33, and Dionisy Pozdynyaev, *Xianggang shouzha 2016 xia* [Hong Kong's diary summer 2016], trans. Lin Sen (Hong Kong: China Orthodox Press, 2017), 32.

31. Dionisy Pozdynyaev, *Gonkongskaia Tetrad'. Zima 2016–2017* [Hong Kong diary's winter 2016–2017] (Hong Kong: China Orthodox Press, 2017), 36–37, and Dionisy Pozdynyaev, *Xianggang shouzha 2016 zhi 2017 nian dong* [Hong Kong's diary winter 2016–2017], trans. Lin Sen (Hong Kong: China Orthodox Press, 2017), 36–38.

32. *Gonkongskaia Tetrad'. Leto 2016*, 49, and *Xianggang shouzha 2016 xia*, 46.

33. Interestingly, this document is only included in the Chinese version of the Autumn 2016 volume, see page *Xianggang shouzha 2016 qiu*, 14. There are other references to documents that are mentioned in both the Russian and Chinese versions such as papers about Father Wen's congregation that are archived in San Francisco. See *Gonkongskaia Tetrad'. Zima 2016–2017*, 49–51, and *Xianggang shouzha 2016 zhi 2017 nian dong*, 47–50.

34. Many Russian-language resources that provide concise and highly comprehensible explanations are also available for both Russophone natives and users who can read them. See, for example, Pravoslavnaia entsiklopediia "Azbuka very" [Orthodox Encyclopedia "ABC of faith"], accessed May 2, 2017, https://azbyka.ru.

35. Frederica Mathewes-Green, *Welcome to the Orthodox Church: An Introduction to Eastern Christianity* (Brewster, MA: Paracelete Press, 2015).

36. English is a language used in many COP publications because many members of the OPASPP congregation use English as a primary language in Hong Kong and because many of the original texts which are translated by the COP are in English.

37. About impagination as a multidisciplinary field of study, see Ku-ming (Kevin) Chang, Anthony Grafton and Glenn W. Most, eds., *Impagination – Layout and Materiality of Writing and Publication: Interdisciplinary Approaches from East and West* (Berlin: De Gruyter, 2021).

38. Yalishanda (Milante) zhujiao [Bishop Alexander Mileant], ed., *Zhengjiaohui* [The Orthodox church] (Hong Kong: OPASPP, 2010). The original text is: [Bishop] Alexander (Mileant), *Orthodox Christianity* (self-pub., CreateSpace, 2016). A comparable example in English is [Archpriest] D. Sokolof [Dimitrii Pavlovich Sokolov], *A Manual of the Orthodox Church's Divine Services* (Jordanville, NY: Holy Trinity Monastery, 2001). This publication is also a historical text, translated from Russian before the Russian Revolution.

39. Yalishanda Duolike shenfu [(Arch) priest Alexander Torik], *Shouxi rujiao: xie gei gangang kaishi zongjiao shenghuo de ren* [Baptism and entry to the faith: written for those who have just started religious life], trans. Tamala Jin [Tamara Jin] (Hong Kong: OPASPP and OFASC, 2011). The original text is [Protoiereus] Alexander Torik, *Churching: For Beginners to Church Life*, trans. Nathan Williams (self-pub., LOGOS Digital Publishing, 2011), Kindle.

40. Dionisy Pozdynyaev/[Da siji] Di'aonixi Boidiniyefu, *Jiaohui, jiaoli, sheng aomi, jiaotang nei de juzhi* [The church, catechism, holy mysteries, and behavior in church], trans. Lin Sen (Hong Kong: China Orthodox Press, 2015). This book and the others introduced in this paragraph are in the same market as such as the Traditional Chinese book *Zhengjiaohui de chongbai*, the title translated in English and provided in the book as "An Introduction to the Liturgical Practice of the Orthodox Church." Originally published in 1999 by the Hong Kong Christian Institute as the Orthodox

section of "Christian Worship Revisited (Expanded Edition)," this 2003 text contains the Lord's Prayer and Apostle's Creed in English and Chinese. See He Xiaoxin, *Zhengjiaohui de chongbai* [An introduction to the liturgical practice of the Orthodox church] (Hong Kong: OMHKSEA, 2003).

The OMHKSEA has also produced informal publications such as "The Power of the Name: the Orthodox Tradition of Jesus Prayer" booklet in English which is undated and unauthored. The booklet is printed on regular photocopy-quality paper with a blue sheet folded in half as the front and back cover. The content is formatted simply as single-spaced text. See "The Power of the Name: The Orthodox Tradition of Jesus Prayer," (Hong Kong: OMHKSEA, n.d.).

The OMHKSEA published a Traditional Chinese version of the booklet with the same title (*Shengming de liliang, shengming* meaning "Holy Name") with a green cover page as the major feature physically distinguishing it from the English version. These publications explain the purpose of worship, seasons of the liturgical year, four major fasting periods, and major holidays.

See *Shengming de liliang* [Power of the Holy Name] (Hong Kong: OMHKSEA, n.d.).

41. Marina V. Rumyantseva, *Russko-kitaiskii slovar' pravoslavnoi leksiki* [Russian–Chinese dictionary of Orthodox vocabulary] (Moscow: Vostochnaia kniga, 2007).

42. Taking the 2015 edition as an example, the Moscow Patriarchate produced book-format calendar that is organized by the months of the year. Each month-based section has entries about each day, with days of the week and corresponding numerical dates, and the Bible verses and notes for worship on those days. The book also features photographs of the Patriarch in different scenarios such as with students or military personnel, and in the back matter, gives photographs and contact information for metropolitans of the Church. See Izdatel'skii Sovet Russkoi Pravoslavnoi Tserkvi, *Patriarshii kalendar'na 2015 god* [Patriarchal calendar for the year 2015] (Moskva: Izdatel'skii Sovet Russkoi Pravoslavnoi Tserkvi, 2014). The format and content of the calendars are fairly similar, with some minor differences, as can be seen if this 2015 edition is compared with the one for the previous year. See Publishing Council of the Russian Orthodox Church, *Pravoslavnyi tserkovnyi kalendar'* 2014 [Patriarchal calendar for the year 2014] (Moskva: Izdatel'stvo Moskovskoi Patriarkhii Russkoi Pravoslavnoi Tserkvi, 2013). Comparable to the COP publications in Chinese are the Japanese-language calendars published by the Orthodox Church of Japan. The 2010 edition, which is in a handbook format like the Moscow Patriarchate versions, starts with an explanation about the calendar, major dates of the year with Julian (first column on left), Gregorian (second column and in bold) dates, and brief titles of the dates/holidays (third column). The official first page starts with the first day of the Gregorian calendar. Each day has one paragraph of information which includes the Gregorian date which is in a larger font size than the corresponding Julian date and the day of the week, and whether fasting should take place. The second to last page of the handbook is a table with the dates of major holidays from 2011 to 2030, and the last page has the dates for the Easter holiday for 2001 to 2100. See Nihon Harisutosu Seikyōkai [Orthodox Church of Japan], *Seikyōkai-reki: shu gōshō 2010-nen*

[Orthodox liturgical calendar: for the year 2010 (CE)] (Tokyo: Nihon Harisutosu Seikyōkai kyōdan).

The Moscow Patriarchate also publishes liturgical instructions for clergy. For a published version, see for example, see Izdatel'skii Sovet Russkoi Pravoslavnoi Tserkvi, *Bogosluzhebnye ukazaniia na 2008 god dlia sviashchenno-tserkovnosluzhitelei* [Liturgical instructions for the year 2008: For clergy] (Moskva: Izdatel'skii Sovet Russkoi Pravoslavnoi Tserkvi, 2007) and more recently, available as an app, "Bogosluzhebnye ukazaniia 2020" [Liturgical instructions 2020], Teoretik, 2020, Vers. 8.3.2, APKPure, https://apkpure.com/cn/%D0%B1%D0%BE%D0%B3%D0%BE%D1%81%D0%BB%D1%83%D0%B6%D0%B5%D0%B1%D0%BD%D1%8B%D0%B5-%D1%83%D0%BA%D0%B0%D0%B7%D0%B0%D0%BD%D0%B8%D1%8F-2020/ru.teoretik.ukazaniya.

43. Orthodox Parish of Apostles Saints Peter and Paul (Moscow Patriarchate) (OPASPP), "Orthodox Christian Calendar+," Apple App Store, Vers. 4.9 (2019), accessed December 17, 2019, https://apps.apple.com/us/app/orthodox-christian-calendar/id1010208102.

44. For many converts, the Julian calendar may be unfamiliar. For an explanation of this calendrical system, see Ludmila Perepiolkina, *The Julian Calendar as the 1000-Years Icon of Time in Russia* (Moscow: Metochion of the Russian Monastery of St. Panteleimon on the Athos, 1996).

45. In addition to the handbooks, one-page calendars, and the app, the COP has published other texts about the significance of time-based elements in Orthodox Christian life. A 2009 Simplified Chinese translated book about the lives of the saints for the month of Epiphany has one section for each day in the month giving extensive explanations for worship, including Bible quotations, psalms, biographies of the saints associated with each day, homilies, ideas for contemplation, and references to sources in footnotes. See Orthodox Parish of Apostles Saints Peter and Paul (Moscow Patriarchate) (OPASPP), *Shengren liezhuan: di wu ce: yi yue (zhu xian yue)* [Lives of the saints, book five: January (month of Epiphany)], trans. Xue Bin (Hong Kong: OPASPP and China Orthodox Church, April 2009).

Another example of a time-based publication is Father Kung's translation of a book about Easter and the twelve major holidays in 2014. These books explain both aspects of Church history and about why daily and annually celebrated rituals are important. See Anatoly Kung (Kung Cheung Ming), trans. *Fuhuojie he shi er zhong da jieri Dongzhengjiao zhuyao jieri jianjie* [Easter and the twelve major holidays: A concise explanation of the main Orthodox holidays] (Hong Kong: OPASPP, 2014). The source text for this book is not stated in the publication.

46. Orthodox Parish of Apostles Saints Peter and Paul (Moscow Patriarchate) (OPASPP), *Zhonghua Zhengjiaohui lishu Shangdi chuangshi qiqian wubai shisi nian Jidu jiangsheng erqian ling liu nian* [Chinese Orthodox Church handbook: 7514 years since God's creation of the world, 2006 since the birth of Christ] (Hong Kong: China Orthodox Press, 2006), 99–108. About the Bible comparison, see 99–101; about frequently recited prayers, 102; about regulations about fasting, 103–108.

47. Orthodox Parish of Apostles Saints Peter and Paul (Moscow Patriarchate) (OPASPP), *Zhonghua Zhengjiaohui lishu Shangdi chuangshi qiqian wubai shiwu*

nian Jidu jiangsheng erqian ling qi nian [Chinese Orthodox Church handbook: 7515 years since God's creation of the world, 2007 since the birth of Christ] (Hong Kong: China Orthodox Press, 2007), 2.

48. Ibid, 142–43.

49. For the common prayers, see OPASPP, *Zhonghua Zhengjiaohui lishu Shangdi chuangshi qiqian wubai shisi nian*, 143–44, for fasting regulations, 124–49.

50. The one-page calendars do not have any titles or other publication information listed on them and are generally available only for distribution within the parish community. The color scheme for fasting has also changed between years. On the 2013 calendar, blue indicated "no meat," purple was for "fish, hot food, and plant oil foods," yellow for "hot food and plant oil cooked foods," green for "hot foods not cooked with oil," pink for "cold foods only," and gray for "complete abstinence from food."

51. The significant presence of people who use Simplified Chinese refers to both the growing proportion of Hong Kong's population that was educated in the PRC mainland using Simplified Chinese and also Hong Kong-born Sinophones who use both Simplified Chinese and Traditional Chinese, or in the case of some people educated in the international schools (private schools that do not follow the local curriculum for primary and secondary education), only Simplified Chinese because many such schools deliver their Chinese-language curricula in that script only.

52. Orthodox Parish of Apostles Saints Peter and Paul (Moscow Patriarchate) (OPASPP), *Annotatsiia k osmoglasiiu* [Annotation for osmoglasia]/*Ba diao ji: zhuri xiao zanci ji fu zanci* [Collection of (works based on the) eight church modes: praises and sub-praises for the Lord's Day], music by Nina Sitaluosijinna [Nina Starostina] (Hong Kong: China Orthodox Press, 2017), 3.

53. Orthodox Parish of Apostles Saints Peter and Paul (Moscow Patriarchate) (OPASPP), *Dimu ke* [Vespers] (Hong Kong: China Orthodox Press, 2016).

54. Orthodox Christianity HK (OPASPP), *Sheng jinkou Yuehan shi feng sheng li (dai yuepu) / Bozhestvennaia Liturgiia Ioanna Zlatousta (s notnym prilozheniem)* [Divine liturgy in honor of Our Father Among the Saints John Chrysostom (with supplementary music)], music by Nina Sitaluosijinna [Nina Starostina], ed. Lin Sen (Hong Kong: China Orthodox Press, 2015). The choral music is on pages 39 to 59, with a table of contents listing the 21 pieces on page 37 and a brief introduction to the composer who is noted for her training in Chinese music, specifically in the *guqin* (seven-string zither), and her credentials from top Russian schools of music, and the significance of these commissioned pieces as original compositions and that include characteristics of traditional Chinese music on page 38. The musical scores are arranged in a similar way as the church mode compositions, with titles given in Chinese characters, Hanyu Pinyin, and Russian, and the lyrics in Traditional Chinese and Hanyu Pinyin.

55. For comparison about bilingual versions of this liturgy, see for example, Greek Orthodox Archdiocese of America, *The Divine Liturgy of St. John Chrysostom Hymnal: A Hymnal with Texts in Greek, English and English Phonetics* (Brookline, MA: Greek Orthodox Archdiocese of America Department of Religious Education, 1977) and for an English-only version for Russian Orthodox worship in the United

States, see St. Tikhon's Monastery, *Book of Needs (Abridged)* (South Canaan, PA: St. Tikhon's Seminary Press, 2002). This version is based on the 1902 Moscow edition of the *Trebnik* and 1864 edition of the *Trebnik* published in Kiev, and in addition to commonly recited prayers, includes instructions for practice outside of the church and emergency situations, such as prayers and blessings for a priest to give.

56. Orthodox Parish of Apostles Saints Peter and Paul (Moscow Patriarchate) (OPASPP), *Bozhestvennyę Litūrgīi vo svętȳkh" oṯtsa nashegō Ĭōanna Zlatoūstagō* (Бжⷭ҇твенныѧ Лїтꙋргі́и во стых҃ъ ѻ҆́тца на́шегѡ І҆ѡа́нна Златоꙋ́стагѡ)/*The Divine Liturgy of Our Father Among Saints John Chrysostom* (Hong Kong: OPASPP, 2013).

57. Orthodox Parish of Apostles Saints Peter and Paul (Moscow Patriarchate) (OPASPP), *Bozhestvennyę Litūrgīi vo svętȳkh" oṯtsa nashegō Ĭōanna Zlatoūstagō / Sheng jinkou Yuehan shi feng sheng li* [Divine liturgy in honor of Our Father Among the Saints John Chrysostom] (Hong Kong: China Orthodox Press, 2014) and Orthodox Parish of Apostles Saints Peter and Paul (Moscow Patriarchate) (OPASPP), *The Divine Liturgy of Our Father Among Saints John Chrysostom / Sheng jinkou Yuehan shi feng sheng li* (Hong Kong: China Orthodox Press, 2014).

58. Orthodox Parish of Apostles Saints Peter and Paul (Moscow Patriarchate) (OPASPP), *Molitvoslov / Zhu wen shu* [Prayer book] (Hong Kong: OPASPP, 2005). The prayer book has two Chinese titles. The title on the outer cover is *"zhu wen shu"* and the one on the inner title page is *"qidao shu."*

59. For the Morning Prayers section, see *Molitvoslov / Zhu wen shu*, 6–63, for the Evening Prayers, 64–119 (same arrangement by language as for Morning Prayers), and for Sacraments (divine liturgy) in honor of Saint John Chrysostom, 120–255. In terms of pagination, the Church Slavonic text is on the even (verso) pages and the Simplified Chinese text is on the odd (recto) pages.

60. Orthodox Parish of Apostles Saints Peter and Paul (Moscow Patriarchate) (OPASPP), *Zhengjiao qidao shu* [Orthodox prayer book] (Hong Kong: China Orthodox Press, 2013).

61. Orthodox Parish of Apostles Saints Peter and Paul (Moscow Patriarchate) (OPASPP), *Zhengjiao qidao shu* [Orthodox prayer book] (Hong Kong: China Orthodox Press, 2016). Incidentally, in the same year, the Russo-Chinese Orthodox Mission of the ROCOR in Australia subsequently published a Simplified Chinese version with a bilingual Simplified Chinese and English table of contents. The title of this version, *Orthodox Daily Prayers in Modern Written Chinese/Baihua xiao qidao shu*, explains its purpose as a reference. The large font text helps in reading while reciting the prayers. See Michael Li and Elias Wen, *Orthodox Daily Prayers in Modern Written Chinese/Baihua xiao qidao shu*, rev. and repr. (Sydney: Russo-Chinese Orthodox Mission of the ROCOR in Australia, 2016).

62. Although they are titled as "prayer books," these books resemble "service books" or the missals used in Roman Catholic Masses. For a comparative example from another Orthodox Church, see Antiochian Orthodox Christian Archdiocese of New York and all North America, *Service Book of the Holy Eastern Orthodox Catholic and Apostolic Church* (New York: Antiochian Orthodox Christian Archdiocese of New York and all North America, 1971).

63. Other publications are similarly only in Chinese translation, not in bilingual versions, the *Synaxarion of Lenten Tradition* published in 2015 and a book of Easter hymns and praise. See Orthodox Parish of Apostles Saints Peter and Paul (Moscow Patriarchate) (OPASPP), *Da zhai qi jihui shu* [Book of worship for the Lenten period]/*Synaxarion of Lenten Triodion* (Hong Kong: China Orthodox Press, 2015) and Orthodox Parish of Apostles Saints Peter and Paul (Moscow Patriarchate) (OPASPP), *Pasiha sheng song dian ji zanci* [Easter hymns and praise] (Hong Kong: China Orthodox Press, 2016).

64. Other examples are the Typica for the Eucharist as performed by laity with Church Slavonic on the verso and Traditional Chinese on the recto of each page. See Orthodox Parish of Apostles Saints Peter and Paul (Moscow Patriarchate) (OPASPP), *Chinoposledovanie Obednitsy dlia soversheniia mirianami*/*Ping xintu dai shengti xue liyi* [Observance of the Eucharist as performed by laity], trans. Ambrose Lam (Lin Sen) (Hong Kong: OPASPP, 2014). Also arranged in this format for daily services are Orthodox Parish of Apostles Saints Peter and Paul (Moscow Patriarchate) (OPASPP), *Xiangchen ke / di yi shi ke* [Morning services for the first hour] (Hong Kong: China Orthodox Press, 2016) and Orthodox Parish of Apostles Saints Peter and Paul (Moscow Patriarchate) (OPASPP), *Di san, liu, jiu shi ke* [Services for the third, sixth, and ninth hours] (Hong Kong: China Orthodox Press, 2016).

65. Orthodox Parish of Apostles Saints Peter and Paul (Moscow Patriarchate) (OPASPP), *Service of the Holy Protomartyrs of China, Slain During the Boxer Rebellion*/*Erbai ershi you er wei Zhonghua xundaozhe zhanli zanci* [Praise for the feast day of the 222 martyrs in China] (Hong Kong: China Orthodox Press, 2015). The English text is on pages 3 to 36, and the Chinese text on pages 39 to 58. The Boxer Rebellion was an uprising from 1899 to 1901 that started as a popular movement against foreigners but was ultimately supported by the government.

66. Orthodox Parish of Apostles Saints Peter and Paul (Moscow Patriarchate) (OPASPP), *Service of the Holy Protomartyrs of China, Slain During the Boxer Rebellion / Sluzhba dvumstam dvadesiati dvum muchenikam pri vosstanii ikhetuanei v Kitae postradavshim* [Service for the 222 martyrs who were victims of the Boxer rebellion in China]/*Erbai ershi you er wei Zhonghua xundaozhe zhanli zanci* [Praise for the feast day of the 222 martyrs in China] (Hong Kong: China Orthodox Press, 2015).

67. Orthodox Parish of Apostles Saints Peter and Paul (Moscow Patriarchate) (OPASPP), *Blagodarstvennyi Moleben*/*Gan'en yigui* [Thanksgiving prayer service] (Hong Kong: China Orthodox Press, 2012).

68. Orthodox Parish of Apostles Saints Peter and Paul (Moscow Patriarchate) (OPASPP), *Sheng yong jing: Shangdi jiangsheng yi qian ba bai qi shi jiu nian sui ci ji mao, Jingdu dong jiao zong beiguan* [Psaltirion: in the 1879th year of the Lord, the Orthodox North Hostel at the capital] (Hong Kong: China Orthodox Press, 2016).

69. [Archpriest] Andrei Dudchenko/da siji Duoteqinke Andelie, *Osnovy Very. Prichastie: chto eto takoe i kak podgotovit'sia?*/*Xinyang de jichu: Sheng can li: ta de hanyi ji zenyang zhunbei?* [Foundations of faith: The holy sacrament—what it is and how to be prepared?], trans. Anatoly Kung (Kung Cheung Ming) (Hong Kong: OPASPP, 2014) and [Archpriest] Andrei Dudchenko/da siji Duoteqinke Andelie,

Osnovy Very. Kak podgotovit'sia k pervoi ispovedi?/Xinyang de jichu: zenyang zhunbei diyici chuanhui liyi? [Foundations of faith: how to prepare for the first time of confession?]. trans. Anatoly Kung (Kung Cheung Ming) (Hong Kong: OPASPP, 2014).

70. Orthodox Parish of Apostles Saints Peter and Paul (Moscow Patriarchate) (OPASPP). *Shouxi guiyu Jidu de yiyi* [What does it mean to be baptized and return to Christ?], trans. Anatoly Kung (Kung Cheung Ming) (Hong Kong: OPASPP, 2014). This book features Father Pozdnyaev on the cover baptizing one baby in one photo and one adult in the open waters of the South China Sea.

71. About the life and significance of Jesus Christ, see Dan Mengxin [Hieromonk Damascene], *Yesu Jidu shi shui? Zhengjiaohui de lijie: Dan Mengxin jiaoshou de yanjiang* [Who is Jesus Christ? The Orthodox understanding: the lecture of Professor Damascene] (Hong Kong: China Orthodox Press, 2014).

72. Danni'er Sishaoyefu shenfu [Father Daniel Sysoev], *Hewei qidao* [Why do we pray?], trans. Anatoly Kung (Kung Cheung Ming) (Hong Kong: China Orthodox Press, 2015). Father Sysoev was murdered by militant Islamists in a Russian Orthodox Church in November 2009.

73. Yilaliweng zong zhujiao [Metropolitan Hilarion (Alfeyev) of Volokolamsk], *Zhengjiao daoshi tan qidao: sa'er jiang* [Orthodox teacher discusses prayer: thirty-two lectures], trans. (shenfu) Aixili'er [(Father) Kiril Chkarboul] (Taipei: Kuangchi Cultural Group, 2009).

74. For example, see Duzhujiao Lilaliyong (La'erfeiyefu) [Metropolitan Hilarion (Alfeyev)], *Zhengxin aoyi: Dongzhengjiao shenxue daolun* [The mystery of faith: introduction to Eastern Orthodox theology], trans. Ambrose Lin, ed. Byron Wong and Ambrose Lin (Hong Kong: OPASPP, 2015) which is the translation of [Metropolitan] Ilarion, *Tainstvo very: Vvedenie v pravoslavnoe dogmaticheskoe bogoslovie* [The sacrament of faith: introduction to Orthodox dogmatic theology] (Moscow: Izdatel'stvo Bratstva Sviatitelia Tikhona, 1996). The translated version was by the Taosheng Press and includes Chinese translations of key terms with the original terms in parentheses and italics organized by chapter. See *Zhengxin aoyi*, 283–89.

75. Antonios Alevisopoulos, *Zhengjiao de jingshen yu lingxing* [The Orthodox church: its faith, worship, and life], trans. Stephen Avramides (Taipei: Tian'en chubanshe, 2002).

Some translations are conscious of the Traditional Chinese and Simplified Chinese scripts like the service books published by the COP. One example is the *Orthodox Mirror* by Saint Dimitry of Rostov (1651–1709) which was translated by Saint Gory of Taurida (Grigory Karpov, 1814–1882) into Chinese. Second and third editions of the translation were published in 1863 and 1913. The ROCOR Russo-Chinese Orthodox Mission in Australia sponsored the fourth edition based on the 1863 version preserved and provided by Bishop Seraphim of the Eastern Diocese of the Orthodox Church of Japan which was published in 2016. The major innovation of the fourth edition was the intra-lingual translation of the original Chinese translation's content, which was rendered in classical Chinese, into modern written Chinese. The fourth edition includes a biography of Saint Gory in Simplified Chinese only (3–4). From pages 6 to 56, each spread is divided into two columns. The left-hand column consists of the original classical Chinese text in Traditional Chinese script and the modern Chinese in Simplified Chinese script is in the right-hand column. A reader can compare the two versions or just read one side. The *Mirror* discusses topics such as the meaning of the cross, the significance of baptism, and the ten mortal sins of the faith. English is used sparingly in this text, primarily for headings such as "Forward," "Introduction," and also for each of the three parts, entitled "About Faith," "About Hope," and "About Love." Some terms of the Russian Ecclesiastical Mission in Beijing that modern Sinophone readers may not understand are explained on page 56 and the final page (58) lists the Chinese priest who helped to edit this version, but interestingly, this explanation is only in English without any reference to the Chinese-language names of Fathers Dimitry Zhang, Nicolas Du, and Michael Zhu. See [Saint] Dmitry of Rostov, *Mirror of Orthodox Confession*, trans. [Saint] Gory of Taurida (Sydney: Russo-Chinese Orthodox Mission of ROCOR in Australia, 2016).

76. Li Liang, *Liyi/Liturgy* (Taipei: Taiwan jidu zhengjiaohui, 2007).

77. Galatea Grigoriadou Soureli, *Mingtian shi libairi: jieshi sheng feng li de gushi* [Tomorrow is Sunday: a story explaining the sacraments], trans. Ivan Shchelokov, Illustrations by Julia Naumova (Hong Kong: China Orthodox Press, 2012).

78. A comparable work is a picture book about the Bible published by the Orthodox Church of Japan. The title uses *hiragana* script for "story" rather than Chinese characters (*kanji*) and the main text includes *furigana* (*hiragana* over Chinese characters) to help young readers. The book is formatted in the traditional Japanese style so that it is read from left to right. It consists of two parts, one about the Old Testament and one about the New Testament. Subsections include explanations about the "creation of the world" and "birth of Jesus" and the text is illustrated with very simple drawings in red, black, and white. See Nihon Harisutosu Seikyōkai [Orthodox Church of Japan], *Seisho monogatari* [The story of the Bible] (Tokyo: Nihon Harisutosu Seikyōkai, 1983).

79. [Archimandrite] Ioann, *Chanhui zhinan: da zhai qijian shenfu guanyu chanhui de xunhui* [Guide to repentance: a priest's exegesis on repentance during major fasts], trans. Wen Jian (Ailaina) (Hong Kong: Saint Apostles Peter and Paul Church of Hong Kong, 2006), originally published as *Opyt postroeniia ispovedi: po desiati zapovediam* [Confession construction: experience ten commandments] (Moscow: Moskovskoe podvor'e Pskovo-Pecherskogo Sviato-Uspenskogo monastyria, 2004).

80. Shanghai de Sheng Yiwang/Sviatitel' Ioann (Maksimovich) Shankhaiskii [Saint John (Maximovitch) of Shanghai], *Zhengjiao dui danshen nü de jingli* [The Orthodox Veneration of Mary the Birthgiver of God], trans. Makarios (Hong Kong: OPASPP, 2007).

81. John (Archbishop of San Francisco), *The Orthodox Veneration of the Mother of God*, 1st edition (Platina, CA: St. Herman of Alaska Brotherhood). Hieromonk Damascene's work includes *Christ the Eternal Tao* (Platina, CA: Valaam Books, 1999).

Other OPASPP and COP publications that provide in-depth theological explanations of worship include Yalishanda Shimeiman da siji [Archpriest Alexander Dmitrievich Schmemann], *Shengzhou liyi chanxiang* [A liturgical explanation of the Holy Week], trans. Lin Sen (Hong Kong: China Orthodox Press, 2015); Yalishanda (Milante) zhujiao [Bishop Aleksandr (Mileant)], *Sheng san yi jie: Shengling jianglin yu zhong shitu zhi ri* [The Feast of the Holy Trinity: the day the Holy Spirit approached the apostles], trans. Lian Qianqi, Xia Ershan, and Lin Sen (Hong Kong: OPASPP, 2014); Sheng Nikela Kawaxilasi [Saint Nicholas Cabasilas], *Shifeng sheng li shi yi* [Commentary on the Divine Liturgy], trans. Makarios (Mogeng), ed. Jingzhao (Hong Kong: OPASPP, 2007). The original versions of these works, respectively, are Alexander Schmemann, *Great Lent: Journey to Pascha*, 2nd ed. (New York: St Vladimir's Seminary Press, 1974); (Bishop) Aleksandr (Mileant), *Prazdnik Sviatoi Troitsy — en' soshestviia Sviatogo Dukha na Apostolov* [The feast of the Holy Trinity: the descent of the Holy Spirit on apostles] (Moscow: Izdatel'stvo khrama Pokrova Presviatoi Bogoroditsy, 1998); Nicholas Cabasilas, *Commentary on the Divine Liturgy*, 14th century, trans. J.M. Hussey and P.A. McNulty (New York: St. Vladimir's Seminary Press, 1960).

82. Publishers in the PRC mainland have produced some translations about Orthodox saints and morality such as Suofuluoni [(Archimandrite) Sophrony], *Eluosi jingshen jujiang zhanglao Xila* [The great master of the Russian spirit, Staretz Selouan], trans. Dai Guiju (Shanghai: Huadong shifan daxue chubanshe, 2007) which is the translation of [Archimandrite] Sophrony, *The Monk of Mount Athos: Staretz Selouan 1866–1938* (Crestwood, NY: St. Vladimir's Seminary Press, 1997).

Other books about living as an Orthodox Christian believer for Sinophone readers include the Traditional Chinese translation of a seminal book by Peter E. Gillquist (1938–2012), an American archpriest in the Antiochian Orthodox Christian Archdiocese. Gillquist explains his own experiences as a convert to Orthodoxy and clergyman in California and Indiana, and outside of the United States, in Romania. Photo spreads in the middle of the book introduce various aspects of church life and include images of religious leaders like the archdiocese primate Metropolitan Philip Saliba (1931–2014). The original version is Peter E. Gillquist, *Becoming Orthodox: A Journey to the Ancient Christian Faith*, 1st ed. (Brentwood, TN: Wolgemuth & Hyatt, 1989). The translated version is Bide Ji'erkuisi [Peter Gilquist], *Chengwei Dongzheng jiaotu: chonghui shanggu jidu xinyang zhi lu* [Becoming an Orthodox believer: the road of returning to ancient Christianity], 1st ed. 1989, rev. ed. 1992 (Xindian: Taipei Jidujiao Zhengjiaohui, 2006), with an introduction by Father Jonah Li Liang, currently pastor of the Taipei Holy Trinity Church and parish.

83. Yelusaling zong zhujiao Sheng Sufeluoni [Patriarch of Jerusalem, St. Sophronius], *Aiji de Sheng Maliya shengping* [The life of St. Mary of Egypt], trans. Makali Wang [Makarios Wang] (Hong Kong: OPASPP, 2014).

84. Yalishanda (Milante) zhujiao [Bishop Alexander (Mileant)], *Xianxing lingji zhe Yiwang da zhujiao: 20 shiji zui weida de shengren zhiyi — Shanghai ji Jiujinshan da zhujiao Yiwang · Makeximoweiqi shengping ji shengji* [Archbishop John the Wonderworker: one of the greatest saints of the twentieth century, the life and miracles of Saint John, Archbishop of Shanghai and San Francisco], trans. Lu Hongti (Hong Kong: China Orthodox Press, 2015).

85. Sheng Nikela Weiliminuoweiqi and Sheng Yousiting Popoweiqi [Saint Nikolai Velimirovich and Saint Justin Popovich], *Shengren liezhuan jianjie* [A brief introduction to the lives of the saints], trans. Xue Bin (Hong Kong: OPASPP and OFASC, 2007).

86. [Saint] Nectarios of Aegina[*Aiyina dao de sheng zhujiao Nieketali*] *Put' k schast'iu/Tongwang xingfu zhi lu* [The road to happiness] (Hong Kong: Chinese Patriarchal Metochion and the Saint Apostles Peter & Paul Orthodox Church, 2016). The full title of the Russian version is *Put'k schast'iu: sviatitel' Nektarii Eginskii* (The road to happiness: St. Nectarios of Aegina).

87. Xin shenxuejia Sheng Ximeng [Saint Symeon the New Theologian], *Chu zao zhi ren* [The first-created man], trans. Salafen Luosi shenfu [Father Seraphim Rose] and Chu Guo, eds. Yifan [Ivan] and Lin Sen (Hong Kong: China Orthodox Press, 2015).

88. Another comparable work of multi-step translation is Damashige de Sheng Yuehan [Saint John of Damascus], *Zhengtong Xinyang chan xiang* [An exact exposition of the Orthodox faith], trans. Shen Xianweizhen, based on the Greek version edited by Du Menggao [M. H. Throop] (Hong Kong: China Orthodox Press, 2015). This Simplified Chinese translated version about the proper exposition of Orthodox faith is based on volume 94 of the *Migne Patrologia Graeca* in the 58. It was translated from Greek into English, as part of the ninth volume of *The Nicene and Post-Nicene Fathers* series, and then into Chinese by Shen Xianweizhen. See Jacques Paul Migne, ed., *Patrologiae Cursus Completus, Series Graeca*, Patrologia Graeca (Google Books), http://patristica.net/graeca/#t001, and Philip Schaff, ed., *Nicene and Post-Nicene Fathers: First Series* (Peabody, MA: Hendrickson Publishers, 1994).

89. Bide Falangshi (Peter France), *Eluosi de zhanglao, senlin zhong de yinzhe* [Elders of Russia, hermits in the forest], trans. Liang Yong'an (Hong Kong: China Orthodox Press, 2016).

90. Other publications about ascetic life include the Simplified Chinese version of 300 sayings of ascetics which was not published by the COP but for which the OPASPP conducted the translation. See Kere'aozesiji de sheng cheng de Xielapiweng Dongzhengjiao chuanjiaohui, *Dongzhengjiao kuxiuzhe 300 tiao* [300 sayings of Orthodox ascetics] (Moscow: Pravslanoe missionerskoe obshchestvo imeni prp. Serapiona Kozheozerskogo [Orthodox Missionary Society of Venerable Serapion Kozheozersky], 2012) and Orthodox Parish of Apostles Saints Peter and Paul (Moscow Patriarchate) (OPASPP), *Dongzhengjiao xiudao zhuyi* [Eastern Orthodox monasticism] (Hong Kong: China Orthodox Press, 2014).

91. Orthodox Parish of Apostles Saints Peter and Paul (Moscow Patriarchate) (OPASPP), *The Icon, History, Symbolism and Meaning/Shengxiang de lishi, xiangzheng he yiyi* (Hong Kong: OPASPP, 2010).

92. Pelagia Yu Chuan, *Byzantine Iconography: The Life of Jesus by Icons* (New Taipei City: Orthodox Church of Taiwan, 2014).

93. Abbey of St. John (Community of John the Baptist), *What Do You Know About Icons?* (Kareas, Attiki, Greece: Holy Monastery of St. John the Baptist, 2001).

94. Abbey of St. John (Community of John the Baptist), *Nin dui shengxianghua you he lijie?* [What do you know about icons?] (Xindian: Taiwan Jidu Zhongjiaohui, 2006).

95. The section of theological questions and answers is on pages 127–50, prayer for icons on page 153, and the bibliography on pages 155–56 of the book. Sources in the bibliography include Leonid Ouspensky, *Theology of the Icon* (New York: St.

Vladimir's Seminary Press, 1978) and Constantine Cavarnos, *Orthodox Iconography* (Boston: Institute for Byzantine and Greek Studies, 1997). A comparable Chinese-language monograph is Xu Fenglin, *Dongzhengjiao shengxiang shi* [History of Orthodox icons] (Beijing: Beijing daxue chubanshe, 2012).

96. Xu, *Dongzhengjiao shengxiang shi*.

97. Yu Juan, *Hunyin zhi huihuang* [The Splendor of the Marriage in the Orthodox Church] (Xindian: Taiwan Jidu Zhengjiaohui, 2012).

98. Alexander (Mileant), *Danshen, jiehun huo "ziyou xing'ai" —gai ruhe xuanze?* [Celibacy, marriage, or "free sexual love"— which way to choose?], trans. Lin Xianhe (Hong Kong: China Orthodox Press, 2014).

Another kind of ethical decision is about the immorality of abortion, as discussed in [Father] Li Liang, *Mitu shuguang* [Lost dawn] (Xinbei shi: Xinbei shi Jidujiao zhengjiao hui, 2013).

99. [Da siji] Di'aonixi and Dimiteli Yiwannuofu, eds., *Jidutu rensheng zhi zhongdian ji yuan he you si* [The end of a Christian life and the meaning of death], trans. Lian Qianqi, ed. Ambrose Lam (Lin Sen) (Hong Kong: China Orthodox Press, 2015).

100. A Yi Aoxibofu [A.I. Osipov], *Cong duanzhan dao yongheng: linghun de laishi* [From brevity to eternity: the afterlife of the soul] (Hong Kong: OPASPP, 2012). The original work is

Aleksei Il'ich Osipov, *Iz vremeni v vechnost': posmertnaia zhizn' dushi* [From time to eternity: the afterlife of the soul] (Moscow: Danilov muzhskoi [Danilov Monastery], 2017). Another well-known work on the same theme is [Father] Seraphim Rose, *The Soul after Death* (Platina, CA: St. Herman of Alaska Brotherhood, 1980).

101. [Archpriest] Oleg Davydenkov, *Katikhizis: Vvedenie v dogmaticheskoe bogoslovie* [Catechism: introduction to dogmatic theology] (Moscow: Izd-vo PSTGU [St. Tikhon's Orthodox University of Humanities Press], 2000).

102. [Archpriest] Oleg Davydenkov, *Zhengjiao jiaoli wenda* [Questions and answers about the Orthodox catechism], trans. Anatoly Kung (Kung Cheung Ming) (Hong Kong: China Orthodox Press, 2017).

103. [Archbishop] Pavel / [Fenlan] da zhujiao Pawei'er, *Kak my veruem* [How we believe]/*Dongzhengjiao xintu ruhe Xinyang zongjiao* [How do Orthodox followers believe in their faith], trans. Sun Ming (Hong Kong: China Orthodox Press, 2015). This book was originally written in Russian and published in 1986, with several editions subsequently produced.

104. The content in the two languages is paginated separately, for the Russian text, including front matter, 5–90, and for the Chinese text, 6–85.

Another COP publication that addresses a fundamental tenet of the faith is Yalishanda (Milante) zhujiao [Bishop Alexander (Mileant)], *Jidu de fuhuo: dui siwang de zhengfu (jiexuan)* [The resurrection of Christ: the conquest of death (excerpts)], trans. Lu Hongshi (Hong Kong: China Orthodox Press, 2015).

The Taiwan Orthodox community has also produced several works about basic concepts such as *Sheng Baoluo lilun zhong de yuanzui* (Original sin in the theory of St. Paul), a translation of the Very Reverend John Romanides' (1927–2001) article in the *St. Vladimir's Seminary Quarterly* in 1956. Published in 2007 by the Taiwan Orthodox

Church, the table of contents is presented in Chinese and then English, and some terms are given in English with Chinese translation such as "Anthropology of St. Paul (*Sheng Baoluo de renleixue*)." See John Romanides, *Sheng Baoluo lilun zhong de yuanzui* [Original sin in the theory of St. Paul] (Xindian: Taiwan Jidu Zhengjiaohui, 2007).

105. Zhang Baichun, *Dangdai Dongzhengjiao shenxue sixiang* [Contemporary theology of the Orthodox churches] (Shanghai: Shanghai Sanlian shudian, 2000) and Zhang Baichun, *Feng suizhe yisi chui: Bie'erjiayefu zongjiao zhexue yanjiu* [As the wind blows: Berdyaev's research on religion and philosophy] (Harbin: Heilongjiang daxue chubanshe, 2011). See also Xu Fenglin, *Eluosi zongjiao zhexue* [Russian religious philosophy] (Beijing: Beijing daxue chubanshe, 2006).

106. C. H. Bu'erjiakefu [Sergei Nikolaevich Bulgakov], *Dongzhengjiao—jiaohui xueshuo gaiyao* [Eastern Orthodoxy—summary of church doctrine] (Beijing: Shangwu yinshuguan, 2005). For the original work, see S. N. Bulgakov, *Pravoslavie: Ocherki ucheniia Pravoslavnoi Tserkvi* [Orthodoxy: essays on the teachings of the Orthodox Church] (Paris: YMCA Press, 1962).

107. Xie'ergai Huoluri [Sergey Khoruzhiy], *Xietong ren xue yu Sulian zhexue: Huoluri zai Beijing Shifan Daxue yanjiang* [Synergetic anthropology and Russian philosophy: the lectures of Sergey Khoruzhiy at Beijing Normal University], trans. Zhang Baichun (Hong Kong: OPASPP, 2010). The COP also published the English-only version of another book by Khoruzhiy in 2010. See Sergey Horujy [Sergei Khoruzhiy], *Orthodox Spiritual Tradition and Russian World* (Hong Kong: OPASPP, 2010).

108. Pajiama de da zhujiao [Metropolitan John Zizioulas (of Pergamon)], *Jidujiao jiaoyi: jiaoyi de xingcheng ji zai dagong huiyi zhong de zhengyi* [Christian doctrine: the formation of doctrine and its controversies in the Ecumenical Council], trans. Lawrence Chin (Xindian: Taiwan jidu zhengjiaohui, 2007) and Pajiama de da zhujiao [Metropolitan John Zizioulas (of Pergamon)], *Jidujiao jiao 2: jiaoyi de xingcheng ji zai dagong huiyi zhong de zhengyi* [Christian doctrine, volume 2: the formation of doctrine and its controversies in the Ecumenical Council] (Xindian: Taiwan jidu zhengjiaohui, 2008).

109. Orthodox Parish of Apostles Saints Peter and Paul (Moscow Patriarchate) (OPASPP), *Zhenli yu jiaoliu (wai yi pian)* [Truth and communication (extra section)], trans. Ren Yanlin (Hong Kong: OPASPP, 2006). This Simplified Chinese publication was based on the OMHKSEA-sponsored Chinese translation produced from 2003 to 2004.

A work similar in scope and accessibility to a diverse reading audience, which is on the concept of theosis, is [Archimandrite] George, *Shengming zhongji mudi: tian ren he yi* [The ultimate goal of human life: theosis], trans. Lucia Chang (Xindian: Taiwan Jidu zhengjiaohui, 2006).

110. The OPASPP has also been the principal organizer of translation and editing of the China Orthodox Library series which includes many books introduced in this chapter, such as *Zhenli yu jiaoliu*, *Yesu Jidu shi shei*, *Chanhui zhinan*, and *Zhengjiao dui danshen nü de jingli*.

111. [Bishop] Alexander (Mileant)/zhujiao Yalishanda (Milante), *Angels: Blessed Messengers of God and End of the World/Tianshi: shangdi mengfu de xinshi shijie*

mori, vol. 1 of *Missionary Leaflets/Zhengxin xuanyang ji*, trans. Gong Lei and Ji Mi Luomannuofu [J. M. Romanov] (Hong Kong: OPASPP and OFASC, 2009); [Bishop] Alexander (Mileant)/zhujiao Yalishanda (Milante), *On the Island of Lepers and Evil Spirits at the Threshold of the Fiery Gehenna: Teachings of the Orthodox Church about God's Judgment about them/Zai ma feng bingren de daoyu shang, diyu menqian xieling ji Shangdi dui qi shenpan de Zhengjiaohui jiaoyi*, vol. 2 of *Missionary Leaflets/Zhengxin xuanyang ji*, trans. unknown (Hong Kong: OPASPP and OFASC, 2009); [Dr.] Malik, Charles/*Cha'ersi Malike boshi*, *These Things I Believe/Wo suo xinyang de zhexie shi*, vol. 3 of *Zhengxin xuanyang ji* (Hong Kong: OPASPP and OFASC, 2010); [Princess] Ileana of Romania (Mother Alexandra of the Holy Transfiguration Monastery)/Luomaniya Yilianna gongzhu bixia, *Introduction to the Jesus Prayer/Yesu daowen jianjie*, vol. 4 of *Zhengxin xuanyang ji*, trans. Ji Mi Luomannuofu [J. M. Romanov] and Yuehan Xu (Hong Kong: OPASPP and OFASC, 2010); [Archpriest] Lev Lebedev and Archimandrite Alexander/Da siji Fu Liebidefu he xiudaoyuan zhang Yalishanda, *What is Most Important/Shenme shi zui zhongyao de*, vol. 5 of *Zhengxin xuanyang ji*, trans. Hieromonk Herman Ciuba and Liang Jiarong (Hong Kong: OPASPP and OFASC, 2010).

112. Kalake Ka'erdun [Clark Carlton], *Zhengdao: Xinjiao xintu dui Zhengjiao xuzhi* [The Way: What Protestants should know about Orthodoxy], trans. Cinde Lee (Li Lishi) (Hong Kong: OPASPP, 2013), 173–76. The original book is Clark Carlton, *The Way: What Every Protestant Should Know About the Orthodox Church* (Salisbury, MA: Regina Orthodox Press, 2007).

113. *Zhengdao: Xinjiao xintu dui Zhengjiao xuzhi*, 177–79.

114. *Zhengdao: Xinjiao xintu dui Zhengjiao xuzhi*, 181–83.

115. Yue'an Weifu [John Whiteford], *Weidu Shengjing ma? Zhengjiao dui Jidu xinjiao zhi jiaodao de pingjia* [The "Exclusive Bible"? The Orthodox evaluation of Protestant theology] (Hong Kong: OPASPP and OFASC, 2009). The original book is John Whiteford, *Sola Scriptura: An Orthodox Analysis of the Cornerstone of Reformation Theology* (Chesterton, IN: Conciliar Press, 1997).

116. The translations of theological texts are significant publications for two reasons. The COP values translations that are accurate in content, use the language most representative or similar to the language of the original text, and are rendered by translators who understand the theology. Therefore, the quality of translation is necessarily higher than translations which concentrate either only on conveying the general meaning of the text or which are direct linguistic translations that do not give cultural context. These publications address a different audience from Sinophone academic studies and translations that focus on Orthodox theology as philosophy, and rather impart the experiential nature of spirituality. As introduced earlier in this chapter, studies and translations that are distinctly more oriented toward academic discourse include Zhang, *Dangdai Dongzhengjiao shenxue* and Xu, *Eluosi zongjiao zhexue*.

117. Although the China Orthodox Press has published many books, the utility of these liturgical and theological texts has not been assessed systematically. A significant question affecting the publication of the Chinese texts is whether to use classical or modern Chinese. Many OPASPP parishioners are not accustomed to reading classical Chinese in most aspects of daily life and may struggle to read liturgical

texts. When one such person told the clergy that it was difficult to understand the classical Chinese recited during services, the church's initial response was that classical Chinese is the appropriate language for liturgical text because it matches the formality and style of Church Slavonic. However, modifications were later made so that the text was closer to modern Chinese and therefore more comprehensible, but the question of whether classical or vernacular forms of Chinese remains one that the COP continues to consider, as well as the usage of Traditional Chinese and Simplified Chinese scripts.

Chapter 5

The OPASPP as a Hong Kong Community

Prominently included in many materials that the OPASPP produces for its members and for outreach to the general public is the crest of the parish which has a lion and a dragon holding up the Orthodox cross with the key and the sword below them, as seen in figure 5.1.[1] The cross, key, and sword are evident symbols of Christianity, as is the lion, but the presence of the dragon is a more nuanced element about the parish's location in Hong Kong as a Chinese place and within a society predominantly consisting of ethnic Chinese people.

In this chapter, we examine how the OPASPP enhances the social and cultural diversity of Hong Kong through its presence as a spiritual community and a hub for information about Russia and China to flow bidirectionally. Building upon the previous chapters about the Russian Language Center (RLC) as a source of knowledge about Russian language and culture and the work of the China Orthodox Press (COP) to produce and disseminate texts that enrich the corpus of Chinese Christianity, this chapter returns to the fundamental purposes of the OPASPP which are to support and nurture the expression of Orthodox Christianity and to act as a social organization which educates both its own members and unaffiliated audiences. In carrying out this composite mission of explicitly religious and secular functions, the OPASPP affects the lives of believers and nonbelievers in Hong Kong as well as the broader Orthodox Christian world. Inculturation, or the adaptation of Christian beliefs and practice to non-Christian locales and societies as introduced earlier in the book, is exemplified and embodied in many aspects of the OPASPP's role as a haven for people seeking conversion into the faith and cradle Orthodox Christians (heritage believers) who want to worship in a familiar environment. The OPASPP also contributes to the spiritual diversity within Hong Kong and facilitates understanding between individuals and groups in China and Russia through in-person contact and its media.

Figure 5.1 Logo of the Orthodox Parish of Saint Apostles Peter and Paul.
Source: Permission granted by the Saint Apostles Peter & Paul Orthodox Church in Hong Kong.

CULTIVATING NEW IDENTITIES AND LIVES: FACILITATING CONVERSION

The OPASPP invites people who are interested in learning about the Orthodox Christian faith to visit the Sheung Wan Church for an informal look around the premises or for a guided orientation and conversation with clergy and staff. Literature about the parish is available outside of the main door so that even visitors who have come when the church and RLC are closed may learn about current events and the history of the church. The standard brochure, which is always available in both English and Chinese, introduces the foundation of the church in 1934 and dates the suspension of parish activities to 1974. This brief explanation also describes the relationship between the Hong Kong parish and believers in mainland China by stating that "Our parish also nourishes the Orthodox communities of Shenzhen and Guangzhou."[2] The brochure shows vibrant color photos of clergymen, the logos of the OPASPP and the RLC side by side, two church singers, and a group of children learning how to sing. The reader can learn about the OPASPP's translation and publication projects and the RLC's curriculum as well as about the services held for worship. Some converts who identify as "Hong Kong (born and raised) Chinese" (HKC) have visited the church because they are interested in Russian culture. They are motivated to learn about Orthodox beliefs and customs because they think that Orthodox Christianity is an essentially Russian religion. Such a view may arise from their experiences reading Russian literature or visiting the Russian Federation where they saw Orthodox churches. In this section, we discuss these reasons for pursuing conversion and the challenges that they face on both the individual and communal levels as they adjust to their new religious identities and also how the OPASPP has addressed some of these issues.

Preparation for conversion is part of religious instruction which is considered as an essential regular function of the parish. Children who attend liturgical services may remain with their families but are often more interested in going to other rooms of the church where they can learn and discuss tenets of the faith through stories and songs. They can enjoy playing and studying with their peers and rejoin their parents and siblings who are mature enough to participate in the full process of worship after the service has ended.

For catechumens, or persons seeking baptism and admission to the faith, the church offers an "Introduction to the Orthodox Faith" course that the instructor leads in Russian, English, Mandarin, or Cantonese, depending on the student's preference.[3] The curriculum consists of subjects such as Christine doctrine, Bible and church history, and elements of worship. The instructor gives lectures about these topics. After the end of each unit, the student takes a quiz. At the end of the course, the student must finish a written examination consisting of fifty questions (out of 100 in a question bank) in 100 minutes. Each question should be answered concisely, in a few words or one sentence. This written examination is worth 60 percent of the student's total score. After passing this examination, the student participates in an oral examination. Three examiners present several envelopes to the student. The student chooses an envelope and after being allowed to prepare for twenty to thirty minutes, is asked to respond to the questions written inside. This examination counts for 40 percent of the student's total score. To ensure that both examinations are fair, an authorized person other than the instructor evaluates the written evaluation, and the three examiners must reach a consensus about the student's performance. The written examination is a facet developed to emulate the Hong Kong practice of examinations for advancement from one level of education to another, such as from primary to secondary school, and to apply for university admission. The oral examination is based on the Russian tradition of testing whether catechumens can demonstrate that they are mentally prepared for baptism.

Systematic education for catechumens is similar to other forms of religious education for adults. The OPASPP also offers a course for training altar servers. The twenty-four-hour course, consisting of fifteen hours of lecture and nine hours of tutorial, teaches students about the physical space of the church, how the divine liturgy is performed, and what tasks altar servers perform during services.[4] Students taking this course must participate in classes taught in English, and practice their skills in the church. Students who successfully pass the course can earn credits that will be applied to earning credentials in theology through a system that the OPASPP is currently developing. The Altar Server course is worth one academic credit, and the Introduction to Orthodox Faith course is worth two credits.

Spiritual fulfillment is the major impetus for some converts to join the faith such as "Peter," a HKC man who was formerly a self-professed atheist. Peter became interested in Orthodox Christianity because he appreciates the spiritual elements in Russian literary works.[5] He was also inspired by his first experience visiting an Orthodox church in Russia. He thinks that the sensorial experience is more profoundly moving than Protestant churches, which from his experience in Hong Kong, place more emphasis on encouraging people to join their congregations. Protestant churches, in Peter's view, are "too corporate."[6] Peter grew up in a family whose members practice different religions, including Chinese folk religions and Roman Catholicism. He learned about Orthodox Christian culture through the OPASPP and YouTube videos, especially those created by the Orthodox Church of America (OCA).

Peter completed the catechumen course after attending lectures and participating in tutorials for three months. In the final lesson, Peter reviewed the rituals of baptism and chrismation.[7] The instructor asked questions that could be part of the examination such as how one differentiates "mystery" and "sacrament." The instructor showed YouTube videos of adult and infant baptism as performed in Russian churches to Peter and explained procedural details such as what gifts Peter's godmother, a mainland Chinese female believer, would give him and what Peter should prepare for the baptism, such as candles. The instructor also explained unique features of the OPASPP parish practices regarding baptism. Russian churches require catechumens to pay set fees for baptism. The OPASPP performs baptisms without collecting such fees. The instructor explained that although Peter would undergo baptism without paying fees, he should still be prepared to treat all the persons attending his baptism to a meal or at least to pass out candies to them because they would share his joy. Another difference is that in Russian churches, all steps of the baptism and chrismation rituals for catechumens occur on the same day. The OPASPP performs these steps on separate days.

Following the lesson, the instructor and Peter reviewed the examination syllabus. The instructor posed questions about the basic tenets of the faith such as the number of sacraments and the characteristics of the Orthodox Bible and aspects of church life like how the church space is arranged and what vestments clergy wear. Many of the examination questions are comparative, distinguishing Orthodox Christian belief and practice apart from the Roman Catholic, Protestant, and even Jewish and Muslim faiths. The examinee must also respond to questions about values such as whether Orthodox Christians may believe in the existence of aliens or associate with non-Christian friends and family members. Some questions test values such as opposition to homosexual marriage. Others are very specific to Hong Kong such as why housing is so expensive and what are the major events in the Hong Kong church's history.

Peter took the examination at the OPASPP on June 18, 2017. He was given thirty minutes to prepare for the orally administered assessment. He was permitted to write notes by hand on lined paper in a blue folder but could not consult electronic media or any other reference materials. Peter was required to answer one question about why he intended to convert to Orthodoxy. He also responded to one of five questions in each of five categories: dogmatic theology, orthodoxy and heterodoxy, worship, Bible and church history, and Orthodoxy in everyday life. Each correct answer was worth five points. After the examination was over, Peter waited while his examiners deliberated. He received a passing grade and was permitted to be baptized.

Other reasons that HKC converts cite for their decision to adopt the faith include the perceptions that Orthodox Christianity is an "exclusive religion" and that it is a "traditional religion." Some converts value the requirement that individuals must renounce all other spiritual belief systems to gain recognition as members of the faith. They think this is more meaningful than performing religious practices without making formal commitments to one particular faith. This understanding is different from the common occurrence in not only China but other East Asian societies of religious syncretism and the composition of families whose members belong to different religious groups rather than following a single faith.[8] The element of "tradition" in their view of Orthodox Christianity is also appealing to some converts because they consider the adoption of a new mindset as an integral aspect of conversion, especially for persons who were not previously raised in Christian families or educated according to Christian precepts. For some HKC converts, the transition to Orthodox Christianity is important because it represents a rejection of "superstition" associated with Asian religions. Other HKC converts do not view their own conversion as a complete break from their past beliefs, but rather as the discovery of new values that are more congruent with their intended goals in life.

Another factor in conversion is the choice of Orthodox Christianity in comparison with other branches of Christianity. One HKC convert chose

Orthodox Christianity explicitly over Roman Catholicism and Protestantism because he believes that the Orthodox interpretation of the Holy Trinity is more than accurate than Roman Catholic and Protestant ones.[9] He was born into a multi-faith family formed by a Daoist master father and Mormon mother and embraced Buddhism before he started to learn about Russian history. He agrees with the Orthodox tolerance for other faiths like Islam and believes that Orthodox Christian doctrine is the most compatible with his family's religious pluralism. He said that there have been no adverse consequences following his decision to convert and has not faced any criticisms from family members or friends.

Other converts have become Orthodox Christians because of and with the support of their families. One such convert is a current member of the OPASPP congregation who will be referred to as "Mrs. Zu." Mrs. Zu had no systematic understanding of Orthodox Christianity before her baptism. She is a Hakka person native to Hong Kong who attended Protestant Christian services regularly from an early age. When she went to the United States as a student, she met her now-husband, a Serbian American, "Mr. Zu." Mr. Zu's mother arranged for Mrs. Zu to be baptized in the Serbian Orthodox church before Mr. and Mrs. Zu's religious wedding. Mrs. Zu remembers that she did not think there was any difference between Protestantism and Orthodox Christianity, and that she agreed to be baptized because she loved her husband. It was only after she returned to Hong Kong that she began to attend church services and learned about how Orthodox faith is expressed and practiced. Mrs. Zu reads scripture aloud during services in her native Hakka language and is one of the few HKC to contribute food to church potlucks.[10] Another example of a married couple in the OPASPP in which one partner helped with the conversion of the other is an HKC man and a Ukrainian woman. They met in England as students. The man started to attend church services with his then-partner and classmate, and eventually received baptism with the encouragement of his wife.[11]

The responses of family members about conversion may also pose challenges. An unnamed man from Zhejiang province whose wife is a devout Buddhist asked Father Kung for help to deal with his wife's opposition to his decision to convert to Orthodox Christianity.[12] Father Kung prayed for him and advised him to convince his wife that his conversion is beneficial for their marriage and family through positive behavior that showed his care and affection for her. Father Kung stressed that this man should not expect his wife to have an immediate change of heart. He should instead express patience and tolerance of his wife's resistance to persuade her.

Father Kung draws upon his own experience learning about and joining the faith as an adult to counsel converts. A native of Yancheng, Jiangsu province, he graduated from the Russian language department of the

Guangdong University of Foreign Studies in 1992. From 1992 to 1995, he worked in the Guangdong provincial tea trade as a manager. He then became a specialist in pharmaceuticals and from 1999 to 2012, conducted trade in Moscow. He decided to retire from business and in 2013, was baptized as an Orthodox Christian. From September of that year, he started his studies at the Khabarovsk Theological Seminary. He was ordained in 2014, an event that marked not only a significant milestone in his religious career but also in the history of the ROC in Hong Kong.[13] His native language of Mandarin has been a crucial tool of outreach and pastoral care to the Chinese-speaking parishioners and visitors to the OPASPP. As discussed in chapter 4, he also translates and supervises the translation of religious texts. In addition to producing these publications, Kung reaches out to a Sinophone audience by writing about religious matters in his social-media channels on Facebook and WeChat. His vivid writings of how he carries out his spiritual duties and pursues his own spiritual development attract many readers in mainland China as well as Hong Kong and other parts of Greater China.[14]

One of the main difficulties for HKC converts in particular and for persons of Chinese background who want to learn more about Orthodox Christianity is the use of language. OPASPP liturgical services are arranged to accommodate believers who are not proficient in Church Slavonic, which is the primary language of worship. Father Kung believes that for most Chinese in Hong Kong, praying in Cantonese and reciting the gospel in Cantonese foster inculturation, as does reading religious materials in Traditional Chinese, as done in many of the COP publications.[15] He thinks that ethnic Chinese participants will naturally feel more comfortable using their primary language in religious services. However, he also recognizes that no one language can realistically be used for the whole congregation. A gathering, whether for a religious service or cultural activity, will bring together a diverse group of persons, so even if the linguistic minority consists of one person, it is better to use more than one language to communicate with the group.

Father Kung furthermore considers linguistic inculturation as a matter of cultural adaptation. He prefers to teach the gospel using examples that many HKC can understand from their daily lives.[16] Father Kung believes that Orthodox Christianity is a multicultural, polyethnic faith, and that HKC do not have to understand Russian culture well in order to learn about Orthodox Christian spirituality. Instead, he emphasizes values that they may understand as Chinese ones such as setting a good example for one's family and exercising restraint in one's conduct.[17] He also encourages believers to communicate with him in the ways they find most comfortable, such as using the social-media application WeChat which most mainland Chinese and many HKC regard as a mode of contact that is more preferable than face-to-face verbal interaction.

Although an individual church member like Mrs. Zu does not feel that she is disadvantaged because she worships in Hakka Chinese rather than Russian, language poses many challenges in church operations and in sustaining the mission. As introduced in chapter 4, a key difference between the PRC mainland and Hong Kong is language. In mainland China, clergy can use Mandarin on the assumption that all participants in a service can understand the language. In Hong Kong, since Cantonese is the predominant Chinese language and used for official and informal communication widely in the region, Mandarin is a relatively less effective tool of communication because it is not the primary language for many prospective converts. Most HKC believers comprehend Mandarin but as non-native users of the language. Therefore, conducting services in Mandarin does not have the emotional resonance of doing so in Cantonese or another native language like Chiuchow (Chaozhou) dialect. Local (Chinese) Christian churches of all denominations generally hold most services in non-Mandarin Chinese languages, with some services in English and Mandarin. Using more Mandarin in the church could attract believers who originate from mainland China but could also alienate HKC members who would prefer to use their native language instead.

The use of English within the OPASPP community is also contentious because it is not the customary language of worship which differentiates the OPASPP from most churches that have polyethnic congregations. Moreover, although English is used for informal communication between OPASPP clergy, staff, and non-Russian-speaking visitors, much of the OPASPP's routine operations is conducted in Russian. For some members, the trilingual (Russian–English–Chinese) environment is acceptable. For others, English is less essential than Chinese as a primary language.

How language affects the OPASPP's inculturation and identity as a church rooted into Hong Kong but not just for people who may be considered as "non-local," "expatriate," or "international," is connected to the broader shifts in language use in Hong Kong. Since 1997, the use of Chinese has been emphasized over English as the main language of daily communication in Hong Kong. This development has been helpful for much of Hong Kong's current population, especially persons who did not attain English-language proficiency during formal education and for migrants from the PRC mainland who were educated entirely in Chinese. The "mother-tongue" policy in education implemented to complement the region's general principle of "biliteralism and trilingualism" has not diminished the prestige and emphasis on learning English from the preschool to secondary levels of education, much less the enduring practice of English as the primary medium of instruction in the eight public universities overseen by the University Grants Committee.[18] Despite the prevalence of English as one of the languages that most Hong

Kongers can speak in varying degrees of fluency, from knowing a few words to conducting conversations about academic subjects, many foreigners, including Russians, believe that people native to Hong Kong speak English poorly. This assumption affects how foreigners interact with Hong Kongers and inhibits the formation of close ties between these groups.

Relations between HKC and non-HKC members of the OPASPP have generally been positive on both the individual and communal levels, but the possibility of conflict within the community became apparent in one incident with lasting consequences. A person who identifies by the name "George Zhu" stirred controversy in October 2016 when he contested the Hong Kong Christian Council (HKCC)'s rejection of his nomination to be elected to the council. He claimed that he represented the whole Orthodox Christian community of Hong Kong and had received the blessing of Metropolitan (Archimandrite) Nektarios, head of OMHKSEA. The HKCC considered George Zhu's assertion to be problematic because Zhu was a member of the OPASPP and because the two Orthodox churches had not previously demonstrated any interest in putting forth a jointly nominated candidate. The HKCC decided that the Orthodox community had lost its right to put forth any candidate and invalidated George Zhu's nomination.[19] This result caused tension within the OPASPP community. Some members, whose identities were anonymized in public media sources, insisted that Father Pozdnyaev discipline George Zhu for embarrassing the church and for causing a rift between the OPASPP and OMHKSEA. At the time of the dispute, Father Pozdnyaev defended George Zhu's intention to maintain his membership in the church. Some members subsequently left the OPASPP, citing the George Zhu incident as a prime reason for their departure.

The George Zhu incident stands out as an exceptional situation within a community that has dealt with multiple cultural differences that are inherent with members who have diverse national and ethnic identities and some who are believers born into the faith and others who have converted into it. As Father Kung has emphasized in his ministry, there are many cultural values in Orthodox Christianity that HKC converts already know from the Confucian traditions that affect social life in China and other parts of East Asia. The conversion of the samurai Sawabe Takuma (1834–1913) after he tried to kill Ivan Dmitrievich Kasatkin/St. Nicholas of Japan is an oft-example of how Orthodox Christianity is comprehensible for people educated according to East Asian philosophical mores. Kasatkin averted his own murder by inviting Sawabe to hear about Christianity. Sawabe became intrigued after the first conversation and was an ardent disciple known by the church name Paul until his death in 1913, just a year after Kasatkin's demise.

Sawabe's case implies that Japanese (and by extension, those of other Confucian societies) culture, at least on the level of an individual, who eventually drew more people into the faith, could be compatible with Orthodox Christianity.[20] It could be that the samurai code (Ja. *bushidō*), often translated directly as "way of the warrior(s)" resonated with Orthodox means of self-discipline. Widely considered as deriving from values and behavior expected of warriors during the Kamakura period (1185–1333) and later the Edo period (1603–1868), the samurai code emphasizes righteousness, bravery, benevolence, ritual, sincerity, honor, fidelity, and endurance. These values are common to many religions, including Orthodox Christianity. How they are expressed in the samurai code, which embodies a combination of principles and behaviors from Buddhism, Shinto, and Confucianism, and Orthodox Christianity are certainly different. However, there are some broad similarities that may have attracted adherents to the samurai code like Sawabe to embrace Orthodox Christianity. The importance of meditation and awakening are important in both traditions. Since the samurai code is not a theistic philosophy, meditation is not to become closer to God as in Orthodox practice. As a method of cleansing one's mind and for a select few, to reach enlightenment, Buddhist meditation is like the Orthodox Christian use of meditation to build up spiritual strength through concentrated mental contact with God.

There are also some appropriate comparisons of Buddhist and Shinto religions with Orthodox Christianity. Buddhism advocates asceticism in the example of the historical Gautama Buddha. Orthodox Christians and Buddhists are not supposed to fear death but prepare for the eventuality by overcoming related fear. Shinto contributed the guiding principle of fidelity to the samurai code. Samurai were expected to die for their lords without question or regret. Orthodox Christianity also requires believers to defend their countries and to be loyal to their political leaders. However as seen in Betsy Perabo's study, Nicholas of Japan tried not to be directly involved in services praying for the Japanese emperor and the imperial army during the Russo-Japanese War (1904–1905) because he felt committed to serving the Japanese Orthodox community.[21]

Confucian precepts of righteousness, benevolence, ritual, and honor, which are familiar to many Chinese persons, are also relatable to values in Orthodox Christianity. To become an exemplary Orthodox Christian believer, a person must subsume his or her own interests and desires and perform good actions to express care and respect for others. This humanistic code of ethics is very similar to how adherents of Confucianism are expected to behave toward other members of their faith community and toward society at large. Understanding Orthodox Christianity through values that are more familiar from Confucian-influenced socialization and education helps some converts appreciate their new faith and their choice to adopt it.

A NATIVE PLACE: PRESERVING FAMILIARITY AND TRADITION

In addition to expanding access to the faith via conversion and facilitating knowledge and reception of beliefs and cultural practices through inculturation, serving the needs of heritage believers or cradle Orthodox Christians, including but not limited to ethnic Russian persons from Russia and the former USSR, is a priority that has been consistently important for the OPASPP and more broadly, in the ROC's past and present missions in China. The narrative of spreading Orthodox Christian moral values and material culture in China is prominent in sources and scholarship regarding the seventeenth century onward.[22] Albazinians, who were mostly descendants of Cossacks who were indigenous inhabitants of the Amur River region, were the earliest native or heritage believers during the eighteenth and nineteenth centuries. Alexander Lomanov describes Albazinians as "magnets" because their friends and relatives by marriage or maternal descent could be possible converts.1[23] Lomanov reasons, however, that these persons could not attract many more new believers once their personal networks had been exhausted.

The ROC also faced increasing challenges during the nineteenth century as the empire-wide mission encountered competition from Protestant missions. Orthodox and Roman Catholic missionaries sought influence and converts during the seventeenth and eighteenth centuries by discussing their faith in terms that Chinese literati could understand. Both missions were hampered by the Qing imperial government's policies limiting their contact with the general populace. However, continual presence in China was ultimately not that advantageous. Although the ROC mission provided education in Chinese to converts and trained native clergy in the mid and late nineteenth centuries, Orthodox Christianity was not as popular as Protestantism, because Protestant missions provided more social services such as education and medical treatment to a larger group of people and therefore became more popular among non-elite Chinese than Roman Catholicism.[24]

Affecting the ROC in the nineteenth century and relevant to the OPASPP now is the inherent bifurcation of a mission to serve "native" and "non-native" believers. Exemplifying this principle was that ROC choirs in the earlier era were divided into Slavonic and Chinese singing groups, placed on the right and left in the choral space, respectively. Differentiation of "natives" and "non-natives" made sense when working with Albazinians, who were in principle born into the faith because of their ancestors, and Chinese (construed in the broad sense, because not all persons would be identifiable as Han Chinese) who had to be taught to accept a faith that set them apart from their relatives and local communities.

For many members of the parish, the OPASPP church is very similar to churches in the now-Russian Federation or other parts of the former USSR. The few obvious differences often noted are that the OPASPP is not housed in its own building, which is significant because some architectural features of an Orthodox church can only be expressed in an independent structure like cupolas on the roof, and that people speak different languages in the OPASPP church instead of just Russian.[25]

These traits affect parishioners' attitudes toward the church community in different ways. Parishioners who are from the Russian Federation or ethnic Russians from other, primarily Baltic, countries, have various opinions about the church's conditions.[26] For some, the OPASPP church resembles a "home church" because it is in a commercial building. This description is generally intended to be a neutral description, meaning not only churches which members congregate in private homes but also those which are not housed in spaces that are solely dedicated for church activities, but also as a justification for why the church is different from ones they attended in their native countries. They recognize the advantages of having a physically small church, even if in a building other than a free-standing purpose-built one, such as that it is new, comfortable, and located in the heart of the city. Some parishioners prefer this kind of an environment to an old, large structure that may be intemperate for older worshipers or a physically remote location that is hard to access by public transportation. Other parishioners think that a defining difference of the OPASPP church iconostasis is unlike what they have seen in Russian churches. They describe the OPASPP iconostasis as minimalistic with Chinese elements, and distinct from the Byzantine Baroque style ubiquitous in other churches. Some of the icons are associated with China and Northeast Asia. Otherwise, they acknowledge that the church is a familiar space of worship. Upon entering, one sees icons to view and venerate. The sanctuary is hidden from plain sight behind ornate doors. There are dark brown wooden boxes that people who want to rest before or during the service can sit on. The nave is a wide-open space for worshippers to stand or kneel throughout the service. The foyer functions as the narthex. What newcomers may find unusual is that there are no chairs or pews, as are found in other Christian churches. Believers who are accustomed to attending churches in other parts of the world, may likewise notice that the OPASPP is exempt from rules about the placement of the entrance into a church to the west with the proper entrance facing north because the church is not in purpose-built space. During the liturgical services, the church is situated in a more visible, although still relatively nuanced, Chinese or multi-cultural context. Holy vessels and implements have Chinese characters embedded in their design with the character for holy (*sheng*) on the Communion cup. Vestments for some of the clergy, notably Father Pozdnyaev, combine characteristics of the Greek style and of Chinese robes. These features of the church do not have any direct effect on religious practice but form an esthetic atmosphere that differs from comparable settings in their countries.

Ritual practice in the OPASPP is also marked by characteristics that distinguish it from congregations in Russian-dominant areas. For Palm Sunday, the clergy bless tea leaves and palm fronds that are distributed to worshippers instead of silver willow (binomial: *Salix alba "Sericea"*) branches that Russian believers prepare on their own and bring to the service. Also, instead of burning the remaining palm fronds and disposing the ashes in a ritually clean place, the OPASPP retains them as decoration during Holy Week and then treats them as regular organic waste. Another distinguishing characteristic of worship during Holy Week is the use of kulich bread made by ethnic Russians in Xinjiang for the Holy Saturday services. The kulich bread is flown from Xinjiang to Shenzhen and then brought to Hong Kong.

As discussed in the previous section, language is another one of the OPASPP's distinctive characteristics. Regular parishioners are accustomed to hearing two or three languages being interspersed through the liturgical services. Although most of these participants will use one of those languages, whether Church Slavonic, Mandarin, Cantonese, or English, to sing, chant, and pray during a service, they accept that officiants will switch from one language to another or that officiants may determine which language will be the principal language depending on who is attending the service. They acknowledge that some first-time visitors may be surprised or confused by the fluidity, which may also be misconstrued as irregularity, of language usage. Although many congregations outside of Russophone countries do use multiple languages, particularly the major languages of where they are situated, the OPASPP deals with a more complicated set of choices about language than a church that adds the national language of its location to conduct bilingual services or holds separate services for different languages.

Another aspect of church life that is interpreted in various ways is the small number of congregants and how these persons interact with each other. The perception of the OPASPP as a "home church" is positive for parishioners who think that the tea reception after a service is an ideal time for fellowship. Although not all persons attending a service are interested in being part of the church community because they are focusing on the religious experience of worship, the relatively small number allows people to feel less anonymous and more motivated to introduce themselves and form relationships with others.[27] This atmosphere is different from that of a large church, such as a city like Moscow, where people will not ask for one another's contact information and may only be connected passively through a social-media group that disseminates announcements about church activities. Another persistent problem in fostering a sense of community during the tea receptions is linguistic and cultural barriers. The congregation divides naturally into smaller groups of "Russians" and "(mainly Chinese-speaking) locals," inhibiting the growth of relationships between parishioners who speak different primary languages or are of different ethnic and national backgrounds.[28] Furthermore, people of the same age group tend to associate exclusively with one another, and people who attend the church with family members are also less likely to engage in spontaneous conversations with people who attend alone.

The choir is an important part of the OPASPP and in principle, entirely traditional and similar with what many heritage believers consider as normal or routine. Choristers sing in Church Slavonic *a cappella*.[29] The composition of the choir depends on the members' schedules. Roman Kremnev and the choir director Svetlana Kremneva were the core members, singing in all services unless they were ill or out of town, until they migrated out of Hong Kong in 2018. Other members include (Matushka) Kira Pozdnyaeva, the wife of Father Dionisy Pozdnyaev, and until 2017, Ksenia Kazarina and Nazar Tabachyshyn.[30]

Learning how to perform music at the OPASPP is done in both Church Slavonic and Chinese. Choir members who are proficient in reading Church Slavonic/Cyrillic script use musical scores produced in the Russian Federation for Russian churches. Those whose first language is Chinese are guided to learn music through scores published by the OPASPP-directed COP. Adapting and publishing church music that simultaneously introduces Chinese-language natives to Orthodox tradition and facilitates these individuals' full participation in choral performance and chanting as general members of the congregation has been a complex challenge. As introduced in chapter 4, the COP published a book of vespers (vesper curriculum) in 2015. The whole book contains only Chinese lyrics with Russian included only for the titles of individual psalms. In the following year, the church produced textbooks to teach music for the hours' services. The first hour was published in one volume with Church Slavonic on the verso and Chinese on the recto of each spread. The text font is large to facilitate quick reading and the first words of each section are rendered in red text.[31] Also published in 2016 was a volume of music for Easter services, titled *Pasiha sheng song dian ji zanci* (Easter hymns and praise).[32] Similar to the scores for the Hours, the first Chinese characters of each section are in red text to guide the singer. Another publication, released in 2017, was a compilation by Nina Starostina entitled *Annotatsiia k osmoglasiiu* (Annotation for osmoglasia) in Russian, and in Chinese, *Ba diao ji: zhu ri xiao zanci ji fu zanci* (literal translation, but not stated in the actual volume: Collection of [works based on the] eight church modes: praises and subpraises for the Lord's Day).[33] This book of Znamenny chant starts with a brief introduction in italicized Chinese on top and in Russian on the bottom of the same page. For each piece, the score consists of the music with Traditional Chinese characters and Romanized Chinese lyrics below. The Romanized Chinese lyrics are in Mandarin.[34]

During her tenure as the OPASPP choirmaster, Svetlana Kremneva maintained very high standards for the choir. She is a professional music teacher, conductor and choirmaster, and was choirmaster of a church in Moscow and taught music in Orthodox church schools in Moscow for over twenty years. Father Pozdnyaev invited Kremneva in 2006 to conduct the OPASPP choir for the Easter service. She moved to Hong Kong in 2014 to work for the OPASPP as a full-time staff member. She trained the choristers individually and demanded a high level of musicianship from each of them. In this regard, the OPASPP choir is unlike many of the choirs in Hong Kong's Protestant churches that treat the choir as a means for church members to socialize rather than to cultivate vocal talent or Roman Catholic churches that solicit volunteers to help lead the general congregation's singing irrespective of musical proficiency.

Kremneva also taught several other types of courses and collaborated with the RLC to arrange classes and performance opportunities for children. She instructed parish members in group classes to help them sing religious hymns and held private classes for individuals interested in nonreligious music. She conducted music classes for children on Saturdays, holding separate classes for students who are ages four to six, and ages seven and above.[35] Each class consisted of six to seven students. Kremneva used the solfeggio music education approach commonly taught in Russian schools, including instructional materials and lesson plans that were minimally modified for Hong Kong–based students. For younger children, she taught singing through games to increase their interest and concentration.

Svetlana Kremneva also taught acting classes to prepare music plays and concerts for festivals, which happened about four times per year. Such festivals include Obzhinki, the Slavic harvest festival, for which children dress up in traditional Slavic costumes and sing folk songs, Christmas, Maslenitsa (Cheesefare Sunday) before the Lenten season, and the Slavic Literature and Culture Day celebrated on May 24, for which the RLC also celebrates the end of the academic year for the children's programs.[36] These events are important for showing parents what their children learned in the courses. Children sing, play instruments like violin, accordion, and piano, and act. For some performances, RLC teachers and some parents play roles as well.

For each festival, Kremneva set different themes for the music plays, usually derived from history or fairy tales rather than stories from the Bible or with purely religious themes, because she finds the latter too difficult for children to interpret. As the children are not professional actors, she believes that it is difficult for them to play complicated characters such as Virgin

Mary, whereas characters in fairy tales, either good or evil, are usually simple enough for kids to understand.

Like the teachers of the school, Kremneva believes that the RLC as primarily an institution that help Russian families to preserve the Russian language and culture in Hong Kong, especially due to the special circumstances of families in which only parent, usually the mother, is Russian, and as such, Russian is rarely used as a home language.[37] She also supports a principal function of the RLC to organize events for the general public, promoting Russian language and culture for non-Russian speaking people, and demonstrating how rich Russian culture can be as well as how it is different from Chinese and other Asian cultures. In that vein, Kremneva's classes for RLC students, non-RLC students, and her leadership of the children's choir "Carousel," that she founded in 2015, all facilitated cultural exchange and communication.

Since language is a crucial element of church music, inclusion of parishioners who do not speak Russian natively in the choir has been the subject of debates and experimentation in the OPASPP. Pronunciation, which influences cadence, and a "feel" for the music are significant obstacles for such persons to perform the music during services.[38] Since Russian and Church Slavonic are languages that most HKC cannot access in formal education or through work, concerns that non-native voices detract from the authenticity of the resulting sound are reasonable. However, a more substantial problem is whether church music should be performed in Chinese or other languages, in addition or in place of Church Slavonic. This dilemma rests in another issue of adaptation, which is the assumption that Russians and Chinese have very different ideas about what music means as a vessel of cultural value. Since Russian and Chinese musical traditions are so different, ethnic Chinese singers joining the church choir are assumed to have less understanding of the music altogether. Although this presumption is due to inherent, if benign, cultural bias, such a premise means that it is necessary to develop better methods to train ethnic Chinese, and potentially other non-Russian-native, members of the church choir, and that preservation of the tradition of singing in Church Slavonic may conflict with whether the church should incorporate music that is sung in Chinese or has been composed in "Chinese style." One option that has been considered is that like the use of three languages for the liturgy, to combine different types of music in each service. Another possibility would be to keep all the instrumental music in its original (set to Church Slavonic) form and translate the lyrics of some pieces to Chinese. Neither possibility has been deliberated in a formal manner within the parish.

Maintaining a regular liturgical schedule in the context of an urban society in which religious activities are usually considered secondary priorities to work and family commitments has also been an ongoing area of adaptation for the OPASPP. The parish schedule of daily, weekly, and yearly services on the OPASPP website provide detailed explanations of what each type of service entails and how long the service is expected to last. This information is insightful for persons who are unfamiliar with Orthodox Christian practices and are also helpful for people who want to know how the OPASPP church functions and can plan their schedules by noting what time a service will begin and approximately when it will end.[39]

The church's daily schedule accounts for the prayer services based on the schedule of hours: first hour at daybreak (starting at 6:00 a.m.), third hour at mid-morning (9:00 or 10:00 a.m.), sixth hour (noon), and ninth hour (3:00 p.m.). In practice, since few parishioners can attend daily services, particularly on weekdays, Father Pozdnyaev performs these services at his discretion. He may perform them even for one or two participants. There is no quorum needed for a service to take place.

Weekly services take place on Saturdays and Sundays. The parish attaches attention to the Saturday night vigil. Core members of the parish gather on Saturday evenings for this service, and then may socialize and eat dinner together. For certain holidays such as Christmas and Easter when services begin at 11:30 p.m. and end after midnight, the clergy and congregants may remain at the church between services on consecutive days because the last service on the first day is only a few hours before the first service on the second day. Such an arrangement means that one must find transportation for returning home, a taxi or private car, that is costlier than daytime or evening options like bus or subway. For members of the parish living on Lamma Island, which is only accessible to other parts of the Hong Kong region by ferry, remaining at church for these occasions can be a pragmatic option.

Services on Sundays are the most significant events on a weekly basis for the OPASPP. Since Sunday is a day of rest for most workplaces in Hong Kong, except for hospitality and retail businesses, most members of the parish can congregate at the church for worship. After a service, parishioners remain at the church to drink tea and converse in small groups. Other activities are scheduled after the service so some people may remain at church for several hours on Sundays.

Holiday seasons, primarily Easter and Christmas, involve both regular and special services. The church expects more participants in these services and publicizes the schedules through Facebook and other media. Visitors to the OPASPP website can also see when the next service will be conducted by glancing at the top left-hand side of any webpage. This corner of the header is available in all linguistic versions of the website, English, Russian, Traditional Chinese, and Simplified Chinese.

Although clergy perform liturgical services and routine rituals without requiring the attendance of a quorum, the scheduling of services nevertheless conflicts with how most people in Hong Kong work and arrange their leisure time. Services are customarily held when Hong Kongers of all ethnic backgrounds are still on duty at their places of employment. The time investment on Sundays is also considered significant for Chinese families who usually only have Sunday as the one day off work per week and would therefore like to get together to socialize rather than to worship and participate in church-centered activities. Attending all-night vigils for two to three hours on Saturday nights, and then returning to church on Sundays for one to two hours for liturgy moreover represents a tremendous commitment for people who adhere to the local customs of socializing during those periods. The parish has been responsive to these habits and their implications for attendance at services. It shifted the 6:00 p.m. start time for Saturday services to 5:00 p.m. starting in October 2017, which could help people who want to make dinner reservations for 7:00 p.m., a customary time for eating dinner in Hong Kong.

PROMOTING SPIRITUAL DIVERSITY IN HONG KONG

Preserving traditions and conventions while also adapting to the expectations and needs of its members has been an ongoing process for the OPASPP.[40] However, arguably more complex than using multiple languages and adjusting the time of services is cultivating awareness and acceptance that the ROC is part of China's religious history and Hong Kong's contemporary society. Outreach to the public within and beyond the space of the church occurs in several ways as will be introduced and discussed in this section. OPASPP clergy regularly participate in many academic events around Hong Kong and mainland China. The OPASPP maintains productive relations with universities and research institutions in the region. Since a relative minority of Hong Kong residents attend intellectual activities, promoting the ROC to a broader audience has taken various forms. One representative activity was an exhibition held in the St. John's Cathedral, the seat of the Anglican diocese of Hong Kong island about "Eastern Orthodox Christianity in China: Past, Present and Future (*Dongzhengjiao zai Zhongguo: guoqu, xianzai yu jianglai*)" from November 22 to 26, 2016. Targeting HKC attendees as a principal audience, Chinese was the main language of introducing the images and other featured artifacts.[41] The exhibition attracted large numbers from the public as well as persons affiliated with the Orthodox communities.

Since the expression of religious beliefs and the study of theology has remained unconstrained by law in Hong Kong as of 2018, production and transmission of knowledge through oral exchanges and publications about religion from an ecumenical approach have been important channels for the OPASPP to contribute a different perspective on Christianity that what may be learned from the Protestant and Roman Catholic churches that are more visible and familiar in everyday life.[42] A project that resulted from collaboration with local partners but with broader impact for an international audience was the Chinese Academic Library of Christian Thought series published over several years. The series has three components: the ancient series and the modern (sixteenth century to the present day) series, both consisting of translations of primary source texts, and the "research series" featuring translations of scholarly analytical works. The board of editors includes experts from the PRC mainland, Hong Kong, and the United States such as Wang Xiaochao of the Tsinghua University philosophy department, Li Qiuling of the Renmin University philosophy department, Stephen Chan affiliated with the theology and religious studies department at Seattle University, and Lai Pan Chiu, professor of cultural and religious studies at CUHK, and academic advisors from the United Kingdom, Germany, Norway, Finland, Sweden, Italy, Denmark, and other countries. The Logos and Pneuma Press, a division of the Institute of Sino-Christian Studies, published the series. The core mission of this press is to make texts about religion accessible to a Sinophone audience.[43] Texts in the Chinese Academic Library of Christian Thought series give readers a comprehensive understanding of Christian theology that transcends the emphasis on a particular branch or sect of the faith. Some of the translated works of scholarship are distinctive for providing in-depth references to original texts such as the Chinese version of Timothy Ware's *The Orthodox Church*.[44]

The series also reflects the different types of contributions that the OPASPP made to this publication project. For some books, the OPASPP jointly contributed financial support with the OFASC.[45] A translation of Vladimir Lossky's *Orthodox Theology: An Introduction* preceded the formal establishment of the OPASPP but reflected the series' aim to foster ecumenical dialogues and to cultivate a breadth of exposure to Christian thought.[46] For some works in the series, the OPASPP provided financial support explicitly to support the cost of translation.[47] The emphasis on translation rather than the creation of new exegetical studies for this series is similar to the "theology as philosophy" approach taken by publishers in the PRC mainland to make texts about religion less sensitive and less likely to be censored or prohibited.[48]

Another important method of public outreach that gives opportunities for Hong Kong residents of all backgrounds to understand the OPASPP's mission is by making many of the parish's events open for visitors. Special services are important ways in which the parish can demonstrate how religious culture aligns with the social identity of the community, such as the Blessing of the Waters of the South China Sea which is a ritual that the OPASPP clergy has performed on a yearly basis. This ceremony affirms the OPASPP's location and connection to Hong Kong and is also an event that brings together believers to appreciate the natural environment and fulfills the obligation of the Feast of Theophany (Epiphany) in which holy water for the parish is blessed on January 6 of the Julian calendar and then a nearby body of water is similarly blessed to represent collective salvation of all living things.

The OPASPP clergy furthermore increases the Hong Kong public's awareness about historical and contemporary relations between China and Russia, as well as about Orthodox Christianity in general by representing the church and faith to the media and at public events held outside of the church. In his capacity as rector of OPASPP, Father Pozdnyaev gave an interview entitled "The Patriarchal Visit to China" about His Holiness Patriarch Kirill's visit to China from May 10 to 15, 2013. Father Pozdnyaev, interviewed on March 14, 2013, explained why the visit was significant as a diplomatic mission and how Orthodox Christianity could be introduced to more people in China.[49]

As head of the COP, Father Pozdnyaev has also served as an interlocutor about Orthodox Christian texts translated and published in Chinese for many events. At the 2012 Beijing Book Fair, he participated in a roundtable with G.M. Gupalo, chief editor of Dar Publishing House and Zhang Baichun, professor at Beijing Normal University.[50] The discussion covered various aspects of the history of Russian books in China such as the early interactions between Russia and China during the mid-Qing dynasty, publications undertaken by the Russian Missions in Beijing, and the publication of works of Russian Sinologists in China. OPASPP clergy furthermore coordinate lectures by lay leaders such as the public lectures by celebrity Archdeacon Andrew Kuraev on November 24, 2012.

In Hong Kong, the OPASPP brought together a diverse audience interested in Orthodox Christianity and books about the faith by cohosting the book release event for the Chinese translation of Patriarch Kirill's *Slovo Pastyria* (original English translated title: *Word of a Pastor*).[51] Held at the Grand Hyatt Hotel on June 26, 2018, the event was cosponsored by the OPASPP, Consulate General of the Russian Federation, and the Russian Club. The organizers provided gift bags for all attendees with pamphlets about the OPASPP and after the event, attendees could take free copies of the book from a table near the venue's front door.

Metropolitan Tikhon (Shevkunov), bishop of Pskov and Porkhov and a celebrity cleric, presided over the event. He moderated the first part of the meeting, greeting participants with his own explanation of how the book was originally published in 1998 which was a "complicated time for Christianity in Russia." He described the book as an output of a television show in which then-Metropolitan Kirill preached to a general audience about his experiences as a pastor. The book is a compilation of transcripts from the show. The next speaker was the book's publisher Lu Dezhi, representing the Wenyuan Press (Wenyuan chubanshe). Lu described the book as a monumental collaboration between the Moscow Patriarchate and Chinese sponsors of the translation. The third speaker was Sun Yue, the translator of the book. Sun is fluent in Russian, apparent in his self-interpretation ability by alternating statements in Chinese and Russian. Sun is a leading expert on Russian culture, professor, and independent translator. Lu and Sun explained how the first draft of the translation was completed in 2015, and how editing and revising took place in 2016 with the support and advice of Russian Sinologists.

Another way in which the OPASPP enhances the diversity of spirituality and religious practices in Hong Kong is its coexistence with the OCSLE as one of two Orthodox communities. The Ecumenical Patriarchate of Constantinople established the Metropolitanate of Hong Kong on August 12, 1969. The metropolitanate held jurisdiction in China, Taiwan, Mongolia, Vietnam, Laos, Cambodia, Thailand, Philippines, and Myanmar. On January 9, 2008, the Holy Synod of the patriarchate redefined the boundaries of the metropolitanate, having included the People's Republic of China and a number of Southeast Asian nations in it, including mainland China and creating a separate Metropolitanate of Singapore. Since its founding, two metropolitans have led the eparchial unit: Nicetas (December 1996 to August 2007) and Nektarios (Nectarius) (January 2008 to present).[52]

Relations between the OPASPP and the OCSLE, which was founded in 1996, seem to have been closer in the past when they jointly organized activities. Now the two communities can be described as maintaining cordial relations but as with Fathers Uspensky and Wen in the 1950s and 1960s, coexisting and serving two different subgroups in the Orthodox population. To use economic terms, the two churches belong to the same sector of the religious market in Hong Kong and can accommodate believers of the same faith while not directly or openly competing for resources like members or private funding.

Persons who have chosen to join the OCSLE after starting their religious journeys in Orthodox Christianity at the OPASPP cite several key differences between the two churches.[53] The first is that English is the medium of worship in the OCSLE. This feature attracts a congregation of members from more diverse ethnic and national backgrounds. These people include socially marginalized populations in Hong Kong such as foreign domestic workers from Southeast Asia. The OCSLE is also considered different from the OPASPP because ethnic Greek members form a minority in the Hong Kong congregation. Another difference is that the current parish priest is ethnic Chinese, Father Jeffrey Yeung. Father Yeung is responsible for regular church and parish operations, under the general supervision of Metropolitan Nektarios. Furthermore, the OCSLE's church schedule consists of fewer services than those held at the OPASPP. Only matins at 9:00 a.m. and the divine liturgy at

10:00 a.m. are performed on Sundays, and there are few activities held during non-holiday seasons.

The differences between the churches offer some choice to believers, including those who participate in services and activities with both congregations. Jean-Michel Sourd, a French resident of Hong Kong for over two decades, feels comfortable associating with both the OPASPP and OCSLE. He attends more liturgical services in the OCSLE but welcomes opportunities to visit the OPASPP for religious and cultural activities.[54] He believes that some of the differences between the parishes are due to practical factors. The OCSLE, like the OPASPP, has a very small staff. Metropolitan Nektarios must supervise parishes throughout Southeast Asia and is therefore only occasionally present at the Hong Kong church. Metropolitan Nektarios is fluent in Greek and English, so English as the main language of the church may be influenced by his own linguistic ability. Sourd believes that the OPASPP has strengths and priorities as a religious institution that the OCSLE does not. Although the OCSLE congregation is welcoming of worshipers from various backgrounds, social exchanges are mainly limited to individual parishioners forming friendships. Due to limitations of time and individual capacity, clergy and lay leaders of the OCSLE are less invested in outreach beyond the congregation. Newcomers to the OCSLE are most likely to be related to current parishioners as family members or friends, rather than persons who were attracted to the church and faith by publicity.

CONNECTING RUSSIA AND HONG KONG

Although the OPASPP embodies both "Russian" and "Orthodox Christian" dimensions of its identity, with significant emphasis on its inclusion in the Orthodox Christian world, it plays an important role as an intermediary source of information about Russia to people in Hong Kong and vice versa, about Hong Kong to Russophone audiences.[55] It therefore complements the efforts of other institutions such as the Consulate General of the Russian Federation and the Russian Club, which were introduced as cosponsors of the book event held in 2018.[56]

Cultivating awareness and accurate understanding of Russian culture has been an ongoing process because many people in Hong Kong do not know much about it. An article about the OPASPP published on December 25, 2016 on the HK01.com news website posed the question, "Why does the Russian Orthodox Church not celebrate Christmas on December 25?"[57] Given the timing of the article, the author selected a fitting headline to discuss the topic of how (Chinese) Hong Kong people are generally unaware that there are Russians living in the region and that the Russian Orthodox community observes certain customs for Christmas which are different from those of other Christian groups. The article showed photos of the church congregation, a Christmas activity for children, and religious objects. Father Pozdnyaev explained how he incorporated Chinese elements into the church and how people in Hong Kong ask him questions about Russian politics and food when he introduces himself as being Russian. The article conveyed two messages, the first that Orthodox Christianity is like other forms of Christianity such as enacting the Nativity as part of the Christmas celebration, but secondly, also emphasizing how unique certain aspects of Orthodox Christian beliefs and culture are from those of other Christian groups. The article also cited Father Pozdnyaev's hope that the congregation would grow from its size (at the time of the article) of thirty Russians and ten local Chinese, and used two striking phrases, that Orthodox Christians constituted a *"xiaozhong de xiaozhong* (a minority among a minority)" and that Hong Kong people regard meeting Russians as like seeing penguins at Ocean Park.

Father Pozdnyaev has been a cultural ambassador by leading and participating in meeting with ROC leaders and communities throughout the world but has similarly educated people in Hong Kong about the past and present of Russian society and culture within Hong Kong. A special issue of the *Post Magazine*, the weekly magazine of the *South China Morning Post* newspaper which is the primary English-language daily in Hong Kong, published on May 7, 2017 featured interviews with Father Pozdnyaev and his wife Kira Pozdnyaeva, as well as Nona Langley (née Pio-Ulski) who was born in Hong Kong in 1947, Paul Astroshenko who was born in Hong Kong and is now an artist in Sydney, and Luba Estes who moved from Hong Kong to the United States.[58] The theme of the issue was about how Russian refugees came to Hong Kong after the 1917 Russian Revolution and formed their own community largely in response to racism and ethnic discrimination. Kira Pozdnyaeva mentioned in her interview that only one White Russian family descended from the refugees has remained in Hong Kong, and that the rest have emigrated to other places.[59]

This detail is significant not only in informing readers how much the composition of the ethnic Russian population in Hong Kong has changed over time, but also because ethnic Russians are largely well-integrated into diverse places of employment, residential areas, and social groups. Members of the OPASPP congregation live in different parts of the region. They have jobs in various sectors of the economy. Father Serafimovich is employed outside of the church on a full-time basis, so he principally serves as the co-officiant at OPASPP services depending on his work schedule. He also provides pastoral care to individual church members, such as visiting patients in hospitals and performing memorial services for the deceased. The wives of Fathers Pozdnyaev and Serafimovich also balance their careers reaching outside of the church with their commitments within the church. Kira Pozdnyaeva describes herself as a matushka (priest's wife) who contributes to the church by supporting and caring for her husband rather than by directly managing the church's social affairs.[60] After completing her university education in history with a specialty in archives, Matushka Kira, as she is known in the parish, has worked in the media industry as an overseas correspondent and freelance editor. She chose her jobs based on the needs of her husband and two sons. In 2018, Matushka Kira became the manager of the RLC. She oversees the daily operations of the RLC and non-language-related events such as monthly meetings for parents to discuss child psychology and educational development. She has also shared her interest in literature by organizing sessions for parents to learn about topics like modern Russian children's literature. Matushka Kira also serves the church by preparing tea for post-liturgy social hours and teaching Sunday School for children.[61] Irina Ustyugova, the wife of Father Serafimovich, is a full-time teacher of the RLC and organizes many activities for the parish and for the public to learn about Russian culture and language. Her significant involvement in both the ROC and Russian-speaking communities of Hong Kong has been discussed in chapter 3.

Teaching Hong Kong residents about Russian culture has been a continuous priority of the OPASPP. Ways to learn about Russian culture are relatively limited for many HKC people who may not seek out credible sources of information or prefer to learn about it through light-hearted entertainment. One example of a popular form of learning is by media such as a video featuring Hong Kong Chinese people identified only by Western given names who seem to be between twenty and forty years old by appearance and only speak in Cantonese, Artem Ansheles, a host of ViuTV's "Joyous Alliance," a program for children, introduces five foods and beverages that are typically consumed in Russia, Eastern Europe, and Central Asia.[62] Ansheles explains at the beginning of the video that he has lived in Hong Kong for four years as of the video's filming, and since he has tried many typical Hong Kong foods, he would like Hong Kong people to try Russian foods. The men and women who taste the foods and beverages generally have mixed reactions, starting with caution or outright disgust and eventually determining that something is edible or potable.[63] The group samples the fermented bread-based beverage kvas which is compared to soy sauce or herbal tea, cottage cheese/quark which is considered bearable but very sour, kefir likened to urine or other bodily waste, birch juice deemed to have a chemical smell and no taste but slight sweetness, and pickles (*zasolka*) that seems to resemble McDonald's pickles as served in sandwiches or like Korean kimchi. The video is humorous, and the participants act in a light-hearted manner, but the prevailing conclusion is that Hong Kong Chinese people could not eat the featured foods on a regular basis.

The OPASPP introduces Russian material culture through food and other forms in structured settings open to the public with events held on a one-time or recurring basis such as the mulled wine party held on December 18, 2016 for members of the parish and visitors to celebrate the winter holiday season.[64] Also associated with religious holidays but emphasizing culture over spiritual values are the events organized for Cheesefare Sunday (*Maslenitsa*) before the Lenten season. During the Cheesefare Sunday held on February 26, 2017, families and their friends of the Russian community, and students of RLC gathered at the church suite to eat Russian blini (crêpes), which were freshly hand made on spot and served with sour cream, different kinds of berry jams, and other traditional side dishes. Participants could taste Russian Suzdal Mead (a branded drink) with floral and honey flavors, sing, and dance as part of the celebration. Many children played games and participated in the workshop with RLC teacher Anastasia Kraeva to make traditional rag dolls.[65]

The Russian Bazaar, which began in 2014, developed into a biannual tradition in 2015 and 2016, and is now part of the Russian Culture Week which is jointly organized by the RLC and the Russian Club of Hong Kong.[66] In 2016, the last year in which it was an independent event, the Russian Bazaar was held twice, on May 18 and November 27. Established as a fundraising event to support RLC and Russian Club activities, the Russian Bazaar featured hands-on activities for adults and children and stalls for selling goods by local merchants. The May event took place in Soho, a neighborhood in the Central district with many restaurants and bars, in the Central district. The November event was held in the Steam Studio in Sheung Wan, close to the OPASPP premises. Most participants were ethnic Russians and Russophones who attended with their families. The RLC teachers served as primary coordinators of the event and hosted art workshops for adults and children, such as coffee-ink and Christmas decoration-making workshops at the November 2016 bazaar. Participants could also learn about traveling in Russia, buy books about Russian culture, and enjoy refreshments like homemade pies and Russian-style tea.

Events such as Cheesefare Sunday and the Russian Bazaar provide an immersive experience in Russian cultural activities with the guidance of experts. The elements of these events are designed to be fun and therefore accessible to children, youth, and adults, such as the matryoshka doll cut-out display seen in figure 5.2 behind which people can stand and take photographs.

The experience of being photographed as part of a matryoshka doll introduces the object to people who have not seen one before, and for those who are familiar with them, the cut-out display is a new and different way to appreciate the doll's characteristics. At the same event where this display was

Figure 5.2 Russian Bazaar Doll Cut-Out Board.
Source: Permission granted by the Saint Apostles Peter & Paul Orthodox Church in Hong Kong and the Russian Language Center, Hong Kong and photograph by Chengyi Zhou.

featured, there was an exhibition of actual matryoshka dolls as seen in figure 5.3, to show the esthetic differences between different sets.

Since 2017, the RLC, with the support of the OPASPP, has increased the scope of its cultural outreach with its involvement as a primary organizer of the Russian Culture Festival, which is a well-publicized event on the Hong Kong social calendar. Russian Culture Festival programs feature performances of Russian music, dance, and theater by artists invited from the Russian Federation and other countries, tastings and workshops about Russian food and beverages, and other events introducing Russian literature, film, and visual arts.[67]

Figure 5.3 Display of Dolls at the Russian Bazaar.
Source: Permission granted by the Saint Apostles Peter & Paul Orthodox Church in Hong Kong and the Russian Language Center, Hong Kong and photograph by Chengyi Zhou.

In addition to acting as a non-governmental source of information about Russia, the OPASPP has developed other ways to employ cultural knowledge to help Hong Kong society. One aspect of the OPASPP that is less well-known but critical to its beneficiaries is pastoral care for Russian-speaking inmates in Hong Kong prisons. Volunteers who visit the inmates give emotional support and distribute goods such as personal care products, foods, and books. The prison mission, led by Father Serafimovich, has been subsidized by the Rus Sidyaschaya Foundation since July 2017.[68] As described on the OPASPP website, the unofficial diplomatic significance of the mission is implied in the call for more volunteers and financial support. Many of the inmates are disadvantaged in the Hong Kong prison system because they do not understand English or Chinese, which is sometimes a factor in why they were convicted for certain crimes committed in Hong Kong, and because they suffer more cultural shock in the prison environment than inmates whose family members and friends are local residents and can visit them occasionally and who are accustomed to Hong Kong–style food.[69] The church mission helps these Russian-speaking inmates adjust and manage their physical and mental conditions during incarceration.

Pilgrimages have been another way to engendering contact and communication between people in Hong Kong and Orthodox Christian communities in other parts of the world. In February 2015, during the Lunar (Chinese) New Year holiday season, Father Kung and Father Dmitry Lukyanov, pastor of the Shenzhen and Guangzhou ROC communities, led five parishioners to Jerusalem and visited historic sites in Moscow on route back to Hong Kong. The pilgrimage, conducted mainly in Russian language, included stops at the Russian Monastery of St. (Equal to the Apostles) Mary Magdalene and the Church of All Nations in the Garden of Gethsemane, and the Church of the Holy Sepulchre in Jerusalem, and the Church of the Nativity of the Blessed Virgin in Moscow. The group engaged in prayer and singing troparia. Two priests, the chief driver, and the tour guide accompanying the group were all Russian. Similarly, in May 2016, Fathers Pozdnyaev and Kung led a group to the Republic of Georgia to visit religious sites.[70] The group interacted with local people during visits to several churches and a rehabilitation center for children. During this trip, Father Kung received an icon of St. Seraphim of Sarov on behalf of the OPASPP.[71] Metropolitan Georgy of Nizhny Novgorod and Amzaras bestowed the gift to Father Kung on May 21, after a liturgical service for which Father Kung served as a co-officiant. Father Kung escorted the icon back to the OPASPP sanctuary, and its arrival on May 28 is documented as a major event in the OPASPP's history.[72] The icon itself is important because it is a relic containing bodily remains of St. Seraphim. Father Kung's receipt of this gift was also meaningful because it reinforced his personal connection to the Russian network of Orthodox Christian clergy and institutions and his role as a cultural intermediary.

In addition to disseminating information about Russian social and cultural practices to audiences in Hong Kong, the OPASPP clergy has also integrated the Hong Kong parish into the worldwide Russian Orthodox diaspora and the Orthodox Christian world.[73] Some of the OPASPP publications have been entirely in Russian such as a book about the life and teachings of Archimandrite Peter (Kamensky) (1765–1845) published in 2013,[74] and two works by historian Vladimir Grigor'evich Datsyshen about Metropolitan Innocent of Peking and the Russian Ecclesiastical Mission in China.[75]

The OPASPP has furthermore developed its identity and public image through the Russophone media as a mission in a special administrative region of the PRC and therefore as part of but also distinct from parishes in the PRC mainland. In the *Khristianskii Mir Azii* (Christian World of Asia) journal featuring Easter celebrations in Asian countries, the description of Hong Kong is set on a background of Hong Kong's high-story buildings with the caption *V Gonkonge* (In Hong Kong) in Cyrillic and *Jidu fuhuo le* (Christ has risen) in Traditional Chinese characters.[76] The description of the Easter celebration in Hong Kong is on a separate page from the one entitled *V Kitaye* (In China) in Cyrillic and *Fuhuojie kuaile* (Happy Easter) in Traditional Chinese characters on a background from the imperial palace in Beijing.[77] Two interesting features of this division of "China" and "Hong Kong" are that both Chinese captions (sans Romanization) are in Traditional Chinese script, rather than the one about China being in Simplified Chinese characters, and that the two are arranged on one spread, with China on the verso and Hong Kong on the recto. In this format, the two descriptions are related but distinct from one another, alluding to Hong Kong's special political status and also the enduring differences between social and cultural norms in mainland China and Hong Kong. In another special section about the "Orthodox spring" in China, the focus is entirely on Hong Kong. It includes photographs of an ethnic Chinese person reading Chinese text facing the altar, photographs of the nightscape, Father Pozdnyaev and Kira Pozdnyaeva, and two signs welcoming people to the church and the RLC.[78]

Both tangible characteristics, like the layout of the church and rice-based kolivo, and intangible ones such as the values imparted through sermons and pastoral care, are vital components of the OPASPP's mission to be a religious community that serves and is part of Hong Kong society. An article published bilingually in Chinese and English in the *Bulletin of the Institute of Sino-Christian Studies* about significant dates in the twenty years from 1995 to 2015 includes the milestone of then-Metropolitan Kirill, in his capacity as Chairman of the Russian Orthodox Church's Department for External Church Relations (DECR), Dmitry Petrovsty (a likely misspelling of Petrovsky) and Father Pozdnyaev's visit to the institute on November 7, 2001.[79] This event was significant for expanding interfaith dialogues in Hong Kong, and presages the increasingly important role of the parish in Greater China as the Chinese Autonomous Orthodox Church has changed in the past two decades. Since the death of Aleksander Du Lifu (1923–2003), the last native-born clergyman working primarily in the PRC mainland, Orthodox communities have started to rely on foreign religious personnel, as well as native-born and trained clergy, to officiate services and serve as rectors, such as Father Sergiy Voronin, rector of The Dormition of the Most Holy Theotokos Church in Beijing. The rector of the Orthodox Church in Taiwan

(Moscow Patriarchate), Father Kiril Chkarboul, is also not Chinese, but an ethnic Russian of Canadian nationality. Since missionary work is highly constrained in the PRC mainland, if not functionally impossible, and official policies toward Christian institutions shift from tolerance to prosecution unsystematically, Hong Kong is more important as a mission for converting and increasing Chinese participation in the Orthodox world. Father Dmitry Lepeshev, a clergyman who has visited the OPASPP several times, believes that the currently small size of the OPASPP is not a weakness but a strength. He contrasts the impersonal scope of some parishes in Russia (Russian Federation) to the Hong Kong OPASPP which is "like a family."[80]

For individual members of the OPASPP, the impact of its existence can be felt in different ways. Converts experience and evaluate what it means to be an Orthodox Christian and the relationship between the faith and Russian culture through their exposure to the OPASPP. They must learn about the precepts and practices through systematic education, which distinguishes them from heritage believers who may be comfortable "carrying out the motions" of religious rituals and cultural customs even if they do not fully understand or agree with the tenets underlying these practices.[81] Since they may perceive and experience concrete consequences of their decision to convert, their spiritual identities and lifestyles may be more purposeful. Lida V. Nedilsky has argued that in Hong Kong, "Christianity is pivotal to individualism because Christianity is pivotal to the individual,"[82] and as seen in the case studies discussed in this chapter, HKC Christians value "transformation, a departure from previous ways of being and doing."[83] For some individuals, converting to Orthodox Christianity may be seen as an act that is at odds with core values of ethnic Chinese culture such as an emphasis on the family of birth as the primary unit of concern and respect for family elders as more important than to authorities of non-family institutions.[84] Martin Go (Go Ziran), when interviewed during his pilgrimage to St. Elisabeth Convent in Minsk explained that although his father is a CCP member, he became an Orthodox Christian after studying philosophy in the United States when he first converted to Roman Catholicism. Go believes that Orthodox Christianity has "preserved Christian traditions better" than Catholicism and has been inspired by Father Pozdnyaev who has also encouraged him to continue studying in Europe.[85]

For both converts and heritage believers, the OPASPP is a center for spiritual nourishment and the practice of Orthodox Christian traditions. While the parish has adapted aspects of its operations such the scheduling of services, it has retained many features that promote the sense of authenticity that provides security to believers who have developed expectations about what it means to worship and to socialize in an Orthodox Christian setting. Intellectual and public outreach are essential methods of expanding access to the faith while serving committed members. As discussed in chapter 4 and in this chapter, translation of liturgical texts, theological exegeses, histories of the church, and handbooks about Orthodox cultural customs is an important part of the parish's mission. Pedagogy and research supplement ritual practices and enhance the cultivation of mind and soul that are integral to the faith. Conveying values and practical knowledge about how to live as an Orthodox Christian believer has been a key component of ROC development since the earliest missions. The OPASPP has also made full use of twenty-first century media such as Facebook as a major tool of outreach since March 2010. Information about OPASPP events and posts by clergy, RLC teachers, and lay members of the parish on social media all reinforce the communal identity of the parish and the individual expressions of faith and cultural identity by its supporters.

Adaptation to local circumstances is certainly not unique to the OPASPP but is expected of all Orthodox Christian missions. In East Asia, Japanese churches have the longest, continuous traditions, minimally disrupted by political strictures on their practices. Japanese is the main language for all forms and purposes of communication. Local materials are used to produce vestments for clergy and lay participants in liturgical services. Women do not cover their hair while worshiping, as is customary, although not mandatory, in Orthodox churches. Language, dependence on local economy, and relaxation of rules that are not commonly followed in the host culture may explain why the three dioceses in present-day Japan serve a robust total population of 25,000 to 30,000 believers.[86]

However, instead of treating inculturation as a fixed process which can be implemented according to preset standards, this study has treated inculturation in this chapter and the previous ones on language education and publication of media as an inherently improvisational and circumstance-driven kind of development. Evaluating inculturation as a series of steps or objectives does not match the reality that the adjustment of any religious mission depends highly on the specific persons, political climate, and social structure at a given time. Inculturation is not only an ongoing priority but also a continual challenge for the OPASPP. Orthodox Christianity is not familiar to most HKC, so the OPASPP must determine whether inculturation means nativization as Father Michael J. Oleksa argues in his observation–participation based study of Orthodox Christianity in Alaska.[87] Nativization, according to Oleksa, requires the deep involvement of persons who self-identify and can be identified by others as natives, and therefore can add elements from their native culture into a blend of beliefs and practices that come from Orthodox Christianity as interpreted in Russian-majority communities. In East Asia, both Japanese and South Korean Orthodox churches have developed according to this model. Similar to Japanese churches, South Korean churches perform services in the national language, conduct pastoral functions according to local customs, and are largely administered by native-born clergy and lay leaders.[88] Such elements of religious organization may explain why there are seven Orthodox parishes, two monasteries, and a seminary in South Korea as of 2015.[89] Another form of inculturation which applies to South Korea and Hong Kong is what may be called internationalization based on Anglophone and "Western" (North American–British–Western European) cultural norms. The South Korean ecumenical patriarchate website can be read in four languages: English, Korean, Greek, and Russian. This arrangement is like the OPASPP's provision of content on its own website in three languages, but in four scripts, since Traditional Chinese and Simplified Chinese versions are presented separately.

This chapter sheds light on how the OPASPP has evolved into a religious community that has consciously maintained its unique identity while also contributing to Hong Kong society's spiritual and cultural diversity. The ways in which it has done so are different from the conventional understanding of Orthodox Christianity as a vehicle of political and cultural diplomacy in China. Cultural influence was certainly part of the calculus of Russian imperial expansion during the eighteenth and nineteenth centuries. Acquiring control over material resources went together with increasing the number of Russian subjects who would provide labor and allegiance to the imperial center. Orthodox Christianity was a tool of the civilizing mission to transform peoples who had been politically autonomous or belonged to other states into such subjects.[90] In practice, Orthodox Christian missions advocated spiritual exclusivity as characteristic of monotheistic faiths but made concessions as needed to gain and maintain their influence. This was true in China, most evidently in the "absorption" of Russian missionaries until 1737 as Chinese civil servants, and official Chinese imperial sponsorship until 1858 reflects how Orthodox missionaries compromised with the host government.[91] The OPASPP is not a governmental institution but as a legal religious organization, it has become a stakeholder of Hong Kong's "spiritual marketplace" and interlocutor between Hong Kong and the Russophone world.

NOTES

1. This crest is on the top left-hand side of the OPASPP's official website. See OPASPP, "Saint Apostles Peter & Paul Orthodox Church in Hong Kong (Moscow Patriarchate)." The keys and sword are commonly associated with the Saints Peter and Paul. The lion embodies attributes such as courage and is also part of the Christian tetramorph. About icons and symbols, see David Coomler, *The Icon Handbook: A Guide to Understanding Icons and the Liturgy Symbols and Practices of the Orthodox Church* (Springfield, IL: Templegate, 1995).

The parish also expresses its identity as belonging to Hong Kong through the Icon of the Most Holy Mother of God of Hong Kong. The depiction of the bauhinia flower, which is the floral emblem of the city serves as the symbol of the place. See Orthodox Parish of Apostles Saints Peter and Paul (Moscow Patriarchate) (OPASPP), "Icon of the Most Holy Mother of God of Hong Kong," Orthodox Christianity Bookstore and Library, accessed August 2, 2020, https://www.orthodoxbookshop.asia/catalogue/icon-of-the-most-holy-mother-of-god-of-hong-kong_340/.

The combination of local and traditional elements in Chinese Christian iconography has been the focus of Roman Catholic artist Wong Wing Kuen's work. Wong graduated from the Faculty of Architecture at the University of Hong Kong in 1991 and has mainly completed work for Roman Catholic churches but has trained in Greece to study the Orthodox tradition. See Tianzhujiao Xianggang jiaoqu liyi weiyuanhui [Hong Kong Diocesan Liturgy Commission], *Beauty Will Save the World / Zhu jiang renjian—mei yin tianxia: Huang Yongquan dongfang shengxianghua huace* [Beauty will save the world/The divine coming down to earth—beauty encompassing the world: a collection of Eastern icons by Wong Wing Kuen] (Hong Kong: Catholic Diocese of Hong Kong, 2011).

2. OPASPP, *Saint Apostles Peter & Paul*, 2.

3. Saint Apostles Peter & Paul Orthodox Church in Hong Kong, "CA17-1: Introduction of Orthodox Faith," Syllabus. As of 2018, two students had taken the course; one passed the course by completing the compulsory final examination.

4. Saint Apostles Peter & Paul Orthodox Church in Hong Kong, "Altar Service Basics for Altar Boy," Syllabus. This document includes the term "altar boy" because no women have been trained to serve in this role.

5. "Peter," interview, June 1, 2017.

6. Ibid.

7. This lesson took place on June 1, 2017 in Loretta Kim's office at the University of Hong Kong so that it could be observed and so that Peter could respond to interview questions after the lesson.

8. For a historical discussion of religious syncretism in China, see Timothy Brook, "Rethinking Syncretism: The Unity of the Three Teachings and their Joint Worship in Late-Imperial China," *Journal of Chinese Religions* 21, no. 1 (2013): 13–44. The study of multifaith families in China and in Hong Kong is a highly underexplored topic but is a common phenomenon.

9. "Augustin," interview, May 20, 20217 through email.

10. Anatoly Kung, interview, April 24, 2017.

11. Ibid.

Another HKC convert, "Anna," was divinely inspired through visions and motivated by the pastoral care her father received during his terminal illness. Anna's father converted to Orthodox Christianity when he was dying. Her mother converted afterward her husband's death. Anna followed a family friend, who she calls "auntie," to the OPASPP church and was moved by the complete sensory immersion into a spiritual world. She felt that Orthodox religious practice, such as the routine use of incense in liturgical services and movement of hands and body, fosters deeper communion with God. After converting, she visited and lived in Russian convents and is contemplating religious life as a nun. Anna was a member of the OPASPP but later decided to join the OCSLE congregation. "Anna," interview, April 28, 2017.

12. Ibid.

13. The presence of Father Kung as an officiant at liturgical services is significant in situating the OPASPP as a place that welcomes ethnic Chinese believers. Father Kung's ordination on December 9, 2014 was celebrated as a milestone not only in his career but also in the church's history. Father Kung became the only ethnic Chinese priest ordained actively serving in Hong Kong and in southern China. Metropolitan Ignatius of Khabarovsk and Priamur performed the ordination. See Orthodox Christianity in China, "Student from Hong Kong at Khabarovsk Seminary is ordained to the diaconate," accessed May 9, 2017, http://orthodox.cn/contemporary/hongkong/20141204hkdiaconate_en.htm.

As introduced in chapter 4, the OPASPP acquired a property in Lamma Island to host visiting clergy and pilgrims in September 2013. This property, a residential space with two bedrooms and a living room, was useful for arranging Father Kung's tenure as a member of the OPASPP clergy because he resides there when he is in Hong Kong for regular and holiday liturgical services.

14. Father Kung's social-media accounts are accessible through customary search engines, so they are not explicitly listed here. Greater China here refers to Hong Kong, Macau, Taiwan, and ethnic Chinese communities in areas outside of the PRC and the ROC.

15. Ibid.

16. Ibid.

17. Ibid.

18. Although Cantonese is the most common Chinese language used in Hong Kong, it does not have the same status as Modern Standard Chinese (*Putonghua*) and English. See Lee Kwai Sang and Leung Wai Mun, "The Status of Cantonese in the Education Policy of Hong Kong," *Multilingual Education* 2, no. 2 (2012), https://link.springer.com/content/pdf/10.1186%2F10.1186%2F2191-5059-2-2.pdf.

19. Most of the open-access sources about this incident have now been removed from the provider websites. One link that was current as of the time this book was written is Chi Wing Sin, "Xiejinhui tu zhuandai, Dongzhengjiao bei quxiao timing zige" [The Hong Kong Christian Council's sudden change, Orthodox Christianity loses its right to nominate], In Media HK, October 25, 2016, accessed March 29, 2018, http://www.inmediahk.net/node/1045394.

20. See Julia Ching, *Confucianism and Christianity: A Comparative Study* (Tokyo: Kodansha, 1978).

21. See Betsy Perabo, *Russian Orthodoxy and the Russo-Japanese War* (Bloomsbury, 2017).

22. For descriptions of Orthodox Christianity as a faith in China in addition to ones cited in previous chapters, see (Hieromonk) Damascene, "Appendix I: Eastern Orthodox Christianity in China," *Christ the Eternal Tao* (Platina, CA: Valaam Books, 1999), 427–44 and Zhang Sui, *Dongzhengjiao he Dongzhengjiao zai Zhongguo* [Orthodox Christianity and Orthodox Christianity in China] (Shanghai: Xuelin chubanshe, 1986). To contextualize the specific experiences in China with

contemporaneous missions, see Alexander Schmemann, *The Historical Road of Eastern Orthodoxy*, trans. Lydia W. Kesich (New York: Holt, Rinehart and Winston, 1963); Stamoolis, *Eastern Orthodox Mission Theology Today*; and Michael Angold, ed., *The Cambridge History of Christianity, vol. 5: Eastern Christianity* (Cambridge: Cambridge University Press, 2006).

23. Alexander Lomanov, "Russian Orthodox Church (Late Qing China)," in *Handbook of Christianity in China, Volume Two: 1800 to the Present*, ed. R.G. Tiedemann (Leiden and Boston: Brill, 2010), 203.

24. Ibid., 207–09.

25. Roman Kremnev, interview, July 6, 2017.

26. Group interview, May 29, 2017. This group included Alexander Dmitrenko, then-PhD candidate of the City University of Hong Kong from Riga, Latvia; Polina Sarafanova, a graduate of the University of Hong Kong and employed in Hong Kong from Moscow; Polina Malkova, then-PhD candidate of The Chinese University of Hong Kong; Dayana Samantseva from Kiev, Ukraine.

27. Dayana Samantseva, part of group interview, May 29, 2017.

28. Alexander Dmitrenko, part of group interview, May 29, 2017.

29. For a concise history and description of Orthodox church music, see Hallick, *Treasured Traditions and Customs*, 21.

30. Ksenia Kazarina resigned from the choir in 2017 when she moved away from Hong Kong because her husband transferred to a job in another place. Nazar Tabachyshyn resigned from his part-time post in the choir due to other commitments.

31. See OPASPP, *Dimu ke*, and OPASPP, *Xiangchen ke / di yi shi ke*. As cited in chapter 4, scores for the third, sixth, and ninth hours were compiled and published in another volume. See OPAASPP, *Di san, liu, jiu shi ke*.

32. OPASPP, *Pasiha sheng song dian ji zanci*.

33. OPASPP, *Annotatsiia k osmoglasiiu*.

34. Given that native speakers of Mandarin significantly outnumber those of Cantonese among ethnic Chinese persons worldwide, these texts are more useful for a greater number of Chinese-speaking people with Mandarin lyrics. However, the actual inclusion of Romanization is interesting because most hymnals in Hong Kong's Christian churches only have Chinese character lyrics. Singers can choose whether to pronounce the characters in Cantonese, Mandarin, or another Chinese spoken language.

35. The OPASPP subsidizes these classes so students do not have to pay tuition fees to participate. The church and RLC charges admissions fees for some performances by children.

36. The Slavic Literature and Culture Day, also known as the Slavonic Literature and Culture Day, is the feast day of Saints Cyril (826–869) and Methodios (815–885), two brothers who are also known as "Apostles to the Slavs" for their work as missionaries to Slavic peoples. See Hallick, *Treasured Traditions and Customs*, 80–81.

37. Svetlana Kremneva, interview, June 24, 2017, Russian Orthodox Church, Sheung Wan, Hong Kong.

38. It is also a point of contention that the use of English and Chinese are discouraged for certain aspects of the service such as the recitation of the Credo, as well as

the singing of some songs. Such a restriction causes discontent in with HKC and other ethnic Chinese worshipers who feel they cannot learn how to pronounce the original versions.

39. Orthodox Parish of Apostles Saints Peter and Paul (Moscow Patriarchate) (OPASPP), "Schedule of Services," revised regularly, https://orthodoxy.hk/schedule.

40. Other religious groups in Hong Kong that do not have roots in Chinese culture also make accommodations and selectively follow "local" (Chinese) customs. Few Parsis employ *feng shui* masters when arranging new spaces like offices and cemeteries but some have done so to confirm that their plans are propitious. See John R. Hinnells, "The Parsis in Hong Kong and the China Seas," in *The Zoroastrian Diaspora: Religion and Migration* (Oxford: Oxford University Press, 2005), 187.

41. Orthodox Parish of Apostles Saints Peter and Paul (Moscow Patriarchate) (OPASPP), "Dongzhengjiao zai Zhongguo tupian zhan [Photo exhibition of Eastern Orthodox Christianity in China], accessed March 7, 2017, https://orthodoxy.hk/hk/news/2016-11-28/fotovystavka_o_pravoslavii_v_kitae.

42. The currently small scope of the field of research about Orthodox Christianity in Hong Kong is proportionate to the relatively few scholars interested and able to research Orthodox Christianity in China due to limitations of language and access to sources. For a rare work of scholarship produced in Hong Kong about this subject, see Liu and Yang, "Dongzhengjiao zai Huaren shehui de fazhan."

By comparison, Protestant and Roman Catholic Christianity are popular topics in the social and cultural history of Hong Kong because there are substantial and easily accessible repositories of sources about them in Hong Kong like the Hong Kong Baptist University (HKBU). See Hong Kong Baptist University (HKBU), "Archives on the History of Christianity in China," accessed April 29, 2017, https://library.hkbu.edu.hk/collections/special-collections-archives/archives-on-the-history-of-christianity-in-china.

43. About the Institute of Sino-Christian Studies and its subunits, see Institute of Sino-Christian Studies, "Yanjiusuo jianjie" [Introduction to the Institute of Sino-Christian Studies], accessed January 21, 2021, https://www.iscs.org.hk/Common/Reader/Channel/ShowPage.jsp?Cid=14&Pid=2&Version=0&page=0.

44. Wei'er [Timothy Ware], *Dongzheng jiaohui daolun* [Doctrine of the Orthodox Church], trans. Tian Yuan (Hong Kong: The Logos and Pneumas Press, 2013). The original version is Timothy Ware, *The Orthodox Church* (Harmondsworth, Middlesex: Penguin Books 1963).

45. These publications include Yuehan Kelimakesi [John Climacus], *Shensheng pandeng de tianti* [The ladder of divine ascent], trans. Xue Liemin (Hong Kong: The Logos and Pneuma Press, 2012), the translation of John Climacus, *The Ladder of Divine Ascent* (Boston: Holy Transfiguration Monastery, 1979); Meiyanduofu [Jean Meyendorff], *Baizanting shenxue zhong de Jidu* [Le Christ dans la théologie byzantine], trans. Tan Lizhu (Hong Kong: The Logos and Pneuma Press, 2011), the translation of Jean Meyendorff, *Le Christ dans la théologie byzantine* (Paris: Cerf, 1969); Fuluoluofusiji [Georges Florovsky], *Jidujiao yu wenhua* [Christianity and Culture], trans. Li Shuqin (Hong Kong: The Logos and Pneuma Press, 2009), the translation of Georges Florovsky, *Christianity and Culture*, vol. 2, *Collected Works of Georges Florovsky* (Boston: Nordland Publishing Company, 1974).

46. Luosiji [Vladimir Lossky], *Dongfang shenxue daolun* [Orthodox theology, an introduction], trans. Yang Deyou (Hong Kong: The Logos and Pneuma Press, 1997). The original work is Vladimir Lossky, *Orthodox Theology: An Introduction* (Crestwood, NY: St. Vladimir's Seminary Press, 1989).

47. An example is Palikan [Jaroslav Pelikan], *Jidujiao chuantong (juan er)—dongfang Jidujiao shijie de jingshen* [The Christian tradition, volume 2—the spirit of Eastern Christendom (600–1700)], trans. Sha Mei (Hong Kong: The Logos and Pneuma Press, 2009), the translation of Jaroslav Pelikan, *The Christian Tradition: A History of the Development of Doctrine, Volume 2: The Spirit of Eastern Christendom (600–1700)* (Chicago: University of Chicago Press, 1971).

48. In addition to texts cited in chapter 4, some examples include (gu Luoma) Aogusiding [St. Augustine of ancient Rome], *Chanhui lu* [Confessions], trans. Ren Xiaojin, Wang Aiju, and Pan Yusha (Beijing: Guangming ribao chubanshe, 2007); [gu Luoma] Anboluoxiu [St. Ambrose of ancient Rome], *Lun Jidujiao xinyang* [Exposition of the Christian faith], trans. Yang Lingfeng, ed. Luo Yufang (Beijing: Sanlian shudian, 2010); [gu Luoma] Youxibiwu [St. Eusebius (of Caesarea)], *Jiaohui shi* [Church history], original translation and commentary by Paul L. Maier, trans. Qu Xutong (Beijing: Sanlian shudian, 2012), adapted from Paul L Maier, *Eusebius: The Church History* (Grand Rapids, MI: Kregel Publications, 1999).

49. Maria Senchukova, "The Patriarchal Visit to China: An Interview with Fr. Dionisy Pozdnyaev," *Pravmir*, May 16, 2013, accessed January 29, 2017, http://www.pravmir.com/the-patriarchal-visit-to-china-an-interview-with-fr-dionisy-pozdnyaev.

50. Nina Tkachuk Dimas, trans., "Orthodox Publications in Chinese Presented at Beijing Book Fair," Orthodox Christianity in China, September 3, 2012, accessed February 8, 2017, http://orthodox.cn/contemporary/beijing/20120903beijing_en.htm.

51. The original book is Kirill, *Slovo pastyria: Bog i chelovek; Istoriia spaseniia; Besedy o pravoslavnoi vere* [The word of the pastor: God and man, the history of salvation, conversations about the Orthodox faith] (Moscow: Moskovskaia Patriarkhiia Ruskoi Pravoslavnoi Tserkvi [Moscow: Moscow Patriarchate of the Russian Orthodox Church], 2004). The Chinese translation is Kirill, *Mushou jiyu* [Word of a pastor] (Beijing: Wenyuan chubanshe, 2018). For related media coverage, see Department for External Church Relations (DECR), "Chinese edition of His Holiness Patriarch Kirill's book Word of a Pastor presented in Hong Kong," June 26, 2018, accessed July 1, 2018, https://mospat.ru/en/2018/06/26/news161375 and *Ta Kung Pao*, "E da mushou zai Xianggang ban xin shu shou fa shi" [Russian high-ranking priest holds a new book launch ceremony in Hong Kong], June 27, 2018, accessed July 1, 2018, http://www.takungpao.com.hk/international/text/2018/0627/180349.html.

52. Demetrius Kiminas, *The Ecumenical Patriarchate: A History of Its Metropolitanates with Annotated Hierarch Catalogs* (Cabin John, MD: The Borgos Press/Wildside Press, 2009), 146. About the current OSCLE community, see Orthodox Church in Hong Kong, Saint Luke Orthodox Cathedral, accessed March 03, 2021, http://www.omhksea.org/metropolis-of-hong-kong/hong-kong/ and http://orthodox.cn/contemporary/omhksea_en.htm.

53. "Anna," interview, April 28, 2017.

Father Kung acknowledges that people may attend OPASPP services for some purposes and OCSLE services for other reasons, and that since both churches are Orthodox Christian, clergy should not monitor or interfere with these choices. Anatoly Kung, interview, April 24, 2017.

54. Jean-Michel Sourd, interview, May 10, 2017.

55. We thank Phillip Calington for his valuable observation that the OPASPP is foremost an Orthodox Christian institution and community, rather than being more narrowly or exclusively "Russian Orthodox Christian."

56. About the Consulate General, see Consulate General of the Russian Federation in the Hong Kong SAR, PRC (official website), accessed November 10, 2017, https://hongkong.mid.ru/web/hongkong-en, and for Russian-literate users, General'noe konsul'stvo Rossiiskoi Federatsii v Spetsial'nom administrativnom raione Gonkong KNR [Consulate General of the Russian Federation in the Hong Kong SAR, PRC] (official website), accessed November 10, 2017, http://hongkong.mid.ru. About the Russian Club, see "Russian Club in Hong Kong," accessed November 10, 2017, http://www.russianclubhk.org/en and for Russian-literate users, Russkii klub v Gonkonge [Russian Club in Hong Kong] (official website), accessed November 10, 2017, http://www.russianclubhk.org.

57. Chan Tsz Wai, "'Tamen de Shengdanjie': shangsha zhong bashi zai de E Dongzheng jiaohui Shengdanjie bushi shi'er yue ershiwu ri? ['Their Christmas': 80 years of Russian Orthodox Church in a commercial building; Why is Christmas not celebrated on 25th December?], Community, HK01, December 25, 2016, accessed January 7, 2017https://www.hk01.com/sns/article/62153.

58. For the Pozdnyaev and Pozdnyaeva interviews, see Stuart Heaver, "The White Tide," *Post Magazine*, May 7, 2017, 12–15. About Nona Langley's experience, see chapter 2 of this book.

59. "The White Tide," 15.

60. Kira Pozdnyaeva, interview, February 12, 2019.

61. For praise of Kira Pozdnyaeva's contributions to the parish, see Piotr Adamek, "'Unworthy to Be Quoted among the Believers—Worthy to be Quoted among the Martyrs': Women in the Orthodox Church in China," *Religions & Christianity in Today's China* volume 8, no. 4 (2017): 25–33.

62. Ansheles maintains an active presence on social media through his own webpage, YouTube channel, and Facebook page. He has produced a series of videos about Russians living in Hong Kong. See "Artem Ansheles (website)," accessed March 13, 2017, http://ansheles.com/eng, "Artem Ansheles (YouTube channel)," accessed March 13, 2017, https://www.youtube.com/user/Kalendorable, and "Artem Ansheles (Facebook page)," accessed March 13, 2017, https://www.facebook.com/anshelesartem. See also "Eluosi nanhai Xianggang di zhuimeng" [Russian boy chasing dreams in Hong Kong], *Ming Pao*, May 12, 2016, http://news.mingpao.com/pns/dailynews/web_tc/article/20160512/s00011/1462990204930 and "Kan shijie: Eluosi yishu xiaozi zai gang cachu huohua" [See the world: Russian art boy sparks in Hong Kong], *Ming Pao*, May 12, 2016, http://news.mingpao.com/pns/dailynews/web_tc/article/20160512/s00011/1462990206131.

63. Artem Ansheles, "Xianggangren shi shi qiguai de Eluosi shiwu!," [The People of Hong Kong Try to Eat the Strange Russian Food!], YouTube video, 6:20, accessed October 26, 2016, https://www.youtube.com/watch?v=2ugpFlrQEd8.

64. Information and a post-event report about the mulled wine party was available right after it took place but was removed from the website after about two months. The link was "Mulled Wine Party (Facebook)," accessed January 2, 2017, https://www.facebook.com/groups/107977518685/permalink/101547769550286.

65. "Cheesefare Sunday (Maslenitsa) (Facebook)," accessed March 13, 2017, https://www.facebook.com/events/415658958770919/permalink/420602504943231.

66. About the 2015 event, see "Russian Bazaar," accessed May 9, 2018, http://www.russianclubhk.org/en/russian-bazaar. About the 2016 event, see "Russian Bazaar (Facebook page)."

67. "Russian Culture Festival," accessed November 29, 2019, http://www.russianclubhk.org/en/category/russian-culture-festival.

68. For information about the foundation, see "Rus' sidiashchaia" [Russia behind bars], accessed November 24, 2017, https://zekovnet.ru.

69. Orthodox Parish of Apostles Saints Peter and Paul (Moscow Patriarchate) (OPASPP), "Prison Mission," accessed November 20, 2017, https://orthodoxy.hk/projects/prison_mission.

70. Denis (Dionisy) Pozdnyaev, "Nachnem nashe palomnichestvo. Gospodi, blagoslovi!" [Let's start our pilgrimage. God bless!], Facebook, May 12, 2016, https://www.facebook.com/photo.php?fbid=10154737843713238&set=a.10150373961628238&type=3&theater, and "Pervyi za 60 let – kak korennoi kitaets stal pravoslavnym sviashchennikom" [The first in 60 years—how a native Chinese became an Orthodox priest], *Pravoslavnoe Khristianstvo* [Orthodox Christianity] (blog), December 7, 2016, https://pravoslavnoe-hristianstvo.mirtesen.ru/blog/43816009885/Pervyiy-za-60-let-%E2%80%93-kak-korennoy-kitayets-stal-pravoslavnyim-svy?nr=1&utm_referrer=mirtesen.ru.

71. Orthodox Parish of Apostles Saints Peter and Paul (Moscow Patriarchate) (OPASPP), "Icon of St. Seraphim of Sarov with a part of the remains of the saint has been gifted to the Hong Kong parish," accessed December 13, 2019, https://orthodoxy.hk/news/2016-05-28/icon_of_st._seraphim_of_sarov.

72. Ibid.

73. About the Russian Orthodox diaspora, see Burlacioiu, "Russian Orthodox Diaspora," 4–24.

74. Vladimir Grigor'evich (V.G) Datsyshen and Anton Borisovich Chegodaev, *Arkhimandrit Petr (Kamenskii)* [Archimandrite Peter (Kamensky)] (Hong Kong: OPASPP, 2013).

75. Vladimir Grigor'evich (V.G.) Datsyshen, *Istoriia Rossiiskoi dukhovnoi missii v Kitae* [History of the Russian Spiritual Mission in China] (Hong Kong: OPASPP, 2010) and Datsyshen, *Mitropolit Pekinskii Innokentii*.

76. The whole special section is "Paskha v stranakh Azii [Easter in Asia]," *Khristianskii Mir Azii* (Christian World of Asia) (April 2016), 6–11. The article about Hong Kong is "V Gonkonge Jidu fuhuo le" [In Hong Kong Christ has risen], *Khristianskii Mir Azii* [Christian World Asia] (May 2016): 11. This section includes descriptions of Easter celebrations in Korea, Japan, and Cambodia.

77. "V Kitae Fuhuojie kuaile" [In China Happy Easter], *Khristianskii Mir Azii* [Christian World Asia] (May 2016): 10.

78. *Kitai. Vesna Pravoslaviia. Zhongguo Dongzhengjiao de chuntian* [China. Orthodox spring.], *Foma: Pravoslavnyi zhurnal dlia somnevaiushchikhsia* [Thomas: Orthodox magazine for doubters] 119, no. 3 (March 2013): 17–27.

79. Daniel H. N. Yeung, Ho Lai Yung, and Jason T. S. Lam, eds., *Hanyu Jidujiao wenhua yanjiusuo tongxun* [Bulletin of the Institute of Sino-Christian Studies], *er shi zhou nian jinian tekan* (1995–2015) [special issue to commemorate the 20th year anniversary (1995–2015)] (Spring 2016).

80. Dmitry Lepeshev, interview, April 21, 2017, through email.

81. The authors acknowledge that there are tremendous variations in the theoretical interpretation and practice of Orthodox Christian spirituality, even by heritage believers. See Sonja Luehrmann, ed., *Praying with the Senses: Contemporary Orthodox Christian Spirituality in Practice* (Bloomington, IN: Indiana University Press, 2017), especially Vlad Naumescu, "Becoming Orthodox: The Mystery and Mastery of a Christian Tradition," 29–53.

82. Nedilsky, *Converts to Civic Society*, 33.

83. Ibid., 50.

84. These values and other principles are often considered as facets of "Confucian culture," but interpreted at variation with the formal precepts of Confucian (Ruist) philosophy.

85. Yanchuk, "The Visitor of St. Elisabeth Convent."

86. About past and current practices of the Japanese Russian Orthodox Church, see Van Remortel and Chang, eds., *St. Nikolai Kasatkin*.

87. Oleksa, *Orthodox Alaska*, chapter 7, 143–68. Father Oleksa is married to a member of the Yup'ik tribe native to Alaska and has served in Alaska for over thirty-five years.

88. See, for example, "Ecumenical Patriarchate / Orthodox Metropolis of Korea," accessed June 2, 2017, https://www.orthodoxkorea.org/home. For concise, summative explanations of how Korean Orthodox Christianity has developed, see Stamoolis, *Eastern Orthodox Mission Theology Today*, 42–43.

89. Ware, *The Orthodox Church*, 183.

90. Regarding the origins and objectives of the Russian civilizing mission, see Ricarda Vulpius, "The Russian Empire's Civilizing Mission in the Eighteenth Century: A Comparative Perspective," in *Asiatic Russia: Imperial Power in Regional and International Contexts*, ed. Uyama Tomohiko (Abingdon, Oxon; New York: Routledge, 2012), 13–31.

91. See Nikolai, *Pravoslavnaia missiia v Kitae*; Widmer, *The Russian Ecclesiastical Mission*; Dina V. Doubrovskaia, "The Russian Orthodox Church in China," in *China and Christianity: Burdened Past, Hopeful Future*, Stephen Uhalley and Xiaoxin Wu (London and New York: Routledge, 2001), 163–76; and Datsyshen, *Istoriia Rossiiskoi dukhovnoi missii v Kitae*.

Epilogue

The study of contemporary history is less conductive to developing conclusions and more suitable to provide some informed prognostication about what lies ahead in the evolving future. The OPASPP and the ROC community of Hong Kong, as encompassing the stakeholders and beneficiaries of the RLC and COP who live in the region but may not be members of the parish, have continued to develop since the ending point for this book in 2018. Several factors have affected these processes, not least the COVID-19 pandemic which has constrained many aspects of daily life in Hong Kong.[1] Instead of scrutinizing this most recent segment of contemporary history, we return to the three areas of significance that motivated us to start this research and to shed light on why this case study, set in the geographical and political periphery of the PRC matters for questions that affect and draw comparisons with other examples within and outside of China.

To start our reflection, we consider two different interpretations about the future of Orthodox Christianity in China. The first is that it is endangered and may disappear. This message is evident in how limited the number of Orthodox Christian churches are in the PRC mainland as of 2020. Churches in Ergune, Urumqi, Ili, and Harbin (particularly the Pokrovsky Cathedral) are among the few hubs of religious and social life for Orthodox Christians.[2] The second interpretation is the opposite but also symbiotic with the first, in that the numbers of churches and their members are not as important as what may be seen as evidence of revival. The current Ergune church was built from the vestiges of the St. Innocent of Irkutsk Church, which was one of eighteen ROC churches that were historically in the area and was consecrated and visited by Patriarch Kirill in 2009. Ten years later, in 2019, Father Pavel Sun Ming returned from his ordination to the church in time for the Pascha midnight service.[3] Father Sun's leadership of the congregation, which is legally bound not to admit new members through conversion, is significant because the church is able to conduct services and sustain the cultural life of the community, two functions which were greatly limited for many years without a priest in residence.

Likewise, our goal for this book has been to demonstrate the OPASPP is important in and of itself, without comparison to any other religious organization in or outside of Hong Kong, and also that the understanding of Orthodox Christianity in China must be broadened and connected to fields other than theology, missiology, and anthropology in which significant contributions have been made. Our perspective as historians elucidates that the OPASPP and the preceding ROC communities of the 1930s through 1970 have been underexamined in connection to Sino-Russian relations and more severely, perhaps by passive omission, in the multidisciplinary fields of Christianity in China and of Religious and Ethnic Diversity in Hong Kong.

We reaffirm that there are as yet distinct differences in legal and political structures, and the social composition of Hong Kong and other parts of China. Therefore, this study shows a particular facet of Orthodox Christianity and about Christianity in general in China. However, the Hong Kong ROC is important in understanding how Christian communities and culture can develop in an environment if PRC citizens have less restrictions on producing and disseminating knowledge and expressing their religious ideas.[4] At the same time, we understand that the ROC community in Hong Kong, as well as other religious groups, will depend on how Hong Kong changes as mainlandization affects the regional government and society's capacity to maintain its autonomy from direct administrative control by the PRC central government.[5]

In light of evidence presented in this book, it is possible to infer that the OPASPP and other ROC communities in China do and will contribute to Sino-Russian relations. The OPASPP clergy play crucial roles in fostering interactions for religious, social, and academic purposes. The OPASPP and its arms, the RLC and the COP, are among the few sources that Hong Kong residents have to learn about Russian culture. It is also vital for Sino-Russian relations that Russians and Chinese can literally come together at religious services and at gatherings such as the cultural events hosted by the community.

Also looking beyond Sino-Russian relations on a state-to-state level, as Christianity becomes more significant in regions that are politically and culturally Chinese, Russian Orthodox Christianity may play a greater role in shaping beliefs and practices of adherents of various backgrounds. As of 2016, estimates of Christians in the PRC include the Protestant Christian population, approximating 20–83.5 million,[6] Roman Catholic population 5.7–10 million,[7] and Orthodox Christian believers (not differentiating between branches) 15,000.[8] The relative smallness of the Orthodox population may account for the tidy figure, but also because Orthodox Christian believers are largely clustered in specific parts of China, including Beijing, Shanghai, Heilongjiang, Inner Mongolia, and Xinjiang. As the number of Christians in mainland PRC is forecasted to grow, the "market share" of Orthodox Christians may increase proportionately.

The potential for Orthodox Christianity to expand its presence in the spiritual marketplace is still ambiguous, in part because of inadequate public recognition. Figures for the Hong Kong Christian community are more definitive because most congregations are accounted by their churches, which have legal recognition and the right of self-governance with minimal oversight from the regional government. For comparison with the PRC figures, 500,000 residents of Hong Kong were registered as members of 1,500 Protestant congregations,[9] 379,000 Catholics in 52 parishes,[10] and 24,856 Mormons (Church of Latter-Day Saints) in four stakes consisting of 40 congregations (in 31 wards and nine branches).[11] There are no definitive figures for the Russian Orthodox, Greek Orthodox (OCSLE), and Coptic Orthodox populations.

Historically speaking, public awareness of Orthodox Christian communities in Hong Kong is yet relatively low. In the post-1997 period, the presence of Orthodox churches has gradually come to light. Using the *Hong Kong Yearbook*, published annually by the HKSAR government as a public report, as a barometer of official recognition, we see how the public profile of the Orthodox communities has evolved. In the first Yearbook (1997), the section on Religion only included information about the Protestant and Roman Catholic Christian communities.[12] In 2001, the Yearbook included one sentence about the establishment of OMHKSEA.[13] The following year, OMHKSEA was not cited as one of the members of the Hong Kong Christian Council (HKCC), but in 2004, the description of the Council included a reference to OMHKSEA. Furthermore, in this edition, OMHKSEA was portrayed as an ecumenical partner with Roman Catholic and Protestant churches.[14] General references to OMHKSEA were included in subsequent editions until 2012. The 2012 Yearbook named specific sects of Orthodox Christianity separately.[15] The next major change about the Orthodox communities is in the 2015 version. OMHKSEA was not named as one of the members of the HKCC.[16]

More significant than whether they are mentioned at all is the relative "lack" of details about the Orthodox sects. For Protestant and Roman Catholic groups, the *Yearbook* includes descriptions of how they are as multidenominational communities as well as their constituent subgroups, citing the number of members and the types of institutions that they manage, such as hospitals, schools, and social services centers. These profiles also contain details about outreach tools such as print and television media.[17] In contrast, the Greek, Russian, and Coptic Orthodox Churches are cited as "having a presence" in Hong Kong.[18]

The phrase "having a presence" implies that the ROC community in Hong Kong is small but we argue that it is not negligible or marginal in quality. It is a node in the Russian Orthodox community of China and also of Orthodox Christian communities in both China and East Asia. It is important within and to Hong Kong because its mission is based on the freedom of religious and cultural practices and it can operate in multiple modes, such as publishing in both Simplified and Traditional Chinese. It has also been vital as a community that connects Hong Kong and by extension the rest of China to Russia and to Orthodox Christian communities around the world. The ways in which the OPASPP has inculturated to fit the needs of its ethnically diverse congregation, as discussed in chapter 5, furthermore reflect how the social composition of Hong Kong has changed considerably since Father Uspensky established the first church in the 1930s. Migration and settlement of different populations are constant forces of change, but after 1997, the conscious political and social mainlandization of the region, the latter through the influx of "new immigrants" from the PRC mainland provinces, means that being "Chinese" and "Hong Konger" are subject to active and contentious debates.

Although the OPASPP has not been directly involved in dialogues and social movements about local identity, the ROC experience in Hong Kong, from the 1930s to the present, shows a parallel development with what has occurred with Orthodox Christianity in the PRC mainland because it has not been influenced by explicit restrictions on proselytization or religious persecution, as well as with other Christian groups in Hong Kong. Rather than seeking converts in large numbers, as Baptist, Methodist, and Catholic missionaries achieved, evidenced in the numerous churches, schools, hospitals, and charitable organizations still operating in Hong Kong today, the first Orthodox Christian mission led by Father Uspensky developed to satisfy the needs of a population that was not part of "mainstream society." During the colonial era, China and even Great Britain could be excluded within the confines of the church. Church, as a space and as an experience, could be a respite from adjustment to a non-native language and culture for some believers. Even parishioners who acclimated to Hong Kong's British-led social environment could seek an authentically Russian atmosphere during religious worship. Since 1997, Hong Kong's atypical political status within the PRC and the cultural legacy of British colonial rule have distinguished the OPASPP from ROC congregations in mainland China. OPASPP clergy and lay leaders have acculturated the church in some respects as introduced below but face many unresolved or ongoing problems about how to be a parish in Chinese political territory but one that is also in a unique area of China as a sociocultural unit.

Epilogue

This study is also a realistic assessment of how the OPASPP in Hong Kong faces many ongoing challenges. Achieving financial stability and providing a comprehensive range of religious and pastoral services with highly limited staff are among the problems that the OPASPP is trying to solve. Evidence from interviews with OPASPP clergy and parishioners reveal that some of these issues stem from cultural differences, such as language barriers and limited connections with other religious entities in Hong Kong.[19] These challenges affect how the OPASPP serves parishioners from the Russian and other Slavic-majority countries, and non-Russian/Slavic parishioners, who are adult converts and are not proficient in Russian language. The OPASPP furthermore faces many obstacles to attract a critical mass of converts who are willing to participate actively and regularly in church rituals and activities and gaining a higher profile in the city's market of religious organizations.

Although the ROC has been a centuries-old institution in China, the ongoing need to redefine its purpose has been most apparent in Hong Kong. Congregations in mainland China, particularly Harbin, Shanghai, and in Xinjiang, have identities based on the long history of the faith in those areas. Comparative cultural homogeneity of those groups makes it relatively easier to develop protocol for liturgical services and social communication. In Hong Kong, which type of spoken Chinese to use, how to accommodate a work-centered culture in which leisure time schedules interfere with religious ones, and how to infuse religious space and social interaction with "Chinese elements" are all challenges.

More positively, the OPASPP does have the potential to become more significant in Hong Kong than the earlier communities led by Fathers Uspensky and Wen were. A sentimental view of these groups is that they were spiritual havens for foreigners that were an ethnic minority even within Hong Kong's non-Chinese population. With the disadvantage of not being native English-language users, expatriate Russians valued the security and familiarity of the Orthodox church community. However, because of their limited size, they did not establish schools, hospitals, and other social institutions that would serve as modes of public outreach. The decision of many Russians to leave Hong Kong and migrate to other parts of the world further diminished the ability of the first mission to sustain its own operations and to instill a stable presence in Hong Kong society. The lack of adequate funding from the Moscow Patriarchate exacerbated the logistical hardships of maintaining a presence with few people. There were also no long-term networks for accumulating capital like the Parsis.[20]

The OPASPP moreover faces the ongoing challenge that not all residents of Hong Kong who identify as Orthodox Christians by heritage or spiritual affinity are interested in participating in religious activities so cultural events become the most effective forms of public outreach. It is a worldwide phenomenon that people who hold religious beliefs may choose not to belong or are not active members of religious institutions.[21] Therefore in Hong Kong, as arguably in other major cities, the OPASPP makes a greater impact through events that are not directly associated with spirituality or require the practice of rituals. Cultural activities do not require parish membership and are natural opportunities for parishioners and nonparishioners to interact socially. Parishioners sometimes introduce nonbeliever friends to the church by bringing them to the events held at the OPASPP complex. Persons who belong to the other two Orthodox churches in Hong Kong occasionally join these activities without facing any discrimination or overt differentiation from OPASPP members. In that sense, public outreach fulfils the dual objectives of serving Russians and ROC believers and attracting prospective converts and community members by demonstrating that material customs associated with Orthodox Christianity are compatible and adaptable to life in Hong Kong.

Another factor that affects that both academic and popular awareness is the evolving complexity of the OPASPP as a church and a sociocultural community as it builds its identity in Hong Kong. A key variable in identity development is evident in the differences between the first and current missions in chapter 2. The first mission served a group that is accurately described as a Russian diaspora. This group consisted of persons migrating to Hong Kong directly from the Soviet Union and their descendants born outside of the Soviet Union. The current mission targets what can be considered a Russian-speaking community. This community consists of persons who identify as ethnic Russian, natives of the Russian Federation or a state formerly part of the Soviet Union, and members of the second generation for the first two categories. These persons may not necessarily identify strongly as adherents to Orthodox Christianity because of their own religious experiences or because they were raised in families that were not religiously active. Many of these people also fit with both recent scholarly interpretations of "diaspora," as observed by Ludmila Isurin, as defined by language and civil identity rather than ethnicity.[22]

The future of the OPASPP and of Orthodox Christianity in Hong Kong, as a region of China, will probably depend not only on changes in Chinese politics and social order but also more global trends of religious practice as well as spiritual and ethnic identity. The general revival of Orthodox Christianity in the Russian Federation during the late twentieth century was a direct impetus for the foundation of the OPASPP and subsequently revival of the ROC in Hong Kong.[23] As such, the Hong Kong mission is very much a part of the ROC's "global mission," which according to Alicja Curanović consists of two vectors, an internal vector about boosting Russia's cultural integrity and an external one about Russia as a leader and role model in the world.[24] Sino-Russian relations will be undoubtedly affected as Orthodox Christianity continues to be an aspect of Russian political identity as the ROC is supported but also monitored by the Russian Federation government.²⁵

What it means to be Russian both within and outside of the Russian political sphere, that could include just the Russian Federation or all the constituent states of the former Soviet Union as well as the Soviet bloc in Eastern Europe, may also influence how Russian Orthodox Christianity is perceived in Hong Kong and the PRC mainland. David Rowley argues that Russian nationalism is relatively new, and that Russian imperialism has dominated the definition and expression of "Russian identity" (or identities, plural) even to the end of the twentieth century.²⁶ As such, elements of Russian identity that were previously intertwined such as language and faith must now be considered separately and in variable combinations for individuals and subgroups.²⁷ The OPASPP faces the ongoing mission of redefining what is Orthodox identity and for Russian believers, what is "Russian and Orthodox" identity. The OPASPP must also guide church members who are not Russian to develop their beliefs and habits in ways that retain what elements of their spiritual and cultural foundations do not conflict with Orthodox Christian teachings and can promote the healthy growth of their faith and sense of belonging in Orthodox Christian communities. The continual presence of the ROC community in Hong Kong entails many ongoing experiments that have profound consequences for Orthodox Christianity in China and more broadly, in East Asia.

NOTES

1. The pandemic has also held broad implications for the PRC mainland and germane to this study, Sino-Russian relations in trade and migration. See Andrew Higgins, "Businesses 'Getting Killed' on Russian Border as Coronavirus Fears Rise," Russia Dispatch, *New York Times*, February 24, 2020, accessed January 12, 2021. https://www.nytimes.com/2020/02/24/world/europe/coronavirus-russia-china-commerce.html.

2. Xuyang Jingjing, "Orthodox Christians in China Seeking Official Recognition," *Global Times*, May 15, 2013, accessed August 29, 2020, http://www.globaltimes.cn/content/781838.shtml#:~:text=Researchers%20predict%20that%20the%20religion,of%20a%20revival%20in%20China.

Other ROC church buildings remaining in the PRC mainland, but which are not occupied by active congregations include St. Alexander Nevsky Church in Wuhan (established in 1893 when the city was called Hankou) which has undergone renovation since 2015 and the Church of St. Nicholas the Wonderworker (Shanghai) which is currently used for non-religious purposes.

3. "Near China's Border with Russia, the Orthodox Church Regains a Toehold," Heaven's Outposts, *The Economist*, May 7, 2020, https://www.economist.com/chin

a/2020/05/07/near-chinas-border-with-russia-the-orthodox-church-regains-a-toehold. Father Pozdnyaev has also expressed judicious optimism about the sustainability of Orthodox Christianity in China. See Pozdynyaev, *Zhongguo dalu Zhengjiaohui*.

4. As of the completion of this book, the Basic Law and certain freedoms that are not granted to PRC mainland residents remain in effect in Hong Kong until 2047. However, discussions about religious life have long considered the possible consequences of eventual "normalization" of political and social institutions in Hong Kong after that point. See, for example, Kwong, *Hong Kong's Religions in Transition*.

5. In the period immediately after the 1997 political transition, the mode of religious organization was considered as neither separation of "church-state" (like the United States) nor "state domination of the church" (like many communist countries). See Leung and Chan, *Changing Church and State Relations in Hong Kong*, 11–21.

6. Katharina Wenzel-Teuber, "2015 Statistical Update on Religions and Churches in the Peoples' Republic of China," *Religions & Christianity in Today's China* 6, no. 2 (2016): 34.

7. Ibid., 35.

8. See Russkaia Pravoslavnaia Tserkov' Ofitsial'nyi sait Russkoi Pravoslavnoi Tserkvi [The official website of the Russian Orthodox Church] and Alan Hunter and Kim-kwong Chan, "Orthodox Church, Chinese," in *Encyclopedia of Chinese History*, ed. Michael Dillon (London: Routledge, 2016), 510–11.

9. "Religion and Custom," in *Hong Kong Yearbook 2015* (Hong Kong: HKSAR, 2015), http://www.yearbook.gov.hk/2015/en/index.html.

10. Ibid.

11. Mormon Newsroom (The Church of Jesus Christ of Latter-Day Saints), "Facts and Statistics: Hong Kong," accessed March 21, 2017, http://www.mormonnewsroom.org/facts-and-statistics/country/hong-kong.

12. "Religion and Custom," in *Hong Kong Yearbook 1997* (Hong Kong: HKSAR, 1997), https://www.yearbook.gov.hk/1997/eindex.htm.

13. "Christianity," in *Hong Kong Yearbook 2001* (Hong Kong: HKSAR, 2001), http://www.yearbook.gov.hk/2001/ehtml/index.html.

14. "Christianity," in Hong Kong Yearbook 2004 (Hong Kong: HKSAR, 2004), http://www.yearbook.gov.hk/2004/en/index.html.

15. "Religion and Custom," in *Hong Kong Yearbook 2012* (Hong Kong: HKSAR, 2012), http://www.yearbook.gov.hk/2012/en/index.html.

16. "Religion and Custom," in *Hong Kong Yearbook 2015* (Hong Kong: HKSAR, 2015), http://www.yearbook.gov.hk/2015/en/index.html.

17. Ibid.

18. The Coptic community is based in the Sheung Wan district, like the OPASPP, at St. Thomas Coptic Orthodox Church. See St. Thomas Coptic Church, accessed December 15, 2019, https://sites.google.com/site/hkcoptic/Home, and St. Thomas Coptic Church HK, "St. Thomas Coptic Church HK's Facebook Page," Facebook, December 15, 2019, https://www.facebook.com/coptichk.

19. The OPASPP and the RLC are still making progress with intangible resources to integrate into Hong Kong local society, and to maintain distinct relationships with the Russian sociocultural world. The OPASPP makes a conscious effort to make

the church accessible to nonbelievers. The church is open throughout most days when members of the clergy or lay staff are on the premises. It also acts as a conduit between Hong Kong and Russia by sponsoring opportunities for Hong Kong residents to make donations to Russian institutions. 2012, the RLC organized a market selling homemade deli foods and books to raise money for a Russian charitable organization called *Volunteers to Help Orphans* (*Volontery v pomoshch' detiam-sirotam*).

20. There is a relative dearth of literature about the Hong Kong Parsi community because non-Parsis generally cannot gain access to information about the group. Parsi wealth and community-building is evident in the establishment and maintenance of an exclusive Parsi cemetery in the Happy Valley district of Hong Kong.

21. For conceptual treatment of this phenomenon and comparable empirical evidence in the case of Great Britain and Italy, see Grace Davie, "Believing without Belonging: Is This the Future of Religion in Britain?," *Social Compass* 37, no. 4 (1990): 455–69; Grace Davie, *Religion in Britain since 1945: Believing without Belonging* (Oxford: Blackwell, 1994); and Robert Marchisio, and Maurizio Pisati, "Belonging without Believing: Catholics in Contemporary Italy," *Religion, State and Society* 33, no. 1 (1999): 35–36.

22. See Ludmila Isurin, *Russian Diaspora Culture, Identity, and Language Change* (Boston: De Gruyter, 2011).

23. About the late twentieth-century revival, see Milena Benovska, *Orthodox Revivalism in Russia: Driving Forces and Moral Quests* (London: Routledge, 2020).

24. Alicja Curanović, "Russia's Mission in the World: The Perspective of the Russian Orthodox Church," *Problems of Post-Communism* 66, no. 4 (2019): 258.

25. About the strategic collaboration between the ROC and the Russian Ministry of Foreign Affairs (Foreign Ministry) since 1997, see Emily Belle Damm and Skye Cooley, "Resurrection of the Russian Orthodox Church: Narrative of Analysis of the Russian National Myth," *Social Science Quarterly* 98, no. 3 (2017): 942–57; and Daniel P. Payne, "Spiritual Security, the Russian Orthodox Church, and the Russian Foreign Ministry: Collaboration or Cooptation?," *A Journal of Church and State* 52, no. 4 (2010): 712–27.

The expansion of PRC economic influence through the Belt and Road Initiative (BRI), started in 2013, is another major factor that has and will likely influence Sino-Russian relations. See Fanqi Jia and Mia M. Bennett, "Chinese Infrastructure Diplomacy in Russia: The Geopolitics of Project Type, Location, and Scale," *Eurasian Geography and Economics* 59, no. 3–4 (2018): 340–77.

26. See David G. Rowley, "Imperial Versus National Discourse: The Case of Russia," *Nations and Nationalism* 6, no. 1 (2000): 23–42.

27. Katja Richters has argued that the ROC has become an influential diplomatic authority and proponent of traditional Russian culture since the end of an official ban on religion in the former Soviet Union. Therefore ROC institutions are not entirely apolitical because some, if not substantial aspects, of their cultural outreach work is endorsed and sponsored by the Russian Federation government. See Richters, *The Post-Soviet Russian Orthodox Church*, especially 18–55.

Glossary

General Terms, Places, Institutions, and Texts

NOTES

1. Each entry in this section of the glossary is arranged in this format:
English
Chinese term (Hanyu pinyin transliteration) Chinese term (characters)
Russian term (Cyrillic) [Russian term (Romanized transliteration)]
2. Chinese-language place names in Hong Kong, particularly those that are transliterations of non-Chinese proper nouns, are usually pronounced orally in Cantonese, but since these terms are also rendered according to the Hanyu pinyin system and therefore in Mandarin (Putonghua). The authors are not making a political statement by doing so, but because Mandarin is the *lingua franca* of China Studies throughout the world.
3. For persons, no Romanizations are given with Cyrillic names in the second rows of entries in which the official name of the person is already the proper Romanized form.s
4. The original names for persons of Greek origin are provided in Greek script.

a minority among a minority
xiaozhong zhong de xiaozhong 小眾中的小眾
меньшинство среди меньшинства [men'shinstvo sredi men'shinstva]

(Benedictine) Abbey of St. John (Müstair, Switzerland)
Mishita'er Benduhui Sheng Yuehan nü xiudaoyuan 米施泰爾的本篤
會聖約翰女修道院
Бенедиктинский монастырь Святого Иоанна [Benediktinskii monastyr' Sviatogo Ioanna]

ABC of Hong Kong
Азбука Гонконга [Azbuka Gonkonga]

Act of Canonical Communion of the Russian Orthodox Church Outside Russia with the Russian orthodox Church Moscow Patriarchate
Sheng can li quanwei fa'an 《聖餐禮權威法案》
Акт о каноническом общении Русской Православной Церкви Заграницей с Русской Православной Церковью Московского Патриархата [Akt o kanonicheskom obshchenii Russkoi Pravoslavnoi Tserkvi Zagranitsei s Russkoi Pravoslavnoi Tserkov'iu Moskovskogo Patriarkhata]

Albazin (Yaksa)
Yakesa 雅克薩
Албазин / Албазино (Якса) [Albazin / Albazino (Iaksa)]

Albazinian
A'erbajin ren 阿爾巴津人
Албазинцы [Albazintsy]

"all can be eaten"
yi qie ke shi 一切可食
«можно есть все» ["mozhno est' vse"]

Annotation for osmoglasia (Ru.) / Collection of eight tones: praises and sub-praises for the Lord's Day (Ch.)
Ba diaoji: zhuri xiao zanci yu fuzanci 《八調集：主日小讚詞與副讚詞》
Аннотация к осмогласию [Annotatsiia k osmoglasiiu]

Anti-Piracy Guards
Fan haidao dui 反海盜隊

Anthropology of St. Paul
Sheng Baoluo de renleixue 聖保羅的人類學
Антропология апостола Павла [Antropologiia apostola Pavla]

archbishop
da zhujiao 大主教
архиепископ [arkhiepiskop]

archimandrite
xiudao yuanzhang 修道院長
архимандрит [arkhimandrit]

Glossary

archpriest
da siji 大司祭
протоиерей [protoierei]

The Basic Law of the Hong Kong Special Administrative Region of the People's Republic of China (Basic Law)
Zhonghua renmin gongheguo Xianggang tebie xingzheng qu jiben fa (Jiben fa) 《中華人民共和國香港特別行政區基本法》（《基本法》）
«Основном законе» Гонконга ["Osnovnom zakone" Gonkonga]

bauhinia flower
yang zijing 洋紫荊

Beijing Foreign Studies University
Beijing waiguoyu daxue 北京外國語大學
Пекинский университет иностранных языков [Pekinskii universitet inostrannykh iazykov]

Beijing Normal University
Beijing shifan daxue 北京師範大學
Пекинский педагогический университет [Pekinskii pedagogicheskii universitet]

bi-literalism and trilingualism
liang wen san yu 兩文三語
билитерализм и трехъязычие [biliteralizm i trekh"iazychie]

Biographies of the Saints
Shengren liezhuan 《聖人列傳》
Жития Святых [zhitiia sviatykh]

birch juice
березовый сок [berezovyi sok]

Bogoyevlensky Church (Church of the Holy Epiphany) (Shanghai)
Богоявленский храм [Bogoiavlenskii khram]

"book of needs"
xuyong jing 需用經
требник [trebnik]

Book of Services of the Twelve Feasts
Shi'er jieri zhanli liyi wenben 《十二節日瞻禮禮儀文本》
Литургические тексты двенадцати праздников [Liturgicheskie teksty dvenadtsati prazdnikov]

Boxer Rebellion (Yihetuan Movement)
Yihetuan yundong 義和團運動
Ихэтуаньское восстание [Ikhetuan'skoe vosstanie]

Carousel (children's choir studio)
Детская хоровая студия Карусель [Detskaia khorovaia studiia Karusel']

Carl Smith Collection (Hong Kong Public Records Office)
Shi Qile mushi cangpin Ji 施其樂牧師藏品集
Коллекция Карла Смита (Государственный архив Гонконга) [Kollektsiia Karla Smita (Gosudarstvennyi arkhiv Gonkonga)]

Cathedral of the Icon of the Mother of God "Surety of Sinners" (Shanghai)
"Women de shengmu – zuiren de baoren" zhujiao zuotang "我們的聖母—罪人的保人"主教座堂
Кафедральный собор иконы Божией Матери «Споручница грешных» в Шанхае [Kafedral'nyi sobor ikony Bozhiei Materi "Sporuchnitsa greshnykh" v Shankhae]

chairman of (the Synodal Department of) the Department for External Church Relations of Russian Orthodox Church
Eluosi Dongzheng jiaohui waijiaobu zhuren 俄羅斯東正教會外交部主任
председатель Отдела внешних церковных связей [predsedatel' Otdela vneshnikh tserkovnykh sviazei]

Cheesefare Sunday
Масленица [Maslenitsa]

Cherikoff Bakery
Cheligefu bingdian 車厘哥夫餅店
Пекарня Черикова [Pekarnia Cherikova]

China Continuation Committee
Zhonghua xu xing wei ban hui 中華續行委辦會

China Orthodox Press (COP)
Zhonghua zhengjiao chubanshe 中華正教出版社
Китайское православное издательство [Kitaiskoe pravoslavnoe izdatel'stvo]

(ethnic) Chinese
Huaren 華人
Китайцы [kitaitsy]

Chinese Academic Library of Christian Thought
Lidai Jidujiao sixiang xueshu wenku 歷代基督教思想學術文庫

Chinese Autonomous Orthodox Church
Zhonghua zizhi zhengjiaohui 中華自治正教會
Китайская Автономная Православная Церковь [Kitaiskaia Avtonomnaia Pravoslavnaia Tserkov']

Chinese Eastern Railway
Zhongdong tielu / Dong qing tielu 中東鐵路 / 東清鐵路
Китайско-Восточная железная дорога [Kitaisko-Vostochnaia zheleznaia doroga]

Chinese Good Tidings / Chinese Good News
Zhongguo fuyin bao 《中國福音報》
Китайский благовестник [Kitaiskii blagovestnik]

Chinese Orthodox Association (Shanghai)
Zhongguo Dongzhengjiao xiehui 中國東正教協會
Китайское Православное братство [Kitaiskoe Pravoslavnoe bratstvo]

Chinese Patriarchal Metochion
Mosike zongzhu jiaoqu zhonghua huiguan 莫斯科宗主教區中華會館
Китайское Патриаршее Подворье в Москве [Kitaiskoe Patriarshee Podvor'e v Moskve]

Chinese University of Hong Kong (CUHK)
Xianggang zhongwen daxue 香港中文大學
Китайский университет Гонконга [Kitaiskii universitet Gonkonga]

Chiuchow dialect
Chaozhou hua 潮州話

Christian Literature Society for China (CLSC)
Guang xue hui 廣學會

Christian World of Asia
Yazhou Jidujiao shijie 《亞洲基督教世界》
«Христианский мир Азии» ["Khristianskii mir Azii"]

Church of All Nations in the Garden of Gethsemane (Jerusalem)
Wanguo jiaotang 萬國教堂
Церковь Всех Наций [Tserkov' Vsekh Natsii]

Church of Japan
Riben zhengjiao hui (Ja. Nihon Harisutosu) 日本正教會 (日本ハリス
 トス正教会)
Японская православная церковь [Iaponskaia pravoslavnaia tserkov']

Church of the Dormition (Beijing)
Shengmu anxi jiaotang (Beijing) 聖母安息教堂（北京）
Церковь в честь Успения Божией Матери на Новом кладбище
 ["Tserkov' v chest' Uspeniia Bozhiei Materi na Novom kladbishche"]

Church of the Dormition (Harbin)
Shengmu anxi jiaotang (Ha'erbin) 聖母安息教堂（哈爾濱）
Церковь в честь Успения Божией Матери на Новом кладбище
 [Tserkov' v chest' Uspeniia Bozhiei Materi na Novom kladbishche]

Church of the Holy Annunciation (Harbin)
Shengmu lingbao jiaotang 聖母領報教堂
Благовещенский собор [Blagoveshchenskii sobor]

Church of the Holy Iveron Icon [St. Ibervel Church] (Harbin)
Sheng Yiwei'er jiaotang 聖伊維爾教堂
Храм в честь Иверской иконы Божией Матери [Khram v chest' Iver-
 skoi ikony Bozhiei Materi]

Church of the Holy Resurrection / Resurrection parish (Hong Kong)
Церковь воскресенского прихода [Tserkov' Voskresenskogo prikhoda]

Church of the Holy Sepulchre (Jerusalem)
Sheng mu jiaotang 聖墓教堂
Храм Гроба Господня [Khram Groba Gospodnia]

Church of the Holy Trinity (Macau)
Sheng sanyi jiaotang 聖三一教堂
Церковь Святой Троицы в Макао [Tserkov' Sviatoi Troitsy v Makao]

Church of the Iberian Icon of the Mother of God (Manila)
Yiwei'er shengmu xiang jiaotang 伊維爾聖母像教堂
Домовой храм в честь Иверской иконы Божией Матери в Маниле (Республика Филиппины) [Domovoi khram v chest' Iverskoi ikony Bozhiei Materi v Manile (Respublika Filippiny)]

Church of the Immaculate Conception (Hong Kong)
Shengmu wu yuanzui zhujiao zuotang 聖母無原罪主教座堂
Собор Непорочного Зачатия Пресвятой Девы Марии [Sobor Neporochnogo Zachatiia Presviatoi Devy Marii]

Church of the Nativity of the Blessed Virgin (Moscow)
Mosike Kaboteniya shengmu shengdan tang 莫斯科卡波特尼聖母聖誕堂
Храм Рождества Пресвятой Богородицы в Капотне [Khram Rozhdestva Presviatoi Bogoroditsy v Kapotne]

Church of St. Nicholas the Wonderworker (Shanghai)
Sheng Nigula tang 聖尼古拉堂
Храм святителя Николая Чудотворца [Khram sviatitelia Nikolaia Chudotvortsa]

Church of the Theophany (Shanghai)
Zhu xian tang 主顯堂
Храм Богоявления Господня [Khram Bogoiavleniia Gospodnia]

Church Bulletin
Церковный бюллетень [Tserkovnyi biulleten']

classical Chinese
wenyan 文言
классический китайский язык (вэньянь) [klassicheskii kitaiskii iazyk (ven'ian')]

College of Foreign Affairs
Waijiao bu hui 外交部會
Коллегия иностранных дел [Kollegiia inostrannykh del]

Confucian Academy
Kong jiao xueyuan 孔教學院

Confucius
Kongzi 孔子
Конфуций [Konfutsii]

convent / monastery
xiudaoyuan 修道院
монастырь [monastyr']

Coordination Council of Russian Compatriots in China
Zai Hua E Qiao xie weiyuanhui 在華俄僑協委員會
Координационный Совет Соотечественников в Китае [Koordinatsionnyi Sovet Sootechestvennikov v Kitae]

cottage cheese / quark
творог [tvorog]

Council of Bishops
zhujiao gonghui 主教公會
Архиерейский собор [Arkhiereiskii sobor]

Crimean War
Kelimiya Zhanzheng 克里米亞戰爭
Крымская война [Krymskaia voina]

Dar Publishing House
Издательство «Дар» [Izdatel'stvo "Dar"]

Daur
Dawo'er 達斡爾
Дауры [daury]

deacon
fuji 輔祭
дьякон [d'iakon]

deanery
xinzhong 信眾
Благочиние [Blagochinie]

Department for External Church Relations (DECR)
Отдел внешних церковных связей [Otdel vneshnikh tserkovnykh sviazei]

divine liturgy in honor of Our Father Among the Saints John Chrysostom
Sheng jinkou Yuehan shi feng sheng li 聖金口約翰事奉聖禮
Божественная Литургия Святителя Иоанна Златоуста [Bozhestvennaia Liturgiia Sviatitelia Ioanna Zlatousta]

Dormition of the Most Holy Theotokos Church (Beijing)
Shengmu Anxi Tang 聖母安息堂
Храм Успения Пресвятой Богородицы (Успенская церковь) [Khram Uspeniia Presviatoi Bogoroditsy (Uspenskaia tserkov')]

East Asian Exarchate
Dongya du zhujiao qu 東亞督主教區
Восточно-Азиатский Экзархат [Vostochno-Aziatskii Ekzarkhat]

Eastern Orthodox Christianity in China: Past, Present, and Future
Dongzhengjiao zai Zhongguo: guoqu, xianzai yu jianglai 《東正教在中國：過去、現在與將來》
Восточная православная церковь в Китае: прошлое, настоящее, будущее [Vostochnaia pravoslavnaia tserkov' v Kitae: proshloe, nastoiashchee, budushchee]

Ecumenical Patriarchate of Constantinople
Junshitandingbao pu shi mushou qu 君士坦丁堡普世牧首區
Константинопольская православная церковь [Konstantinopol'skaia pravoslavnaia tserkov']

Edo period
Jianghu shidai (Ja. Edo jidai) 江戶時代
Период Эдо [Period Edo]

eparchy
zhujiao qu 主教區
епархия [eparkhiia]

eparchial council
jiaoqu weiyuanhui 教區委員會
епархиальный совет [eparkhial'nyi sovet]

eparchial court
jiaoqu fating 教區法庭
епархиальный суд [eparkhial'nyi sud]

Ethnic Identification Project
Minzu shibie gongcheng 民族識別工程

ethno-religious communities
minzu zongjiao tuanti 民族宗教團體
этнорелигиозные группы [etnoreligioznye gruppy]

evening prayers
wan dao 晚禱
вечерние молитвы [vechernie molitvy]

expatriate churches
qiao min jiaohui 僑民教會
церкви для экспатриантов [tserkvi dlia ekspatriantov]

Family Art Picnic
Семейный арт-пикник [Cemeinyi art-piknik]

family holiday
семейный праздник [semeinyi prazdnik]

fasting day
zhai ri 斋日
постный день [postnyi den]

Feast of Theophany / Epiphany
zhu xian jie 主顯節
Богоявление [Bogoiavlenie]

"fifty years of no change"
wushi nian bu bian 五十年不變

"Finest, the Brave Falcon"
Финист-ясный сокол [Finist-iasnyi sokol]

The Frigate Pallada
Zhanji "Balada" Hao 《戰機"巴拉達"號》
фрегат «Паллада» [fregat "Pallada"]

Glossary

Gantimur
Gentemu 根特木
Гантимур [Gantimur]

Gantimurov family
Gentemu jiazu 根特木家族
Гантимуровы [Gantimurovy]

General Church Court
jiaohui zong fating 教會總法庭
Общецерковный суд [Obshchetserkovnyi sud]

German Bethesda Chapel (Hong Kong)
Xi Ying Pan Deguo libai tang 西營盤德國禮拜堂

graduation
выпускной [vypusknoi]

Great Lent
Da zhai qi 大齋期
Великий пост [Velikii post]

Great Proletariat Cultural Revolution
Wu chan jieji wenhua da geming 無產階級大革命
Великая пролетарская культурная революция [Velikaia proletarskaia kul'turnaia revoliutsiia]

Greater China
Da Zhonghua 大中華
Большой Китай [Bol'shoi Kitai]

Guangdong province
Guangdong sheng 廣東省

Провинция Гуандун [Provintsiia Guandun]

Guangdong University of Foreign Studies
Guangdong waiyu waimao xueyuan (daxue) 廣東外語外貿學院 (大學)
Гуандунский университет иностранных языков и внешней торговли [Guandunskii universitet inostrannykh iazykov i vneshnei torgovli]

Hakka
Kejia 客家
Хакка [Khakka]

Heavenly Bread
Хлеб Небесный [Khleb Nebesnyi]

hegumen / protoiereus
zhangyuan / dianyuan 掌院 / 典院
игумен / протоиерей [igumen / protoierei]

Hechuan (Chongqing, Sichuan province)
Hechuan (Sichuan sheng Chongqing shi) 合川 (四川省重慶市)
Хэчуань (Чунцин, провинция Сычуань) [Khechuan' (Chuntsin, provintsiia Sychuan')]

"hello"
Привет [privet]

hieromonk
xiushi siji 修士司祭
иеромонах [ieromonakh]

holy
sheng 聖
святой [sviatoi]

Holy Communion
Sheng can 聖餐
Евхаристия [Evkharistiia]

Holy Scriptures
Sheng yong jing 聖詠經
Священное писание [Sviashchennoe pisanie]

Holy Monastery of Zografos (also known as Saint George the Zograf Monastery)
Zuogelafu xiudaoyuan 佐格拉夫修道院
Зографский монастырь [Zografskii monastyr']

Holy Synod of the Russian Orthodox Church (Moscow Patriarchate)
Eluosi zhengjiao hui zhi sheng zhujiao gonghui 俄羅斯正教會至聖主教公會

Священный синод Русской православной церкви [Sviashchennyi sinod Russkoi pravoslavnoi tserkvi]

Holy Trinity Church (parish) (Taipei)
Taibei Sheng san yi tang 台北聖三一堂
Свто-Троицкий приход в Тайбэе [Svto-Troitskii prikhod v Taibee]

Holy Virgin "The Joy of All Who Sorrow" Cathedral (San Francisco)
Радосте-Скорбященский собор [Radoste-Skorbiashchenskii sobor]

holy water (Blessing of the Waters of the South China Sea)
агиасма [agiasma]

homeland
родина [Rodina]

Hong Kong Adventist Hospital
Xianggang gang'an yiyuan 香港港安醫院
Гонконгский госпиталь адвентистов [Gonkongskii gospital' adventistov]

Hong Kong Baptist University (HKBU)
Xianggang Jin hui daxue 香港浸會大學
Гонконгский Баптистский Университет [Gonkongskii Baptistskii Universitet]

Hong Kong Buddhist Association
Xianggang fojiao lianhe hui 香港佛教聯合會
Буддийская ассоциация Гонконга [Buddiiskaia assotsiatsiia Gonkonga]

Hong Kong Cemetery
Xianggang fen chang 香港墳場
Гонконгское кладбище [Gonkongskoe kladbishche]

Hong Kong Chinese Christian Churches Union (formerly Hong Kong Christian Churches Union)
Xianggang Huaren Jidujiao lianhui (Xianggang Jidujiao lianhui) 香港華人基督教聯會 (香港基督教聯會)
Союз Китайских христианских церквей Гонконга (ранее известный как Союз христианских церквей Гонконга) [Soiuz Kitaiskikh khristianskikh tserkvei Gonkonga (ranee izvestnyi kak Soiuz khristianskikh tserkvei Gonkonga)]

Hong Kong Christian Council (HKCC)
Xianggang Jidujiao xiejin hui 香港基督教協進會
Христианский Совет Гонконга [Khristianskii Sovet Gonkonga]

Hong Kong Government Census and Statistics Department
Xianggang zhengfu tongjichu 香港政府統計處
Департамент переписи населения и статистики Гонконгского правительства [Departament perepisi naseleniia i statistiki Gonkongskogo pravitel'stva]

Hong Kong Handbook / *Hong Kong Notebook*
Xianggang shouzha 《香港手札》
Гонконгскаиа Тетрадь [Gonkongskaia Tetrad']

Hong Kong Orthodox Association
Xianggang zhengjiao xiehui 香港正教協會
Православная ассоциация Гонконга [Pravoslavnaia assotsiatsiia Gonkonga]

Hong Kong Public Records Office (PRO)
Xianggang lishi dang'anguan 香港歷史檔案館

Hong Kong Special Administrative Region (HKSAR)
Xianggang tebie xingzhengqu 香港特別行政區
Специальный административный район Гонконг [Spetsial'nyi administrativnyi raion Gonkong]

Hong Kong Taoist Association
Xianggang daojiao lianhe hui 香港道教聯合會
Гонконгская Ассоциация последователей даосизма [Gonkongskaia Assotsiatsiia posledovatelei daosizma]

"I am Dasha. I am six years old. I love my school in Hong Kong. And I love my friends in my school."
Я Даша, мне 6 лет. Я люблю мою школу в Гонгонге. Также я люблю моих подружек в моей школе. [Ia Dasha, mne 6 let. Ia liubliu moiu shkolu v Gongonge. Takzhe ia liubliu moikh podruzhek v moei shkola.]

"I Understand the World."
Я познаю мир [Ia poznaiu mir]

Icon of the Ark of Salvation (Image of our Holy Orthodox Church)
Zhengjiao fangzhou 正教方舟
Икона «Образ Святой нашей Церкви» (Православной), или «Корабль спасения» [Ikona "Obraz Sviatoi nashei Tserkvi" (Pravoslavnoi), ili "Korabl' spaseniia"]

Icon of the Mother of God "Joy of All Who Sorrow" Church (Guangzhou)
Zhong aishang zhe zhi huanle shengmu xiang tang 眾哀傷者之歡樂聖母像堂
Домовый храм в честь иконы Матери Божией «Нечаянная радость» в Гуанчжоу [Domovyi khram v chest' ikony Materi Bozhiei "Nechaiannaia radost'" v Guanchzhou]

indigenous religion
bentu zongjiao 本土宗教
коренные религии [korennye religii]

Inner Mongolia Autonomous Region
Neimenggu zi zhi qu 內蒙古自治區
Внутренняя Монголия [Vnutrenniaia Mongoliia]

Institutio Ad Fidem Christi
Tian shen hui ke 《天神會課》
Тяньшэнь хуэй кэ («Беседы в собрании ангелов») [Tian'shen' khuei ke ("Besedy v sobranii angelov")]

Institute of Sino-Christian Studies

Hanyu Jidujiao wenhua yanjiusuo 漢語基督教文化研究

International Association of Teachers of Russian Language and Culture (MAPYRAL)
Международная ассоциация преподавателей русского языка и литературы [Mezhdunarodnaia assotsiatsiia prepodavatelei russkogo iazyka i literatury]

Johnston House
Zhuangshidun lou 莊士敦樓
Джонстон Хауз [Dzhonston Khauz]

Kamakura period
Liancang shidai (Ja. Kamakura jidai) 鎌倉時代
Период Камакура [Period Kamakura]

kathisma
duan zuo song ci 端坐誦詞
кафисма [kafisma]

kefir
кефир [kefir]

Khabarovsk (formerly known as Boli)
Habaluofusike (Boli) 哈巴羅夫斯克（伯力）
Хабаровск [Khabarovsk]

Khabarovsk Theological Seminary
Habaluofusike shenxueyuan 哈巴羅夫斯克神學院
Хабаровская духовная семинария [Khabarovskaia dukhovnaia seminariia]

Khanty
Hante 漢特
ханты [khanty]

koliva
коливо [kolivo]

Korean Orthodox Church (Metropolis of Korea)
Hanguo zhengjiao hui (Ko. Hanguk Jeonggyohoe) 韓國正教會
Корейская митрополия [Koreiskaia mitropoliia]

Kronstadt
Kalangshitade 喀琅施塔得
Кронштадт [Kronshtadt]

Kulich (kalich) bread
kuliqi mianbao 庫利奇麵包
кулич [kulich]

kvas
квас [kvas]

Ladushki
Ладушки [ladushki]

The Legislative Council of the Hong Kong Special Administration Region (LegCo)
Xianggang li fa hui 香港立法會
Законодательный совет Гонконга [Zakonodatel'nyi sovet Gonkonga]

Lingnan University
Lingnan daxue 嶺南大學
Университет Линнань [Universitet Linnan']

Liturgical instructions
liyi zhinan 禮儀指南
Богослужебные указания [Bogosluzhebnye ukazaniia]

Local Council
Difang gonghui 地方公會
Поместный собор [Pomestnyi sobor]

The Logos and Pneuma Press
Daofeng shushe 道風書社

Lord's Prayer
Zhudao wen 祝禱文
Отче наш [Otche nash]

"main unifying sign"
основным объединяющими признаком [osnovnym ob"ediniaiushchimi priznakom]

Manchuria / Manchukuo
Man zhou li / Man zhou guo 滿洲里 / 滿洲國
Маньчжурия / Маньчжоу-го [Man'chzhuriia / Man'chzhou-go]

Mansi
Manxi 曼西
Манси [Mansi]

Masha and the Bear
Маша и Медведь [Masha i Medved]

Matushka (mother)
Матушка [matushka]

"Messenger of the Orthodox Parish of Apostles Saints Peter and Paul in Hong Kong"
Xianggang Sheng Bide Sheng Baoluo Jiaotang Tongbao 《香港聖彼聖得保羅教堂通報》
Свято-Петропавловский Вестник [Sviato-Petropavlovskii Vestnik]

metochion
huiguan 會館
подворье [podvor'e]

metropolitan
du zhujiao / fu zhujiao 都主教 / 府主教
Митрополит [mitropolit]

Minzu University of China
Zhongyang minzu daxue 中央民族大學
Китайский университет Миньцзу [Kitaiskii universitet Min'tszu]

Mirror of Orthodox Confession
Зерцало православного исповедания [Zertsalo pravoslavnogo ispovedaniia]

Modern Standard Chinese
Putonghua 普通話
Путунхуа [Putunkhua]

month of Epiphany
zhu xian yue 主顯月
месяц Крещения Господня [mesiats Kreshcheniia Gospodnia]

morals
daode 道德
Мораль [moral']

morning prayers
chengqi qidao 晨起祈禱
молитвы утренние [molitvy utrennie]

Moscow, I love you!
Москва, я люблю тебя! [Moskva, ya lyublyu tebya!]

Moscow Patriarchate
Mosike zongzhu jiaoqu 莫斯科宗主教區
Московский Патриархат [Moskovskii Patriarkhat]

Moscow Patriarchate Krutitsy Metochion
Mosike zong zhujiao Kelujici jijinhui huiguan 莫斯科宗主教克魯季茨基金會會館
Крутицкое Патриаршее подворье в Москве [Krutitskoe Patriarshee podvor'e v Moskve]

Mother of God of Tabyn Icon
Shengmu shengxiang 聖母聖像
Табынский образ Божией Матери [Tabynskii obraz Bozhiei Materi]

Mount Athos
Asusi shan 阿索斯山
Афон [Afon]

multitudinous (Russian) congregation
xuduo Eluosi jiaohui de zuzhi 許多俄羅斯教會的組織
множество организаций Русской Православной Церкви [mnozhestvo organizatsii Russkoi Pravoslavnoi Tserkvi]

Museum Sinicum
Zhongwen bolan 《中文博览》

New Testament (translation into Chinese)
Xin yizhao shengjing 《新遺詔聖經》

New Territories
Xinjie 新界
Новые территории [Novye territorii]

The News of the Brotherhood of the Orthodox Church in China
Известия Братства православной церкви в Китае [Izvestiia Bratstva pravoslavnoi tserkvi v Kitae]

North Hostel / Russian Hostel / Capital Eastern Orthodox North Hostel
Eluosi Guan / Bei Guan / Jingdu dong jiaozong bei guan 北館 / 俄羅斯館 / 京都東教宗北館 Русский дом [Russkii dom]

"One Child, Two Languages"
Один ребёнок-два языка [Odin rebenok-dva iazyka]

Old Russian Life
Древнерусская жизнь [Drevnerusskaia zhizn']

Orthodox Church in Taiwan (Moscow Patriarchate)
Taiwan Jidu zhengjiaohui (Mosije da mu shou zuo) 台灣基督正教會（莫斯科大牧首座）Православная Церковь в Тайване [Pravoslavnaia Tserkov' v Taivane]

Orthodox Church in Taiwan (OMHKSEA)
Taiwan Jidu zhengjiaohui (Zhengjiaohui pushi zongzhu jiao sheng tong) 台灣基督正教會（正教會普世宗主教聖統）
Тайваньская православная церковь [Taivan'skaia pravoslavnaia tserkov']

Orthodox Prayer Book
Zhengjiao qidao shu 《正教祈禱書》
Молитвослов [molitvoslov]

The Orthodox Mirror
Dongjiao zong jian 《東教宗鑑》
Зеркало Православия [Zerkalo Pravoslaviia]

Our Mother of Kazan monastery
Казанско-Богородицкий мужской монастырь [Kazansko-Bogoroditskii muzhskoi monastyr']

Orthodox Fellowship of All Saints of China (OFASC)
Zheng jiaohui Zhonghua zhu sheng hui 正教會中華諸聖會
Православное Братство всех китайских святых [Pravoslavnoe Bratstvo vsekh kitaiskikh sviatykh]

(Ecumenical Patriarchate) Orthodox Metropolitanate of Hong Kong and South East Asia (OMHKSEA)
Zhengjiaohui pushi zongzhu jiao sheng tong Xianggang ji Dongnanya du zhujiao qu 正教會普世宗主教聖統香港及東南亞都主教教區
Митрополия Гонконга и Юго-Восточной Азии [Mitropoliia Gonkonga i Iugo-Vostochnoi Azii]

parish
tang qu 堂區
приход [prikhod]

parish assembly
tang qu huiyi 堂區會議
приходское собрание [prikhodskoe sobranie]

parish audit committee
shenji weiyuanhui 審計委員會
ревизионная комиссия [revizionnaia komissiia]

parish council
tang qu weiyuanhui 堂區委員會
приходской совет [prikhodskoi sovet]

The Path of Youth
Путь Молодежи [Put' Molodezhi]

patriarch
mushou / zong zhujiao / zong zhujiao 牧首 / 總主教/宗主教
патриарх [patriarch]

Pedder's Hill
Bida shan 畢打山
Педдерс Хилл [Pedders Khill]

Pereslavl
Переславль [Pereslavl']

(Russian style) pickles
Засолка [zasolka]

Podolsk
Подольск [Podol'sk]

Praise for the feast day of the 222 martyrs in China
Erbai ershi you er wei Zhong hua xundaozhe zhanli zanci 二百二十又二位中華殉道者瞻禮讚詞

Служба двумстам двадцати двум мученикам при восстании ихэтуаней в Китае пострадавшим [Sluzhba dvumstam dvadtsati dvum muchenikam pri vosstanii ikhetuanei v Kitae postradavshim]

prayer book
zhuwen shu 祝文書
молитвослов [molitvoslov]

priest
shenfu / siji 神父 / 司祭
священник [sviashchennik]

Profession of Faith
Xuan xin ci 宣信辭
Тридентский Символ веры [Tridentskii Simvol very]

Protection (Pokrov) of the Theotokos Church (Harbin)
Ha'erbin shengmu pingmeng (shouhu) tang 哈爾濱聖母帡幪（守護）堂
Храм в честь Покрова Пресвятой Богородицы в Харбине [Khram v chest' Pokrova Presviatoi Bogoroditsy v Kharbine]

(Book of) Psalms (translation into Chinese)
Sheng yong jing 聖詠經
Псалмы (перевод на китайский язык) [Psalmy (perevod na kitaiskii iazyk)]

Pskov-Caves Monastery (Pskovo-Pechersky Dormition Monastery)
Pusike-Peiqie'ersiji xiudaoyuan 普斯科-佩切爾斯基修道院
Псково-Печерский Успенский монастырь [Pskovo-Pecherskii Uspenskii monastyr']

(Diocese of) Pskov and Porkhov
Pusikefu he Bo'erhuofu jiaoqu 普斯科夫和波爾霍夫教區
Псковская и Порховская епархия [Pskovskaia i Porkhovskaia eparkhiia]

Pyongyang Church of the Life-Giving Trinity
Pingrang zhenbai siyuan (Ko. Pyongyang Jongbaek sawon) 平壤貞栢寺院 / 평양정백사원
Храм Троицы Живоначальной [Khram Troitsy Zhivonachal'noi]

Qing empire (dynasty)
Qingchao 清朝
Империя Цин [Imperiia Tsin]

Queen's Café
Huanghou fandian 皇后飯店
Куинс Кафе [Kuins Kafe]

"real social instrument"
реальный социальный инструмент [real'nyi sotsial'nyi instrument]

Red Fangzi at the Russian Embassy in Beijing: An Islet of Orthodoxy in China
Eluosi zhu Beijing dashiguan de hong fangzi: zai Zhongguo Dongzhengjiao de xiaodao 《俄羅斯駐北京大使館的紅房子：在中國東正教的小島》
Красная Фанза Российского Посольства в Пекине: Островок Православия в Китае [Krasnaia Fanza Rossiiskogo Posol'stva v Pekine: Ostrovok Pravoslaviia v Kitae]

Religious Affairs Bureau (predecessor of SARA)
Guowuyuan zongjiao shiwu ju 國務院宗教事務局

Renovationist Church / Living Church
gexin jiaohui / huo jiaohui 革新教會 / 活教會
Обновленческая церковь / Живая Церковь [Obnovlencheskaia tserkov' / Zhivaia Tserkov']

Ruist (Confucian) thought
Rujia sixiang 儒家思想
конфуцианская мысль [konfutsianskaia mysl']

Rus Sidyaschaya Foundation
Благотворительный фонд помощи осужденным и их семьям «Русь Сидящая» [Blagotvoritel'nyi fond pomoshchi osuzhdennym i ikh sem'iam "Rus' Sidiashchaia"]

Russian (ethnic group in the PRC)
Eluosi zu 俄羅斯族
русские (этническая группа в КНР) [russkie (etnicheskaia gruppa v KNR)]

Russian Culture Association (RCA)
Eguo wenhua xiehui 俄國文化協會
Ассоциация Русской культуры [Assotsiatsiia Russkoi kul'tury]

Russian Culture Week in Hong Kong
Xianggang Eluosi wenhua zhou 香港俄羅斯文化週
Неделя Русской культуры в Гонконге [Nedelia Russkoi kul'tury v Gonkonge]

Russian Ecclesiastical Mission in China / Spiritual Mission in Beijing
Eluosi Dongzhengjiao Zhongguo chuan jiao tuan 俄羅斯東正教中國傳教團
Русская духовная миссия в Пекине [Russkaia dukhovnaia missiia v Pekine]

Russian Language: 5 Elements
Русский Язык: 5 Элементов [Russkii Iazyk: 5 Elementov]

Russian Language Center (RLC)
Eluosi yuyan zhongxin 俄羅斯語言中心
Центр русского языка [Tsentr russkogo iazyka]

Russian Monastery of St. (Equal to the Apostles) Mary Magdalene / Church of St. Mary Magadalene (Jerusalem)
Modalade Maliya jiaotang 抹大拉的馬利亞教堂
Церковь Святой Марии Магдали́ны в Гефсимании [Tserkov' Sviatoi Marii Magdalíny v Gefsimanii]

Russian Orthodox Church Outside Russia (ROCOR)
Eluosi yu wai Dongzhengjiao hui 俄羅斯域外東正教會
Русская православная церковь заграницей [Russkaia pravoslavnaia tserkov' zagranitsei]

Russian Orthodox Mission College (Beijing)
Eluosi chuanjiao tuan fushu xuexiao 俄羅斯傳教團附屬學校
Русская духовная миссия в Пекине [Russkaia dukhovnaia missiia v Pekine]

Russian soup (borscht)
luosong tang 羅宋湯
борщ [borshch]

Russian Soviet Federative Socialist Republic
Eluosi Suweiya duli guojia lianheti guo 俄羅斯蘇維埃獨立國家聯合體國
Российская Советская Федеративная Социалистическая Республика
 [Rossiiskaia Sovetskaia Federativnaia Sotsialisticheskaia Respublika]

Russian-speaking population
Русскоязычное население [Russkoiazychnoe naselenie]

Russian Theological Seminary (Beijing)
Eluosi chuanjiao tuan fushu shenxueyuan 俄羅斯傳教團附屬神學院
духовная семинария при русской духовной миссии в Пекине [dukhovnaia seminariia pri russkoi dukhovnoi missii v Pekine]

Russkiy Mir Foundation
Фонд «Русский Мир» [Fond "Russkii Mir"]

Russo-Chinese Bank (later Russo-Asiatic Bank)
Hua-E Daosheng yinhang (E-Ya yinhang) 華俄道勝銀行 (俄亞銀行)
Русско-Китайский банк (Русско-Азиатский банк) [Russko-Kitaiskii bank (Russko-Aziatskii bank)]

Saint (Apostles) Peter and Paul Church of Hong Kong
Xianggang Sheng Bide Sheng Baoluo tang 香港聖彼得聖保羅堂
Храм святых апостолов Петра и Павла в Гонконге [Khram sviatykh apostolov Petra i Pavla v Gonkonge]

Saint Luke Orthodox Cathedral in Hong Kong / Orthodox Cathedral of Saint Luke the Evangelist (OCSLE)
Xianggang Sheng Lujia zhengjiao zuotang / Sheng Lujia xuan dao zhe zhengjiao da jiao tang 香港聖路加正教座堂/ 聖路加宣道者正教大教堂

samurai code
wushi dao (Ja. bushidō) 武士道
кодекс самурая [kodeks samuraia]

Saturday of the Souls
jinian wangzhe zhou liu 紀念亡者週六
Родительская суббота [Roditel'skaia subbota]

Seraphim of Sarov
Saluofu de Sheng Sailafen 薩羅夫的聖塞拉芬
Серафим Саровский [Serafim Sarovskii]

seven-string Chinese zither
guqin 古琴
Цисяньцинь [tsisian'tsin']

Shanghai China Orthodox Association
Shanghai Zhongguo zhengjiao xiehui 上海中國正教協會
Ассоциация Китайской Православной церкви в Шанхае [Assotsiatsiia Kitaiskoi Pravoslavnoi tserkvi v Shankhae]

Simplified Chinese script
jiantizi 簡體字
упрощенные китайские иероглифы [uproshchennye kitaiskie ieroglify]

Slavic harvest festival
Обжинки [Obzhinki]

Slavic Literature and Culture Day
День славянской письменности и культуры [Den' slavianskoi pis'mennosti i kul'tury]

The Snow Queen
Снежная королева [Snezhnaia koroleva]

sound
yin 音
звук [zvuk]

South China Morning Post (SCMP)
Nan hua zao bao 《南華早報》

Sower
Сеятель [Seiatel']

soy sauce Western
chiyou xican 豉油西餐
соевый соус в западной кухне [soevyi sous v zapadnoi kukhne]

St. Aleksejev Church (Harbin)
Sheng Aliekexieyefu jiaotang 聖阿列克謝耶夫教堂
Свято-Алексеевский храм [Sviato-Alekseevskii khram]

St. Alexander Nevsky Church (Hankou)
Aliekesangde Niefu tang / Sheng Aliekesangde datang / Yalishanda Niefusiji jiaotang 阿列克桑德聶夫堂 / 聖阿列克桑德大堂 / 亞歷山大·涅夫斯基教堂
Церковь Александра Невского [Tserkov' Aleksandra Nevskogo]

St. Andrew's Church (Hong Kong)
Sheng Andelie tang 聖安德烈堂
Церковь Святого Андрея в Гонконге [Церковь Святого Андрея в Гонконге]

"St. Andrew's Church for westerners"
Xiren Sheng Andelie tang 西人聖安德烈堂
«Церковь святого Андрея для граждан стран Запада» ["Tserkov' sviatogo Andreia dlia grazhdan stran Zapada"]

St. Danilov Monastery
Danninuofu xiudaoyuan 丹尼諾夫修道院
Свято-Данилов монастырь [Sviato-Danilov monastyr']

St. Elisabeth Convent
Sheng Yilishabai xiudaoyuan 聖伊利莎白修道院
Свято-Елисаветинский монастырь [Sviato-Elisavetinskii monastyr']

St. Gabriel's Church (Shanghai)
Sheng Jiabailie jiaotang 聖加百列教堂
Храм Святого Гавриила в Шанхае [Khram Sviatogo Gavriila v Shankhae]

St. Innocent of Irkutsk Church (Ergune)
Sheng Yingnuokenti tang 聖英諾肯提堂
Храм Святителя Иннокентия Иркутского [Khram Sviatitelia Innokentiia Irkutskogo]

St. John's Cathedral (Hong Kong)
Shenggonghui Sheng Yuehan zuotang 聖公會聖約翰座堂
Собор Святого Иоанна в Гонконге [Sobor Sviatogo Ioanna v Gonkonge]

St. Joseph's Church (Hong Kong)
Sheng Ruose tang 聖若瑟堂

St. Nicholas Church (Harbin)
Sheng Nigula jiaotang 聖尼古拉教堂

Никольский / Свято-Николаевский собор в Харбине [Nikol'skii sobor / Sviato Nikolaevskii sobor v Kharbine]

St. Nicholas Church (Ili)
Yining shi Dongzhengjiao tang 伊寧市東正教堂
Храм святителя Николая [Khram sviatitelia Nikolaia]

St. Nicholas Church (Tianjin)
Sheng Nigula tang 聖尼古拉堂
Свято-Николаевская церковь в Тяньцзине [Sviato-Nikolaevskaia tserkov' v Tian'tszine]

St. Nicholas Church (Urumqi)
Wulumuqi shi Dongzhengjiao tang 烏魯木齊市東正教堂
Храм святителя Николая [Khram sviatitelia Nikolaia]

St. Nicholas the Wonderworker Prayer House (Xiamen)
Xianling shengji zhe Sheng Nigula qidao suo 顯靈聖跡者聖尼古拉祈禱所
Молитвенный дом святителя Николая Чудотворца [Molitvennyi dom sviatitelia Nikolaia Chudotvortsa]

St. Peter and St. Paul Orthodox Church (OPASPP, Hong Kong) (formerly Church of Saints Peter and Paul)
Sheng Bide Sheng Baoluo Dongzheng jiaotang 聖彼得聖保羅東正教堂
Свято-Петропавловский храм [Sviato-Petropavlovskii khram]

St. Peter's Church (Hong Kong)
Sheng Boduolu tang 聖伯多祿堂

St. Petersburg University
Shengbidebao guoli daxue 聖彼得堡國立大學
Санкт-Петербурский государственный универстет [Sankt-Peterburskii gosudastvennyi universtet]

St. Sergius of Radonezh Parish (Shenzhen)
Sheng Se'erji tang 聖塞爾吉堂
Приход преп. Сергия Радонежского [Prikhod prep. Sergiia Radonezhskogo]

St. Sophia Cathedral
Sheng Suofeiya jiaotang 聖索菲亞教堂
Софийский собор [Sofiiskii sobor]

St. Teresa's Hospital
Sheng Deleisa yiyuan / Faguo yiyuan 聖德肋撒醫院 / 法國醫院
Госпиталь Святой Терезы [Gospital' Sviatoi Terezy]

St. Thomas Coptic Church (Hong Kong)
(Sheng Duomasi) kepute zhengjiao Xianggang fenhui （聖多瑪斯）科普特正教香港分會
Коптская Церковь Святого Фомы [Koptskaia Tserkov' Sviatogo Fomy]

St. Tikhon's Orthodox University of Humanities
Православный Свято-Тихоновский гуманитарный университет [Pravoslavnyi Sviato-Tikhonovskii gumanitarnyi universitet]

State Administration for Religious Affairs (SARA)
Guojia zongjiao shiwu ju 國家宗教事務局
Государственное управление по делам религий [Gosudarstvennoe upravlenie po delam religii]

Supreme Church Council
zuigao jiaohui weiyuanhui 最高教會委員會
Высший церковный совет [Vysshii tserkovnyi sovet]

Taipei Orthodox Church
Taibei Jidu zhengjiaohui 台北基督正教會
Тайбэйская православная церковь [Taibeiskaia pravoslavnaia tserkov']

Taosheng Publishing House
Daosheng chubanshe 道聲出版社

Ten Commandments
Banbu shijie 頒布十誡
Десять заповедей [Desiat' zapovedei]

Thanksgiving service
gan'en yigui 感恩儀軌
благодартвенный молебен [blagodartvennyi moleben]

Theological Question and Answer
Shenxue wen da 《神學問答》
Вопросы и ответы о теологии [Voprosy i otvety o teologii]

theosis
shenhua 神化
теозис [teozis]

"there"
Вот [vot]

Three-Self Patriotic Church
San zi aiguo jiaohui 三自愛國教會

Tianjin
Tianjin 天津
Тяньцзинь [Tian'tszin']

Tkachenko Restaurant
Tekaqinke canting 特卡琴科餐廳
Кафе-ресторан братьев Ткаченко [Kafe-restoran brat'ev Tkachenko]

Traditional Chinese script
fantizi 繁體字
традиционные китайские иероглифы [traditsionnye kitaiskie ieroglify]

Treaty of Nerchinsk
Nibuchu tiaoyue 《尼布楚條約》
Нерчинский договор [Nerchinskii dogovor]

underground church
di xia jiaohui 地下教會

Union Church (Hong Kong)
Xianggang you ning tang 香港佑寧堂

The United Front Work Department of CPC Central Committee
Zhonggong zhongyang tongyi zhanxian gongzuo bu 中共中央統一戰線工作部
Департамент Единого фронта ЦК КПК [Departament Edinogo fronta TsK KPK]

University of Hong Kong (HKU)
Xianggang daxue 香港大學
Университет Гонконга [Universitet Gonkonga]

vicar bishop
fu zhujiao 副主教
викарный епископ [vikarnyi episkop]

vicarate
fu zhujiao jigou 副主教機構
викариатство [vikariatstvo]

Vladimir School of Theology
духовная семинария во Владимире [dukhovnaia seminariia vo Vladimire]

Vladimir-Suzdal diocese
Владимиро-Суздальская епархия [Vladimiro-Suzdal'skaia eparkhiia]

Volunteers to Help Orphans
Волонтеры в помощь детям-сиротам [Volontery v pomoshch' detiam-sirotam]

WeChat
Weixin 微信
Вичат [Vichat]

Western cuisine
xican 西餐
Западная кухня [Zapadnaia kukhnia]

"wine and oil may be consumed"
jiu you ke shi 酒油可食
«разрешено есть масло и пить вино» ["razresheno est' maslo i pit' vino"]

"Winter Branches"
Зимние ветки [Zimnie vetki]

Xiamen (Amoy)
Xiamen 廈門
Сямэнь [Siamen']

Xinjiang Uyghur Autonomous Region
Xinjiang Weiwu'er zizhiqu 新疆維吾爾自治區

Синьцзянь-Уйгурский автономный район [Sin'tszian'-Uigurskii avtonomnyi raion]

Yancheng (Jiangsu province)
Yanchen (Jiangsu sheng) 鹽城 (江蘇省)
Яньчэн (Провинция Цзянсу) [Ian'chen (Provintsiia Tsziansu)]

Yenching University
Yanjing daxue 燕京大學
Яньцзинский университет [Ian'tszinskii universitet]

Yi ethnic group
Yizu 彝族

Zaraisk
Зарайск [Zaraisk]

Zhili
Zhili 直隸
Чжили [Chzhili]

Zhuang ethnic group
Zhuangzu 壯族

Znamenny chant
Знаменное пение, знаменный распев [Znamennoe penie, znamennyi raspev]

12 Essex Crescent, Kowloon Tong
Jiulong Tang Yaxishi dao 12 hao 九龍塘雅息士道12號
Эссекс Крессент 12, Коулун Тунг [Esseks Kressent 12, Koulun Tung]

216 Nathan Road, Yau Ma Tei
Youmadi Midun dao 216 hao 油麻地彌敦道216號
Нэтэн Роад 216, Яуматэй [Neten Road 216, Iaumatei]

(year of our Lord's birth) 1879
Shangdi jiangsheng yi qian ba bai qi shi jiu nian 上帝降生一千八百七十九年
1879 год от Рождества Христова [1879 god ot Rozhdestva Khristova]

Glossary

PERSONS

Notes

1) Russian names below are presented in "given name–(patronym)–surname order" instead of the customary "surname–given name–patronym" order.
2) Transliterations are not given after the Cyrillic versions if the name has been already been introduced on the preceding line in the standard transliterated form.
3) Names separated by the slash mark are two names for the same person.

Religious/Clergy, Living and Deceased (Alphabetized by Given Name)

Aidan (Keller) 艾丹（凱勒）

Alexander (Mileant) 亞歷山大（米蘭特）

Alexander Yu Shi 亞歷山大•遇石
Александр Ю Ши [Aleksandr Iu Shi]

Alexy I
Алексий [Aleksii]

Aleksander Du Lifu 阿里克桑德尔•杜
Александра Ду Лифу [Aleksandra Du Lifu]

Anastasius
Анастасий [Anastasii]

Anton Serafimovich
Антоний Серафимович [Antonii Serafimovich]

Antonios Alevisopoulos 安多尼•阿勒維所波洛斯
Αντώνιος Αλεβιζόπουλος [Antónios Alevizópoulos]

Anatoly Kung 安那托利•龔 / Kung Cheung Ming 龔長明
Анатолий Кун [Anatolii Kun]

Arkady Tyshchuk
Аркадий Тыщук [Arkadii Tyshchuk]

Sergei Nikolaevich Bulgakov [Сергей Николаевич Булгаков]

Cyril 西里爾
Кирилл [Kirill]

Damascene (John Christensen)
Дамаскин [Damaskin]

Daniel Alexeyevich Sysoev
Даниил Алексеевич Сысоев [Daniil Alekseevich Sysoev]

Dionisy Pozdnyaev
Дионисий Поздняев [Dionisii Pozdniaev]

Dmitry Lepeshev
Дмитрий Лепешев [Dmitrii Lepeshev]

Dmitry Lukyanov 德米特里·魯卡亞諾夫
Дмитрий Лукьянов [Dmitrii Luk'ianov]

Dmitry Mikhailovich Uspensky 德米特里·烏斯賓斯基
Дмитрий Михайлович Успенский [Dmitrii Mikhailovich Uspenskii]

Dmitry of Rostov (Danila Savvich Tuptalo)
Димитрий Ростовский [Dimitrii Rostovskii] / Данила Саввич Туптало [Danila Savvich Tuptalo]

Elias (Ilia) Wen 文子正
Илия Вэнь Цзычжэн [Iliia Ven' Tszychzhen]

Ephraim of Bikin (Roman Prosyanok)
Бикинский Ефрем / Роман Просянок [Bikinskii Efrem / Roman Prosianok]

Feodor Du Runchen 杜潤臣
Симеон [Simeon]

Germogen Orekhov
Гермоген Орехов [Germogen Orekhov]

Georgy, metropolitan of Nizhny Novgorod and Arzamas
митрополит Нижегородский и Арзамасский Георгий [mitropolit Nizhegorodskii i Arzamasskii Georgii]

Grigorij Zhu Shipu 格里高利·朱世樸
Григорий Чжу Шипу [Grigorii Chzhu Shipu]

Guri Karpov 固利乙 (Gurii of Taurida)
Григорий Платонович Карпов [Grigorii Platonovich Karpov]

Hilarion (Alfeyev)
Иларион (Алфеев) [Ilarion (Alfeev)]

Iakinf / Nikita Yakovlevich Bichurin 雅金甫 (皮丘林)
Иакинф / Никита Яковлевич Бичурин [Nikita Iakovlevich / Bichurin]

Ignatius, metropolitan of Khabarovsk and Priamur
митрополит Хабаровский и Приамурский Игнатий [mitropolit Khabarovskii i Priamurskii Ignatii]

Igor Filyanovsky
Игорь Филяновский [Igor' Filianovskii]

Innocent
Иннокентий / Иван Апполонович Фигуровский [Innokentii / Ivan Appolonovich Figurovskii]

Ioann (Krestiankin) 約安•克列斯季揚京

Ioann Vostorgov
Иван Иванович Восторгов [Ivan Ivanovich Vostorgov]

Jeffrey Yeung 楊澤

John Maximovitch
Иоанн Максимович [Ioann Maksimovich]

John Romanides
Ιωάννης Σάββας Ρωμανίδης [Ioánnis Sávvas Romanídis]

Jonah Li Liang 李亮

Juvenaly Poyarkov
Ювеналий Поярков [Iuvenalii Poiarkov]

Kiril Chkarboul 愛西里爾

Kirill (Vladimir Mikhailovich Gundiaev)
Кирилл / Владимир Михайлович Гундяев

Maxim Leontiev
Максим Леонтьев [Maksim Leont'ev]

Methodios 美多德
Мефодий [Mefodii]

Michael Li 李奉慈

Nestor / Nikolai Aleksandrovich Anisimov
Нестор / Николай Александрович Анисимов

Mikhail Yerokhin
Михаил Ерохин [Mikhail Erokhin]

Nectarios of Aegina
Άγιος Νεκτάριος Αιγίνης [Ágios Nektários Aigínis]

Nektarios
Νεκτάριος [Nektários]

Nicholas of Japan
Иван Дмитриевич Касаткин [Ivan Dmitrievich Kasatkin]

Nicholas the Miracle Worker (Nikolaos of Myra)
Николай Чудотворец [Nikolai Chudotvorets]

Nicetas
Νικήτας

Nikitas Lulias
Никита Лулиас

Nikodim
Никодим [Nikodim]

Oleg Davydenkov 奧列格•達維傑恩科夫
Олег Давыденков

Pavel Sun Ming 巴維爾•孫明
Павла Сунь Мин [Pavla Sun' Min]

Peter E. Gillquist 彼得•基爾魁斯

Glossary

[Saint] Polycarp 聖頗利卡爾普 Sheng Polika'erpu / 聖坡旅甲 Sheng Polǚjia
Поликарп Смирнский [Polikarp Smirnskii]

Semyon
Семён [Semen]

Sergiy Voronin
Сергей Николаевич Воронин [Sergei Nikolaevich Voronin]

Stephen Avramides 阿夫拉米德

Stephen of Perm
Стефан Пермский [Stefan Permskii]

Tikhon (Shevkunov)
Тихон (Георгий Александрович Шевкунов) [Tikhon (Georgii Aleksandrovich Shevkunov)]

Vasily Yao (Yao Fu'an 姚福安, born as Yao Shuanglin 姚雙林)
Василий Яо [Vasilii Yao]

Viktor Chernykh
Виктор Черных [Viktor Chernykh]

Viktor Svyatin 魏克托爾·斯維亞金
Виктор Святин [Viktor Sviatin]

Vladimir Sviatoslavich the Great
Владимир I Святославич [Vladimir I Sviatoslavich]

Yevgeny Lutchev
Евгений Лутчев [Evgenii Lutchev]

Historical Personalities (Including Persons Presumed to Be Deceased)

Nikolai Berdyaev
Николай Александрович Бердяев [Nikolai Aleksandrovich Berdiaev]

Nicholas Belanovsky
Николай Александрович Белановский [Nikolai Aleksandrovich Belanovskii]

Tatiana Ivanovra Belanovsky
Татьяна Ивановра Белановский [Tat'iana Ivanovra Belanovskii]

(Mr. and Mrs.) Birinkoff
Биринков [Birinkov]

Serge Nikolaevich Bolshakoff
Сергей Николаевич Большаков [Sergei Nikolaevich Bol'shakov]

John Bowring 寶寧 / 寶靈 / 包令

Chan Bing Yim 陳炳炎

Anton [Pavlovich] Chekhov
Антон Павлович Чехов [Anton Pavlovich Chekhov]

Chiang Kai-shek / Jiang Jieshi 蔣介石

Harold T. Creasy

William Des Vœux 德輔

Du Bining 杜碧寧

Adelaide Dmitryevna Fogt
Аделаида Дмитриевна Фогт [Adelaida Dmitrievna Fogt]

(Mr. and Mrs.) Gavidoff
Гавидов [Gavidov]

Constantine Golden (Goldin)
Сонстантине Голдин [Constantine Goldin]

Anastasia Goldin (Golden)
Анастасия Голдина [Anastasiia Goldina]

Ivan [Aleksandrovich] Goncharov
Иван Александрович Гончаров [Ivan Aleksandrovich Goncharov]

(Miss) D. Goroskenko (sic.)
Д. Горосченко [Goroschenko]

D. A. Kaluzhny
Д. А. Калюжный [D. A. Kaliuzhnyi]

Michael A. Koodiaroff
Михаил А. Кудияров [Mikhail A. Kudiiarov]

Aleksandr Aleksandrovich Kuzminskii 亞歷山大・庫茲明斯基
Александр Александрович Кузминский

Sergey Khoruzhiy
Сергей Сергеевич Хоружий [Sergei Sergeevich Khoruzhii]

Lai Wai Suen 黎慧宣

James Legge 理雅各

William Legge 威廉・列格

Liu Yüeh-sheng [Lin Yuesheng] 劉粵聲

Rudolf Löwenthal 羅文達

Murray MacLehose 麥理浩

Nicholas II
Николай II [Nikolai II]

Lila Nozadze
Лила Нозадзе [Lila Nozadze]

Peter I (Peter the Great)
Пётр I [Petr I]

George Pio-Ulski
Георгий Пио-Ульский [Georgii Pio-Ul'skii]

E. V. Putiatin 普提雅廷 / 葉夫菲米・瓦西里耶維奇・普佳京
Евфимий Васильевич Путятин [Evfimii Vasil'evich Putiatin]

Alexander S. Pushkin
Александр С. Пушкин [Aleksandr S. Pushkin]

Antonina Riasanovsky
Антонина Рязановский [Antonina Riazanovskii]
née Антонина Федоровна Подгоринова [Antonina Fedorovna Podgorinova]

Nicholas Valentine Riasanovsky
Николай Валентинович Рязановский [Nikolai Valentinovich Riazanovskii]

I. A. Rogachev 羅高壽
Игорь Алексеевич Рогачёв [Igor' Alekseevich Rogachev]

George V. Smirnov
Георгий Витальевич Смирнов [Georgii Vital'evich Smirnov]

Sawabe Takuma 沢辺 琢磨

A. P. Tkachenko
Аю Пю Ткаченко [A. P. Tkachenko]

Niculau Theodor Turin
Нисолау Теодор Турин [Nicolau Teodor Turin] / Нисула Теодор Турин [Nicula Theodor Turin]

V. V. Vaganoff
В.В. Ваганов [V. V. Vaganov]

Mischa Yu 于永富

Stanley Yu 于德義

Living Persons (Alphabetized by Surname)
Note: Chinese names are presented in "surname, given name" order.

Stephen Chan [Chen Zuoren] 陳佐人

Nelson Mitrophan Chin 米特洛凡•陳

Ingrid Chow

Anoush Georgievna Davis
Ануш Георгиевна Дейвис (Павлова) [Anush Georgievna Deivis (Pavlova)]

Alexander Dmitrenko
Александр Анатольевич Дмитренко [Aleksandr Anatol'evich Dmitrenko]

Tatiana Erohina
Татиана Ерохина [Tatiana Erokhina]

Dmitry Ivanov
Дмитрий Иванов [Dmitrii Ivanov]

Ksenia Kazarina
Ксения Казарина

Vladimir A. Kalinin
Владимир А. Калинин

Natalia Koval
Наталья Коваль

Anastasia Kraeva
Анастасия Александровна Краева [Anastasiia Aleksandrovna Kraeva]

Roman Kremnev
Роман Кремнев [Roman Kremnev]

Svetlana Kremneva
Светлана Алексеевна Кремнева [Svetlana Alekseevna Kremneva]

Andrew Kuraev
Андрей Кураев [Andrei Kuraev]

Lai Pan Chiu [Lai Pinchao] 賴品超

Nona Pio-Ulski Langley
Нона Пио-Ульский Лэнгли [Nona Pio-Ul'skii Lengli]

Li Qiuling 李秋零

Lin Sen / Ambrose Lam 林森

Lu Dezhi 盧德之

Polina Malkova
Полина Юрьевна Малкова [Polina Iur'evna Malkova]

Tatiana Manakova 塔季揚娜•馬納克科娃
Татьяна Манакова [Tat'yana Manakova]

Sergio Min 謝爾蓋•明
Сергей Мэн [Sergei Men]

Leonid Patorsky
Леонид Паторский

Anna Petrova
Анна Петрова

Liudmila Popova
Людмила Попова

Kira Pozdnyaeva
Кира Поздняева

Tatiana Pugacheva
Татьяна Сергеевна Пугачева [Tat'iana Sergeevna Pugacheva]

Anna Rayton

Dayana Samantseva
Даяна Ігорівна Самарцева [Daiana Igorivna Samartseva]

Polina Sarafanova
Сарафанова Полина Михайловна [Polina Mikhailovna Sarafanova]

Jean-Michel Sourd

Nina Starostina 妮娜•斯塔羅斯金娜
Нина Старостина

Nazar Tabachyshyn
Назар Табачишин [Nazar Tabachishin]

Susanna Tsang 曾佩珊

Irina Ustyugova
Устюгова Ирина Сергеевна [Irina Sergeevna Ustiugova]

Nadezhda Sperantova
Надежда Сретенская [Nadezhda Sretenskaia]

Wan Tsz Ming (Wen Ziming) 溫子銘

Lino Wong Wing Kuen (Huang Yongquan) 黃永權

Wang Xiaochao 王曉朝

Wen Jian 溫健

Bishop Seraphim [Tsujie] of Sendai [Eastern Diocese of Japan]
セラフィム辻永昇
Sun Yue 孫越

Daniel H.N. Yeung [Yang Xinan] 楊熙楠

Zhang Baichun 張百春

"George Zhu" 喬治•朱

"Mrs. Zu" 祖太太

Bibliography

NOTES

1. Authors/compilers for eponymous websites are not named. Such websites are alphabetized by the titles. Likewise, individual translators are not mentioned by their own names if they worked on teams on behalf of the commissioning publisher.
2. For details about interviews, refer to the relevant citations in the text. Following stylistic convention, such information is not included in this section of the book.
3. Access dates for websites are not given if the purpose of the reference is to indicate the presence of such websites rather than to refer to content that is time specific.
4. Cyrillic is added to an author's name and the book/article title only when the book/article is written in the Russian language. In some cases, the English translation of the publisher is provided in []. The original (pre-ordination) names of Orthodox priests are generally not included in the citations. If a book/article is a translation by English/Chinese, Cyrillic is omitted. Parentheses () are used to delineate Cyrillic names more visibly from the transliterations in Latin alphabet, and to distinguish from square brackets [] used for English translation.
5. The Asian-language version of an author's name and the book/article title only when the book/article is written in an Asian language.
6. Entries with Chinese characters present the type of characters used in the original publication, either traditional or simplified. However, there are some publications that are in simplified characters, but which have titles and/or author names in traditional characters. In these cases, the details of the books are presented in the bibliography as they are printed in the

original publications, so these citations contain both traditional and simplified characters.
7. Names of translators that are only cited Chinese characters in the publications are Romanized in Hanyu Pinyin according to Mandarin pronunciation of the characters. However, some of these persons may use other names or forms of these names, including Cantonese Jyutping romanizations.
8. "Orthodox Church of Taiwan" as a publisher is sometimes translated into English in the case of bilingual English/Chinese publications or English as primary language publications, whereas it remains in Chinese for Chinese-language works.

A Yi Aoxibofu 阿•伊•奧西波夫 (А.И. Осипов) [A. I. Osipov]. *Cong duanzhan dao yongheng: linghun de laishi* 從短暫到永恆：靈魂的來世 [From brevity to eternity: the afterlife of the soul]. Hong Kong: OPASPP, 2012.

Abbey of St. John (Community of John the Baptist). *What Do You Know About Icons?* Kareas, Attiki, Greece: Holy Monastery of St. John the Baptist, 2001.

Abbey of St. John (Community of John the Baptist) 聖約翰修道院修女們 [Sheng Yuehan xiudaoyuan xiunümen]. *Nin dui shengxianghua you he lijie?* 您對聖像畫有何理解？[What do you know about icons?]. Xindian: Taiwan Jidu Zhengjiaohui, 2006.

Adamek, Piotr. "'Unworthy to Be Quoted among the Believers—Worthy to be Quoted among the Martyrs': Women in the Orthodox Church in China." *Religions & Christianity in Today's China* 8, no. 4 (2017): 25–33.

Afinogenov, Gregory. *Spies and Scholars: Chinese Secrets and Imperial Russia's Quest for World.* Cambridge, MA: The Belknap Press of Harvard University Press, 2020.

Aidan (Keller). *A Pocket Church History for Orthodox Christians.* Austin, TX: St. Hilarion's Press, 1994.

[Xiushi siji] Aidan (Keller) 修士司祭艾丹 (凱勒) [Father Hieromonk Adrian (Keller)]. *Zhengjiao Jidutu de jiaohui lüeshi* 正教基督徒的教會略史 [A concise history of the church for Orthodox Christians]. Translated by Peter Lu 彼得·陸 (陸宏湜). Hong Kong: China Orthodox Press, 2016.

Alevisopoulos, Antonios. *Zhengjiao de jingshen yu lingxing* 正教的精神與靈性 [The Orthodox church: its faith, worship, and life]. Translated by Stephen Avramides. Taipei: Tian'en chubanshe, 2002.

[Bishop] Aleksandr (Mileant) (Александр [Милеант]). *Prazdnik Sviatoi Troitsy — en' soshestviia Sviatogo Dukha na Apostolov* (Праздник Святой Троицы — день сошествия Святого Духа на Апостолов) [The feast of the Holy Trinity: the descent of the Holy Spirit on apostles] Moscow: Izdatel'stvo khrama Pokrova Presviatoi Bogoroditsy, 1998.

[Bishop] Alexander (Mileant) / zhujiao Yalishanda (Milante) 主教亚历山大 （米兰特）. *Angels: Blessed Messengers of God and End of the World / Tianshi: shangdi mengfu de xinshi shijie mori* 天使：上帝蒙福的信使，世界末日. Vol. 1 of *Missionary Leaflets / Zhengxin xuanyang ji* 正信宣扬集. Translated by Gong

Lei 龚蕾 and Ji Mi Luomannuofu 季·米·罗曼诺夫 [J. M. Romanov]. Hong Kong: OPASPP and OFASC, 2009.

———. *On the Island of Lepers and Evil Spirits at the Threshold of the Fiery Gehenna: Teachings of the Orthodox Church about God's Judgment about them / Zai ma feng bingren de daoyu shang, diyu menqian xieling ji Shangdi dui qi shenpan de Zhengjiaohui jiaoyi* 在麻疯|病人的岛屿上, 地狱门前邪灵及上帝对其审判的正教会教义. Vol. 2 of *Missionary Leaflets / Zhengxin xuanyang ji* 正信宣扬集. Translator(s) unknown. Hong Kong: OPASPP and OFASC, 2009.

———. *Orthodox Christianity*. Self-published, CreateSpace, 2016.

Alexeeva, Olga, and Michael Black. "Chinese Migration in the Russian Far East: A Historical and Sociodemographic Analysis." *China Perspectives* 75, no. 3 (2008): 20–32.

[Gu Luoma] Anboluoxiu （古罗马）安波罗修 [St. Ambrose of ancient Rome]. *Lun Jidujiao xinyang* 论基督教信仰 [Exposition of the Christian faith]. Translated by Yang Lingfeng 杨凌峰. Edited by Luo Yufang 罗宇芳. Beijing: Sanlian shudian, 2010.

Angold, Michael, ed. *The Cambridge History of Christianity, vol. 5: Eastern Christianity*. Cambridge: Cambridge University Press, 2006.

Anonymous. "Nekrolog" (Некролог) [Obituary]. *Zhurnal Moskovskoi Patriarkhii* (Журнала Московской Патриархии) [Journal of the Moscow Patriarchate], no. 5 (1970): 48.

———. "Paskha v stranakh Azii" (пасха в странах азии) [Easter in Asia]. *Khristianskii Mir Azii* (христианский мир Азии) [Christian World of Asia] (April 2016): 6–11.

———. "V Gonkonge Jidu fuhuo le" (В Гонконге 基督復活了) [In Hong Kong Christ has risen]. *Khristianskii Mir Azii* (Христианский Мир Азии) [Christian World Asia] (May 2016): 11.

———. "V Kitae Fuhuojie kuaile" (В Китае 復活節快樂) [In China Happy Easter]. *Khristianskii Mir Azii* (Христианский Мир Азии) [Christian World Asia] (May 2016): 10.

Ansheles, Artem (Артём Аншелес). "Xianggangren shi shi qiguai de Eluosi shiwu!," 香港人試食奇怪的俄羅斯食物! [The People of Hong Kong Try to Eat the Strange Russian Food!]. YouTube video. 6:20. Accessed October 26, 2016. https://www.youtube.com/watch?v=2ugpFlrQEd8.

———. "Artem Ansheles (Facebook page)." Accessed March 13, 2017. https://www.facebook.com/anshelesartem.

———. "Artem Ansheles (website)." Accessed March 13, 2017. http://ansheles.com/eng.

———. "Artem Ansheles (YouTube channel)." Accessed March 13, 2017. https://www.youtube.com/user/Kalendorable.

Antiochian Orthodox Christian Archdiocese of New York and all North America. *Service Book of the Holy Eastern Orthodox Catholic and Apostolic Church*. New York: Antiochian Orthodox Christian Archdiocese of New York and all North America, 1971.

[Gu Luoma] Aogusiding （古罗马） 奥古斯丁 [St. Augustine of ancient Rome]. *Chanhui lu* 忏悔录 [Confessions]. Translated by Ren Xiaojin 任晓晋, Wang Aiju 王爱菊, and Pan Yusha 潘玉莎. Beijing: Guangming ribao chubanshe, 2007.

Baddeley, John F. *Russia, Mongolia, China, being some record of the relations between them from the beginning of the XVIIth century to the death of the Tsar Alexei Mikhailovich, A.D. 1602–1676, rendered mainly in the form of narratives dictated or written by the envoys sent by the Russian tsars, or their voevodas in Siberia to the Kalmuk and Mongol khans & princes; and to the emperors of China; with introductions, historical and geographical, also a series of maps, showing the progress of geographical knowledge in regard to Northern Asia during the XVIth, XVIIth, & early XVIIIth centuries, the texts mainly taken more especially from manuscripts in the Moscow Foreign Office Archive*s. London: Macmillan, 1919.

Baker, Kevin. *A History of the Orthodox Church in China, Korea and Japan*. Lewiston, NY: Edwin Mellen, 2006.

Bard, Solomon. *Voices from the Past: Hong Kong 1842–1918*. Hong Kong: Hong Kong University Press, 2002.

Barua, Ankur, and M. A. Basilio. *Buddhism Flourishes in Hong Kong: The History of Buddhism in Hong Kong Dates Back to the Fifth Century A.D*. Saarbrücken: VDM, Verlag Dr. Müller, 2010.

Bayer, Theophilus Siegfried. *Museum Sinicum: in quo Sinicae linguae et literaturae ratio explicatur*. 2 vols. Petropoli: Typogr. acad. Imperatoriae, 1730.

Bays, Daniel H. *A New History of Christianity in China*. The Global Christianity Series. Chicester: Wiley-Blackwell, 2011.

———. *Christianity in China: From the Eighteenth Century to the Present*. Stanford University Press, 1999.

Benovska, Milena. *Orthodox Revivalism in Russia: Driving Forces and Moral Quests*. London: Routledge, 2020.

Bickers, Robert. *Britain in China: Community, Culture and Colonialism 1900–1949*. Manchester: Manchester University Press, 1999.

Bide Falangshi 彼得•法郎士 [Peter France]. *Eluosi de zhanglao, senlin zhong de yinzhe* 俄羅斯的長老，森林中的隱者 [Elders of Russia, hermits in the forest]. Translated by Liang Yong'an 梁永安. Hong Kong: China Orthodox Press, 2016.

Bide Ji'erkuisi 彼得•基爾魁斯 [Peter Gilquist]. *Chengwei Dongzheng jiaotu: chonghui shanggu jidu xinyang zhi lu* 成為東正教徒：重回上古基督信仰之路 [Becoming an Orthodox believer: the road of returning to ancient Christianity]. Originally published 1989. Revised edition 1992. Xindian: Taipei Jidujiao Zhengjiaohui, 2006.

Billington, James H. *The Icon and the Axe: An Interpretive History of Russian Culture*. New York: Vintage Books, 1970.

"Bogosluzhebnye ukazaniia 2020" (Богослужебные указания 2020) [Liturgical instructions 2020]. Teoretik, 2020. Vers. 8.3.2. APKPure. https://apkpure.com/cn/%D0%B1%D0%BE%D0%B3%D0%BE%D1%81%D0%BB%D1%83%D0%B6%D0%B5%D0%B1%D0%BD%D1%8B%D0%B5-%D1%83%D0%BA%D0%B0%D0%B7%D0%B0%D0%BD%D0%B8%D1%8F-2020/ru.teoretik.ukazaniya.

Bojanowska, Edyta M. *A World of Empires: The Russian Voyage of the Frigate Pallada*. Cambridge, MA: Belknap Press of Harvard University Press, 2018.

Bolshakoff, Serge. *The Foreign Missions of the Russian Orthodox Church*. London: Society for Promoting Christian Knowledge; New York: The Macmillan Co., 1943.

———. "Les Missions étrangeres dan l'Eglise orthodox russe" [Foreign missions of the Russian Orthodox Church]. *Irénikon* 28 (1955): 159–75.

Brand Hong Kong. "Brand Hong Kong." Accessed December 21, 2018. www.brandhk.gov.hk/en/index.html.

Braun, Elihai. "Hong Kong Virtual Jewish History Tour." Jewish Virtual Library: A Project of AICE. Accessed March 3, 2021. https://www.jewishvirtuallibrary.org/hong-kong-virtual-jewish-history-tour.

Brook, Timothy. "Rethinking Syncretism: The Unity of the Three Teachings and their Joint Worship in Late-Imperial China." *Journal of Chinese Religions* 21, no. 1 (2013): 13–44.

Bulgakov, S. N. (С. Н. Булгаков). *Pravoslavie: Ocherki ucheniia Pravoslavnoi Tserkvi* (Православие: Очерки учения Православной Церкви) [Orthodoxy: essays on the teachings of the Orthodox Church]. Paris: YMCA Press, 1962.

Burlacioiu, Ciprian. "Russian Orthodox Diaspora as a Global Religion after 1918." *Studies in World Christianity* 24, no. 1 (April 2018): 4–24.

C. H. Bu'erjiakefu C. H. 布尔加科夫 [Sergei Nikolaevich Bulgakov]. *Dongzhengjiao —jiaohui xueshuo gaiyao* 东正教——教会学说概要 [Eastern Orthodoxy— summary of church doctrine]. Beijing: Shangwu yinshuguan, 2005.

Cabasilas, Nicholas. *Commentary on the Divine Liturgy*. 14th century. Translated by J. M. Hussey and P. A. McNulty. New York: St. Vladimir's Seminary Press, 1960.

Cai Hongsheng 蔡鸿生. *Eluosi guan jishi* 俄罗斯馆纪事 [Accounts of the Russian Hostel]. Guangzhou: Guangdong renmin chubanshe, 1994.

Carlton, Clark. *The Way: What Every Protestant Should Know About the Orthodox Church*. Salisbury, MA: Regina Orthodox Press, 2007.

Carroll, John M. *A Concise History of Hong Kong*. Lanham, MD: Rowman & Littlefield, 2007.

Cary, Otis. *Roman Catholic and Greek Orthodox Missions*. Vol.1 of *A History of Christianity in Japan*. Rutland, VT and Tokyo, Japan: Charles. Tuttle Company, 1976.

Cavarnos, Constantine. *Orthodox Iconography*. Boston: Institute for Byzantine and Greek Studies, 1997.

Chan, Shun Hing. "The Development of Christian Social Services in Hong Kong." In *A Carnival of Gods Studies of Religions in Hong Kong*, edited by Chan Shun Hing, 351–68. Hong Kong: Oxford University Press, 2002.

Chan Tsz Wai 陳芷慧. "'Tamen de Shengdanjie': shangsha zhong bashi zai de E Dongzheng jiaohui Shengdanjie bushi shi'er yue ershiwu ri? 【他們的聖誕】商廈中80的俄東正教會聖誕不是12月25日? ['Their Christmas': 80 years of Russian Orthodox Church in a commercial building; Why is Christmas not celebrated on 25th December?]. Community, HK01, December 25, 2016. Accessed January 7, 2017. https://www.hk01.com/sns/article/62153.

Chang, Felix B., and Sunnie T. Rucker-Chang, eds. *Chinese Migrants in Russia, Central Asia and Eastern Europe*. Routledge Contemporary Russia and Eastern Europe Series 28. London and New York: Routledge, 2012.

Chang, Ku-ming (Kevin), Anthony Grafton, and Glenn W. Most, eds. *Impagination – Layout and Materiality of Writing and Publication: Interdisciplinary Approaches from East and West*. Berlin: De Gruyter, 2021.

"Cheesefare Sunday (Maslenitsa) (Facebook)." Accessed March 13, 2017. https://www.facebook.com/events/415658958770919/permalink/420602504943231.

Chekhov, Anton Pavlovich (Антон Павлович Чехов). *Letters of Anton Tchehov to his Family and Friends*. Translated by Constance Garnett. London: Chatto & Windus, 1920.

Chen, Vincent. *Sino-Russian Relations in the Seventeenth Century*. The Hague: Martinus Nijhoff, 1966.

Chen Yuping 陈玉萍. "Zhong E hunyin jiating guanxi luetan" 中俄婚姻家庭关系略谈 [Brief discussion on Chinese-Russian marriage and family relationship]. *Chizi*, no. 7 (2015): 48.

Chi Wing Sin 池永賢. "Xiejinhui tu zhuandai, Dongzhengjiao bei quxiao timing zige" 協進會突轉軚東正教被取消提名資格 [The Hong Kong Christian Council's sudden change, Orthodox Christianity loses its right to nominate]. In *Media HK*, October 25, 2016. Accessed March 29, 2018. http://www.inmediahk.net/node/1045394.

Ching, Julia. *Confucianism and Christianity: A Comparative Study*. Tokyo: Kodansha, 1978.

Choi, Jiyoon (Pilateus). *Kratkii Ocherk Istorii Koreiskoi Pravoslavnoi Tserkvi* (Краткий Очерк Истории Корейской Православной Церкви) / *Hanguk jeonggyohoe yaksa* 한국정교회약사 / *Hanguo Zhengjiaohui lüeshi* 韓國正教會略史 [A short history of Orthodox Christianity in Korea]. Hong Kong: China Orthodox Press, 2015.

Chu, Cindy Yik-yi. *The Chinese Sisters of the Precious Blood and the Evolution of the Catholic Church*. London: Palgrave Macmillan, 2016.

Clark, Anthony E. *China's Christianity: From Missionary to Indigenous Church*. Studies in Christian Mission 50. Leiden: Brill, 2017.

Climacus, John. *The Ladder of Divine Ascent*. Boston: Holy Transfiguration Monastery, 1979.

Cole, David B. "Russian Oregon: A History of the Russian Orthodox Church and Settlement in Oregon, 1882–1976." Master's thesis, Portland State University, 1976. PDXScholar (Paper 2334).

(Hong Kong) Confucian Academy. "Kongjiao xueyuan" 孔教學院 [Confucian Academy]. Accessed July 7, 2018. http://confucianacademy.com.

Consulate General of the Russian Federation in the Hong Kong SAR, PRC (official website). Accessed November 10, 2017. https://hongkong.mid.ru/web/hongkong-en.

Coomler, David. *The Icon Handbook: A Guide to Understanding Icons and the Liturgy Symbols and Practices of the Orthodox Church*. Springfield, IL: Templegate, 1995.

Couling, Samuel, ed. *The Encyclopaedia Sinica*. Shanghai: Kelly and Walsh, Limited, 1917.

Council of Europe (European Council). "Common European Framework of Reference for Languages: Learning, Teaching, Assessment (CEFR)." Accessed January 16, 2017. https://www.coe.int/en/web/common-european-framework-reference-languages.

Cressy, Earl Herbert. *City Churches in Hong Kong: With a Supplementary Survey of All Churches in the Colony*. Hong Kong: Earl Herbert Cressy, 1956.

———. *Urban Church Growth in Hong Kong 1955–1958: Second Hong Kong Study*. Self-published, Hong Kong: Earl Herbert Cressy, 1960.

Crouch, Archie R., et al., eds. *Christianity in China: A Scholars Guide to Resources in the Libraries and Archives of the United States*. Armonk, NY: M.E. Sharpe, 1989.

Crow, Carl. *The Travelers' Handbook for China (including Hong Kong)*, 3rd ed. New York: Dodd, Mead & Co.; Shanghai: Carl Crow, 1921.

Curanović, Alicja. "Russia's Mission in the World: The Perspective of the Russian Orthodox Church." *Problems of Post-Communism* 66, no. 4 (2019): 253–67.

Damascene. *Christ the Eternal Tao*. Platina, CA: Valaam Books, 1999.

Damashige de Sheng Yuehan 大馬士革的聖約翰 [Saint John of Damascus]. *Zhengtong Xinyang chan xiang* 正統信仰闡詳 [An exact exposition of the Orthodox faith]. Translated by Shen Xianweizhen 沈鲜维桢. Based on the Greek version edited by Du Menggao 都孟高 [M. H. Throop]. Hong Kong: China Orthodox Press, 2015. Content written in simplified Chinese.

Damm, Emily Belle, and Cooley, Skye. "Resurrection of the Russian Orthodox Church: Narrative of Analysis of the Russian National Myth." *Social Science Quarterly* 98, no. 3 (2017): 942–57.

Dan Mengxin 单萌心 [Hieromonk Damascene]. *Yesu Jidu shi shui? Zhengjiaohui de lijie: Dan Mengxin jiaoshou de yanjiang* 耶稣基督是谁？正教会的理解：单萌心教授的演讲 [Who is Jesus Christ? The Orthodox understanding: the lecture of Professor Damascene]. Hong Kong: China Orthodox Press, 2014.

Danni'er Sishaoyefu shenfu 丹尼爾·思紹耶夫神父 [Father Daniel Sysoev]. *Hewei qidao* 何為祈禱 [Why do we pray?]. Translated by Anatoly Kung (Kung Cheung Ming 龔長明). Hong Kong: China Orthodox Press, 2015.

Datsyshen, Vladimir Grigor'evich (Владимир Григорьевич Дацышен). *Istoriia Rossiiskoi dukhovnoi missii v Kitae* (История Российской духовной миссии в Китае) [History of the Russian Spiritual Mission in China]. Hong Kong: OPASPP, 2010.

———. *Mitropolit Pekinskii Innokentii* (Митрополит Пекинский Иннокентий) [Metropolitan Innokenty of Peking]. Hong Kong: OPASPP, 2011.

Datsyshen, Vladimir Grigor'evich (Владимир Григорьевич Дацышен) and Anton Borisovich Chegodaev (Антон Борисович Чегодаев). *Arkhimandrit Petr (Kamenskii)* (Архимандрит Петр [Каменский]) [Archmandrite Peter (Kamensky)]. Hong Kong: OPASPP, 2013.

Davie, Grace. "Believing without Belonging: Is This the Future of Religion in Britain?" *Social Compass* 37, no. 4 (1990): 455–69.

———. *Religion in Britain since 1945: Believing without Belonging.* Oxford: Blackwell, 1994.

[Archpriest] Davydenkov, Oleg 奧列格•達維傑恩科夫大神父. *Zhengjiao jiaoli wenda* 正教教理問答 [Questions and answers about the Orthodox catechism]. Translated by Anatoly Kung 安那托利•龔 (Kung Cheung Ming龔長明). Hong Kong: China Orthodox Press, 2017.

[Archpriest] Davydenkov, Oleg (Олег Давыденков). *Katikhizis: Vvedenie v dogmaticheskoe bogoslovie* (Катихизис: Введение в догматическое богословие) [Catechism: introduction to dogmatic theology]. Moscow: Izd-vo PSTGU [St. Tikhon's Orthodox University of Humanities Press], 2000.

Demidova, N. F. (Н. Ф. Демидова), and V. S. Miasnikov (В. С. Мясников), eds. *Russko-kitaiskie otnosheniia v XVII veke: Materialy i dokumenty, 1608–1691* (Русско-китайские отношения в XVII веке: Материалы и документы) [Russo-Chinese relations in the seventeenth century: materials and documents, 1608–1691]. 2 vols. Moscow: Nauka, 1969.

Department for External Church Relations (DECR). "Chinese edition of His Holiness Patriarch Kirill's book Word of a Pastor presented in Hong Kong," June 26, 2018. Accessed July 1, 2018. https://mospat.ru/en/2018/06/26/news161375.

———. "Department for External Church Relations, Moscow Patriarchate," www.mospat.ru.

DeWolf, Christopher. "Why do Hong Kong Restaurants Serve Borscht? The Overlooked History of Russian Hong Kong." *Zolima Citymag*, October 4, 2017. Accessed December 10, 2017. https://zolimacitymag.com/why-do-hong-kong-restaurants-serve-borscht-the-overlooked-history-of-russian-hong-kong.

[Da siji] Di'aonixi 大司祭迪奧尼西, and Dimiteli Yiwannuofu 迪米特里•伊萬諾夫, eds. *Jidutu rensheng zhi zhongdian ji yuan he you si* 基督徒人生之終點及緣何有死 [The end of a Christian life and the meaning of death]. Translated by Lian Qianqi 連阡淇. Edited by Ambrose Lam (Lin Sen) 林森. Hong Kong: China Orthodox Press, 2015. Content written in simplified Chinese.

Dimas, Nina Tkachuk, trans. "Orthodox Publications in Chinese Presented at Beijing Book Fair," Orthodox Christianity in China. September 3, 2012. Accessed February 8, 2017. http://orthodox.cn/contemporary/beijing/20120903beijing_en.htm.

[Saint] Dmitry of Rostov. *Mirror of Orthodox Confession.* Translated by [Saint] Gory of Taurida. Sydney: Russo-Chinese Orthodox Mission of ROCOR in Australia, 2016.

Dmytryshyn, Basil, E. A. P. Crownhart-Vaughan, and Thomas Vaughan, eds. and trans. *Russia's Conquest of Siberia, 1558–1700: A Documentary Record.* Portland: Oregon Historical Society Press, 1990.

The Dormition of the Most Holy Theotokos Church in Beijing. Russian Orthodox Church Moscow Patriarchate. Accessed October 28, 2017. http://orthodoxbj.com/en.

Doubrovskaia, Dina V. "The Russian Orthodox Church in China." In Stephen Uhalley and Xiaoxin Wu, *China and Christianity: Burdened Past, Hopeful Future*, 163–76. London and New York: Routledge, 2001.

Du Zhongqi (Ду Чжунци). *Du Bining zai Zhongguo: gui si nian Eluosi houyi "zongjiao xungen zhi lü"* 杜碧宁在中国——癸巳年俄罗斯后裔「宗教寻根之旅」[Du Bining in China: "The journey for seeking religious roots" by descendants of Russians in the Gui si year (2013)]. N.p.: Self-published, 2014.

[Archpriest] Dudchenko, Andrei (Андрей Дудченко) / da siji Duoteqinke Andelie 大司祭多特琴科·安德烈. *Osnovy Very. Prichastie: chto eto takoe i kak podgotovit'sia?* (Основы Веры. Причастие: что это такое и как подготовиться?) / *Xinyang de jichu: Sheng can li: ta de hanyi ji zenyang zhunbei?* 信仰的基礎：聖餐禮：它的含義及怎樣準備？ [Foundations of faith: The holy sacrament—what it is and how to be prepared?]. Translated by Anatoly Kung (Kung Cheung Ming 龔長明). Hong Kong: OPASPP, 2014.

———. *Osnovy Very. Kak podgotovit'sia k pervoi ispovedi?* (Основы Веры. Как подготовиться к первой исповеди?) / *Xinyang de jichu: zenyang zhunbei diyici chuanhui liyi?* 信仰的基礎：怎樣準備第一次懺悔禮儀？ [Foundations of faith: how to prepare for the first time of confession?]. Translated by Anatoly Kung (Kung Cheung Ming 龔長明). Hong Kong: OPASPP, 2014.

Duzhujiao Lilaliyong (La'erfeiyefu) 都主教伊拉里雍（阿爾菲耶夫）[Metropolitan Hilarion (Alfeyev)]. *Zhengxin aoyi: Dongzhengjiao shenxue daolun* 正信奧義：東正教神學導論 [The mystery of faith: introduction to Eastern Orthodox theology]. Translated by Ambrose Lin 林森. Edited by Byron Wong 黃柏祥 and Ambrose Lin 林森. Hong Kong: OPASPP, 2015.

The Economist. "Near China's Border with Russia, the Orthodox Church Regains a Toehold." Heaven's Outposts. May 7, 2020. Accessed August 25, 2020. https://www.economist.com/china/2020/05/07/near-chinas-border-with-russia-the-orthodox-church-regains-a-toehold.

———. "Protestant Christianity is booming in China: President Xi does not approve." Daily chart. September 15, 2020. Accessed February 18, 2021. https://www.economist.com/graphic-detail/2020/09/15/protestant-christianity-is-booming-in-china.

"Ecumenical Patriarchate / Orthodox Metropolis of Korea." Accessed June 2, 2017. https://www.orthodoxkorea.org/home.

Elleman, Bruce A. *Diplomacy and Deception: The Secret History of Sino-Soviet Diplomatic Relations, 1917–1927.* Armonk, NY and London: M.E. Sharpe, 1997.

Ellis, Jane. *The Russian Orthodox Church: A Contemporary History.* Bloomington, IN: Indiana University Press, 1986.

Eluosi zu jianshi bianxie zu 《俄罗斯族简史》编写组, ed. *Eluosi zu jianshi* 俄罗斯族简史 [A brief history of the Russian ethnic group]. Ürümqi: Xinjiang renmin chubanshe, 1987.

Embassy of Russia (Russian Federation) to the DPRK. "Orthodox Church of the Live-Giving (sic.) Trinity in Pyongyang." Accessed June 16, 2018. http://www.rusembdprk.ru/en/russia-and-dprk/orthodox-church-in-pyongyang.

Erni, John Nguyet, and Lisa Yuk-ming Leung. *Understanding South Asian Minorities in Hong Kong.* Hong Kong: Hong Kong University Press, 2014.

Erohina, Tatiana. *Growing Up Russian In China: A Historical Memoir.* Bloomington, IN: iUniverse, 2011.

Esmantova, Tat'iana L. (Татьяна Л. Эсмантова). *Russkii iazyk: 5 elementov* (Русский язык: 5 элементов) [Russian language: 5 elements], 4th ed. 4 vols. St. Petersburg: Zlatoust, 2014.

Federova, Nina. *The Family.* Boston: Little, Brown, and Company, 1940.

Florovsky, Georges. *Christianity and Culture.* Vol. 2 of *Collected Works of Georges Florovsky.* Boston: Nordland Publishing Company, 1974.

France, Peter. *Hermits: The Insights of Solitude.* Self-published, Vintage Digital, 2014. Kindle.

Franklin, Simon. *Writing, Society and Culture in Early Rus, c.950–1300.* Cambridge and New York: Cambridge University Press, 2002.

Freeze, G. L. (Gregory L.). "Handmaiden of the State? The Church in Imperial Russia Reconsidered." *Journal of Ecclesiastical History* 36, no. 1 (1985): 82–102.

Friesen, Aileen. "Building an Orthodox Empire: Archpriest Ioann Vostorgov and Russian Missionary Aspirations in Asia." *Canadian Slavonic Papers* 57 (2015): 56–75.

Forsyth, James. *A History of the Peoples of Siberia: Russia's North Asian Colony, 1581–1990.* Cambridge: Cambridge University Press, 1992.

Fulton, Brent. *China's Urban Christians: A Light That Cannot Be Hidden.* Eugene, OR: Pickwick Publications, 2015.

Fuluoluofusiji 弗洛羅夫斯基 [Georges Florovsky]. *Jidujiao yu wenhua* 基督教與文化 [Christianity and Culture]. Translated by Li Shuqin 李樹琴. Hong Kong: The Logos and Pneuma Press, 2009.

Gao Liqin 高莉琴 and Teng Chunhua 滕春华. "Xinjiang Eluosi zu wenhua bianqian yanjiu" 新疆俄罗斯族文化变迁研究 [Research about the cultural development of ethnic Russians in Xinjiang]. *Xinjiang daxue xuebao* 38, no. 5 (2010): 73–77.

García, Ofelia, Rakhmiel Peltz, and Harold F. Schiffman with Gella Schweid Fishman. *Language Loyalty, Continuity and Change: Joshua A. Fishman's Contributions to International Sociolinguistics.* Clevedon: Multilingual Matters, 2006.

Carter, James. "The Future of Harbin's Past." *Itinerario* 35, no. 3 (December 2011): 73–85.

Ge Zhaoguang, and Michael Hill. *What Is China?: Territory, Ethnicity, Culture, and History.* Cambridge, MA: Belknap Press of Harvard University Press, 2018.

Ge Zhaoguang 葛兆光. *He wei Zhongguo?: Jiangyu, minzu, wenhua yu lishi* 何為中國？：疆域, 民族, 文化與歷史 [What Is China?: Territory, Ethnicity, Culture, and History]. Hong Kong: Oxford University Press, 2014.

General'noe konsul'stvo Rossiiskoi Federatsii v Spetsial'nom administrativnom raione Gonkong KNR (Генеральное консульство Российской Федерации в Специальном административном районе Гонконг КНР) [Consulate General of the Russian Federation in the Hong Kong SAR, PRC] (official website). Accessed November 10, 2017. http://hongkong.mid.ru.

[Archimandrite] George. *Shengming zhongji mudi: tian ren he yi* 生命終極目的：天人合一 [The ultimate goal of human life: theosis]. Translated by Lucia Chang. Xindian: Taiwan Jidu Zhengjiaohui, 2006.

Geraci, Robert P. "Going Abroad or Going to Russia?: Orthodox Missionaries in the Kazakh Steppe, 1881–1917." In *Of Religion and Empire: Missions, Conversion, and Tolerance in Tsarist Russia*, edited by Robert P. Geraci, and Michael Khodarkovsky, 115–43. Ithaca, NY: Cornell University Press, 2001.

Gernet, Jacques. *China and the Christian Impact: A Conflict of Cultures*. Cambridge: Cambridge University Press, 1985.

Gerrare, Wirt. *Greater Russia: The Continental Empire of the Old World*. New York and London: Macmillan, 1903.

Gillquist, Peter E. *Becoming Orthodox: A Journey to the Ancient Christian Faith*, 1st ed. Brentwood, TN: Wolgemuth & Hyatt, 1989.

———— [Ji'er Kuisi Bide 基爾魁斯•彼得]. *Chengwei Dongzheng jiaotu: chonghui shanggu Jidu xinyang zhi lu* 成為東正教徒：重回上古基督信仰之路 [Being an Orthodox believer: returning to the path of ancient Christian belief]. Translator(s) unspecified. Xindian: Taiwan Jidu Zhengjiaohui, 2007.

Goncharov, Ivan Aleksandrovich (Иван Александрович Гончаров). *Fregate "Pallada"* (Фрегат «Паллада») [The Frigate *Pallada*]. St. Petersburg, 1858.

————. *The Frigate Pallada*. Translated by Klaus Goetze. New York: St. Martin's Press, 1987.

GovHK. "Xianggang bianlan—Zongjiao yu fengsu" 香港便覽——宗教與風俗 [Hong Kong: the facts—religion and custom]. May 2016. https://www.gov.hk/sc/about/abouthk/factsheets/docs/religion.pdf.

Greek Orthodox Archdiocese of America. *The Divine Liturgy of St. John Chrysostom Hymnal: A Hymnal with Texts in Greek, English and English Phonetics*. Brookline, MA: Greek Orthodox Archdiocese of America Department of Religious Education, 1977.

Gurvich, I. S. (И. С. Гурвич). *Narody Dal'nego Vostoka SSSR v XVII–XX vv. Istoriko-etnograficheskie ocherki* (Народы Дальнего Востока СССР в XVII–XX вв.: Историко-этнографические очерки) [The peoples of the Soviet Far East from the seventeenth to the twentieth century: Historical and ethnographic essays]. Moscow: Nauka, 1985.

Gwulo.com. "Nicholas BELANOVSKY [1889–1997]." Submitted by Dmitry Belanovsky on September 11, 2011, 01:34. https://gwulo.com/node/9220.

Hallick, Mary Paloumpis. *Treasured Traditions and Customs of the Orthodox Church*. Edina, MN: Light and Life Publishing, 2001.

Hammond, Philip E. *Religion and Personal Autonomy: The Third Disestablishment in America*. Columbia, SC: University of South Carolina Press, 1992.

He Hongmei 何红梅, Ma Buning 马步宁, and Li Qinghua 李庆华, eds. *Quanxin daxue Eyu zonghe jiaocheng* 全新大学俄语综合教程 [The new comprehensive course of Russian language for university]. 12 vols. Beijing: Gaodeng chubanshe, 2009.

He Xiaoxin 何曉炘. *Zhengjiaohui de chongbai* 正教會的崇拜 [An introduction to the liturgical practice of the Orthodox church]. Hong Kong: OMHKSEA, 2003.

Heaver, Stuart. "How the White Russian Refugee Crisis Unfolded in China a Century Ago, and the Lucky Ones Who Made It to Hong Kong." *South China Morning Post*, May 7, 2017. Accessed May 17, 2017. http://www.scmp.com/magazines/

post-magazine/long-reads/article/2092988/how-white-russian-refugee-crisis-unfolded-china.

———. "The White Tide." *Post Magazine*, May 7, 2017, 12–15.

Higgins, Andrew. "Businesses 'Getting Killed' on Russian Border as Coronavirus Fears Rise." Russia Dispatch, *New York Times*. February 24, 2020. Accessed January 12, 2021, https://www.nytimes.com/2020/02/24/world/europe/coronavirus-russia-china-commerce.html.

Higuchi, Kenichiro 樋口謙一郎, and Kwong Yan Kit 江仁傑. "Honkon zaijū korian no gengo kyōiku to gengo shiyō" 香港在住コリアンの言語教育と言語使用 [Language education and language use of Koreans living in Hong Kong]. *Journal of the School of Culture-Information Studies (Sugiyama Jogakuen University)* 9, no. 2 (September 2009): 71–79.

Hinnells, John R. "The Parsis in Hong Kong and the China Seas." In *The Zoroastrian Diaspora: Religion and Migration*, 145–88. Oxford: Oxford University Press, 2005.

Ho Lawrence K.K. 何家騏 and Chu Yiu Kong 朱耀光. *Xianggang jingcha: lishi jianzheng yu zhifa shengya* 香港警察：歷史見證與執法生涯 [The Hong Kong police: witnesses to history and careers in law enforcement]. Hong Kong: Joint Publishing, 2011.

Ho, Wai-Yip. *Islam and China's Hong Kong: Ethnic Identity, Muslim Networks, and the New Silk Road*. New York: Routledge, 2013.

Hong Kong Baptist University (HKBU). "Archives on the History of Christianity in China." Accessed April 29, 2017. https://library.hkbu.edu.hk/collections/special-collections-archives/archives-on-the-history-of-christianity-in-china.

———. "Hong Kong Baptist University Vision and Mission." Accessed April 10, 2019. https://www.hkbu.edu.hk/eng/about/mission.jsp.

Hong Kong Buddhist Association. "Xianggang Fojiao lianhehui" 香港佛教聯合會 [The Hong Kong Buddhist Association]. Accessed July 7, 2018. http://wwwhkbuddhist.org/zh.

Hong Kong Chinese Christian Churches Union. "Xianggang Huaren Jidujiao lianhui" 香港華人基督教聯會 [The Hong Kong Chinese Christian Churches Union]. Accessed July 9, 2018. http:/www.hkcccu.org.hk.

Hong Kong Christian Council, "Xianggang Jidujiao xiejinhui" 香港華人基督教協進會 [Hong Kong Christian Council]. Accessed July 9, 2018. http://www.hkcc.org.hk.

Hong Kong Christian Service 香港基督教服務處. Accessed January 17, 2021. http://www.hkcs.org/about/overview-e.html.

Hong Kong Daily Press. 1938. "Russian Orthodox Church." July 2, 1938.

Hong Kong [Special Administrative Region] Government. "Asia's World City." Accessed September 9, 2017. http://www.info.gov.hk/info/sar5/easia.htm.

———. The Basic Law of the Hong Kong Special Administrative Region of the People's Republic of China.

Hong Kong [Special Administrative Region] Government Census and Statistics Department. "Demographic Characteristics." Accessed July 19, 2018. https://www.censtatd.gov.hk/hkstat/sub/gender/demographic/index.jsp.

Hong Kong History Museum. "Secrets of the Russian Monarchs: Nicholas II's Visit to Hong Kong." Accessed June 16, 2017. http://hk.history.museum/documents/54401/2823302/Nicholas+II+Visit+to+Hong+Kong.pdf.

Hong Kong Legislative Council. *The Orthodox Metropolitanate of Hong Kong and South East Asia Ordinance (Cap. 1163). L.N. 562 of 1996.* Operated 2 January 1997. Accessed November 29, 2019. https://www.elegislation.gov.hk/hk/cap1163.

Hong Kong Public Records Office. Carl Smith Collection.

Hong Kong Taoist Association. "Xianggang Daojiao lianhehui" 香港道教聯合會 [Hong Kong Taoist Association]. Accessed July 7, 2018. http://www.hktaoist.org.hk.

Hong Kong Unison. "Hong Kong Unison." Accessed November 20, 2018. http://www.unison.org.hk.

Hong Kong Yearbook 1997. Hong Kong: HKSAR, 1997. https://www.yearbook.gov.hk/1997/eindex.htm.

Hong Kong Yearbook 2001. Hong Kong: HKSAR, 2001. http://www.yearbook.gov.hk/2001/ehtml/index.html.

Hong Kong Yearbook 2004. Hong Kong: HKSAR, 2004. http://www.yearbook.gov.hk/2004/en/index.html.

Hong Kong Yearbook 2012. Hong Kong: HKSAR, 2012. http://www.yearbook.gov.hk/2012/en/index.html.

Hong Kong Yearbook 2015. Hong Kong: HKSAR, 2015. http://www.yearbook.gov.hk/2015/en/index.html.

Horujy, Sergey (Сергей Хоружий) [Sergei Khoruzhiy]. *Orthodox Spiritual Tradition and Russian World.* Hong Kong: OPASPP, 2010.

Hovorun, Cyril / Xiushi da siji Jili'er boshi (Guowolong) 修士大司祭基里爾博士（郭臥龍）[Archimandrite Dr. Cyril (Hovorun)]. *From Antioch to Xi'an: An Evolution of "Nestorianism" / You Antia dao Xi'an: Niesituoli pai de yanbian* 由安提阿到西安——聶斯托利派的演變. Hong Kong: China Orthodox Press, 2014.

Huang Guangyu 黄光域. *Jidujiao zhuan xing Zhongguo ji nian: 1807–1949* 基督教传行中国纪年（1807–1949）[Chronicle of Protestant missions development in China (1807–1949)]. Guilin: Guangxi shifan daxue chubanshe, 2017.

Huang Lanlan, and Li Qiao. "China's New Regulation for Religious Groups Emphasizing Party Leadership Could Better Serve Communities: Observers." *Global Times*, January 20, 2020. Accessed February 2, 2021. https://www.globaltimes.cn/content/1177478.shtml.

Hunter, Alan, and Kim-kwong Chan. "Orthodox Church, Chinese." In *Encyclopedia of Chinese History*, edited by Michael Dillon, 510–11. London: Routledge, 2016.

Huntington, Samuel P. *The Clash of Civilizations and the Remaking of World Order.* New York: Simon & Schuster, 1996.

[Princess] Ileana of Romania (Mother Alexandra of the Holy Transfiguration Monastery) / Luomaniya Yilianna gongzhu bixia 罗马尼亚伊莲娜公主陛下. *Introduction to the Jesus Prayer / Yesu daowen jianjie* 耶稣祷文简介. Vol. 4 of *Zhengxin xuanyang ji* 正信宣扬集. Translated by Ji Mi Luomannuofu 季·米·罗

曼诺夫 [J. M. Romanov] and Yuehan Xu 约翰·徐. Hong Kong: OPASPP and OFASC, 2010.

[Metropolitan] Ilarion (Иларион). *Pravoslavie* (Православие) [Orthodoxy]. Moscow: Sretenskogo monastyria, 2008.

——. *Tainstvo very: Vvedenie v pravoslavnoe dogmaticheskoe bogoslovie* (Таинство веры. Введение в православное догматическое богословие) [The sacrament of faith: introduction to Orthodox dogmatic theology]. Moscow: Izdatel'stvo Bratstva Sviatitelia Tikhona, 1996.

Indenture of Assignment between Lai Wai Suen and the Colony of Hong Kong, concerning the Lease of New Kowloon Inland Lot No. 725 (commencing 1st day of July 1898). Registered Vol: CJX., Fol:53. Prepared by the Land Office (Hong Kong, 5 November 1930). Printed at Noronha & Co., Hong Kong.

Indenture of Assignment between Lai Wai Suen (the Vendor) and Chan Bing Yim (the Purchaser), concerning New Kowloon Inland Lot No. 725 (No. 12 Essex Crescent). Instrumented on 25 April 1962. Registered as Memorial No. 367371. Land Office of the Colony of Hong Kong, Hong Kong, 12 May 1962.

Indenture of Assignment between Chan Bing Yim (the Vendor) and Electro Enterprises and Advertising Company Limited (the Purchaser), concerning New Kowloon Inland Lot No. 725 (No. 12 Essex Crescent). Instrumented on 23 September 1974. Registered as Memorial No. 1113283. Land Office of the Colony of Hong Kong, Hong Kong, 18 October 1974.

[Archimandrite] Innocent. "The Russian Orthodox Mission in China." *The Chinese Recorder* (American Presbyterian Mission Press) 47, no. 10 (1916): 678–85.

Institute of Sino-Christian Studies 漢語基督教文化研究所. "Yanjiusuo jianjie" 研究所簡介 [Introduction to the Institute of Sino-Christian Studies]. Accessed January 21, 2021. https://www.iscs.org.hk/Common/Reader/Channel/ShowPage.jsp?Cid=14&Pid=2&Version=0&page=0.

[Archimandrite] Ioann (Архимандрит Иоанн). *Chanhui zhinan: da zhai qijian shenfu guanyu chanhui de xunhui* 懺悔指南：大齋期間神父關於懺悔的訓誨 [Guide to repentance: a priest's exegesis on repentance during major fasts]. Translated by Wen Jian 溫健 (Ailaina 艾萊納). Hong Kong: Saint Apostles Peter and Paul Church of Hong Kong, 2006. Originally published as *Opyt postroeniia ispovedi: po desiati zapovediam* (Опыт построения исповеди: по десяти заповедям) [Confession construction: experience ten commandments] (Moscow: Moskovskoe podvor'e Pskovo-Pecherskogo Sviato-Uspenskogo monastyria [Moscow Compound Holy Assumption Pskov-Pechersky Monastery], 2004.

Isurin, Ludmila. *Russian Diaspora Culture, Identity, and Language Change*. Boston: De Gruyter, 2011.

Ivanov, P. M. (П.М. Иванов). *Gonkong: Istoriia i sovremennost'* (Гонконг: История и современность) [Hong Kong: History and Modernity]. Moscow: Nauka Glavnaia redaktsiia vostochnoi literatury, 1990.

Izdatel'skii Sovet Russkoi Pravoslavnoi Tserkvi (Издательство Московской Патриархии Православной Церкви) [Publishing Council of the Russian Orthodox Church]. *Bogosluzhebnye ukazaniia na 2008 god dlia sviashchenno-tserkovnosluzhitelei* (Богослужебные указания на 2008 год для священно-церковнослужителей) [Liturgical instructions for the year 2008: For clergy]. Moskva: Izdatel'skii Sovet Russkoi Pravoslavnoi Tserkvi, 2007.

———. *Patriarshii kalendar' na 2015 god* (Патриарший календарь на 2015 год) [Patriarchal calendar for the year 2015]. Moskva: Izdatel'skii Sovet Russkoi Pravoslavnoi Tserkvi, 2014.

Jia, Fanqi, and Mia M. Bennett. "Chinese Infrastructure Diplomacy in Russia: The Geopolitics of Project Type, Location, and Scale." *Eurasian Geography and Economics* 59, no. 3–4 (2018): 340–77.

[Saint] John Maximovitch (Archbishop of San Francisco). *The Orthodox Veneration of the Mother of God*, 1st ed. Platina, CA: St. Herman of Alaska Brotherhood.

———. Shanghai de Sheng Yiwang 上海的圣伊望/Sviatitel' Ioann (Maksimovich) Shankhaiskii Святитель Иоанн (Максимович) Шанхайский [Saint John (Maximovitch) of Shanghai]. *Zhengjiao dui danshen nü de jingli* 正教对诞神女的敬礼 [The Orthodox Veneration of Mary the Birthgiver of God]. Translated by Makarios (Μακάριος / Makários). Hong Kong: OPASPP, 2007.

Joske, Alex. "Reorganizing the United Front Work Department: New Structures for a New Era of Diaspora and Religious Affairs Work." *China Brief* 19, no. 9. The Jamestown Foundation. May 9, 2019. Accessed January 15, 2021. https://jamestown.org/program/reorganizing-the-united-front-work-department-new-structures-for-a-new-era-of-diaspora-and-religious-affairs-work/.

Kalake Ka'erdun 卡拉克·卡爾頓 [Clark Carlton]. *Zhengdao: Xinjiao xintu dui Zhengjiao xuzh*i 正道：新教信徒對正教須知 [The Way: What Protestants should know about Orthodoxy]. Translated by Cinde Lee (Li Lishi 李麗詩). Hong Kong: OPASPP, 2013.

Kalkandjieva, Daniela. *The Russian Orthodox Church, 1917–1948: Decline to Resurrection*. London: Routledge, 2014.

Kan, Sergei. *Memory Eternal: Tlingit Culture and Russian Orthodox Christianity Through Two Centuries*. Seattle: University of Washington Press, 1999.

Kapustin, D. (Д. Капустин) "Gonkong—pervyi port zagranichnogo puteshestviia Chekhova" (Гонконг—первый порт заграничного путешествия Чехова) [Hong Kong—the first port abroad in Chekhov's travels]. *Problemy Dal'nego Vostoka*, no. 3 (2009): 155–67.

Keller, Adrian. *A Pocket Church History for Orthodox Christians*. Austin, TX: St. Hilarion Press, 1994.

Kere'aozesisiji de sheng cheng de Xielapiweng Dongzhengjiao chuanjiaohui 科熱奧澤斯斯基的聲成德謝拉皮翁東正教傳教 (Православное миссионерское общество имени прп. Серапиона Кожеозерского). *Dongzhengjiao kuxiuzhe 300 tiao* 東正教苦修者格言300條 [300 sayings of Orthodox ascetics]. Moscow: Pravslanoe missionerskoe obshchestvo imeni prp. Serapiona Kozheozerskogo [Orthodox Missionary Society of Venerable Serapion Kozheozersky], 2012.

Khabarovsk Pravoslavnyi (Хабаровск Православный) [Khabarovsk Orthodox]. "V Kitae mnogie gotovy byli by priniat' Pravoslavie" (В Китае многие готовы были бы принять Православие) [In China many would be willing to accept Orthodoxy].

Last modified September 30, 2010. Accessed February 9, 2018. http://pravostok.ru/blog/v-kitae-mnogie-gotovi-bili-bi-prinyat-pravoslavie.

Khodarkovsky, Michael. "The Conversion of Non-Christians in Early Modern Russia." In *Of Religion and Empire: Missions, Conversion, and Tolerance in Tsarist Russia*, edited by Robert P. Geraci, and Michael Khodarkovsky, 115–43. Ithaca, NY: Cornell University Press, 2001.

Kim, Loretta E. *Ethnic Chrysalis: China's Orochen People and the Legacy of Qing Borderland Administration*. Cambridge, MA: Harvard University Asia Center, 2019.

———. "From Residency to Citizenship: Chinese Nationalism and Changing Criteria for Political and Legal Interpretations of Hong Kong Identity in the Post-1997 Era." In *Reimagining Nation and Nationalism in Multicultural East Asia*, edited by Sungmoon Kim and Hsin-Wen Lee, 123–40. London and New York: Routledge, 2018.

Kiminas, Demetrius. *The Ecumenical Patriarchate: A History of Its Metropolitanates with Annotated Hierarch Catalogs*. Cabin John, MD: The Borgos Press/Wildside Press, 2009.

[Metropolitan] Kirill (Митрополит Кирилл). *Slovo pastyria: Bog i chelovek; Istoriia spaseniia; Besedy o pravoslavnoi vere* (Слово пастыря: Бог и человек; История спасения; Беседы о православной вере) [The word of the pastor: God and man, the history of salvation, conversations about the Orthodox faith]. Moscow: Moskovskaia Patriarkhiia Ruskoi Pravoslavnoi Tserkvi [Moscow: Moscow Patriarchate of the Russian Orthodox Church], 2004.

———. 莫斯科及全俄至圣大牧首基里尔. *Mushou jiyu* 牧首寄语 / *Slovo Pastyria* (Слово Пастыря) [Word of a pastor]. Beijing: Wenyuan chubanshe, 2018.

Kitai. Vesna Pravoslaviia. Zhongguo Dongzhengjiao de chuntian (Китай. Весна Православия. 中国 东正教的春天) [China. Orthodox spring.]. *Foma: Pravoslavnyi zhurnal dlia somnevaiushchikhsia* (Фома: Православный журнал для сомневающихся) [Thomas: Orthodox magazine for doubters] 119, no. 3 (March 2013): 17–27.

"Kitaiskaia Avtonomnaia Pravoslavnaia Tserkov'" (Китайская Автономная Православная Церковь) [Chinese Autonomous Orthodox Church]. Accessed March 21, 2017. http://www.orthodox.cn/localchurch/pozdnyaev/5_ru.htm.

Kollman, Paul. "At the Origins of Mission and Missiology: A Study in the Dynamics of Religious Language." *Journal of the American Academy of Religion* 79, no. 2 (June 2011): 425–58.

Kung, Anatoly (Kung Cheung Ming) 龔長明, trans. *Fuhuojie he shi er zhong da jieri Dongzhengjiao zhuyao jieri jianjie* 復活節和十二重大節日：東正教主要節日簡介 [Easter and the twelve major holidays: a concise explanation of the main Orthodox holidays]. Hong Kong: OPASPP, 2014.

Kwok, Pui-lan. *Chinese Women and Christianity, 1860–1927*. Atlanta: Scholars Press, 1992.

Kwong, Chun-wah. *Hong Kong's Religions in Transition: Confucianism, Taoism, Buddhism, and Christianity, and the Restructuring of Their Public Roles during Hong Kong's Incorporation into Mainland China (1984–1998)*. Waco, TX: Tao Foundation, 2000.

———. *The Public Role of Religion in Post-colonial Hong Kong: An Historical Overview of Confucianism, Taoism, Buddhism and Christianity.* Vol. 53 of *Asian Thought and Culture.* New York: Peter Lang, 2002.

Ladds, Catherine. "Eurasians in Treaty-port China: Journeys across Racial and Imperial Frontiers." In *Migrant Cross-Cultural Encounters in Asia and the Pacific,* edited by Jacqueline Leckie, Angela McCarthy, Angela Wanhalla, 19–35. Abingdon: Routledge, 2016.

Laitin, David D. *The Russian-speaking Populations in the Near Abroad.* Ithaca, NY: Cornell University Press, 1998.

Langley, Nona Pio-Ulski. "Pio-Ulski." Accessed January 20, 2018. https://pio-ulski.com.

Latourette, Kenneth Scott. *A History of Christian Missions in China.* London: Society for Promoting Christian Knowledge, 1929.

Lau, Stephen, and Lewis Choi, eds. *Literature on Chinese Christianity and Society since the Inception of the People's Republic of China: An index of writings located in Hong Kong.* 2 vols. Hong Kong: sn, 1996.

Law, Kam-yee, and Lee Kim-ming. "Citizenship, Economy and Social Exclusion of Mainland Chinese Immigrants in Hong Kong." *Journal of Contemporary Asia* 36, no. 2 (2006): 217–42.

Lee, Chinyun. "From Kiachta to Vladivostok: Russian Merchants and the Tea Trade." *Region* 3, no. 2 (2014): 195–218.

Lee Kam Keung 李金強. *Jindai Zhongguo mushi qunti de chuxian* 近代中國牧師群體的出現 [The emergence of the community of pastors in modern China]. Taipei: Wanjuanlou, 2020.

Lee Kwai Sang 李貴生, and Leung Wai Mun 梁慧敏. "The Status of Cantonese in the Education Policy of Hong Kong." *Multilingual Education* 2, no. 2 (2012), https://link.springer.com/content/pdf/10.1186%2F10.1186%2F2191-5059-2-2.pdf.

Lee, Robert H. G. *The Manchurian Frontier in Ch'ing History.* Cambridge, MA: Harvard University Press, 1970.

Lee, Vicky. *Being Eurasian: Memories Across Racial Divides.* Hong Kong: Hong Kong University Press, 2004.

Legge, William. *A Guide to Hongkong with some Remarks upon Macao and Canton.* Hong Kong: Walter W. Brewer, 1893. Microform.

Leung, Beatrice, and Shun-hing Chan. *Changing Church and State Relations in Hong Kong, 1950–2000.* Hong Kong: University of Hong Kong Press, 2003.

[Archpriest] Lev Lebedev and Archimandrite Alexander / Da siji Fu Liebidefu he xiudaoyuan zhang Yalishanda 大司祭弗列比德弗和修道院长亚历山大. *What is Most Important / Shenme shi zui zhongyao de* 什么是最重要的. Vol. 5 of *Zhengxin xuanyang ji* 正信宣扬集. Translated by Hieromonk Herman Ciuba and Liang Jiarong 梁家荣. Hong Kong: OPASPP and OFASC, 2010.

Levin, Ned. "Hong Kong Democracy Protests Carry a Christian Mission for Some." *The Wall Street Journal.* Updated October 3, 2014. Accessed October 25, 2016. https://www.wsj.com/articles/hong-kong-democracy-protests-carry-a-christian-mission-for-some-1412255663.

Li Fengbo 李风波. "Xinjiang Eluosi zu renkou de shuliang biandong yu fengbu bianqian yanjiu (1949–2000 nian)" 新疆俄罗斯族人口的数量变动与分布变迁研究（1949–2000年）[Research on the demographic change and distribution of the Russian ethnic group in Xinjiang (1949–2000)]. *Xibei renkou*, no. 1 (2006): 60–63.

[Father] Li Liang 李亮神父. *Liyi* 禮儀 / *Liturgy*. Taipei: Taiwan Jidu Zhengjiaohui, 2007.

———. *Mitu shuguang* 迷途曙光 [Lost dawn]. Xinbei shi: Xinbei shi Jidujiao zhengjiao hui, 2013.

Li Pingye 李平曄, and Wang Xiaozhao 王曉朝. *Jidu zongjiao zai dangdai Zhongguo de shehui zuoyong ji qi yingxiang* 基督宗教在當代中國的社會作用及其影響 [Social effect and impact of Christian religion in contemporary Chinese society]. Xianggang: Lun jin shenxue chuban youxian gongsi, 2011.

Li Qifang 李齊芳. *Zhong E guanxi shi* 中俄關係史 [History of China and Russian relation]. Taipei: Lian jing chuban shiye gongsi, 2000.

Li Ting 李婷. "Xi Xinjiang Eluosi zu de wenhua bianqian" 析新疆俄罗斯族的文化变迁 [Analysis of the cultural development of ethnic Russians in Xinjiang]. *Yuwen xuekan*, no. 13 (2011): 78–80.

Li, Ji. *God's Little Daughters: Catholic Women in Nineteenth-Century Manchuria*. Seattle: University of Washington Press, 2015.

Li, Michael [Li Fengci] 李奉慈, and Elias Wen [Wen Zizheng] 文子正. *Orthodox Daily Prayers in Modern Written Chinese / Baihua xiao qidao shu* 白話小祈禱書. Revise and reprint, Sydney: Russo-Chinese Orthodox Mission of the ROCOR in Australia, 2016.

Lim, Susanna Soojung. "From Albazin to Nagasaki: Russia's First Contacts with China and Japan, 1685–1813." In *China and Japan in the Russian Imagination, 1685–1922: To the Ends of the Orient*, 31–55. London: Routledge, 2013.

Lin, Yuexin Rachel. "The Opportunity of a Thousand Years: Chinese Merchant Organizations in the Russian Civil War." *Kritika* 19, no. 4 (2018): 745–68.

Lipman, Jonathan N. *Familiar Strangers: A History of Muslims in Northwest China*. Seattle: University of Washington Press, 1998.

Liu Chih-hao 劉智豪, and Yang Jia 楊佳. "Dongzhengjiao zai Huaren shehui de fazhan: yi Xianggang Eluosi Dongzheng jiaohui wei hexin de kaocha" 東正教在華人社會的發展：以香港俄羅斯東正教會為核心的考察 [The development of Orthodox Christianity in Chinese society: the Saint Apostles Peter and Paul Orthodox Parish in Hong Kong as a case study]. Unpublished manuscript, last modified December 18, 2016. Portable Document Format File.

Liu Minsheng 刘民生, Meng Xuanzhang 孟宪章, and Bu Ping 步平, eds. *Shiqi shiji Sha-E qinlüe Heilongjiang liuyu shi ziliao* 十七世纪沙俄侵略黑龙江流域史资料 [Historical materials on the invasion of the Heilongjiang river basin by Russian Tsarist forces during the seventeenth century]. Harbin: Heilongjiang jiaoyu chubanshe, 1992.

Liu Yüeh-sheng [Liu Yuesheng] 劉粵聲. *Xianggang Jidujiao shi* 香港基督教會史 [The history of Christian churches in Hong Kong]. Hong Kong: Xianggang Jidujiao lianhui, 1941.

Lo, Andrea. "East Meets West: Best Soy Sauce Western in Hong Kong." *Ovolo Hotels*. Accessed August 29, 2017. https://www.ovolohotels.com/east-meets-west-best-soy-sauce-western-hong-kong.

Lo, Lung-Kwong 卢龙光, and Tang Xiaofeng 唐晓峰. *Jidu zongjiao yu Zhongguo shehui: lishi huisu yu quyu yanjiu* 基督宗教与中国社会：历史回溯与区域研究 [Christianity and Chinese society: a historical review and regional research]. Beijing: Zongjiao wenhua chubanshe, 2018.

Lodwick, Kathleen L. *How Christianity Came to China: A Brief History*. Understanding World Christianity Series. Minneapolis, MN: Fortress Press, 2016.

Lomanov, Alexander. "Chinese Orthodox Church (People's Republic, Hongkong, Macao, Taiwan)." In *Handbook of Christianity in China, Volume Two: 1800 to the Present*, edited by R.G. Tiedemann, 826–36. Leiden and Boston: Brill, 2010.

———. "Russian Orthodox Church (Late Qing China)." In *Handbook of Christianity in China, Volume Two: 1800 to the Present*, edited by R.G. Tiedemann, 193–211. Leiden and Boston: Brill, 2010.

———. "Russian Orthodox Church (Republican China)." In *Handbook of Christianity in China, Volume Two: 1800 to the Present*, edited by R.G. Tiedemann, 553–63. Leiden and Boston: Brill, 2010.

Lossky, Vladimir. *Orthodox Theology: An Introduction*. Crestwood, NY: St. Vladimir's Seminary Press, 1989.

Löwenthal, Rudolf. *The Religious Periodical Press in China*. Peking [Beijing]: Synodal Commission in China, 1940.

Lu Su 鲁速, ed. *Eyu shangwu xinhan jiaocheng* 俄语商务信函教程 / *Kommercheskaia korrespondentsiia na russkom iazyke* (Коммерческая корреспонденция на русском языке) [Commercial correspondence in Russian language]. Beijing: Beijing daxue chubanshe, 2016.

Luehrmann, Sonja, ed. *Praying with the Senses: Contemporary Orthodox Christian Spirituality in Practice*. Bloomington, IN: Indiana University Press, 2017.

Luo, Weihong. *Christianity in China*. Translated by Zhu Chengming. Beijing: China Intercontinental Press, 2004.

Luosiji 洛斯基 [Vladimir Lossky]. *Dongzhengjiao shenxue daolun* 東正教神學導論 [Orthodox theology, an introduction]. Translated by Yang Deyou 楊德友. Hong Kong: The Logos and Pneuma Press, 1997.

Lutz, Jessie G. and Rolland Ray Lutz. *Hakka Chinese Confront Protestant Christianity, 1850–1900: With the Autobiographies of Eight Hakka Christians, and Commentary*. Armonk, NY: M.E. Sharpe, 1998.

Lyutko, Eugene I. "Church History and the Predicament of the Orthodox Hierarchy in the Russian Empire of the Early 1800s." *Slověne* 6, no. 2 (2017): 385–99.

Ma Fuzhen 马福珍, ed. *Eluosi guoqing yu wenhua* 俄罗斯国情与文化 / *Stranovedenie i Kul'tura Rossii* (Страноведение и Культура России) [National studies and culture of Russia]. Harbin: Harbin gongye daxue chubanshe, 2008.

MacGillivray, Donald, ed. *The China Mission Year Book: Being "the Christian Movement in China", 1910*. Shanghai: Christian Literature Society for China and the China Continuation Committee, 1910.

———. *The China Mission Year Book: Being "the Christian Movement in China"*, *1915*. Shanghai: Christian Literature Society for China and the China Continuation Committee, 1915.

Maier, Paul L. *Eusebius: The Church History*. Grand Rapids, MI: Kregel Publications, 1999.

[Dr.] Malik, Charles / *Cha'ersi Malike boshi* 查尔斯·马力克博士. *These Things I Believe / Wo suo xinyang de zhexie shi* 我所信仰的这些事. Vol. 3 of *Zhengxin xuanyang ji* 正信宣扬集. Hong Kong: OPASPP and OFASC, 2010.

Manakova, Tatiana (Татьяна Манакова). *Krasnaia Fanza Rossiiskogo Posol'stva v Pekine: Ostrovok Pravoslaviia v Kitae* (Красная Фанза Российского Посольства в Пекине: Островок Православия в Китае) [Red fangzi of the Russian embassy in Beijing: An islet of Orthodoxy in China]. Beijing and Moscow: n. p., 2007.

Mancall, Mark. *Russia and China: Their Diplomatic Relations to 1728*. Cambridge, MA: Harvard University Press, 1971.

"MAPYRAL." Accessed September 25, 2017. https://ru.mapryal.org/internationalassociation-of-teachers-of-russian-language-and-literature-mapryal.

Marchisio, Robert, and Maurizio Pisati. "Belonging without Believing: Catholics in Contemporary Italy." *Religion, State and Society* 33, no. 1 (1999): 35–36.

Mathewes-Green, Frederica. *Welcome to the Orthodox Church: An Introduction to Eastern Christianity*. Brewster, MA: Paracelete Press, 2015.

Meiyanduofu 梅延多夫 [Jean Meyendorff]. *Baizanting shenxue zhong de Jidu* 拜占庭神學中的基督 [*Le Christ dans la théologie byzantine*]. Translated by Tan Lizhu 譚立鑄. Hong Kong: The Logos and Pneuma Press, 2011.

Meng Ssu-ming (Meng Siming) 孟思明. "The E-luo-ssu kuan (Russian Hostel) in Peking." *Harvard Journal of Asiatic Studies* 23 (1960–1961): 19–46.

Meyendorff, Jean. *Le Christ dans la théologie byzantine*. Paris: Cerf, 1969.

Migne, Jacques Pau., ed. *Patrologiae Cursus Completus, Series Graeca*, Patrologia Graeca (Google Books). http://patristica.net/graeca/#t001.

Ministry of Education and Science of the Russian Federation. "Level of Competence in Russian as a Foreign Language." Accessed May 12, 2017. http://en.russia.edu.ru/russian/levels.

Ming Pao. "Eluosi nanhai Xianggang di zhuimeng" 俄羅斯男孩香港地追夢 [Russian boy chasing dreams in Hong Kong]. May 12, 2016, http://news.mingpao.com/pns/dailynews/web_tc/article/20160512/s00011/1462990204930.

———. "Kan shijie: Eluosi yishu xiaozi zai gang cachu huohua" 看世界:俄羅斯藝術小子在港擦出火花 [See the world: Russian art boy sparks in Hong Kong]. May 12, 2016, http://news.mingpao.com/pns/dailynews/web_tc/article/20160512/s00011/1462990206131.

Minzu University of China Museum [Zhongyang minzu daxue bowuguan] 中央民族大学博物馆. "Jidujiao" 基督教 [Christianity]. Permanent exhibit.

"Mulled Wine Party (Facebook)." Accessed January 2, 2017. https://www.facebook.com/groups/107977518685/permalink/101547769550286.

Mormon Newsroom (The Church of Jesus Christ of Latter-Day Saints). "Facts and Statistics: Hong Kong." Accessed March 21, 2017. http://www.mormonnewsroom.org/facts-and-statistics/country/hong-kong.

Mullaney, Thomas S. *Coming to Terms with the Nation: Ethnic Classification in Modern China*. Berkeley: University of California Press, 2011.

Mungello, David E. *The Spirit and the Flesh in Shandong, 1650–1785*. Lanham, MD: Rowman & Littlefield, 2001.

National Religious Affairs Administration [Guojia zongjiao shiwu ju] 国家宗教事务局. Accessed January 15, 2021. http://www.sara.gov.cn/gjzjswjhtml/index.html.

Naumescu, Vlad. "Becoming Orthodox: The Mystery and Mastery of a Christian Tradition." In *Praying with the Senses: Contemporary Orthodox Christian Spirituality in Practice*, edited by Sonja Luehrmann, 29–53. Bloomington, IN: Indiana University Press, 2017.

[Saint] Nectarios of Aegina (Нектарий). *Put' k schast'iu* (Путь к счастью) / *Tongwang xingfu zhi lu* 通往幸福之路 [The road to happiness]. Hong Kong: Chinese Patriarchal Metochion and the Saint Apostles Peter & Paul Orthodox Church, 2016.

Nedilsky, Lida V. *Converts to Civil Society: Christianity and Political Culture in Contemporary Hong Kong*. Waco, TX: Baylor University Press, 2014.

Ng, Ka Shing 伍嘉誠. "Changing Church-state Relations in Colonial and Postcolonial Hong Kong." *Ta bunka syakai kenkyū* 多文化社会研究 [Journal of global humanities and social sciences], no. 4 (March 2018): 251–74. http://hdl.handle.net/10069/38009.

———. "Religion and Social Welfare in Hong Kong: An Overview." *Journal of Graduate Students of Letters* 14 (December 2014): 249–66. http://hdl.handle.net/2115/57709.

Ni Mi Nikelisiji 尼·米·尼克利斯基 [Nikolay Mikhaylovich Nikolsky]. *Eguo jiaohui shi* 俄国教会史 [History of the Russian Church]. Translated by Ding Shichao 丁士超, Yuan Yibo 苑一博, and Du Like 杜立克. Edited by Ding Shichao 丁士超. Beijing: Shangwu yinshuguan, 2000.

Nihon Harisutosu Seikyōkai 日本ハリストス正教会 [Orthodox Church of Japan]. *Seikyōkai-reki: shu gōshō 2010-nen* 正教会暦：主降生2010年 [Orthodox liturgical calendar: for the year 2010 (CE)]. Tokyo: Nihon Harisutosu Seikyōkai kyōdan, 2010.

———. *Seisho monogatari* 聖書ものがたり [The story of the Bible]. Tokyo: Nihon Harisutosu Seikyōkai, 1983.

Nikol'skii, Nikolai Mikhailovich (Николай Михайлович Никольский). *Istoriia russkoi tserkvi* (История русской церкви) [History of the Russian Church]. Moscow: Politicheskaia literatura, 1988.

[Bishop] Nikolai (Епископ Николай). *Pravoslavnaia missiia v Kitae za 200 let ee sushchestvovaniia: istoriia Pekinskoi Dukhovnoi missii v pervyi i vtoroi periody ee deiatel'nosti* (Православная миссия в Китае за 200 лет её существования: история Пекинской Духовной миссии в первый и второй периоды её деятельности) [Two hundred years of the Russian Orthodox Mission in China: the history of the Beijing Ecclesiastical Mission in the first and second periods of its activities]. Kazan: Tipografiia Imperatorskogo universiteta [Kazan: Imperial University Printing House], 1887.

Njoroge, John N. "Towards an African Orthodoxy: A Call for Inculturation." *Ortodoksia* 56 (2016): 65–85.

Noren, Loren E. *Urban Church Growth in Hong Kong 1958–1962: Third Hong Kong Study*. Hong Kong: s.n., 1963. (the "s.n." here stands for the lack of publisher)

O'Connor, Paul. *Islam in Hong Kong: Muslims and Everyday Life in China's World City*. Hong Kong: Hong Kong University Press, 2012.

Oleksa, Michael. *Orthodox Alaska: A Theology of Mission*. Crestwood, NY: St. Vladimir's Seminary Press, 1992.

OpenRice. "Queen's Cafe." Accessed October 8, 2017. https://www.openrice.com/en/hongkong/r-queens-cafe-wan-chai-russian-r152809.

Orthodox Christianity in China. "Student from Hong Kong at Khabarovsk Seminary is ordained to the diaconate." Accessed May 9, 2017. http://orthodox.cn/contemporary/hongkong/20141204hkdiaconate_en.htm.

Orthodox Church in Hong Kong. Saint Luke Orthodox Cathedral. Accessed March 03, 2021. http://www.omhksea.org/metropolis-of-hong-kong/hong-kong/ and http://orthodox.cn/contemporary/omhksea_en.htm.

Orthodox Church of Japan, "The Orthodox Church of Japan." Accessed June 19, 2018, http://www.orthodoxjapan.jp.

Orthodox Fellowship of All Saints of China (OFASC). "Icon of the Mother of God 'Joy of All Who Sorrow' Church in Guangzhou," *Orthodox Christianity in China*. Accessed January 17, 2017. http://www.orthodox.cn/contemporary/guangdong/guangzhou_en.htm.

———. "In Memoriam: Protopresbyter Elias Wen." Accessed May 18, 2017. http://www.orthodox.cn/localchurch/shanghai/eliaswen_en.htm.

———. "Orthodox Fellowship of All Saints of China." Accessed August 8, 2017. http://www.orthodox.cn/ofasc.

———. "St. Sergius of Radonezh Parish," *Orthodox Christianity in China*. Accessed March 31, 2017. http://orthodox.cn/contemporary/guangdong/shenzhen_en.htm.

Orthodox Metropolitanate of Hong Kong and South East Asia (OMHKSEA). "The Power of the Name: The Orthodox Tradition of Jesus Prayer." Hong Kong: OMHKSEA, n.d.

———. *Shengming de liliang* 聖名的力量 [Power of the Holy Name]. Hong Kong: OMHKSEA, n.d.

Orthodox Parish of Apostles Saints Peter and Paul (Moscow Patriarchate) (OPASPP). *Annotatsiia k osmoglasiiu* (Аннотация к осмогласию) [Annotation for osmoglasia] / *Ba diao ji: zhuri xiao zanci ji fu zanci* 八調集：主日小讚詞及副讚詞 [Collection of (works based on the) eight church modes: praises and sub-praises for the Lord's Day]. Music by Nina Sitaluosijinna 妮娜˙斯塔羅斯金娜 [Nina Starostina]. Hong Kong: China Orthodox Press, 2017.

———. "Archpriest Dmitry Uspensky." Accessed April 28, 2017. https://orthodoxy.hk/parish/archpriest_dmitry_uspensky.

———. *Blagodarstvennyi Moleben* / *Gan'en yigui* (Благодарственный Молебен) 感恩儀軌 [Thanksgiving prayer service]. Hong Kong: China Orthodox Press, 2012.

———. *Bozhestvennye Liturgīi vo svętykh" ottsa nashegō Ioanna Zlatoustagō* (Бж҃е́ственныѧ Лїтꙋргі́и во ст҃ы́хъ ѻ҆тца̀ на́шегw І҆ѡа́нна Златоꙋ́стагw) / *Sheng jinkou Yuehan shi feng sheng li* 聖金口約翰事奉聖禮 [Divine liturgy in honor of Our Father Among the Saints John Chrysostom]. Hong Kong: China Orthodox Press, 2014.

———. *Bozhestvennye Liturgīi vo svętykh" ottsa nashegō Ioanna Zlatoustagō* (Бж҃е́ственныѧ Лїтꙋргі́и во ст҃ы́хъ ѻ҆тца̀ на́шегw І҆ѡа́нна Златоꙋ́стагw) / *The Divine Liturgy of Our Father Among Saints John Chrysostom*. Hong Kong: OPASPP, 2013.

———. *Chinoposledovanie Obednitsy dlia soversheniia mirianami* (Чинопоследование Обедницы для совершения мирянами) / *Ping xintu dai shengti xue liyi* 平信徒代聖體血禮儀 [Observance of the Eucharist as performed by laity]. Translated by Ambrose Lam (Lin Sen) 林森. Hong Kong: OPASPP, 2014.

———. *Da zhai qi jihui shu* 大齋期集會書 [Book of worship for the Lenten period] / *Synaxarion of Lenten Triodion*. Hong Kong: China Orthodox Press, 2015.

———. *Di san, liu, jiu shi ke* 第三、六、九時課 [Services for the third, sixth, and ninth hours]. Hong Kong: China Orthodox Press, 2016.

———. *Dimu ke* 抵暮課 [Vespers]. Hong Kong: China Orthodox Press, 2016.

———. *The Divine Liturgy of Our Father Among Saints John Chrysostom* / *Sheng jinkou Yuehan shi feng sheng li* 聖金口約翰事奉聖禮. Hong Kong: China Orthodox Press, 2014.

———. *Dongzhengjiao xiudao zhuyi* 東正教修道主義 [Eastern Orthodox monasticism]. Hong Kong: China Orthodox Press, 2014.

———. "Dongzhengjiao zai Zhongguo tupian zhan" 東正教在中國圖片展 [Photo exhibition of Eastern Orthodox Christianity in China]. Accessed March 7, 2017. https://orthodoxy.hk/hk/news/2016-11-28/fotovystavka_o_pravoslavii_v_kitae/.

———. *The Icon, History, Symbolism and Meaning* / *Shengxiang de lishi, xiangzheng he yiyi* 圣象的历史，象征和意义. Hong Kong: OPASPP, 2010.

———. "Icon of the Most Holy Mother of God of Hong Kong." Orthodox Christianity Bookstore and Library. Accessed August 2, 2020. https://www.orthodoxbookshop.asia/catalogue/icon-of-the-most-holy-mother-of-god-of-hong-kong_340/.

———. "Icon of St. Seraphim of Sarov with a part of the remains of the saint has been gifted to the Hong Kong parish." Accessed December 13, 2019. https://orthodoxy.hk/news/2016-05-28/icon_of_st._seraphim_of_sarov.

———. *Molitvoslov* (Молитвослов) / *Zhu wen shu* 祝文書 [Prayer book]. Hong Kong: OPASPP, 2005.

———. "Orthodox Christian Calendar+." Apple App Store, Version. 4.9 (2019). Accessed December 17, 2019. https://apps.apple.com/us/app/orthodox-christian-calendar/id1010208102.

———. "Orthodox Christianity Bookstore and Library." Accessed September 10, 2017. http://www.orthodoxbookshop.asia/catalogue.

———. *Pasiha sheng song dian ji zanci* 葩斯哈聖頌典及讚詞 [Easter hymns and praise]. Hong Kong: China Orthodox Press, 2016.

———. *Pravoslavnyi khram Pervoverkhovnykh Apostolov Petra i Pavla v Gonkonge* (Православный храм Первоверховных Апостолов Петра и Павла в Гонконге) / *Xianggang Sheng Bide Sheng Baoluo jiaotang* 香港聖彼得聖保羅教堂 [Orthodox Church of Apostles Saints Peter and Paul in Hong Kong]. Hong Kong: China Orthodox Press, 2016. Available in hard copy and online. Accessed January 2, 2021, http://www.orthodoxbookshop.asia/catalogue/orthodox-church-of-apostles-saints-peter-and-paul-in-hong-kong_273/.

———. *Prazdnovanie 300-letiia Rossiiskoi Dukhovnoi Missii v Kitai* (Празднование трехсотлетия Русской Духовной Миссии в Китае) [300th Anniversary of the Russian Ecclesiastical Mission to China]. Hong Kong: China Orthodox Press, 2013.

———. "Prison Mission." Accessed November 20, 2017. https://orthodoxy.hk/projects/prison_mission.

———. "Saint Apostles Peter & Paul Orthodox Church in Hong Kong (Moscow Patriarchate)." Accessed January 15, 2017. https://www.orthodoxy.hk.

———. *Saint Apostles Peter & Paul Orthodox Church in Hong Kong* / *Xianggang Sheng Bide Sheng Baoluo jiaotang* 香港圣彼得圣保罗教堂. Hong Kong: China Orthodox Press, 2016. Available in hard copy and online. Accessed January 15, 2017. http://www.orthodoxbookshop.asia/catalogue/orthodox-church-of-apostles-saints-peter-and-paul-in-hong-kong_319.

———. "Schedule of Services." Revised regularly. https://orthodoxy.hk.schedule.

———. *Service of the Holy Protomartyrs of China, Slain During the Boxer Rebellion* / *Erbai ershi you er wei Zhonghua xundaozhe zhanli zanci* 二百二十又二位中華殉道者瞻禮讚詞 [Praise for the feast day of the 222 martyrs in China]. Hong Kong: China Orthodox Press, 2015.

———. *Service of the Holy Protomartyrs of China, Slain During the Boxer Rebellion* / *Sluzhba dvumstam dvadesiati dvum muchenikam pri vosstanii ikhetuanei v Kitae postradavshim* (Служба двумстам двадцати двум мученикам при восстании ихэтуаней в Китае пострадавшим) 二百二十又二位中華殉道者瞻禮讚詞 [Service for the 222 martyrs who were victims of the Boxer rebellion in China] / *Erbai ershi you er wei Zhonghua xundaozhe zhanli zanci* [Praise for the feast day of the 222 martyrs in China]. Hong Kong: China Orthodox Press, 2015.

———. *Sheng jinkou Yuehan shi feng sheng li (dai yuepu)* 聖金口約翰事奉聖禮（帶樂譜）/ *Bozhestvennaia Liturgiia Ioanna Zlatousta (s notnym prilozheniem)* (Божественная Литургия Иоанна Златоуста [с нотным приложением]) [Divine liturgy in honor of Our Father Among the Saints John Chrysostom (with supplementary music)]. Music by Nina Sitaluosijinna 妮娜•斯塔羅斯金娜 [Nina Starostina]. Edited by Lin Sen 林森. Hong Kong: China Orthodox Press, 2015.

———. *Sheng yong jing: Shangdi jiangsheng yi qian ba bai qi shi jiu nian sui ci ji mao, Jingdu dong jiao zong beiguan* 聖詠經：上帝降生一千八百七十九年歲次己卯 京都東教宗北館 [Psaltirion: in the 1879th year of the Lord, the Orthodox North Hostel at the capital]. Hong Kong: China Orthodox Press, 2016.

———. *Shengren liezhuan: di wu ce: yi yue (zhu xian yue)* 圣人列传，第五册：一月（主显月） [Lives of the saints, book five: January (month of Epiphany)].

Translated by Xue Bin 学斌. Hong Kong: OPASPP and China Orthodox Church, April 2009.

———. *Shouxi guiyu Jidu de yiyi* 受洗歸於基督的意義 [What does it mean to be baptized and return to Christ?]. Translated by Anatoly Kung (Kung Cheung Ming 龔長明). Hong Kong: OPASPP, 2014.

———. *Xiangchen ke / di yi shi ke* 嚮晨課 / 第一時課 [Morning services for the first hour]. Hong Kong: China Orthodox Press, 2016.

———. *Zhengjiao qidao shu* 正教祈禱書 [Orthodox prayer book]. Hong Kong: China Orthodox Press, 2013.

———. *Zhengjiao qidao shu* 正教祈祷书 [Orthodox prayer book]. Hong Kong: China Orthodox Press, 2016.

———. *Zhenli yu jiaoliu (wai yi pian)* 真理与交流（外一篇）[Truth and communication (extra section)]. Translated by Ren Yanlin 任炎林. Hong Kong: OPASPP, 2006.

———. *Zhonghua Zhengjiaohui lishu Shangdi chuangshi qiqian wubai shisi nian Jidu jiangsheng erqian ling liu nian* 中华正教会历书：上帝创世七千五百十四年 基督降生二千零六年 [Chinese Orthodox Church almanac: 7514 years since God's creation of the world, 2006 since the birth of Christ]. Hong Kong: China Orthodox Press, 2006.

———. *Zhonghua Zhengjiaohui lishu Shangdi chuangshi qiqian wubai shiwu nian Jidu jiangsheng erqian ling qi nian* 中华正教会历书：上帝创世七千五百十五年 基督降生二千零七年 [Chinese Orthodox Church almanac: 7515 years since God's creation of the world, 2007 since the birth of Christ]. Hong Kong: China Orthodox Press, 2007.

Orthodox Wiki. "Orthodoxy in Taiwan." Accessed February 18, 2021. https://orthodoxwiki.org/Orthodoxy_in_Taiwan.

———. "Russian Orthodox Church Outside Russia." Accessed August 27, 2017. https://orthodoxwiki.org/Russian_Orthodox_Church_Outside_Russia.

Osipov, Aleksei Il'ich (Алексей Ильич Осипов). *Iz vremeni v vechnost': posmertnaia zhizn' dushi* (Из времени в вечность: посмертная жизнь души) [From time to eternity: the afterlife of the soul]. Moscow: Danilov muzhskoi monastyr' (Данилов мужской монастырь) [Danilov Monastery], 2017.

Otdel vneshnikh tserkovnykh sviazei Moskovskogo patriarkhata (Отдел внешних церковных связей Московского патриархата) [External Liaison Office of the Moscow Patriarchate]. *Pravoslavie v Kitae* (Православие в Китае) 東正教在中國 [Orthodox Christianity in China]. Moscow: Moscow Patriarchate, 2010.

Ouspensky, Leonid. *Theology of the Icon*. New York: St. Vladimir's Seminary Press, 1978.

Ouyang Zhesheng 欧阳哲生. "Eguo Dongzhengjiao chuanjiao tuan zai jing huodong shu ping (1716–1859)" 俄国东正教传教团在京活动述评（1716–1859）[Review of the Russian Orthodox mission in Beijing (1716–1859)]. *Anhui shi xue*, no. 1 (2016): 124–33.

Paine, S. C. M. *Imperial Rivals: China, Russia, and Their Disputed Frontier, 1858–1924*. Armonk, NY: M. E. Sharpe, 1996.

Pajiama de da zhujiao 帕加馬的大主教 [Metropolitan John Zizioulas (of Pergamon)]. *Jidujiao jiaoyi: jiaoyi de xingcheng ji zai dagong huiyi zhong de zhengyi* 基督教教義：教義的形成及在大公會議中的爭議 [Christian doctrine: the formation of doctrine and its controversies in the Ecumenical Council]. Translated by Lawrence Chin. Xindian: Taiwan Jidu Zhengjiaohui, 2007.

———. *Jidujiao jiao 2: jiaoyi de xingcheng ji zai dagong huiyi zhong de zhengyi* 基督教教義 2：教義的形成及在大公會議中的爭議 [Christian doctrine, volume 2: the formation of doctrine and its controversies in the Ecumenical Council]. Xindian: Taiwan Jidu Zhengjiaohui, 2008.

Palikan 帕利坎 [Jaroslav Pelikan]. *Jidujiao chuantong—dagong chuantong de xingcheng* 基督教傳統——大公傳統的形成 [The Christian tradition—a history of the development of doctrine]. Translated by Weng Shaojun 翁紹軍. Edited by Chen Zuoren 陳佐人. Hong Kong: The Logos and Pneuma Press, 2002.

———. *Jidujiao chuantong (juan er) —dongfang Jidujiao shijie de jingshen* 基督教傳統 (卷二) 東方基督教世界的精神 [The Christian tradition, volume 2—the spirit of Eastern Christendom (600–1700)]. Translated by Sha Mei 沙湄. Hong Kong: The Logos and Pneuma Press, 2009.

Pang, Tatiana A. "The 'Russian Company' in the Manchu Banner Organization." *Central Asiatic Journal* 43, no. 1 (1999): 132–39.

Papadakis, Aristeides, and John Meyendorff. *The Christian East and the Rise of the Papacy: The Church AD 1071–1453*. New York: St Vladimir's Seminary Press, 1994.

Park, Alyssa M. *Sovereignty Experiments: Korean Migrants and the Building of Borders in Northeast Asia, 1860–1945*. Studies of the Weatherhead East Asian Institute, Columbia University. Ithaca, NY: Cornell University Press, 2019.

[Archbishop] Pavel (Архиепископ Павел) / [Fenlan] da zhujiao Pawei'er （芬蘭）大主教帕維爾. *Kak my veruem* (Как мы веруем) [How we believe] / *Dongzhengjiao xintu ruhe Xinyang zongjiao*東正教信徒如何信仰宗教 [How do Orthodox followers believe in their faith]. Translated by Sun Ming 孫明. Hong Kong: China Orthodox Press, 2015.

Payne, Daniel P. "Spiritual Security, the Russian Orthodox Church, and the Russian Foreign Ministry: Collaboration or Cooptation?" *A Journal of Church and State* 52, no. 4 (2010): 712–27.

Pechatat' Dozvoliaetsia Hachal'nik Missii Episkopi Innokentii [Printing allowed by the Head of Mission Bishop Innocent]. *Kratkaia istoriia Russkoi pravoslavnoi missii v Kitae: sostavlennaia po sluchaiu ispolnivshegosia v 1913 godu dvukhsotletnego iubileia ee sushchestvovaniia* (Краткая история Русской православной миссии в Китае: составленная по случаю исполнившегося в 1913 году двухсотлетнего юбилея ее существования) [A short history of the Russian Orthodox Mission in China: compiled in 1913 on the occasion of the 200th anniversary of its existence]. Peking: Tipografiia Uspenskago monastyria, 1916.

Peck, John. "300 Years of Orthodox Christianity in China." Accessed May 19, 2017. https://journeytoorthodoxy.com/2013/02/300-years-of-orthodoxy-in-china.

Pelikan, Jaroslav. *The Christian Tradition: A History of the Development of Doctrine, Volume 1: The Emergence of the Catholic Tradition, 100–600*. Chicago: University of Chicago Press, 1971.

———. *The Christian Tradition: A History of the Development of Doctrine, Volume 2: The Spirit of Eastern Christendom (600–1700)*. Chicago: University of Chicago Press, 1971.

Perabo, Betsy. *Russian Orthodoxy and the Russo-Japanese War*. Bloomsbury, 2017.

Perepiolkina, Ludmila. *The Julian Calendar as the 1000-Years Icon of Time in Russia*. Moscow: Metochion of the Russian Monastery of St. Panteleimon on the Athos, 1996.

Pianciola, Niccolò. "Orthodoxy in the Kazakh Territories (1850–1943)." Translated by Susan Finnel. In *Kazakhstan: Religions and Society in the History of Central Eurasia*, edited by Gian Luca Bonora, Niccolò Pianciola, and Paolo Sartori, 237–54. Turin, London, Venice and New York: Umberto Allemandi, 2010.

Plüss, Caroline. "Constructing Globalized Ethnicity: Migrants from India in Hong Kong." *International Sociology* 20, no. 2 (2005): 201–24.

Polinsky, Maria. "Heritage Language Narratives." In *Heritage Language Education: A New Field Emerging*, edited by Donna M. Brinton, Olga Kagan, and Susan Bauckus, 149–64. New York: Routledge, 2008.

Powers, John. *The Buddha Party: How the People's Republic of China Works to Define and Control Tibetan Buddhism*. Oxford: Oxford University Press, 2017.

[Archpriest] Pozdnyaev, Denis (Dionisy) (Дионисий Поздняев). *Gonkongskaia Tetrad'. Leto 2016* (Гонконгская Тетрадь. Лето 2016) [Hong Kong's diary summer 2016]. Hong Kong: China Orthodox Press, 2016.

———. *Gonkongskaia Tetrad'. Osen' 2016* (Гонконгская Тетрадь. Осень 2016) [Hong Kong's diary autumn 2016]. Hong Kong: China Orthodox Press, 2016.

———. *Gonkongskaia Tetrad'. Vesna 2016* (Гонконгская Тетрадь. Весна 2016) [Hong Kong's diary spring 2016]. Hong Kong: China Orthodox Press, 2016.

———. *Gonkongskaia Tetrad'. Zima 2016–2017* (Гонконгская Тетрадь. Зима 2016–2017) [Hong Kong's diary winter 2016–2017]. Hong Kong: China Orthodox Press, 2017.

———. "Nachnem nashe palomnichestvo. Gospodi, blagoslovi!" (Начнем наше паломничество. Господи, благослови!) [Let's start our pilgrimage. God bless!]. Facebook, May 12, 2016. https://www.facebook.com/photo.php?fbid=10154737843713238&set=a.10150373961628238&type=3&theater.

———. *Pravoslavie v Kitae (1900–1997)* (Православие в китае) [Orthodox Christianity in China (1900–1997)]. Moscow: Izd. Sviato-Vladimirskogo Bratstva, 1998. Accessed June 28, 2017. http://www.orthodox.cn/localchurch/pozdnyaev/index_ru.html.

[Archpriest] Pozdynyaev, Dionisy / [Da siji] Di'aonixi Bozidiniyefu 大司祭迪奥尼西·波茨德尼耶夫. *Jiaohui, jiaoli, sheng aomi, jiaotang nei de juzhi* 教会、教理、圣奥秘、教堂内的举止 [The church, catechism, holy mysteries, and behavior in church]. Translated by Lin Sen 林森. Hong Kong: China Orthodox Press, 2015.

———. *Xianggang shouzha 2016 chun* 香港手札 2016春 [Hong Kong's diary spring 2016]. Translated by Lin Sen 林森. Hong Kong: China Orthodox Press, 2017.

———. *Xianggang shouzha 2016 qiu* 香港手札 2016秋 [Hong Kong's diary autumn 2016]. Translated by Lin Sen 林森. Hong Kong: China Orthodox Press, 2017.

———. *Xianggang shouzha 2016 xia* 香港手札 2016夏 [Hong Kong's diary summer 2016]. Translated by Lin Sen 林森. Hong Kong: China Orthodox Press, 2017.

———. *Xianggang shouzha 2016 zhi 2017 nian dong* 香港手札2016年至2017年冬 [Hong Kong's diary winter 2016–2017]. Translated by Lin Sen 林森. Hong Kong: China Orthodox Press, 2017.

———. *Zhongguo dalu Zhengjiaohui zai zizhi kuangjia xia jiaohui shengming de fuhuo* 中國大陸正教會：在自治框架下教會生命的復活 [Orthodox Christianity in the People's Republic of China: revival of church life within the framework of an autonomous church]. Translated by Sun Yue 孫越. Hong Kong: China Orthodox Press, 2015.

———. *Zhongguo dalu Zhengjiaohui zai zizhi kuangjia xia jiaohui shengming de fuhuo* 中国大陆正教会：在自治框架下教会生命的复活 [Orthodox Christianity in the People's Republic of China: revival of church life within the framework of an autonomous church]. Translated by Sun Yue 孙越. Hong Kong: China Orthodox Press, 2015.

Pravoslavnaia entsiklopediia "Azbuka very' (Православная энциклопедия «Азбука веры») [Orthodox Encyclopaedia "ABC of faith"]. Accessed May 2, 2017. https://azbyka.ru.

Pravoslavnaia Tserkov' v Taivane (Православная Церковь в Тайване) [Orthodox Church of Taiwan]. "Ofitsial'nyi sait patriarshego podvor'ia russkoi pravoslavnoi tserkvi khram spasitelia v Taibze" (Официальный сайт патриаршего подворья русской православной церкви храм спасителя в Тайбзе) [Official website for Orthodox Church in Taiwan (also known as the official site of the Patriarchal Metochion of the Russian Orthodox Church in Taipei)]. Accessed March 14, 2017. http://orthodoxchurch.com.tw.

Pravoslavnoe Khristianstvo (Православное Христианство) [Orthodox Christianity] (blog). "Pervyi za 60 let – kak korennoi kitaets stal pravoslavnym sviashchennikom" (Первый за 60 лет – как коренной китаец стал православным священником) [The first in 60 years—how a native Chinese became an Orthodox priest]. December 7, 2016. https://pravoslavnoe-hristianstvo.mirtesen.ru/blog/43816009885/Pervyiy-za-60-let-%E2%80%93-kak-korennoy-kitayets-stal-pravoslavnyim-svy?nr=1&utm_referrer=mirtesen.ru.

Publishing Council of the Russian Orthodox Church (Издательский Совет Русской Православной Церкви). *Pravoslavnyi tserkovnyi kalendar'* 2014 [Patriarchal calendar for the year 2014]. Moskva: Izdatel'stvo Moskovskoi Patriarkhii Russkoi Pravoslavnoi Tserkvi, 2013.

Ramet, Sabrina P. *Nihil Obstat: Religion, Politics, and Social Change in East-Central Europe and Russia.* Durham, NC: Duke University Press, 1998.

———. "Religious Policy in the Era of Gorbachev." In *Religious Policy in the Soviet Union*, edited by Sabrina Petra Ramet, 31–52. Cambridge: Cambridge University Press, 1992.

Reinders, Eric. *Borrowed Gods and Foreign Bodies: Christian Missionaries Imagine Chinese Religion.* Berkeley: University of California Press, 2004.

Richters, Katja. *The Post-Soviet Russian Orthodox Church Politics, Culture and Greater Russia.* London: Routledge, 2012.

Romanides, John. *Sheng Baoluo lilun zhong de yuanzui* 聖保羅理論中的原罪 [Original sin in the theory of St. Paul]. Xindian: Taiwan Jidu Zhengjiaohui, 2007.

[Father] Rose, Seraphim. *The Soul after Death*. Platina, CA: St. Herman of Alaska Brotherhood, 1980.

Rowley, David G. "Imperial Versus National Discourse: The Case of Russia." *Nations and Nationalism* 6, no. 1 (2000): 23–42.

Rumyantseva, Marina V. (Марина В. Румянцева). *Russko-kitaiskii slovar' pravoslavnoi leksiki* (Русско-китайский словарь православной лексики) [Russian-Chinese dictionary of Orthodox vocabulary]. Moscow: Vostochnaia kniga, 2007.

"Rus' sidiashchaia" (Русь Сидящая) [Russia behind bars]. Accessed November 24, 2017. https://zekovnet.ru.

Russian Orthodox Church Outside of Russia (website). "Hieromonk Aidan (Keller) / Ieromonakh Aidanii (Keller) [Иеромонах Айданий (Келлер)]." ROCOR Parish and Clergy Directory. Last modified January 31, 2012. http://directory.stinnocentpress.com/viewclergy.cgi?Uid=470&lang=en.

"Russian Bazaar (Facebook page)." Accessed May 5, 2018. https://www.facebook.com/russianbazaarhk.

"Russian Bazaar." Accessed May 9, 2018. http://www.russianclubhk.org/en/russian-bazaar.

Russian Club in Hong Kong (official website). Accessed November 10, 2017. http://www.russianclubhk.org/en.

Russian Culture Association. "Courses." Accessed October 10, 2017. http://www.russian-hk.org/courses.html.

"Russian Culture Festival." Accessed November 29, 2019. http://www.russianclubhk.org/en/category/russian-culture-festival.

Russian Language Center in Hong Kong. "Kusochki Azbuki" (Кусочки Азбуки) [A piece of the ABC]. Facebook, September 1, 2017. https://www.facebook.com/rlchk/photos/gm.1151718191829811/1660583110679782/.

Russkaia Pravoslavnaia Tserkov' Ofitsial'nyi sait Russkoi Pravoslavnoi Tserkvi (Русская Православная Церковь Официальный сайт Русской Православной Церкви) [The official website of the Russian Orthodox Church]. Accessed March 21, 2017. http://www.patriarchia.ru/db/text/1143899.html.

Russkii klub v Gonkonge (Русский клуб в Гонконге) [Russian Club in Hong Kong] (official website). Accessed November 10, 2017. http://www.russianclubhk.org.

Russkiy Mir (Русский мир) [Russian World]. Accessed March 10, 2021. https://russkiymir.ru/.

Ryazanova-Clarke, Lara, ed. *The Russian Language Outside the Nation*. Edinburgh: Edinburgh University Press, 2014.

Ryazantsev, S. V. (С.В. Рязанцев). "Emigranty iz Rossii: Russkaia diaspora ili russkogovoriashchie sobshchestva?" (Эмигранты из России: русская диаспора или русскоговорящие сообщества?) [Emigrants from Russia: Russian diaspora abroad or Russian-speaking communities?]. *Sotsiologicheskie Issledovaniya* 12 (2016): 84–94.

Rzhevsky, Nicholas, ed. *The Cambridge Companion to Modern Russian Culture.* Cambridge: Cambridge University Press, 2012.

Sablina, Eleonora. "Pathways of a Pilgrim from Russia." In *St. Nikolai Kasatkin and the Orthodox Mission in Japan: A Collection of Writings by an International Group of Scholars about St. Nikolai, his Disciples and the Mission*, edited by Michael Van Remortel and Peter Chang, 37–80. Point Reyes Station, CA: Divine Ascent Press, Monastery of St. John of Shanghai and San Francisco, 2003.

Saint Apostles Peter & Paul Orthodox Church in Hong Kong. "Altar Service Basics for Altar Boy." Syllabus.

———. "CA17-1: Introduction of Orthodox Faith." Syllabus.

———. "Icon of St. Seraphim of Sarov with a Part of the Remains of the Saint Has Been Gifted to the Hong Kong Parish." Accessed August 10, 2018. https://orthodoxy.hk/news/2016-05-28/icon_of_st._seraphim_of_sarov.

Schaff, Philip, ed. *Nicene and post-Nicene Fathers: First series.* Peabody, MA: Hendrickson Publishers, 1994.

Schimmelpenninck van der Oye, David. *Russian Orientalism: Asia in the Russian Mind from Peter the Great to the Emigration.* New Haven, CT: Yale University Press, 2010.

Schineller, Peter. *A Handbook on Inculturation.* New York: Paulist Press, 1990.

Schmemann, Alexander. *The Historical Road of Eastern Orthodoxy.* Translated by Lydia W. Kesich. New York: Holt, Rinehart and Winston, 1963.

———. *Great Lent: Journey to Pascha*, 2nd ed. New York: St Vladimir's Seminary Press, 1974.

Schorkowitz, Dittmar. "The Orthodox Church, Lamaism, and Shamanism among the Buriats and Kalmyks, 1825–1925." In *Of Religion and Empire: Missions, Conversion, and Tolerance in Tsarist Russia*, edited by Robert P. Geraci and Michael Khodarkovsky, 201–25. Ithaca, NY: Cornell University Press, 2001.

"Scuola Italiana Manzoni." Accessed July 6, 2017. http://www.manzoni.edu.hk/index.php/2011-09-09-04-09-55.

Sebes, Joseph, S. J. *The Jesuits and the Sino-Russian Treaty of Nerchinsk (1689): The Diary of Thomas Pereira, S. J.* Rome: Institutum Historicum S. I., 1961.

Selivanovsky, Victor. *Orthodoxy in China.* Edited by Eric S. Peterson. Translated by Olga V. Trubetskoy. California: CreateSpace Independent Publishing Platform, 2015.

———. (Виктор Селивановский). *Pravoslavie v Kitae: Sbornik materialov vystavki* (Православие в Китае: Сборник материалов выставки) [Orthodoxy in China: collection of exhibition materials]. Blagoveshchensk: Missionerskii otdel Blagoveshchenskoi eparkhii RPTs (Миссионерский отдел Благовещенской епархии РПЦ) [Missionary department of the Blagoveshchensk diocese of the Russian Orthodox Church], 2013.

Senchukova, Maria (Мария Сеньчукова). "The Patriarchal Visit to China: An Interview with Fr. Dionisy Pozdnyaev." *Pravmir*, May 16, 2013. Accessed January 29, 2017. http://www.pravmir.com/the-patriarchal-visit-to-china-an-interview-with-fr-dionisy-pozdnyaev.

Shanghai shi difangzhi bangongshi 上海市地方志办公室 [Shanghai City Gazetteer Office]. "Di'er jie Dongzhengjiao" 第二节：东正教 [Section 2: Eastern Orthodox Christianity]. Accessed February 20, 2017. www.shtong.gov.cn/node2/node2247/node79044/node79333/node79336/userobject1ai103744.html.

Share, Michael B. *Where Empires Collided: Russian and Soviet Relations with Hong Kong, Taiwan, and Macao*. Hong Kong: Chinese University Press, 2007.

Sheng Nikela Kawaxilasi 圣尼科拉•卡瓦西拉斯 [Saint Nicholas Cabasilas]. *Shifeng sheng li shi yi* 事奉圣礼释义 [Commentary on the Divine Liturgy].Translated by Makarios (Mogeng 默耕). Edited by Jingzhao 景昭. Hong Kong: OPASPP, 2007.

Sheng Nikela Weiliminuoweiqi 圣尼科拉•维利米若维奇, and Sheng Yousiting Popoweiqi 圣犹斯廷•颇颇维奇 [Saint Nikolai Velimirovich and Saint Justin Popovich]. *Shengren liezhuan jianjie* 圣人列传简介 [A brief introduction to the lives of the saints]. Translated by Xue Bin 学斌. Hong Kong: OPASPP and OFASC, 2007.

Shepherd, Bruce. *A Hand-book to Hongkong: Being A Popular Guide to the Various Places of Interest in the Colony, for the Use of Tourists*. Hongkong [Hong Kong]: Kelly & Walsh, 1893.

Shevzov, Vera. "Letting the People into Church: Reflections on Orthodoxy and Community in Late Imperial China." In *Orthodox Russia: Belief and Practice under the Tsars*, edited by Valerie A. Kivelson and Robert H. Greene, 59–77. University Park, PA: Pennsylvania State University Press, 2003.

———. "The Russian Tradition." In *The Orthodox Christian World*, edited by Augustine Casiday, 15–40. London: Routledge, 2012.

Shorter, Aylward. *Toward a Theology of Inculturation*. Maryknoll, NY, Orbis Books, 1988.

Siu, Kwok Kin 蕭國健. Xianggang lishi yanjiu 香港歷史研究 [Study of the history of Hong Kong]. Hong Kong: Xian zhao shushi, 2004.

Skvirskaja, Vera. "'Russian Merchant' Legacies in Post-Soviet Trade with China: Moral Economy, Economic Success and Business Innovation in Yiwu." Supplement, *History and Anthropology* 29, no. S1 (2018): S48–66.

Slagle, Amy. *The Eastern Church in the Spiritual Marketplace: American Conversions to Orthodox Christianity*. DeKalb, IL: Northern Illinois University Press, 2011.

"SMIRNOV Iurii (Georgii) Vital'evich." Accessed June 4, 2018. http://www.artrz.ru/menu/1804657343/1804871053.html.

Smith, Carl T. *Chinese Christians: Elites, Middlemen, and the Church in Hong Kong*. Oxford: Oxford University Press, 1985. Reprint, Hong Kong: Hong Kong University Press, 2005.

———. "The Hong Kong Situation as it Influenced the Protestant Church." In *A Carnival of Gods Studies of Religions in Hong Kong*, edited by Chan Shun Hing, 338–50. Hong Kong: Oxford University Press, 2002.

Smyslova, Alla. "Low-proficiency Heritage Speakers of Russian: Their Interlanguage System as a Basis for Fast Language (Re)building." In *Russian Language Studies in North America: New Perspectives from Theoretical and Applied Linguistics*, edited by Veronika Makarova, 161–92. London: Anthem Press, 2012.

[Archpriest] Sokolof, D. (Дмитрий Павлович Соколов) [Dimitrii Pavlovich Sokolov]. *A Manual of the Orthodox Church's Divine Services*. Jordanville, NY: Holy Trinity Monastery, 2001.

Solovieva, Olga V., and Sho Konishi, eds. *Japan's Russia: Challenging the East-West Paradigm*. Amherst, New York: Cambria Press, 2021.

Sone, Akiko. "'Being Japanese' in a Foreign Place: Cultural Identities of Japanese in Hong Kong." Master's thesis, Chinese University of Hong Kong, 2002.

Song Xiaolü 宋晓绿. "Zai Eluosi zou gangsi—1994–1999 nian Mosike de Zhongguo shangren" 在俄罗斯走钢丝绳——1994–1999年莫斯科的中国商人 [Wire walking in Russia—Chinese merchants in Moscow, 1994–1999]. *Zhongguo xiangzhen qiye*, no. 3 (2000): 24–33.

Song Yanchen 宋彦忱, ed. *Zhongguo diyu wenhua tonglan – Heilongjiang juan* 中国地域文化通览：黑龙江卷 [Overview of Chinese regional cultures – Heilongjiang volume]. Beijing: Zhonghua shuju, 2014.

[Archimandrite] Sophrony. *The Monk of Mount Athos: Staretz Selouan 1866–1938*. Crestwood, NY: St. Vladimir's Seminary Press, 1997.

Soureli, Galatea Grigoriadou 嘎拉迪亞格莉郭麗雅度一素勒里. *Mingtian shi libairi: jieshi sheng feng li de gushi* 明天是禮拜日，解釋聖俸禮的故事 [Tomorrow is Sunday: a story explaining the sacraments]. Translated by Ivan Shchelokov 施義凡. Illustrations by Julia Naumova 尤麗亞●娜吳莫娃. Hong Kong: China Orthodox Press, 2012.

South China Morning Post. "Archbishop John, Head of Orthodox Church in China, Resettlement Plans." July 24, 1949.

Spiegel Online. "North Korea Builds an Orthodox Church." Accessed June 20, 2018. https://www.spiegel.de/international/kim-jong-il-and-religion-north-korea-builds-an-orthodox-church-a-431310.html.

St. Andrew's Church Kowloon, Hong Kong. "Our History." Accessed September 8, 2017. http://standrews.monkpreview2.com/about-us/our-history.

St. Thomas Coptic Church. Accessed December 15, 2019. https://sites.google.com/site/hkcoptic/Home.

St. Thomas Coptic Church HK. "St. Thomas Coptic Church HK's Facebook Page." Facebook, December 15, 2019. https://www.facebook.com/coptichk.

St. Tikhon's Monastery. *Book of Needs (Abridged)*. South Canaan, PA: St. Tikhon's Seminary Press, 2002.

Stamoolis, James J. *Eastern Orthodox Mission Theology Today*. Maryknoll, NY: Orbis Books, 1986.

Standaert, Nicolas, ed. *Handbook of Christianity in China, Volume One: 635–1800*. Leiden and Boston: Brill, 2000.

Suofuluoni 索福罗尼 [(Archimandrite) Sophrony]. *Eluosi jingshen jujiang zhanglao Xila* 俄罗斯精神巨匠长老西拉 [The great master of the Russian spirit, Staretz Selouan]. Translated by Dai Guiju 戴桂菊. Shanghai: Huadong shifan daxue chubanshe, 2007.

The Synod of Bishops of the Russian Orthodox Church Outside of Russia. "Act of Canonical Communion." March 5, 2021. https://web.archive.org/web/20070614175937/http://www.russianorthodoxchurch.ws/synod/engdocuments/enmat_akt.html.

Sweeten, Alan Richard. *Christianity in Rural China: Conflict and Accommodation in Jiangxi Province, 1860–1900*. Ann Arbor: Center for Chinese Studies, University of Michigan, 2001.

Ta Kung Pao. "E da mushou zai Xianggang ban xin shu shou fa shi" 俄大牧首在港辦新書首發式 [Russian high-ranking priest holds a new book launch ceremony in Hong Kong]. June 27, 2018. Accessed July 1, 2018. http://www.takungpao.com.hk/international/text/2018/0627/180349.html.

Taiwan Jidu Zhengjiaohui [Orthodox Church in Taiwan (Moscow Patriarchate)]. Accessed March 14, 2017. http://orthodoxchurch.tw/%E5%8F%B0%E7%81%A3%E6%AD%A3%E6%95%99%E6%9C%83.

Taiwan Jidu Zhengjiaohui 台灣基督正教會 / The Orthodox Church in Taiwan (OMHKSEA). Accessed February 19, 2021. https://theological.asia/.

Tang, Ge 唐戈. *Eluosi wenhua zai Zhongguo: Renlei xue yu lishi xue de yanjiu* 俄罗斯文化在中国：人类学与历史学的研究 [Russian culture in China: anthropological and historical research]. Harbin: Beifang wenyi chubanshe, 2010.

Tang, Ka Jau 鄧家宙. *Ershi shiji Xianggang fojiao zhi fazhan* 二十世紀香港佛教之發展 [Development of Hong Kong Buddhism in the twentieth century]. Hong Kong: Xianggang fojiao yu wenhua lishi xuehui, 2007.

Tang, Ka Jau 鄧家宙, Li Kwok Chu 李國柱, Chin Kin Wing 錢建榮, Chan Kok Chung 陳覺聰, Wong King Chung 黃競聰, Cheng Wing Piu 鄭榮標, Sze Chi Ming 施志明, and Desiwen 德斯文 (Steivan Defilla), eds. *Xianggang lishi tanjiu* 香港歷史探究 / Exploring the history of Hong Kong. Hong Kong: Xianggang shixue hui, 2011.

Telyuk, A. V. (А. В. Телюк), ed. *Pravoslavie v Kitae* (Православие в Китае) [Orthodoxy in China]. Blagoveshchensk: Izd-vo OAO Amurskaia iarmarka ["Amur Fair" publishing house], 2013.

Teng, Emma Jinhua. *Eurasian: Mixed Identities in the United States, China, and Hong Kong, 1842–1943*. Berkeley: University of California Press, 2013.

Tianzhujiao Xianggang jiaoqu liyi weiyuanhui 天主教香港教區禮儀委員會 [Hong Kong Diocesan Liturgy Commission]. *Beauty Will Save the World / Zhu jiang renjian——mei yin tianxia: Huang Yongquan dongfang shengxianghua huace* 主降人間——美蔭天下：黃永權 東方聖像畫畫冊 [Beauty will save the world / The divine coming down to earth — beauty encompassing the world: a collection of Eastern icons by Wong Wing Kuen]. Hong Kong: Catholic Diocese of Hong Kong, 2011.

Tiedemann, R. G., ed. *Handbook of Christianity in China, Volume Two: 1800 to the Present*. Leiden and Boston: Brill, 2010.

Tikhvinskii, Sergei Leonidovich (С. Л. Тихвинский), et al., eds. *Istoriia Rossiiskoi Dukhovnoi missii v Kitae: Sbornik statei* (История Российской Духовной миссии в Китае: Сборник статей) [History of the Russian Ecclesiastical Mission in China: collected articles]. Predisl. S. L. Tikhvinskogo [With a preface by S. L. Tikhvinskogo]. Moscow: Izd-vo Sviato-Vladimirskogo bratstva, 1997.

Ting Sun Pao Joseph 丁新豹, and Lo Shuk-ying 盧淑櫻. *Fei Wo zuyi: Zhanqian Xianggang de waiji zuqun* 非我族裔：戰前香港的外籍族群 [Not of my kind: foreign communities in Hong Kong before World War Two]. Hong Kong: Joint Publishing, 2014.

Tong, Wai Ki 湯偉奇, Mai Kam Hang 麥錦恆, Yau Chi-On 游子安, and Leung Tak Wah 梁德華. *Li wu ji shi: Xianggang Daojiao cishan shiye zonglan* 利物濟世：香港道教慈善事業總覽 / *Reaching out with Benevolence: Overview of Taoist Charitable Work in Hong Kong*. Hong Kong: Xianggang Daojiao lianhehui, 2011.

[Protoiereus] Torik, Alexander. *Churching: For Beginners to Church Life*. Translated by Nathan Williams. Self-published, LOGOS Digital Publishing, 2011. Kindle.

"Training and Testing Language Language Center for Foreigners." Accessed November 28, 2017. http://russian-test.com/eng/center/about_the_center.html.

Tsang, Iris Y. L. 曾燕玲. "Zongjiao ziyou yu Jibenfa" 宗教自由與基本法 [Religious freedom and the Basic Law]. In *Xianggang de zongjiao* 香港的宗教 [Hong Kong religions], edited by Hong Kong Catholic Social Communications Office, 118–25. Hong Kong: Holy Spirit Study Centre and Hong Kong Catholic Social Communications Office, 1988.

Tsang, Steve. *A Modern History of Hong Kong: 1841–1997*. London: I.B. Tauris, 2003.

Ular, Alexandre. *Un Empire Russo-Chinois*. Paris: Félix Juven, 1902.

The United Front Work Department of CPC Central Committee 中共中央统一战线工作部. Accessed January 15, 2021. http://www.zytzb.gov.cn/html/index.html.

United Nations Population Fund. "World Population Dashboard." Accessed June 16, 2019. https://www.unfpa.org/data/world-population-dashboard.

Ustav Tserkovnykh pravoslavnykh obshchin gorodov Iuzhnogo Kitaia i filippinskikh ostrovov (Устав Церковных православных общин городов Южного Китая и филиппинских островов) [Charter of the Orthodox church communities of the cities of South China and the Philippine Islands]. Shanghai, 1939.

Van Remortel, Michael, and Peter Chang, eds. *St. Nikolai Kasatkin and the Orthodox Mission in Japan: A Collection of Writings by an International Group of Scholars about St. Nikolai, his Disciples and the Mission*. Point Reyes Station, CA: Divine Ascent Press, Monastery of St. John of Shanghai and San Francisco, 2003.

Vermander, Benoît. "Sinicizing Religions, Sinicizing Religious Studies." *Religions* 10, no. 2 (2019): 137. https://doi.org/10.3390/rel10020137.

Voinarskii, Boris Pavlovich (Борис Павлович Войнарский). *Bei-guan': Rossiiskaia Dukhovnaia Missiia v Kitae* (Бэй-гуань: Российская Духовная Миссия в Китае) [Bei-guan: The Russian Ecclesiastical Mission in China]. Tianjin: Ideal Press, 1939.

"Volontery v pomoshch' detiam-sirotam" (Волонтеры в помощь детям-сиротам) [Volunteers to help orphans]. Accessed September 14, 2017. https://www.otkazniki.ru.

Voskressenski, Alexei D. *Russia and China: A Theory of Inter-State Relations*. London: Routledge, 2002.

Vulpius, Ricarda. "The Russian Empire's Civilizing Mission in the Eighteenth Century: A Comparative Perspective." In *Asiatic Russia: Imperial Power in Regional and International* Contexts, edited by Uyama Tomohiko, 13–31. Abingdon, Oxon; New York: Routledge, 2012.

Walters, Philip. "A Survey of Soviet Religious Policy." In *Religious Policy in the Soviet Union*, edited by Sabrina Petra Ramet, 3–30. Cambridge: Cambridge University Press, 1992.

Waluokelamusike du zhujiao Yilaliyong 沃洛柯拉姆斯克都主教伊拉里雍 [Metropolitan of Volokolamsk Hilarion], et al. *Chushi Dongzhengjiao: Gei juzhu zai Eluosi de Zhongguoren* 初識東正教：給居住在俄羅斯的中國人 [Introduction to Orthodox Christianity: for Chinese living in Russia]. Moscow: Eluosi Dongzheng jiaohui Mosike zongzhujiao bangongting chubanshe, 2016 / Hong Kong: China Orthodox Press, 2016. Content written in simplified Chinese.

Wang Yingjia 王英佳, ed. *Eluosi shehui yu wenhua* 俄罗斯社会与文化 [Russian society and culture]. Wuhan: Wuhan daxue chubanshe, 2001.

Wang Zhicheng 汪之成. *Jindai Shanghai Eguo qiaomin shenghuo* 近代上海俄国侨民生活 [The life of Russian émigrés in modern Shanghai]. Shanghai: Shanghai cishu chubanshe, 2008.

Ware, Timothy. *The Orthodox Church*. Harmondsworth, Middlesex: Penguin Books 1963.

———. *The Orthodox Church: An Introduction to Eastern Christianity*, 3rd ed. London: Penguin Books, 2015.

Wei'er 韋爾 [Timothy Ware]. *Dongzheng jiaohui daolun* 東正教導論 [Doctrine of the Orthodox Church]. Translated by Tian Yuan 田原. Hong Kong: The Logos and Pneumas Press, 2013.

Wen Guannan 温冠男, and Hu Boya 胡博雅. "Ha'erbin hua e houyi de xianzhuang diaocha" 哈尔滨华俄后裔的现状调查 [Investigation on the current situation of the Chinese-Russian descendants in Harbin]. *Heilongjiang sheng shehui zhuyi xueyuan xuebao*, no. 4 (2011): 45–49.

Wenzel-Teuber, Katharina. "2015 Statistical Update on Religions and Churches in the Peoples' Republic of China." *Religions & Christianity in Today's China* 6, no. 2 (2016): 20–43.

Werth, Paul W. *At the Margins of Orthodoxy: Mission, Governance, and Confessional Politics in Russia's Volga-Kama Region, 1827–1905*. Ithaca, NY: Cornell University Press, 2002.

———. "Orthodoxy as Ascription (and Beyond): Religious Identity on the Edges of the Orthodox Community, 1740–1917." In Valerie A. Kivelson and Robert H. Greene, *Orthodox Russia: Belief and Practice under the Tsars*, 239–51. University Park, PA: Pennsylvania University Press, 2003.

Whiteford, John. *Sola Scriptura: An Orthodox Analysis of the Cornerstone of Reformation Theology*. Chesterton, IN: Conciliar Press, 1997.

Wickeri, Philip L., and Yik-fai Tam. "The Religious Life of Ethnic Minority Communities." In *Chinese Religious Life*, edited by David A. Palmer, Glenn Shive, and Philip L. Wickeri, 50–66. New York: Oxford University Press, 2011.

Widmer, Eric. *The Russian Ecclesiastical Mission in Peking during the Eighteenth Century*. Cambridge, MA: East Asian Research Center, Harvard University Press, 1976.

Wolff, David. *To the Harbin Station: The Liberal Alternative to Russian Manchuria, 1898–1914*. Stanford, CA: Stanford University Press, 1999.

Wong, Timothy Man-kong. "Protestant Missionaries' Images of Chinese Buddhism: A Preliminary Study of the Buddhist Writings of Joseph Edkins, Ernest John Eitel, and James Legge." *The HKBU Journal of Historical Studies* 1 (1999): 183–204.

———. "The Rendering of God in Chinese by the Chinese: Chinese Responses to the Term Question in the *Wanguo Gongbao*." In *Mapping Meanings: The Field of New Learning in Late Qing China*, edited by Michael Lackner, and Natascha Vittinghoff, 589–614. Leiden: Brill, 2004.

World Council of Churches. "Orthodox churches (Eastern)." Accessed February 18, 2021, https://www.oikoumene.org/church-families/orthodox-churches-eastern.

Wu Zhenchun 吴震春. *Jidujiao yu Zhongguo wenhua* 基督教与中国文化 [Christianity and Chinese culture]. Beijing: Shangwu yinshuguan, 2015.

Xiao Yuqiu 肖玉秋. *Eguo chuanjiao tuan yu Qingdai Zhong E wenhua jiaoliu* 俄国传教团与清代中俄文化交流 [The Russian Orthodox Mission in Beijing and Sino-Russian cultural exchange in the Qing dynasty]. Tianjin: Tianjin renmin chubanshe, 2009.

Xie'ergai Huoluri 谢尔盖•霍鲁日 [Sergey Khoruzhiy]. *Xietong ren xue yu Sulian zhexue: Huoluri zai Beijing Shifan Daxue yanjiang* 协同人学与苏联哲学：霍鲁日在北京师范大学演讲 [Synergetic anthropology and Russian philosophy: the lectures of Sergey Khoruzhiy at Beijing Normal University]. Translated by Zhang Baichun 张百春. Hong Kong: OPASPP, 2010.

Xieliwanuofusiji 谢利瓦诺夫斯基 [Selivanovsky, V.]. *Dongzhengjiao hui zai Zhonghuo* 东正教会在中国 [The Orthodox Church in China]. Translated by Gao Yongsheng 高永生. Edited by Ambrose Lam (Lin Sen) 林森. Hong Kong: China Orthodox Press, 2014.

Xin shenxuejia Sheng Ximeng 新神学家圣西蒙 [Saint Symeon the New Theologian]. *Chu zao zhi ren* 初造之人 [The first-created man]. Translated by Salafen Luosi shenfu 塞拉芬•罗斯神父 [Father Seraphim Rose] and Chu Guo 初果. Edited by Yifan 一凡 [Ivan] and Lin Sen 林森. Hong Kong: China Orthodox Press, 2015.

Xu Fenglin 徐凤林. *Dongzhengjiao shengxiang shi* 东正教圣像史 [History of Orthodox icons]. Beijing: Beijing daxue chubanshe, 2012.

———. *Eluosi zongjiao zhexue* 俄罗斯宗教哲学 [Russian religious philosophy]. Beijing: Beijing daxue chubanshe, 2006.

Xuyang Jingjing. "Orthodox Christians in China Seeking Official Recognition." *Global Times*. May 15, 2013. Accessed August 29, 2020. http://www.globaltimes.cn/content/781838.shtml#:~:text=Researchers%20predict%20that%20the%20religion,of%20a%20revival%20in%20China.

Yalishanda Duolike shenfu 亚历山大•多利克神父 [(Arch) priest Alexander Torik]. *Shouxi rujiao: xie gei gangang kaishi zongjiao shenghuo de ren* 受洗入教：写给刚刚开始宗教生活的人 [Baptism and entry to the faith: written for those who have just started religious life]. Translated by Tamala Jin 塔玛拉•金 [Tamara Jin]. Hong Kong: OPASPP and OFASC, 2011.

Yalishanda (Milante) zhujiao 亞歷山大（米蘭特）主教 [Bishop Alexander (Mileant)]. *Jidu de fuhuo: dui siwang de zhengfu (jiexuan)* 基督的復活：對死亡的政府（節選）[The resurrection of Christ: the conquest of death (excerpts)]. Translated by Lu Hongshi 陸宏湜. Hong Kong: China Orthodox Press, 2015.

———. [Bishop Aleksandr (Mileant)]. *Sheng san yi jie: Shengling jianglin yu zhong shitu zhi ri* 聖三一節：聖靈降臨於眾使徒之日 [The Feast of the Holy Trinity: the day the Holy Spirit approached the apostles]. Translated by Lian Qianqi連阡淇, Xia Ershan 夏爾杉, and Lin Sen 林森. Hong Kong: OPASPP, 2014.

———. *Xianxing lingji zhe Yiwang da zhujiao: 20 shiji zui weida de shengren zhiyi — Shanghai ji Jiujinshan da zhujiao Yiwang Makeximoweiqi shengping ji shengji* 顯行靈蹟者伊望大主教：20世紀最偉大的聖人之一——上海及舊金山大主教聖伊望ᴦ馬克西莫維奇生平及聖蹟 [Archbishop John the Wonderworker: one of the greatest saints of the twentieth century, the life and miracles of Saint John, Archbishop of Shanghai and San Francisco]. Translated by Lu Hongti 陸宏湜. Hong Kong: China Orthodox Press, 2015.

Yalishanda (Milante) zhujiao 亚历山大（米兰特）主教 [Bishop Alexander (Mileant)]. *Danshen, jiehun huo "ziyou xing'ai" —gai ruhe xuanze?* 单身，结婚或「自由性爱」— 该如何选择？ [Celibacy, marriage, or "free sexual love" — which way to choose?]. Edited by Xie'ergai Jisiliefu谢尔盖•吉斯列夫 [Sergei Kislev]. Translated by Lin Xianhe 林显河. Hong Kong: China Orthodox Press, 2014.

———. *Zhengjiaohui* 正教会 [The Orthodox church]. Hong Kong: OPASPP, 2010.

Yalishanda Shimeiman da siji 亞歷山大•施梅曼大司祭 [Archpriest Alexander Dmitrievich Schmemann]. *Shengzhou liyi chanxiang* 聖週禮儀闡詳 [A liturgical explanation of the Holy Week]. Translated by Lin Sen 林森. Hong Kong: China Orthodox Press, 2015.

Yalisidilisi Babalaqisi boshi 亞里斯迪黎思•巴巴拉啟斯博士 [Dr. Aristeides Papadakis]. *Jiaohui lishi* 教會歷史 [History of the Church]. Xindian: Taiwan Jidu Zhengjiaohui, 2006.

Yanchuk, Vadim. "The Visitor of St. Elisabeth Convent Tells about Orthodoxy in China." *The Catalogue of Good Deeds* (blog). March 5, 2019, https://blog.obitel-minsk.com/2019/03/the-visitor-of-st-elisabeth-convent-tells-about-orthodoxy-in-china.html.

Yang Duojie 杨多杰. "Qingdai Beijing de Eluosi qiren" 清代北京的俄罗斯旗人 [Russian bannermen in the Qing dynasty Beijing]. *Shijie bolan*, no. 22 (2008): 54–59.

Yang Chuang 杨闯. *Bai nian Zhong E guanxi* 百年中俄关系 [A century of China and Russia relation]. Beijing: Shijie zhishi chubanshe, 2006.

Yang Jia 杨佳. "Dongzhengjiao jisi fushi de dongyahua chutan" 东正教祭祀服饰的东亚化初探 [A preliminary inquiry into the Asianization of Orthodox liturgical vestments]. Paper presented at the 2014 Ph.D. Candidates Academic Conference on Social Change and Cultural Adaptation—Religious Study in Asia-Pacific, Department of Philosophy, Peking University, Beijing, October 2014.

Yao Mingquan 姚民权, and Luo Wei 罗伟. *Zhongguo Jidujiao jianzhi* 中国基督教简史 [A brief history of Christianity in China]. Beijing: Zongjiao wenhua chubanshe, 2000.

Yau, Chi-On 游子安, and Ngai Ting Ming 危丁明. *Daofeng bainian: Xianggang Daojiao yu daoguan* 道風百年：香港道教與道觀 [The Daoist wind in a century: Hong Kong Daoism and Daoist temples] . Xianggang: Peng ying xian guan Daojiao wenhua ziliaoku, Liwen chubanshe, 2002.

Yeung, Brian. "'Da' to the Language." *South China Morning Post*, November 26, 2013, 16.

Yeung, Daniel H. N. 楊熙楠, Ho Lai Yung 何麗蓉, and Jason T. S. Lam 林子淳, eds. *Hanyu Jidujiao wenhua yanjiusuo tongxun* 漢語基督教文化研究所通訊 [Bulletin of the Institute of Sino-Christian Studies]. *Er shi zhou nian jinian tekan (1995–2015)* 二十週年紀念特刊（1995–2015）[special issue to commemorate the 20th year anniversary (1995–2015)] (Spring 2016).

Yelusaling zong zhujiao Sheng Sufeluoni 耶路撒冷宗主教聖索弗羅尼 [Patriarch of Jerusalem, St. Sophronius]. *Aiji de Sheng Maliya shengping* 埃及的聖瑪利亞生平 [The life of St. Mary of Egypt]. Translated by Makali Wang 瑪喀里·王 [Makarios Wang]. Hong Kong: OPASPP, 2014.

[Zong zhujiao] Yilaliweng 伊拉里翁總主教 [Metropolitan Hilarion (Alfeyev) of Volokolamsk]. *Zhengjiao daoshi tan qidao: sa'er jiang* 正教導師談祈禱：卅二講 [Orthodox teacher discusses prayer: thirty-two lectures]. Translated by (shenfu) Aixili'er（神父）愛西里爾 [(Father) Kiril Chkarboul]. Taipei: Kuangchi Cultural Group, 2009.

[Gu Luoma] Youxibiwu （古罗马）优西比乌 [St. Eusebius (of Caesarea)]. *Jiaohui shi* 教会史 [Church history]. Original translation and commentary by Paul L. Maier 保罗•L•梅尔. Translated by Qu Xutong 瞿旭彤. Beijing: Sanlian shudian, 2012.

Yu Chunjiang 于春江. "Zhongguo Eluosi zu minzu guocheng yanjiu—yi Neimenggu E'erguna shi Shiwei Eluosi minzu xiang wei ge'an yanjiu" 中国俄罗斯族民族过程研究——以内蒙古额尔古纳市室韦俄罗斯民族乡为个案研究 [Research on the ethnicization of China's Russian ethnic group—a case study of the Shiwei Russian Ethnic Minority County of Ergun City in Inner Mongolia]. Master's thesis, Zhongyang minzu daxue, 2009.

Yu Juan 于涓. *Hunyin zhi huihuang* 婚姻之輝煌 [The Splendor of the Marriage in the Orthodox Church]. Xindian: Taiwan Jidu Zhengjiaohui, 2012.

Yu, Pelagia Chuan. *Byzantine Iconography: The Life of Jesus by Icons*. New Taipei City: Orthodox Church of Taiwan, 2014.

Yu Tao 于涛. *Huashang taojin Mosike: yige qianyi qunti de kuaguo shengcun xingdong* 华商淘金莫斯科：一個迁移群体的跨国生存行动 [Chinese businessmen in Moscow: the survival behaviour of a transnational migration group]. Beijing: Social Sciences Academic Press, 2016.

Yue Feng 乐峰. *Dongzhengjiao shi* 东正教史 [History of Eastern Orthodox Christianity], 2nd ed. Beijing: Zhongguo shehui kexue chubanshe, 2005.

———. "Dongzhengjiao chuanjiaoshi yu Zhongguo wenhua" 东正教传教士与中国文化 [Eastern Orthodox missionaries and Chinese culture]. *Shijie zongjiao wenhua*, no. 2 (1995): 37–39.

Yue'an Weifu 约安•威福 [John Whiteford]. *Weidu Shengjing ma? Zhengjiao dui Jidu xinjiao zhi jiaodao de pingjia* 唯独圣经吗？正教对基督新教之教导的评价 [The "Exclusive Bible"? The Orthodox evaluation of Protestant theology]. Hong Kong: OPASPP and OFASC, 2009.

Yuehan Kelimakesi 約翰•克利馬科斯 [John Climacus]. *Shensheng pandeng de tianti* 神聖攀登的天梯 [The ladder of divine ascent]. Translated by Xue Liemin 許列民. Hong Kong: The Logos and Pneuma Press, 2012.

Zatsepine, Victor. *Beyond the Amur: Frontier Encounters between China and Russia, 1850–1930*. Vancouver: University of British Columbia Press, 2017.

Zhang Baichun 张百春. *Dangdai Dongzhengjiao shenxue sixiang* 当代东正教神学思想 [Contemporary theology of the Orthodox churches]. Shanghai: Shanghai Sanlian shudian, 2000.

———. *Feng suizhe yisi chui—Bie'erjiayefu zongjiao zhexue yanjiu* 风随着意思吹——别尔嘉耶夫宗教哲学研究 [As the wind blows—Berdyaev's research on religion and philosophy]. Harbin: Heilongjiang daxue chubanshe, 2011.

Zhang Sui 张绥. *Dongzhengjiao he Dongzhengjiao zai Zhongguo* 东正教和东正教在中国 [Orthodox Christianity and Orthodox Christianity in China]. Shanghai: Xuelin chubanshe, 1986.

Zhang Xiaobin 张晓兵. *Neimenggu Eluosi zu* 内蒙古俄罗斯族 [Ethnic Russians in Inner Mongolia]. Hulunbuir: Neimenggu wenhua chubanshe, 2015.

Zhang Xuefeng 张雪峰. *Qingchao qianqi Eguo zhu Hua zongjiao chuandaotuan yanjiu* 清朝前期俄国驻华宗教传道团研究 [Research on Russian religious missions in China during the early Qing]. Xinbei: Hua Mulan wenhua chubanshe, 2012.

Zhebokritskaia, Larisa (Лариса Жебокритская). "Prazdnik russkogo iazyka v Gonkonge" (Праздник русского языка в Гонконге) [Russian Language Day in Hong Kong]. *Koordinatsionnyi Sovet Sootechestvennikov v Kitae* (Координационный Совет Соотечественников в Китае) [The Coordination Council of Compatriots in China]. Accessed May 15, 2017. http://www.russianchina.org/news/2017/05/15/8158#more-8158.

Zheng Yongwang 郑永旺. *Eluosi Dongzhengjiao yu Heilongjiang wenhua: Longjiang dadi shang Eluosi Dongzhengjiao de lishi* 俄罗斯东正教与黑龙江文化：龙江大地上俄罗斯东正教的历史回声 [The Russian Orthodox Church and Heilongjiang culture: the historical echo of the Russian Orthodox Church in Heilongjiang]. Harbin: Heilongjiang chubanshe, 2010.

Zhong Guofa 钟国发. *Xianggang Daojiao* 香港道教 [Hong Kong Daoism]. Beijing: Zongjiao wenhua chubanshe, 2010.

Zhou, Xun. "Collaborating and Conflicted: Being Jewish in Secular and Multicultural Hong Kong." In *Judaism, Christianity, and Islam: Collaboration and Conflict in the Age of Diaspora*, edited by Sander L. Gilman, 99–114. Hong Kong: Hong Kong University Press, 2014.

———. "'Cosmopolitan from Above': A Jewish Experience in Hong Kong." *European Review of History / Revue Européene D'histoire* 23, no. 5–6 (2016): 897–911.

Zhu He 祝贺. "Dui Zhong E hunyin he jiating guanxi de chanshi" 对中俄婚姻和家庭关系的阐释 [Explanation on Russian-Chinese marriage and family relationship]. *Shanxi qingnian*, no. 20 (2017): 202.

Index

ABC of Hong Kong, 55, 73
Act of Canonical Communion of the Russian Orthodox Church Outside Russia with the Russian orthodox Church Moscow Patriarchate, 45
Africa, 23, 41, 70
Aidan (Keller), 85, 106–7
Albazin (Yaksa), 9
Albazinian, 3, 6, 7, 9, 45, 133
Alevisopoulos, Antonios, 99
Alexander (Mileant), 89, 100, 102
Alexy I, 37
"all can be eaten", 92
Anastasius, 36
Anglo-European, 28
Anglophone, 12, 88, 154
Annotation for osmoglasia, 136
Anthropology of St. Paul, 120
Anti-Piracy Guards, 31
archbishop, xxxii
archdiocese, xxvii, 48, 112–13, 117
archimandrite, 4, 6, 18
archpriest, xxxii
Asia, 50, 70, 151
Australia, xxiv, xxxiii, 29, 33, 39–40, 45, 70, 113, 115
Avramides, Stephen, 99

The Basic Law of the Hong Kong Special Administrative Region of the People's Republic of China (Basic Law), 13, 170
bauhinia flower, 155
Beijing, xx, 2–4, 6–8, 14, 29, 32–33, 35–36, 43, 45, 47, 52, 80–81, 103, 105, 116, 142, 151, 165
Beijing Foreign Studies University, 106
Beijing Normal University, 103, 142
Beiping (Beijing), 69
Belanovsky, Nicholas, 60, 77
Belanovsky, Tatiana Ivanovra, 39
Belt and Road Initiative (BRI), 171
(Benedictine) Abbey of St. John (Müstair, Switzerland), 102
Berdyaev, Nikolai, 103
bi-literalism and trilingualism, 130
Biographies of the Saints, 111
birch juice, 146
[Bishop] Seraphim [Tsujie] of Sendai, 115
Bogoyevlensky Church, 36
Bolshakoff, Serge Nikolaevich, 2
"book of needs", 113
(Book of) Psalms (translation into Chinese), 81, 98, 111, 136
Book of Services of the Twelve Feasts, 106
Bowring, John, 31
Boxer Rebellion (Yihetuan Movement), 6, 97, 114

British colony, xxiii, 27, 31–32, 35–36, 50
British Commonwealth, xxiv
British–Russian peace treaty, 31
Buddhism, 2, 9, 13–14, 25, 82, 128, 132
Bulgakov, Sergei Nikolaevich, 103

Cambodia, 143
Cantonese, 14, 45, 62, 70, 75, 83, 92–94, 125, 129–30, 135, 145, 156–57
Carl Smith Collection (Hong Kong Public Records Office), 27, 39
Carousel (children's choir studio), 65, 73, 138
Cathedral of the Icon of the Mother of God "Surety of Sinners" (Shanghai), 8, 36, 47, 60
Catholic, xx, 2–3, 6, 8–10, 13–14, 23–24, 27–29, 31, 47, 82, 90, 104, 113, 127–28, 133, 137, 141, 158, 164–66
Catholicism, xviii, 126, 128, 133, 152, 155
Central Asia, 19, 146
chairman of (the Synodal Department of) the Department for External Church Relations of Russian Orthodox Church, 151
Chan, Bing Yim, 37, 51
Cheesefare Sunday, 62, 137, 147
Chekhov, Anton [Pavlovich], 41
Cherikoff Bakery, 32, 40
Chernykh, Viktor, 8
Chiang, Kai-shek, 7
China Continuation Committee, 6
China Orthodox Press (COP), xviii, xxvi, xxix, xxxi, xxxv, 1, 44, 46, 57, 76, 79, 80, 82–89, 92, 94, 96–107, 109–11, 115–16, 118–23, 129, 136, 142, 163–64
China proper, 7, 8
Chinese Academic Library of Christian Thought, 141
Chinese Autonomous Orthodox Church, 7, 43, 50, 85, 101, 151
Chinese Christianity, xxi–xxii, 10, 86, 123

Chinese Communist Party (CCP), xx–xxi, 11, 152
Chinese Eastern Railway, 18
Chinese elements, 167
Chinese Good Tidings/Chinese Good News, 81
Chinese morals, xxii, 133
Chinese Orthodox Association (Shanghai), 36
Chinese Patriarchal Metochion, 101
Chinese society, xix, 8, 10, 82
Chinese-speaking, 129, 136, 157
Chinese style, 138
Chinese University of Hong Kong (CUHK), 56, 86, 141
Chinese value, xxi, 133
Chiuchow dialect, 130
Chkarboul, Kiril, 152
choir, 33, 49, 57, 65–66, 73, 87, 133, 136–38, 157
Chow, Ingrid, 62
Christian Literature Society for China (CLSC), 6
Christian World of Asia, 151, 161
Church Bulletin, 81, 106
Church of All Nations in the Garden of Gethsemane (Jerusalem), 150
Church of Japan, xxvii, xxxii, 110, 115–16
Church of St. Nicholas the Wonderworker (Shanghai), 169
Church of the Dormition (Beijing), 8, 45, 47, 151
Church of the Dormition (Harbin), 47
Church of the Holy Annunciation (Harbin), 47
Church of the Holy Iveron Icon [St. Ibervel Church] (Harbin), 6, 47
Church of the Holy Resurrection/ Resurrection parish (Hong Kong), 34, 36–37
Church of the Holy Sepulchre (Jerusalem), 150
Church of the Holy Trinity (Macau), 32
Church of the Iberian Icon of the Mother of God (Manila), 32

Church of the Immaculate Conception
    (Hong Kong), 28
Church of the Nativity of the Blessed
    Virgin (Moscow), 150
Church of the Theophany (Shanghai),
    47
(Church) Slavonic, 45, 70, 79, 81–82,
    89, 94–96, 106, 113–14, 122, 129,
    135–36, 138
classical Chinese, 115–16, 121–22
clergyman, 32, 35, 50, 117, 151
Cold Store company, 39
College of Foreign Affairs, 4
colonial government, xx, 13, 29, 32, 38
colonial Hong Kong, 28
Common European Framework of
    Reference for Languages (CEFR),
    61, 77
Confucian Academy, 29
Confucius, 82
congregation, xvii, xxiii, 7, 11, 14, 34,
    37–38, 42–45, 49, 59, 86, 94, 108–9,
    126, 128–30, 135–37, 143–45, 156,
    163, 165–67, 169
convent/monastery, xxxii, 155
convert, xix, xxvi–xxviii, xxxi, 5–6, 12,
    15, 24, 30, 35–36, 42, 70, 84, 88–89,
    111, 117, 125–33, 152, 155, 166–68
Coordination Council of Russian
    Compatriots in China, 73
Coptic Orthodox, 165–66, 170
cottage cheese/quark, 146
Council of Bishops, xxxii
Creasy, Harold T., 33
Crimean War, 31
Cyril, 106, 157
Cyrillic, 81, 106, 136, 151

Dairen (Dalian), 30
Dairy Farm Ice, 39
Damascene (John Christensen), 100,
    116
Daoism, 2, 9, 13–14, 25
Dar Publishing House, 142
Daur, 5, 16

Davis, Anoush Georgievna, 76
Davydenkov, Oleg, 102
Deacon, 6, 36
deanery, xxxii, 32–33, 49, 50
Democratic People's Republic of Korea
    (DPRK), xxiv, xxvii
Department for External Church
    Relations (DECR), 44, 53, 151
Des Vœux, William, 31
diaspora, 32, 68–69, 78, 82, 150, 161,
    168
diocese, xx, xxvii, xxxii, xxxv, 7, 29,
    32–33, 43, 48, 115, 140, 153
(Diocese of) Pskov and Porkhov, 142
divine liturgy in honor of Our Father
    Among the Saints John Chrysostom,
    94, 112, 113
Dmitrenko, Alexander, 157
Dmitry of Rostov (Danila Savvich
    Tuptalo), 80
Dormition of the Most Holy Theotokos
    Church (Beijing), 45, 47, 151
double minority, xxv
Du, Bining, 9
Du, Lifu Aleksander, 151
Du, Runchen Feodor, 7

East Asia, xviii, xxiv–xxviii, xxxiv, 11,
    46, 127, 131, 153, 166, 169
East Asian Exarchate, 7, 33
Easter (holiday), 65, 67, 110–11, 139
Eastern Europe, xix, 19, 62, 146, 169
*Eastern Orthodox Christianity in China:
    Past, Present, and Future*, 140
Ecumenical Patriarchate of
    Constantinople, xxviii, xxxiii, 143
(Ecumenical Patriarchate) Orthodox
    Metropolitanate of Hong Kong and
    South East Asia (OMHKSEA),
    xxxiii, 11, 44, 83, 99, 110, 120, 131,
    165
Edo period, 132
eparchial council, xxxii
eparchial court, xxxii
eparchy, xxxii

Ephraim of Bikin (Prosyanok, Roman), 45, 106
Erohina (Erokhina), Tatiana, 30
Ethnic Identification Project, xxii, xxxiii
(ethnic) Chinese, xix, xxii, xxiii, xxiv, xxv, xxvi, 1, 7, 10, 14, 36, 42, 45, 75, 102, 123, 129, 138, 143, 151–52, 156–58
ethnic identity, 30, 63, 168
ethnic minority, xix, xxiii–xxiv, xxxi, 1, 8–9, 22, 167
ethno-religious communities, 11
Eurasian, 28
Europe, xxi, xxiv, 6, 28, 40–41, 61, 70, 152, 154
evening prayers, 96
exclusive religion, 127
exotic, xxv, 40
expatriate, xix, xxiv, xxv, xxvi, 11, 15, 69, 130, 167
expatriate churches, xix, 11

Family Art Picnic, 73
family holiday, 73
fasting day, 90, 92, 110, 112
Feast of Theophany/Epiphany, 142
Federova, Nina (pseudonym of Antonina Riasanovsky), 30
"fifty years of no change", 12
Filyanovsky, Igor, 44
"Finest, the Brave Falcon", 66
Fogt, Adelaide Dmitryevna, 38
foreigner, xix, xxiv–xxv, 3, 9, 13, 31, 38–39, 114, 131, 167
foreign religion, xx, 10–11, 14, 82
The Frigate Pallada, 40

Gantimur, 5, 18
Gantimurov family, 5
General Church Court, xxxii
Georgy (metropolitan of Nizhny Novgorod and Arzamas), 150
German Bethesda Chapel (Hong Kong), 28
Gillquist, Peter E., 117

Golden (Goldin), Constantine, 39
Goldin (Golden), Anastasia, 39
Goncharov, Ivan [Aleksandrovich], 40
graduation (vypusknoi), 65, 66
Great Britain, xxiv, 166
Greater China, xx, xxx, xxxi, 1, 14, 43, 45–46, 79, 129, 151, 156
Great Lent, xxii
Great Proletariat Cultural Revolution, 8
Greek, 53, 79, 82, 99, 101–2, 118, 143–44, 154
Greek Orthodox, xviii, xxvii–xxviii, xxxv, 112, 165–66
Guangdong province, 11, 14, 35, 86
Guangdong University of Foreign Studies, 129
Guangzhou, 11, 23, 32, 39, 48–49, 124, 150

Hakka, 128, 130
Han (Chinese), xxi, xxii, 133
Hanyu Pinyin, 89, 93, 112
Happy Valley, 37, 87, 171
Heavenly Bread, 81
Hechuan (Chongqing, Sichuan province), 106
Heilongjiang, 20, 165
"hello", 72
heritage believer, xix, xxvi, xxviii, xxxi, 9, 30, 123, 133, 136, 152
Hilarion (Alfeyev), 86, 99, 108
Hinduism, 2, 13
holy *(sheng)*, 134
Holy Communion, xxii, 45, 98, 134
Holy Monastery of Zografos (also known as Saint George the Zograf Monastery), 91
Holy Scriptures, 98
Holy Synod of the Russian Orthodox Church (Moscow Patriarchate), 7, 33, 143
Holy Trinity Church (parish) (Taipei), xxxiii, 117

Holy Virgin "The Joy of All Who Sorrow" Cathedral (San Francisco), 36
holy water (Blessing of the Waters of the South China Sea), 115, 141–42
homeland, 32, 38, 41
Hong Kong(-born) Chinese (HKC), 14, 125, 129–30, 138, 140, 146, 152, 158
Hong Kong Adventist Hospital, xxxiv
Hong Kong Baptist University (HKBU), xxiii, 158
Hong Kong Buddhist Association, 13, 29
Hong Kong Cemetery, xvii, 27, 37–40, 60
Hong Kong Chinese Christian Churches Union (formerly Hong Kong Christian Churches Union), 29
Hong Kong Christian Council (HKCC), 29, 131, 165
Hong Konger, xxiv, 131, 140, 166
Hong Kong Government Census and Statistics Department, xxxiv, 68
Hong Kong Island, xvii, 17, 29, 38, 40, 58, 140
Hong Kong Orthodox Association, 34
Hong Kong proper, 38
Hong Kong Public Records Office (PRO), 27
Hongkong Shanghai Banking Corporation (HSBC), 31, 40
Hong Kong Special Administrative Region (HKSAR), xx, 12, 14, 48, 165
Hong Kong Taoist Association, 13, 29
Hong Kong Tramways, 40
Hubei, xx, 6
Hunan, 6

Iakinf (Bichurin, Nikita Yakovlevich), 12, 24, 80
"I am Dasha. I am six years old. I love my school in Hong Kong. And I love my friends in my school.", 55

Icon of the Ark of Salvation (Image of our Holy Orthodox Church), 91
Icon of the Mother of God "Joy of All Who Sorrow" Church (Guangzhou), 11, 32
Ignatius (metropolitan of Khabarovsk and Priamur), 156
imperial government, 5, 29, 31, 80, 133
indigenous religion, 29, 30
Indochina, 2
Indonesia, 2
Inner Mongolia Autonomous Region, xx, 9, 14, 165
Innocent (Figurovskii, Iv n Apoll novich), 6–7, 81, 84–85, 150
Institute of Sino-Christian Studies, 45, 141, 151
Institutio Ad Fidem Christi, 80
International Association of Teachers of Russian Language and Culture (MAPYRAL), 60
Ioann (Krestiankin), 160
Islam, 2, 11, 13–14, 25, 28, 82, 115, 128
"I Understand the World.", 73
Ivanov, Dmitry, 76

Japan and Japanese, xx, xxvii–xxviii, xxx, xxxii, xxxv, 6, 9, 11, 14, 26, 30–31, 33, 40, 50, 70, 80, 83, 110, 115–16, 131–32, 153, 161–62
Jew and Jewish, 28, 68, 76, 127
Jiangsu province, xx, 6, 128
Johnston House, 31
Judaism, 2, 13–14, 25

Kalinin, Vladimir A., 71
Kaluzhny, D. A., 39
Kamakura period, 132
Karpov, Guri (Gurii of Taurida), 80
Kathisma, 98
Kazarina, Ksenia, 136, 157
Kefir, 146
Khabarovsk (formerly known as Boli), 35

Khabarovsk Theological Seminary, 45, 129
Khanty, 5
Khoruzhiy, Sergey, 107
Kirill (Gundiaev, Vladimir Mikhailovich), 152
koch, 61
Koliva, xxxiii
Koodiaroff, Michael A., 39
Korea and Korean, 14, 26, 49, 83, 146, 154
Korean Orthodox Church (Metropolis of Korea), xxviii, xxxv
Koval, Natalia, 74
Kowloon, xvii, xxxiv, 27, 28, 33, 38, 40, 49, 58, 76
Kowloon Tong, 33–34
Kraeva, Anastasia, 55, 58, 63–67, 71–72, 74–76, 100, 147
Kremnev, Roman, 83, 136
Kremneva, Svetlana, 66, 78, 136–38
Kronstadt, 40
kulich (kalich) bread, 135
Kung, Cheung Ming Anatoly, xxvi, 12, 45, 58, 99, 102, 105–6, 111, 128–29, 131, 150, 156, 159
Kuraev, Andrew, 142
Kuzminskii, Aleksandr Aleksandrovich, 31, 40
kvas, 146

Ladushki, 64
Lai, Pan Chiu, 141
Lai, Wai Suen, 37, 50
Lamma Island, 57–58, 72, 83, 106, 139, 156
Langley (née Pio-Ulski), Nona, 40, 145
Laos, 143
Latin, 6, 82
Legge, James, 23, 28
Legge, William, 28
The Legislative Council of the Hong Kong Special Administration Region (LegCo), 11
Leontiev, Maxim, 45

Lepeshev, Dmitry, 152
Li, Liang Jonah, 99, 117
Li, Michael, 45
Li, Qiuling, 141
Lingnan University, 56
Lin/Lam, Sen Ambrose, 83, 101, 106
Liturgical instructions, 111
Liu, Yüeh-sheng, 42
Local Council, xxxii
local identity, 166
local society, 28, 170
The Logos and Pneuma Press, 141
Lord's Prayer, 101, 110
Löwenthal, Rudolf, 81
Lu, Dezhi, 142
Lukyanov, Dmitry, 150
Lulias, Nikitas, 44
Lutchev, Yevgeny, 49

Macau, xx, 14, 32, 60, 156
MacLehose, Murray, 38
mainland (PRC China), xviii, xix–xxiii, xxv, xxvii, xxxiii, 8–12, 14, 26, 29–31, 36, 38, 42, 52, 70, 79–80, 82, 85, 92, 100–101, 103, 105, 112, 117, 124, 129–30, 140–41, 143, 151–52, 163–67, 169–70
mainlandization, xxx, 13, 28, 166
mainstream society, 14, 166
"main unifying sign", 69
Malkova, Polina, 157
Manakova, Tatiana, 107
Manchuria/Manchukuo, 2, 6, 18, 30, 35
Mandarin, 15, 70, 82–83, 92–94, 125, 129–30, 135, 137, 157
Manila, 32, 41, 49–50
Mansi, 5
Masha and the Bear, 67
matushka (title for wife of priest), 57, 136, 146
Maximovitch, John, 7, 36–37, 50, 87, 91, 100
"Messenger of the Orthodox Parish of Apostles Saints Peter and Paul in Hong Kong", 88

Methodios, 157
metropolitan, xxxii, 110, 143
migration, xix, xxx, 28, 30, 32, 37, 41, 166, 169
Min, Sergio, 44, 57
a minority among a minority, 145
minority group, xviii, xix, xxiii, xxxi, xxxv, 41, 68
Minzu University of China, xxi
Mirror of Orthodox Confession, 80, 116
(Miss) Goroskenko, D., 39
Modern Standard Chinese, 82, 93, 156
Mongolia, 6–7, 143
month of Epiphany, 111
morals, xxii, 86
morning prayers, 96, 113
Moscow, I love you!, 71
Moscow Patriarchate, xvii, xx, xxi, xxvii, 7, 29, 33–34, 36–38, 43–45, 50, 85, 89, 95, 101, 110–11, 143, 152, 167
Moscow Patriarchate Krutitsy Metochion, 95
Mother of God of Tabyn Icon, 86
Mount Athos, 91, 101
(Mr. and Mrs.) Birinkoff, 39
(Mr. and Mrs.) Gavidoff, 39
"Mrs. Zu", 128, 130
multitudinous (Russian) congregation, 86
Museum Sinicum, 6
Myanmar, 143

native religion, 3, 11, 14
nativization, 10–11, 153
Nectarios of Aegina, 101
Nektarios, 131, 143–44
Nelson Mitrophan Chin, 44
Nestor (Anisimov, Nikolai Aleksandrovich), 7
The News of the Brotherhood of the Orthodox Church in China, 81
New Territories, xxxiv, 38
New Testament (translation into Chinese), 81

Nicetas, 143
Nicholas II, 31, 38
Nicholas of Japan, 20, 131–32
Nicholas the Miracle Worker (Nikolaos of Myra), 49
Nikodim, 37
North America, xxiv, xxv, xxviii, xxxiii, 29, 33, 38, 76, 113, 154
Northeast Asia, xxiii, xxxiii, 19, 30, 49, 134
North Hostel/Russian Hostel/Capital Eastern Orthodox North Hostel, 4, 16–17
nostalgia, and nostalgic, xxv, 27, 30
Nozadze, Lila, 40

Old Russian Life, 73
"One Child, Two Languages", 74
Oregon, xxviii, 30
Orekhov, Germogen, 37
Orthodox Church in Taiwan (Moscow Patriarchate), xxi, xxxiii, 45, 102
Orthodox Church in Taiwan (OMHKSEA), 99
Orthodox Church of America (OCA), xxviii, 126
Orthodox Fellowship of All Saints of China (OFASC), 23, 44, 104, 141
The Orthodox Mirror, 80
Orthodox Prayer Book, 96
Our Mother of Kazan monastery, 81
Orthodox Parish of Apostles Saints Peter and Paul (OPASPP), Orthodox Brotherhood of Apostles Saints Peter and Paul, Orthodox Parish of Saint Apostles Peter and Paul, Saint [Apostles] Peter and Paul Church of Hong Kong, St. Peter and St. Paul Orthodox Church, Saint Apostles Peter and Paul Orthodox Church in Hong Kong, Saint Apostles Peter & Paul Orthodox Church in Hong Kong, Church of Saints Peter and Paul, xvii–xviii, xix, xxii, xxv–xxvi, xxviii–xxxii, 1, 10–12, 14, 31,

34–35, 37, 43–46, 49, 56–60, 62, 65, 69, 70, 73, 76, 79, 82–84, 86–89, 92, 94–95, 97–102, 104–6, 109, 123–60, 163–64, 166–70

Parish, xviii, xix, xxii, xxvi, xxvii, xxviii, xxix, xxx–xxxiii, 11–12, 14, 29, 32–33, 35, 37, 43–46, 57, 59, 63, 67, 69–70, 79, 87–88, 106, 108, 112, 117, 121, 123–25, 134, 137–39, 141–44, 146–47, 151–55, 160, 163, 165–66, 168
parish assembly, xxxii
parish audit committee, xxxii
parish council, xxxii, 37
parishioner, xxvi–xxvii, 11–12, 33, 35–38, 45, 50, 57, 60, 69, 87, 121, 129, 134–36, 139, 144, 150, 166–68
Parish of Christ the Savior in Taipei, xxi
pastor, xvii, 14, 23, 32, 35–37, 42–43, 51, 88, 117, 129, 142, 149–51, 153, 155, 159, 167
The Path of Youth, 81
Patorsky, Leonid, 76
patriarch, xxxii, 90, 110
patriotic, xxi, 13
Pedder's Hill, 31
Peiping (Beijing), 81
People's Republic of China (PRC), xviii, xix–xxvii, 7–10, 12–14, 28–29, 33–34, 42–43, 68, 70, 80, 82, 92, 100–103, 105, 112, 117, 130, 141, 151–52, 156, 163–66, 169–71
Pereslavl, 7
Peter I (Peter the Great), 16, 24
Petrova, Anna, 74
Philippines, 2, 32, 143
Pio–Ulski, George, 40
Podolsk, 37
polyethnic, xvii, xxv, 11, 129–30
Popova, Liudmila, 65
Poyarkov, Juvenaly, 37
Pozdnyaev, Dionisy, xvii, xx, xxvi, xxx, 43–45, 52, 57, 59, 63, 70, 76, 85,

87–89, 102, 105–6, 115, 131, 134, 136–37, 139, 142, 145, 150–52, 170
Pozdnyaeva, Kira, xvii, 76, 136, 145–46, 151
Praise for the feast day of the, 222 martyrs in China, 97, 114
prayer book, 95–97, 113
priest, xx, xxi, xxvi, xxxii, 5–6, 8, 27, 34–36, 43–45, 49, 57, 80, 87–88, 92, 100, 113, 116, 143, 146, 150, 156, 164
private company, 57
Profession of Faith, 45
Protection (Pokrov) of the Theotokos Church (Harbin), 8, 14, 47
Protestant, xviii, xxxiii, 2, 6, 8–10, 13–14, 27, 42, 52, 80, 92, 104, 126–28, 133, 137, 141, 158, 164–65
Pskov-Caves Monastery (Pskovo-Pechersky Dormition Monastery), 100
Pugacheva, Tatiana, 58, 60, 62, 72, 76
Pushkin, Alexander S., 66
Putiatin, E. V., 31
Pyongyang Church of the Life-Giving Trinity, xxvii, xxxiv

Qing empire (dynasty), 3–5, 7, 12, 16, 18, 80–81, 92, 133, 142
Queen's Café, 32, 40, 51

Rayton, Anna, 64–65
"real social instrument", 69
Red Fangzi at the Russian Embassy in Beijing: An Islet of Orthodoxy in China, 107
refugee, 29–30, 32–33, 39–40, 49
Religious Affairs Bureau (predecessor of SARA), 13
Renovationist Church/Living Church, 29
Republic of Korea (ROK), xxvii
Riasanovsky, Antonina (née Antonina Fedorovna Podgorinova), 30, 48

Riasanovsky, Nicholas Valentine, 48
Rogachev, I. A., 43
Romanides, John, 119
Ruist (Confucian) thought, 82, 162
Russian (ethnic group in the PRC), 8–9
Russian Club in Hong Kong, 60, 142, 144, 147
Russian Consulate General of Hong Kong, 60, 67, 142, 144, 160
Russian Culture Association (RCA), 56, 62
Russian Culture Week in Hong Kong, xxxii, 60, 147
Russian Ecclesiastical Mission in China/ Spiritual Mission in Beijing, 3, 7, 16, 32–33, 45, 80–81, 86, 97, 116, 150
Russian Language: 5 Elements, 62, 77
Russian Language Center (RLC), xvii, 1, 55–76, 79, 87, 100, 106, 123–25, 137–38, 146–48, 151, 153, 157, 163–64, 170–71
Russian Monastery of St. (Equal to the Apostles) Mary Magdalene/Church of St. Mary Magadalene (Jerusalem), 150
Russian Orthodox Church (ROC), xvii–xviii, xx, xxii, xxv, xxvi–xxxii, 1, 3, 6–12, 14–15, 17–18, 21, 27, 29–30, 32–33, 35–36, 38, 42, 45, 47, 80–81, 83–86, 89, 105, 107, 129, 133, 140, 145–46, 150, 153, 156, 163–64, 166–69, 171
Russian Orthodox Church Outside Russia (ROCOR), xxxii, 2, 7, 34, 36, 45, 100, 107, 113, 115
Russian Orthodox community, xviii, xix, xxi, xxv, xxix, xxx, 1, 8, 10, 12, 14–15, 27–29, 31, 35, 39–40, 42–43, 49–50, 70, 76, 84, 144, 166
Russian Orthodox congregation, xx, 37
Russian Orthodox Mission College (Beijing), 35
Russian proper, 8
Russian soup (borscht), 40
Russian Soviet Federative Socialist Republic, 31
Russian-speaking, 43, 55–56, 61, 63, 66–69, 73–75, 78, 81, 130, 138, 146, 149–50, 168
Russian-speaking population, 68, 75, 78
(Russian style) pickles, 146
Russian Theological Seminary (Beijing), 35
Rus Sidyaschaya Foundation, 149
Russkiy Mir Foundation, 60, 62, 69, 77
Russo-Chinese Bank (later Russo-Asiatic Bank), 31
Russo-Japanese War, 6, 132
Russophone, 12, 69, 73–74, 109, 135, 144, 147, 151, 154

Saint Luke Orthodox Cathedral in Hong Kong/Orthodox Cathedral of Saint Luke the Evangelist (OCSLE), 11–12, 14, 23–24, 31, 35, 43, 143–44, 156, 159, 165
[Saint] Polycarp, 90
Samantseva, Dayana, 157
samurai code, 132
San Francisco, 36, 50, 100, 109
São Paulo (Brazil), 30
Sarafanova, Polina, 157
Saturday of the Souls, xxii
Semyon, xx
Serafimovich, Anton, 57–58, 83, 145–46, 149
Seraphim of Sarov, 150
seven-string Chinese zither, 112
Shanghai, xx, xxv, xxxiv, 7, 8, 14, 29, 30, 33, 36–38, 40–41, 43, 47, 49–50, 60, 81, 100, 165, 167, 169
Shanghai China Orthodox Association, 36, 50
Shenzhen, 11, 23, 124, 135, 150
Siberia, 2–3, 5, 8, 30, 32
Sichuan province, 100
Sikh, 13, 28

Simplified Chinese (script), 82, 84, 89, 90, 92–93, 102, 104, 112, 115–16, 122, 151, 154
Singapore, 41, 69, 82, 143
Sinicization, 11
Sinophone, xviii, xxxviii, 12, 76, 79, 83, 85, 88, 101, 103, 105, 112, 116–17, 121, 129, 141
Sino-Russian, xix–xx, xxx, 1–5, 7, 15–17, 57, 75, 86, 164, 168, 169, 171
Slavic, xix, xxv–xxvi, xxviii, xxx–xxxi, xxxiv, 9, 15, 28, 31, 41, 66–67, 71, 73, 99, 137, 157, 167
Slavic harvest festival, 137
Slavic Literature and Culture Day, 66, 137, 157
Smirnov, George V., 60
The Snow Queen, 66
sound (*yin*), 93
Sourd, Jean–Michel, 144
South Asia, 15
South China Morning Post (SCMP), 20, 145
Southeast Asia, xxiii, xxiv, 31–32, 70, 143–44
South Korean Orthodox church, 153, 162
Soviet Union (Union of Soviet Socialist Republics) (USSR), xix, xxv, xxxiii, 7–8, 29, 31, 43, 50, 62, 67–69, 133–34
Sower, 81
soy sauce Western, 51, 146
Sperantov, Nadezhda a, 76
St. Aleksejev Church (Harbin), 47
St. Alexander Nevsky Church (Hankou), 169
St. Andrew's Church (Hong Kong), 27, 32, 34, 40, 42, 49–50, 87
St. Andrew's Church for westerners", 42
Starostina, Nina, 92, 94, 136
State Administration for Religious Affairs (SARA), 13
St. Danilov Monastery, xxxii

St. Elisabeth Convent, 152
Stephen, Chan, 141
Stephen of Perm, 106
St. Gabriel's Church (Shanghai), 36
St. Innocent of Irkutsk Church (Ergune), 14, 163
St. John's Cathedral (Hong Kong), 28, 39, 51, 140
St. Joseph's Church (Hong Kong), 28
St. Nicholas Church (Harbin), 14, 47
St. Nicholas Church (Ili), 14
St. Nicholas Church (Tianjin), 47
St. Nicholas Church (Urumqi), 14
St. Nicholas the Wonderworker Prayer House (Xiamen), 49
St. Peter's Church (Hong Kong), 28
St. Petersburg University, 103
St. Sergius of Radonezh Parish (Shenzhen), 11, 23
St. Sophia Cathedral, 47
St. Teresa's Hospital, xxxiv
St. Thomas Coptic Church (Hong Kong), 170
St. Tikhon's Orthodox University of Humanities, 102
Sun, Ming Pavel, 14, 163
Sun, Yue, 143
Supreme Church Council, xxxii
Sviatoslavich, Vladimir, 73
Svyatin, Viktor, 7, 49
Sysoev, Daniil Alexeyevich, 99

Tabachyshyn, Nazar, 157
Taipei, xx, xxi, xxxiii, 43, 45
Taipei Orthodox Church, xx
Taiwan, xviii, xx, xxi, 43, 45, 80, 82–83, 99, 101–2
Taiwanese, xx
Takuma, Sawabe, 131
Taosheng Publishing House, 102, 104
Ten Commandments, 101
Test of Russian as a Foreign Language (TORFL), 77
Thailand, 143
Thanksgiving service, 97

Index

Theological Question and Answer, 102, 118
theosis, 120
"there", 72
Three-Self Patriotic Movement, 13
Tianjin, 7, 14, 29, 35, 43, 47, 52, 84
Tibet, 7
Tikhon (Shevkunov), 142
Tkachenko, A. P., 36
Tkachenko Restaurant, 36
Tokyo, xxvii, 37
Tokyo Orthodox Seminary, xxvii
Traditional Chinese (script), 82, 84, 89, 92–93, 97–98, 104, 108, 112–16, 122, 151, 154
traditional religion, 127
Treaty of Nerchinsk, 3
Treaty of Tianjin, 84
Tsang, Susanna, 40
tsar, 5, 18
tsardom, 3, 16
Tsarist Empire, 17
Turin, Niculau Theodor, 39
12 Essex Crescent, Kowloon Tong, 33
216 Nathan Road, Yau Ma Tei, 34
Tyshchuk, Arkady, 37

underground church, xxi
Union Church (Hong Kong), 28, 39
The United Front Work Department of CPC Central Committee, 24
United Sates, xxiv, 70
University of Hong Kong (HKU), 13, 24, 56
Uspensky, Dmitry Mikhailovich, 32, 34–40, 42, 44–45, 49–51, 87, 143, 166–67
Ustyugova, Irina, 57, 61–62, 65, 68, 74, 76, 146

Vaganoff, V. V., 39
Vasily (Yao, Fu'an), 7, 33
vicarate, xxxiii
vicar bishop, xxxii
Vietnam, 143
Vladimir School of Theology, 32
Vladimir-Suzdal diocese, 32
Volunteers to Help Orphans, 71, 171
Voronin, Sergiy, 151
Vostorgov, Ioann, 9

"Wampoa", 41
Wan, Tsz Ming, 62
Wang, Xiaochao, 141
WeChat, 129
Wen, Jian, 100
Wen, Zizheng Elias (Ilia), 35–39, 42, 45, 108–9, 143
Western cuisine, 40
Western Europe, xxiv, xxv, 29, 32, 38, 39, 76
White Russian, 32, 39, 145
"wine and oil may be consumed", 92
"Winter Branches", 66
Wong, Lino Wing Kuen, 155
World War II, xx, xxiii, xxx, 33, 70

Xiamen (Amoy), 49
Xinjiang Uyghur Autonomous Region, xx, 2, 14, 33, 43, 135, 165, 167

Yancheng (Jiangsu province), 128
(year of our Lord's birth) 1879, 98
Yenching University, 81
Yerokhin, Mikhail, 49
Yeung, H. N. Daniel, 162
Yeung, Jeffrey, 143
Yi ethnic group, xxii
Yu, Mischa, 40, 51
Yu, Shi Alexander, 5
Yu, Stanley, 51

Zaraisk, 37
Zhang, Baichun, 103, 142
Zhejiang province, xx, 128
Zhili, 6
Zhu, George, 131
Zhu, Shipu Grigorij, 8, 14
Zhuang ethnic group, xxii
Zhuyin Fuhao, 93
Znamenny chant, 136

About the Authors

Loretta E. Kim is associate professor and coordinator of the China Studies–Arts Stream program at the School of Modern Languages and Cultures, University of Hong Kong. She is a historian of late imperial and modern China. Her primary research areas include the comparative history of borderlands and frontiers, Sino-Russian cultural relations, and Chinese ethnic minority languages and literatures. Her other publications include *Ethnic Chrysalis: China's Orochen People and the Legacy of Qing Borderland Administration* (Harvard University Asia Center, 2019).

Chengyi Zhou is a PhD candidate (China Studies) in the School of Modern Languages and Cultures, University of Hong Kong (HKU). Holding BA and MPhil degrees (School of Chinese, HKU) concentrating in Chinese history and philosophy, she has worked as a teaching and research assistant in the Faculty of Arts (HKU). Her research areas include China's late imperial history, names and naming practices of non-Han Chinese people, and Chinese ethnic minority identities. Her dissertation project takes an onomastic approach to study gender and ethnic identity of the Manchu people during the Qing dynasty.